# War, Image and Legitimacy

In a world where the power of the moving image is evident all around us and images can be transmitted seconds after they are taken, the relationship between images, legitimacy and war is of critical importance. Recall the striking images of the collapsing Twin Towers of September 11, the hooded figure in a web of electrodes at the Abu Ghraib prison in Iraq, frozen images of beheadings available to those seeking them on the internet, the emaciated Bosnian Muslim at the barbed wire fence of a Bosnian-Serb concentration camp, the dancing flashes of detonations across the skylines of some capital – Baghdad, Belgrade, or elsewhere – as US-led air bombardment deals blows to another 'rogue' regime and its long-suffering people; these images define contemporary warfare.

Drawing on a wide range of examples from fiction and factual film, current affairs and television news, as well as new digital media, concerning the US, the UK, the 'Global War on Terror', the Yugoslav war, former Soviet conflicts, the Middle East and Africa, this book examines the power of the moving image and the relationship between images, legitimacy and war. It introduces the radically novel proposition that moving images are the key weapons of contemporary warfare. Crucially, the book demonstrates how moving image representation of conflict can affect the legitimacy, conduct and outcome of contemporary warfare. Just as with other weapons of war, the moving image is a blunt instrument. Whilst it lacks the outwardly destructive kinetic force of more conventional weapons, it operates decisively in an era where the traditional Clausewitzian 'war trinity' has become multidimensional.

This book will be of great interest to students of war and security studies, media and communication studies, and international relations in general.

**Dr Milena Michalski** is a founding member of the Russian Cinema Research Group at the School of Slavonic and East European Studies, University College London, where she also taught. She has published on Russian and Yugoslav film, and is co-author of the British Film Institute study *After September 11*. **Professor James Gow** is Director of the International Peace and Security Programme, King's College London, and is an associate of the Liechtenstein Institute, Woodrow Wilson School, Princeton University. He is author of several books, including most recently *Defending the West*.

# Contemporary security studies

# War, Image and Legitimacy

Viewing contemporary conflict

**Milena Michalski and James Gow**

Routledge
Taylor & Francis Group

LONDON AND NEW YORK

First published 2007
by Routledge
2 Park Square, Milton Park, Abingdon, Oxon OX14 4RN

Simultaneously published in the USA and Canada
by Routledge
270 Madison Ave, New York, NY 10016

*Routledge is an imprint of the Taylor & Francis Group, an informa business*

© 2007 Milena Michalski and James Gow

Typeset in Baskerville by Wearset Ltd, Boldon, Tyne and Wear
Printed and bound in Great Britain by TJI Digital, Padstow, Cornwall

*British Library Cataloguing in Publication Data*
A catalogue record for this book is available from the British Library

*Library of Congress Cataloging in Publication Data*
War, image and legitmacy: viewing contemporary conflict/by Milena
Michalski and James Gow.
p. cm.
Includes bibliographical references and index.
1. Mass media and war. I. Gow, James. II. Title.
P96.W35M53 2007
070.4'333–dc22                                        2006101510

ISBN10: 0-415-40101-1 (hbk)
ISBN10: 0-203-08922-7 (ebk)

ISBN13: 978-0-415-40101-2 (hbk)
ISBN13: 978-0-203-08922-4 (ebk)

**For GAMG**

# Contents

# Preface

This research began in a small way as a joint paper on the Yugoslav War and film, developed at the Woodrow Wilson International Center for Scholars, during 1999, and was first presented at the Indiana University, Bloomington, that spring, although even then there is a 'pre-history' in work associated with the British Film Institute (BFI) earlier in the 1990s. While there was always a background intention to develop this work, it took off only when events impelled the more emphatic source of the research, giving it particular impetus and new dimensions, which emerged during the *After September 11* project organised by Richard Paterson at the British Film Institute on transnational television news and audiences, funded variously by the Broadcasting Standards Commission, the ESRC and the British Film Institute. The British Film Institute published the findings in summary form – *After September 11: TV News and Multicultural Audiences* (London: British Film Institute, 2002). Michalski was one of the principal researchers and authors of that report (along with Alison Preston, on the content analysis side, and Marie Gillespie and Tom Cheeseman, on the audience research side). That study did not have space – with a 5,000-word limit for each part – to include all the research findings; Gow was one of the twenty-strong team that contributed research. Michalski and Preston subsequently published findings separately in a Belgian comparative study: Milena Michalski and Alison Preston, 'Le 11 septembre vu de Grande Bretagne: Comparaison des journaux télévisés', in Marc Lits ed. *Du 11 septembre à la riposte: les débuts d'une nouvelle guerre médiatique* (Brussels: De Boeck, 2004), pp. 61–85. Parts of the present volume draw on research from that project, which was not used in the earlier publications as well as some material that draws on that study, including Alison Preston's work, at certain points. The overwhelming majority of the material from the initial project presented here is original work for which Michalski was responsible, that had to be excluded from the *After September 11* report published by the BFI.

Building on the *After September 11* project, a successful application was made to the ESRC New Security Challenges Programme by Gillespie and Gow, with Andrew Hoskins (who had also been a researcher on the original project), partly reflected in the present volume: ESRC New Security Challenges Programme, ESRC Award RES-223–25–0063, 'Shifting Securities: Television News Cultures Before and After Iraq 2003'. This research comprises three strands: dealing with publics and audiences, content and discourse, and security and news practitioners, respectively. The empirical research for the project is located under protected access (initially at least) at www.mediatingsecurity.com. References to this research throughout the present volume are identified collectively as 'Shifting Securities Project', preceded by particular details. The present volume results from development of the earlier research, begun during the original British Film Institute project and continued in the interim, thanks to support from the Marchmont Trust and assistance from Ivan Zveržhanovski, who was later research associate to Gow on Strand C of the Shifting Securities Project, which provides empirical material for some parts of the present analysis, although he had no direct role in this particular study (Gow and Zveržhanovski are responsible for a further book related to Strand C of the Shifting Securities Project, *Watching War Crimes* (London: Hurst and Co, 2007)).

The present volume is based almost entirely on new research of two broad types: empirically based, qualitative, interpretive criticism of texts, a form of content analysis; and empirical, qualitative social research, using semi-structured open interviews and focus groups. We share joint responsibility for the book, having worked on it in equal parts, either in terms of research, or writing (although Chapter 2 owes more to Michalski and particular parts of Chapters 6 and 7 owe more to Gow, we take equal responsibility for these sections, as for the whole, where the division of labour was 50-50), although Michalski rendered the final version of the manuscript – albeit keeping some of Gow's clumsiness.

As ever with a study of this kind, there are numerous people to thank, who have supported and influenced it in the making. There is no chance that we would have done this work without Richard Paterson's influence, both his generosity and his imaginative ambition in bringing people from different backgrounds together in projects. Alison Preston has been another friendly influence throughout, both as a collaborator and adviser, who emerged originally in the Petrie dish provided by Richard at the BFI. We are grateful for their kindness and collaboration. The BFI context provided by Richard is also where we first came into contact with Marie Gillespie and, later, Andrew Hoskins, giving rise to the challenging ESRC research project that informs this book. We are grateful, again, for the support they have offered, which, in Marie's case also ran to personal encouragement in other, more important aspects of life, which affected us in the course of the project and writing this book. The Shifting Securities Project involved a large number of researchers and assistants in different capacities. We are grateful to all of them for the work they put in on the different parts of the project. Particular thanks go to Zebbie Yousuf,

Habiba Noor, Nourredine Miladi, Olivia Allison, Thomas Horn Hansen, and Louise Wise. Special thanks go also to Ben O'Loughlin, who was, in many ways, the mainstay and linchpin of the project, keeping the various parts of it in touch with each other somehow, and whose work, while not central to the present volume, made certain parts of it considerably easier. His affable, good-natured support and readiness to discuss ideas and seek to develop them is greatly valued. The person to whom we owe the greatest immediate debt, in terms of the project, is Ivan Zveržhanovski, who participated in directly, or even carried out himself, significant parts of the research which underpin this book. While not part of the ESRC Project itself, as Director of the New Security Challenges Programme, which funded the project, and as both source of warm wisdom and helpful advice, credit and thanks go to Stuart Croft. His support for the project and great enthusiasm for this book, in particular (expressed one evening in a Westminster pub as he came or went from some parliamentary event) probably ensured that it was completed, when other factors might have led to abandoning it – though of course, his excitement for it does not, in any way, make him responsible for it. Julian Graffy also deserves special thanks for all his friendship and support over the years. Gratitude to Andrew Humphrys, who was patient, helpful and supportive; Marjorie Francois, who moved on before we finally got to the end of this; and Katie Gordon, who took over with lightness and alacrity – and a dose of patience too! – all at Routledge-cum-Taylor & Francis. Numerous others also deserve gratitude for their advice, support and assistance in various ways – we hope that we have not missed anyone out, and if we have, that they will forgive us for the oversight: Peter Busch, Peter Neumann, Michael Clarke, Lawrence Freedman, John Glover, Mark Hobart, Ray Eiriz, Leonid Sitnikov, Evgenii Tsymbal, Ian Christie, Dodge Billingsley, Leslie Woodhead, Fiona Lloyd Davies, Jim Richardson, Steve Chisnall, Ann Lane, Vesselin Popovski and Rachel Kerr. We wish also to acknowledge the value of discussion with various classes taught and individual students over the years, who have engaged in discussion of moving images, or war, or the two of them together.

Finally, we have to acknowledge that this has been quite a creative journey, and immense, immeasurable thanks go to the family – including those parents and grandparents who are not around to see the project finished. Dušica, Peter, Petra, Franz, Helen, Marjorie, Patricia – and even Don – all helped get us through, in some way, at some time, as the confluence of two major creative activities threatened to burst the banks of time and energy – one source, the river of writing the book, the other, that of discovering the joys of parenthood. The biggest thanks go to whoever made Gabriel possible and to him – although he could not understand what he has had to put up with, he learned the vital importance of computers, films and the treasure of writing.

# 1 Introduction

The collapsing Twin Towers of September 11, the hooded figure in a web of electrodes at the Abu Ghraib prison in Iraq, the frozen images on moving screens of those whose beheadings were available to those seeking them out on the internet, the emaciated Bosnian Muslim figure at the barbed wire fence of a Bosnian Serb concentration camp, the dancing flashes of detonations across the skylines of some capital – Baghdad, Belgrade, or elsewhere – as US-led air bombardment dealt blows to another 'rogue' regime and its long-suffering people: these images define contemporary conflict. More than that, they – and whichever other images become available – dominate the various environments in which the legitimacy of armed campaigns in an era of rapid international and transnational change is contested – politically, socially, legally and communicatively. There is a competition over images – the images, rightly or wrongly, appear to distil the essence of a conflict. They are the short cuts to understanding, and so at the heart of the competition for hearts and minds in different quarters in modern war. Images are the key weapons in contemporary warfare.

This is why the relationship between war and moving images matters, and why both that relationship and the nature of moving images as weapons warrants investigation. How does image affect war? How does image affect our understanding of war? And this means, really, how does image affect our plural understandings of war – of war as it happens, of war in history, of war in memory, of war in general, and of war in one of its specific manifestations? Crucially, how can moving-image representation of conflict affect the legitimacy, nature and conduct of contemporary warfare? What is the nature of this most important of weapons? What are its characteristics? These questions of relationship and qualities are vital to understanding how images work as weapons, and so how their use can be controlled or countered, as far as these might be possible.

This volume explores the nature of moving-image media and their relationship to legitimacy and war. Legitimacy is the key to success in war; the image is the key to the formation of legitimacy, or critical challenges to it. This book maintains that the key weapon of war in the contemporary era, therefore, is the moving image – but, just as with other weapons of war, it is a blunt instrument. It is a kinetic force, but of a different type to the outwardly destructive kinetic force of more conventional weapons – as shown below. The moving image is a blunt instrument because of the means of delivery, its nature and its constraints. Our aim is to show how image and human experience are salient in the fictional representation of war, and how, in the nature of moving-image media, these same elements are vital in constructing, shaping and defining interpretation and understanding in non-fictional film, whether current affairs and documentary, or television news. Images are inevitably a short cut in the quest for detailed comprehension and accuracy. Whether they generally support or deny the bulk of other empirical material, moving images, by their nature, are limited yet powerful.

## Media and war: moving images and meaning

Images are not new; war is certainly not new; and nor are the links between images and war.[1] But there is something, it seems to us, altogether new in the salience of the image in understanding contemporary war. The images of commercial jets as cruise missiles and the collapsing towers of the World Trade Center emphasised the importance of images – or their absence – in reporting and interpretation, whether actuality or fictional, of contemporary conflict, as well as making Usama bin Ladin (hereafter UBL[2]) a household name.[3] The overriding importance of the image – above all the moving image – is a feature of the contemporary era. At the same time, the character of contemporary war also presents new issues of legitimacy. The confluence of these two trends makes them central in the study of contemporary conflict.

Although there is a strong body of literature on the broad theme of media and war,[4] with the greater part of that attention focused on issues of media influence on war, including propaganda and the so-called 'CNN effect', treating fiction and factual forms together is distinctive, if not quite unique – and the systematic approach to the nature of different moving-image media and the relationship between fictional and actuality forms taken here is, we believe, unprecedented. Where others have made reference to the relevance of fictional representation, this has been incidental and connected to memory,[5] or (developing from memory work) more focused discussion of the place of drama and documentary in discursive practices,[6] or consciously addressed, but in an unsystematic way, as in the work of Susan Carruthers.[7]

Carruthers' work was more or less the first attempt to create an overview of the relationship of news and entertainment media to war, and is a retrospective survey of the twentieth century. Her emphasis is not on understanding war, but, in the end, on the way post-conflict fictional treatment has dealt with reporting and interpretation of particular conflicts, rather than the conflicts themselves. Carruthers' book is the closest to our volume in many senses; yet it is already notably different in a number of respects, each of which constitutes an important area of our agenda. While, in some senses, the book broadly explores the same field as Carruthers', in structure and contemporary coverage it goes well beyond the scope of her study. First, regarding the integrated treatment of the fictional form and the relationship to understanding war, whether in particular cases or more generally, Carruthers' book is structured by chapters relating to different types or degrees of conflict – total war, limited war, terrorism – with various information and entertainment media addressed in an undifferentiated way. Our systematic treatment of the different types of moving-image media to uncover the nature of moving images as weapons, focused on contemporary conflict from the very end of the twentieth into the twenty-first century, is embedded in the structure of our book, which is shaped by consideration of different moving-image forms – fiction, current affairs/documentary and television news.

Our work differs from Carruthers' and others' in another crucial respect. Her work emerges from study of propaganda and communications relating to war, and is for the most part concerned with journalism – even where she is treating fictional material. In contrast, the focus in our study is on the nature of moving-image media and their potential impact on legitimacy as the crucial element in contemporary conflict, and so the volume does not deal directly with either journalism (the reporting of war[8]) or propaganda (the intentional efforts by belligerents to shape understanding of conflict, as, for example, treated by Stephen Badsey and Philip Taylor[9]). Although it is necessary to consider propaganda, the concern is not with propaganda as such. In the words of Philip Taylor, propaganda is the 'deliberate attempt to influence people to think and behave in a desired way'.[10] This is about as good a definition of propaganda as could be desired. It is about material being disseminated.

It is important to be aware of propaganda and that it overlaps with the focus here on images as weapons, but that this is not the concern per se. In propaganda the key element is intent, but the present analysis of image is not necessarily connected with intent. Indeed, one aspect of this is that, even where there is intent, the effect is uncontrollable. For example, the CIA dropped matchbooks with a picture of UBL all over Afghanistan, with a text in relevant languages indicating that he was deemed to be a bad guy and that there was a $5m reward (later increased to $25m) for information leading to his apprehension. This was clearly an object with intent to spread the word that UBL was unsavoury and to lead to his capture. However, the real point of interest as an instrument of propaganda is the address on the flip side: Rewards for Justice, PO Box 96781, email heroes@heroes.net. However, in Afghanistan under the Taliban, where there were something like 64 computers in the whole country, otherwise they were banned, and, for large parts of the time, there was no power. In this context, it is hard to imagine an Afghan tribesman on his hilltop with his herd having one of these matchbooks land on his head, and saying, 'my goodness, I must pick up my satellite and send a quick email to heroes@heroes.net'. This is propaganda, it has intention, but the intention is not calibrated to cultural environment in which it is intended to have effect. The intention is there. It is certainly deliberate – to get someone to think and act in a particular way. But, it is hard to imagine that the effect and impact were anything other than negligible.[11]

The key point is that the concern here is not about propaganda per se, because it is not purely about *intentional* efforts to control information and shape understanding intent. Of course, the present analysis has some relationship to propaganda, but its scope is wider. It is about legitimacy. Nor is our analysis concerned directly with the reporting of war, which has various other dimensions (including print journalism and radio), where images do not necessarily impinge – or can only ever do so contingently, as inter-textual discussion of moving-image media. Indeed, it is one of our concerns that, once the nature of moving-image media is taken into account, as well as that of contemporary conflict, legitimacy will be affected at least as much by the *un*intentional as by the *intentional.*

This will make it at once all the more important for protagonists to seek control, but even harder for them to achieve this. While policy and news producers can attempt at times carefully to choose what to feed to the public, there is such a plurality of channels available that no one provider can guarantee to control the agenda, and even less chance that, if they manage to set the agenda, they will be able to control how material is then used, interpreted, understood and relayed by others.[12] Crucially, it is the nature of the media that counts, not conscious or direct intention – although the impact on legitimacy will, of course, have implications for one or another actor's propagandistic purpose. While moving images are key in the battle for legitimacy at the heart of contemporary conflict, they can often constitute an unguided, imprecise and largely uncontrollable weapon. Thus, while both news reporting and propaganda have relevance for the present study, and relevant material is addressed contingently, the focus is on the nature of moving images and the types of narrative they determine – and so the kind of weapon they constitute.

This study focuses on the nature of moving images, how the key media are structured by their dependence on such images, and how this produces particular output with a potential impact on our understanding of war. The impact of images on conflict is not, of course, a novelty of the twenty-first century. For example, the impact of images at the political level can be seen in the case of two British army sergeants in Palestine, who were hanged in 1948, precipitating the end of the Mandate territory, in face of Jewish, proto-Israeli terrorist attacks and insurgency.[13] One national newspaper, the *Daily Express,* carried an account with a picture on the front page, and it became a *cause célèbre* in the House of Commons, very much in a way more characteristic of later times. This was the straw that broke the camel's back. It was the first time that dead bodies had been shown, and they were booby trapped so that when the troops went to cut them down they were injured. That image really resonated at breakfast time and people had had enough. But, in fact, over three years, although around 300 people had been killed, this image set the agenda.

Earlier than this John Hartfield[14] recognised the power of images, both as they were being used by the Nazis and as a means of combating them; he incorporated Nazi images into counter-Nazi work against them. Hartfield is important because he had already identified that, in strategic engagement with opponents, given the increasing availability and means of distributing images, hearts and minds will be most affected by retinal impact. The extent to which this is true has grown during the course of the twentieth and into the twenty-first century. The thing that is going to cut through everything else will be the one that has instant impact on the retina – what, for Hartfield, was the retinal flash. The battle for hearts and minds, so often cited in the context of anti-terrorist and counter-insurgency campaigns, and increasingly in the context of all armed conflict in the contemporary era, notably in the 'Global War on Terrorism' and the engagement of US-led forces in Iraq, is not just that. It is a battle for hearts, minds and retinas.[15]

Retinal impact and moving images hold a vital place in contemporary armed conflict, as may be seen from this brief overview. The characteristics of contemporary warfare differ from previous eras. Contemporary armed conflict is characterised by issues of asymmetry, atrocity, variegated *loci* of political control, as well as issues such as ethnicity, political community, mass migration and, crucially, sovereignty, law, human rights and morality in more fluid environments than ever before.[16] These features of contemporary conflict may be seen in the major cases throughout the 1990s and beyond 2000 – Iraq and the broader Middle East, al-Qa'ida, Africa, the former Soviet Union and the former Yugoslavia (all of which feature to a greater or lesser extent later in this book, particularly in the chapters on different types of moving-image media). The character of contemporary conflict makes the certainties of war in even the recent past of limited or even no relevance. In these circumstances, legitimacy is central to success – a conceptualisation and an argument developed in Chapter 7.

Legitimacy is key because the political, legal and operational framework for using armed force has changed and is changing further, particularly as Western governments, post-September 11, may be required to take 'pre-emptive' action based on secret information, but will not be able to make that information public. This requires public and media trust (both arenas would later damn governments shown to have failed to act when there was knowledge of threats); but the events surrounding Iraq suggest that public and media support may not be available, absent images, as evidence or means of creating memory and understanding. Whereas most discussion of war and the media in recent years has focused primarily on issues of accuracy in factual reporting and fictional depiction, or their impact on policy making or on public opinion, this volume argues that in television, cinema and the increasingly important World Wide Web, these other aspects are of limited significance – it is image and experience that are salient in shaping and defining interpretation and understanding.

In this context, waging war and mounting military operations became far less a matter of a single armed force amassing sufficient physical strength to overwhelm an opponent – although the capability to do so, where necessary, remained important. It became a matter not of victory in battle, but success in interpreting events. Lawrence Freedman in an excellent and concise condensation of the key literature surrounding this trend emphasised the importance of cultural aspects and argued that the source of victory in contemporary conflicts lay in 'strategic narratives'.[17] Defining narratives as 'compelling story lines which can explain events convincingly and from which inferences can be drawn', he argued that these were vital in maintaining cultural networks, where dispersed or diverse groups cohere around the given narratives, as well as being important for framing issues and the responses to them, based on the analysis that 'opinions are shaped not so much by the information received, but by the constructs through which that information is interpreted and understood'. He wisely supplements this with the observation that effective narratives work because of an appeal to the 'values, interests and prejudices of the intended audience', warning that this can be undermined if later information or events 'expose' it as false, or weak, in any way. In summary, narratives are 'implied with every reference to a battle for "hearts and minds"'. The key to successful strategy then shifts from destroying an enemy's assets to undermining the narratives, which give appeal to that enemy and mobilise support for it.

Freedman's excellent analysis remains limited, because the discussion of narrative does not extend to a developed understanding of the salience of images – that the battle for 'hearts and minds' is also one for 'retinas' – and the image- and experience-dependent nature of moving-image media. He does, in passing, acknowledge that governments have become aware that 'images revealing large scale suffering can push them into "doing something", while images exposing the cost of that "something" may impede action',[18] and that the 'pictures of torture at Abu Ghraib were undoubtedly a public relations disaster for the United States'.[19] This is something of an understatement, as the scenes from Abu Ghraib were undoubtedly the biggest blow to the US campaign in Iraq and its Global War on Terror (as we discuss in Chapters 5 and 7). This is why Freedman's excellent analysis remains incomplete, and why it is essential to recognise that images are not just contingent in the battle for hearts and minds, or the struggle for success and legitimacy; they are central and imperative. Analysis and understanding of strategic narratives must comprehend that the critical framework is moving-image media, and that there is a fundamental need to appreciate the determinants and character of moving-image media. Our mission in this book is to explore these issues and to develop understanding of moving-image narratives and modern war, where, as we argue, images are the key weapons.

## Weapons for winning: construction and kinesis

It important to lay out a key assumption in our argument: that images can constitute weapons. This notion is not entirely novel. It is reflected, for example, in the claims of the 'Bond villain' in the 007 film *Tomorrow Never Dies*, played by the excellent Jonathan Pryce, a media magnate, inevitably set on dominating the world by provoking major armed conflict among major powers by using the power he has through broadcast media, who declares that 'words are the new bullets' and 'satellites the new artillery'. Of course, he misses saying that images are weapons, but only a little further reflection would lead to the conclusion that what the satellites deliver with real force is images.

At first glance, this idea might be rejected.[20] Use of the term 'weapon' might initially conjure up images of instruments created with the specific purpose of inflicting physical wounds on an opponent (or, even, just another living being), such as knives, swords, spears or pistols. However, while undoubtedly this received understanding of what constitutes a weapon is not unreasonable, nor is it developed or refined enough. The notion of a weapon can include anything that serves to disrupt the enemy or gain an advantage in a conflict (hence, the *Concise Oxford English Dictionary* includes examples such as irony – as a dual-edged weapon, or the weapon of labour strikes to illustrate devices that fit this sense). This leads towards the key point, which is that weapons are constructions, physical and social. We understand certain objects to be weapons because this is the purposive interpretation that has been placed upon them – a tank is a weapon because it is an instrument that has been designed with the intention of being able to inflict blows on an enemy. But, stripped of this received interpretation-built-into-design, the tank (somewhat absurdly, for effect) could be 'a very big paperweight'.[21] Equally, anyone who recalls the parlour game of Cluedo, or who is a veteran of murder-mystery weekends, or fictional (film or novel) variants, would recognise that the murder weapon might invariably be the candlestick or the telephone – nearly always an object, which, as a text, has a received reading and understanding as being for a particular social purpose, but which is adapted to become a weapon. Thus, it is the use to which an instrument is put and the interpretation of it that defines status as a weapon. When used to inflict blows of any kind, in order to get the better of an opponent in a conflict, anything becomes a weapon.

This is an argument that, without the same purpose as ours, has been played out in exchanges between Grint and Woolgar on one side, and Rob Kling on the other.[22] The former title of Chapter 6 of their book, 'What's social about being shot?', which is an ironic play on the dual sense of 'social', as it is not a sociable act, on one hand, and their point is to demonstrate that it is, on the other, a social phenomenon. Their exchanges with Kling, part of a wider discussion of 'technology', centre on the empirical, physical characteristics of weapons: guns, Kling would maintain, can shatter bones in a way that other instruments, such as rose stems, cannot. While Kling is perfectly correct on this point, as is his attempt to bring a sober approach to the more extreme interpretations of his intellectual opponents, Grint and Woolgar are broadly right, nonetheless. The rose stems can be weapons – instruments to inflict blows, as anyone unfortunate enough to be beaten by them, thorns drawing blood, could attest. Kling's analysis makes sense as far as the intended purpose built into the design of an instrument is taken at face value and in a limited way, and insofar as the degree of damage caused by a weapon is taken as a measure of its status. However, neither of these points can withstand significant interrogation. If degree of damage is the test, then it could be possible to construct a case by which the daggers, swords, spears and pistols that Kling would recognise as weapons would be declassified as such, because they could not inflict destructive blows in anything like the degree to which a howitzer, or a JDAM, or a nuclear device could. Clearly, degree of destructive impact cannot be a measure – particularly as this would exclude instruments clearly recognised as weapons systems, such as electromagnetic impulse systems, which disrupt rather than destroy.

There is undoubtedly basic sense in maintaining lexical and conceptual coherence in recognising that a category – weapons – exists, which generally, and rightly, contains recognised instruments which fit clearly within that category under normal circumstances. Words, of course, have to mean something and there is great benefit in clarity. However, this does not mean that we should not understand that a hand pistol, for example, does not occur naturally but is a product of human social design and construction for purpose; Kling's point would only be wholly appropriate if weapons of this type were to occur naturally (and even then their use and understanding would remain a matter of social construction). Nor does it exclude the possibility that other instruments, normally, or more obviously categorised in a different manner, can acquire a particular status – in this case that of a weapon – if their socially constructed role, determination and actual use make this so. This understanding must be seen to cover the whole range of 'dual-use' technologies, including computers and nuclear, which can constitute weapons, which nobody would deny (except, perhaps, those involved in subterfuge and clandestine schemes to pretend that nuclear knowledge was purely for the peaceful purpose of generating electricity, when it was really for the creation of weapons), if they are construed in that way.

Following from this, it should be evident that images, especially those channelled by moving-image media, can and should be seen as weapons in the context of contemporary warfare. While images can have other purposes and can be constructed in radically different ways, it would not make sense to suggest that their use in, or impact on, armed conflict should not be seen as inflicting blows on an enemy – moral and psychological, at least – and, certainly, as getting the better of that enemy, if possible (or being on the receiving end of strategic image management and delivery by that enemy). The evidence is clear that images can serve as weapons – their status is a matter of context. And, in the contexts of 9/11, Abu Ghraib or filmed suicide operations, the pictures are just as much weapons – instruments dealing blows, or getting the better of an opponent – as the means which they depict. Images, as with any other device, may be used as weapons. And, whether initially weapon-ised or not, just as with any other technical means, they can be adapted within the social context of conflict, to outmanoeuvre an opponent.[23]

Moving images share a particular quality with more conventional weapons – both are kinetic. While this term for physical movement is understood readily by soldiers as applying to the use of destructive armed force – they talk of 'kinetic' operations in contrast to others – it also applies to moving images. Indeed, kinesis lies at the root of one prominent branch of the moving-image media – cinema, or, originally 'kinema', which provides the stem of 'kino', which is the word for cinema in a variety of languages, including German, Russian and Serbian. Both are kinetic forces, but while one operates kinetically against other objects, the other operates kinetically in itself. However, the sense in which the physical movement in moving-image media is the passing of frames, one to another, means it also has a quasi-kinetic force through perceptual, emotional or psychological impact.[24] Indeed, 'moving images', on a certain level, means both the physical movement of the visual, but also capacity to 'move' in terms of sentiment and value, that is, emotionally, or psychologically. The human experience-emotion aspect means a double sense for 'moving' images – those which move physically, and those which move emotionally. One describes the action of the images themselves, the other describes their impact.

The impact of moving images depends on their character, or nature. Our purpose, in the course of the present volume, is to demonstrate the character of moving-image media, determined by images and human, emotional experience. In doing so, we are examining the nature of the key weapon in contemporary armed conflict. Successful strategy may well depend on a judicious balance of these twin kinetic forces.

## Approaches

This volume argues, through analysis of fictional, current affairs-documentary and news moving-image media, that the dominance of the moving image has led to an age where discourse on military action is shaped by understanding of political, ethical and legal issues, which frame legitimacy in the context of such action; that legitimacy determines success – or the approximation of victory, where victory, as such, cannot be achieved, in conventional terms; and that this understanding of those issues is framed predominantly by moving-image media, which means that images are the key weapons of modern warfare. The previous section established the relationship between contemporary warfare and the vital importance of moving-image narratives, the departure point for the remainder of the book. Before undertaking that analysis, however, there are several matters which should be addressed concerning the approach we take.

Our analysis uses two broad approaches to research, as noted above: empirical interpretation of texts; and empirical social research, combining semi-structured, open interviews and focus groups. The second of these significantly supplements the first at times – empirical social research carried out as part of the Shifting Securities Project (see above), mainly from Strand C of the project. Strand C research involved a mixture of focus groups and interviews with practitioners in a particular field relevant to broadcast media and war – journalists, producers, directors, military personnel, policy makers, lawyers, and various types of specialist, or 'expert',[25] with relevance to media and security. This empirical research underpins parts of the analysis at various points in the book and strengthens the analysis overall, but is not appropriate throughout.

The principal approach is rooted in the traditions of literary study and involves individual (or dual, as the literal case maybe) interpretation of texts. This involves taking particular texts as empirical phenomena, and using the empirical evidence to be found within them to develop interpretation of them. This is consistent with the interpretive approach adopted elsewhere in the study of war and film, focusing on manifest, rather than latent content (the latter corresponding more to the dominant schools of film and media studies noted above).[26] In doing this, and calling on the literary heritage, we could be seen to be going against the tide of what has come to be understood to constitute film studies and media studies, as areas of enquiry, as each has taken directions involving significant teleological, social, political, economic, psychological and theoretical aspects, reading texts for what they are deemed to reveal about the contexts in, or from, which they emerge – that is, what they are assumed to be, depending on the ideological or analytical standpoint of the critic, and not purely on what may be derived from the text itself. We follow Richard Dyer in noting that the dominant strands of what have come to constitute film studies, for example, are constructions, and that a range of other matters could – and quite possibly should – really be the focus of study.[27] This was also the philosophy which underpinned the creation at the start of the twenty-first century of a new journal by Ian Christie and Michael Grant, who judged that film studies had been 'prematurely academised' in ways which meant that various avenues were cut off,[28] including straight film criticism, of the kind we seek to offer here, where individual interpretations of filmic texts had their place. While we would not reject the established body of literature on film theory, for example (indeed, we build analysis on parts of it in Chapter 2), we believe that an empirical approach to interpretation offers the soundest basis for analysis in itself, and especially with reference to the steadfastly empirical character of war, the theme, or topic, with which our analysis of moving-image media is entwined. This is not to say that subjective personal influences, or cultural idioms, do not affect any analysis – they do, no doubt including this study. But it is to allow the texts, rather than the assumptions, to have precedence in the analysis.

In line with the literary tradition of film criticism, we devote time within each of the chapters to particular interpretation of individual texts, each of which provides a self-standing reading.[29] The chapters are defined by the typology already identified above, which structure the book (feature fiction, current affairs, and documentary and television news), Therefore in each case we also use our readings to draw out the salience of image and experience in the construction of moving-image narratives. The texts were selected, in part, using a 'convenience' methodology,[30] developing samples that came to our attention directly or through the advice of others, which appeared to have utility for the research, and which, where possible, were available for comparative review by others. There were many texts considered that could have been useful, but which we have not, in the end, addressed in this book, judging that those included had greater merit for our analysis, either in terms of their content or their availability, or both. At times our readings are fairly lengthy, a necessary by-product of an approach to analysis operated in one medium about another. This means that significant amounts of description occur at various points in order to establish the material about which we are writing.

We considered the inclusion of sample images as part of the book, but two factors made us decide against this. The pragmatic and more intellectually feeble of these concerned the various difficulties, such as increased production costs for publishers, of including plates, where these would be few in relation to the amount of material actually covered in the book. The more important reason for the decision not to include actual still images in a book where images are a central concern is that our concern is with moving-image media – and there was no way, short of, perhaps, creating a commercial DVD, in which we could incorporate moving images – but this would have been prohibitively expensive, given the cost of copyright clips for use in documentaries (as one interviewee noted[31]) and anything else would have been deeply unsatisfactory. Instead, for the most part, we have tried to focus on examples where the moving-image texts themselves are fairly easily available in one form or another, although this is not true of all cases, inevitably. This should make the material accessible in terms of both comparable research and educational use.

The volume is intended to be both a research volume of interest and use to others working in the various fields that focus on media and war, and a book with some educational value in war studies, as well as film studies, media studies, cultural studies and area studies. In this context, as noted, and acknowledging Richard Taylor's ever valid comment that with a visual medium the most important thing is to have seen films, not to have simply read or heard about them,[32] in each of the substantive chapters we treat examples extensively that are either available for purchase or for hire from libraries or commercially, or that can be expected, on the basis of experience, to be repeated at regular intervals on television in a niche-market, multi-channel environment, thus facilitating either study or further research. This is in marked contrast to other volumes on media and war, where the twin problems of not having images in the book and writing about phenomena that readers cannot follow up are present.[33]

## The book

Having established the initial and basic link between contemporary armed conflict and the roles both of strategic narrative dependent on moving images and of images as weapons, and having laid the foundation for our work in this Introduction, the rest of the book takes up the exploration of the moving images–modern war nexus. Chapter 2 establishes the basic typology of moving-image media already noted above (feature fiction, actuality long-format, or current affairs and documentary, and actuality short-format in television news) used to structure the subsequent chapters. It also examines the nature of moving-image media narratives – and so the nature of the weapon we are considering, including the limitations on what the media can do, imposed by that nature. Finally, the chapter considers the way in which the nature of these media relates to the study of war, including their evident limitations.

Chapter 3 examines the fictional representation of contemporary conflicts. It includes analysis of films concerning the Yugoslav War, such as the Cannes prize-winner *Underground* by Emir Kusturica, and the Oscar-winning *No Man's Land* by Danis Tanović. It also includes analysis of films on the post-Soviet conflict in Chechnya, including the internationally celebrated and commercially available *Prisoner of the Mountain* by Sergei Bodrov, and *War*, or *Voina*, by Aleksei Balabanov, a success in the West. The chapter also considers two films about the American engagement over Iraq, David O. Russell's *Three Kings* and Sam Mendes' *Jarhead*. The chapter will conclude with a study of *Black Hawk Down* by Ridley Scott, winner of two Oscars and by an Oscar-winning director, one of the most commercially successful war-related films ever, on US operations in Somalia in the early 1990s, which is a *locus classicus* for understanding the issues involved in representing armed conflict through moving images. This last film provides a solid foundation for studying both the interaction between fictional and non-fictional modes – and, indeed, their conflation, and the salience of moving images regarding legitimacy in armed conflict. The chapter as a whole demonstrates that moving-image media, by their nature, generally focus on personal experience and the emotional, as well as on the visual, whatever their interpretation and understanding of conflict or particular conflicts. This defines representation on screen, rather than any other factor.

Chapter 4 examines long-format actuality films related to contemporary conflict. The texts considered include the two major documentary series *The Death of Yugoslavia* (aka *Yugoslavia: Death of a Nation*) and *The Fall of Milošević* on the Yugoslav War, made by the same production company and shown extensively and regularly repeated in both the UK and the US. We show that it is the availability of images, not information, that shapes the films made, and so the material available for interpretation and understanding. The chapter also considers a range of actuality films relating to post-Soviet conflict, and the events of September 11 and their aftermath in the 'Global War on Terror', including the campaign in Iraq. This includes interpretation of the Naudet brothers' fortuitous *911*, where a documentary film already underway on the New York Fire Department was transformed into a memorial of September 11. We conclude the chapter by examining Michael Moore's *Fahrenheit 911*, the most successful non-fiction narrative film of recent times, receiving a wide theatrical release, high audiences and wide exposure, in part trading on its relevance to the US 2004 Presidential elections, where its attack on US engagement in Iraq had an impact. The chapter overall confirms that it is the nature of factual texts, as with fiction, that determines the nature of documentary and current affairs output – despite some differences of style and tone. This makes it an unreliable, unpredictable device for representing, interpreting and understanding contemporary conflicts.[34]

Building on the preceding chapters, Chapter 5 examines the most immediate, widespread and influential form of moving-image media – television news – demonstrating that the same elements which define narrative and selection of material in fictional representations, and also in documentary and current affairs films, also determine television news. It is the moving-image content that defines presentation of contemporary conflict, and other issues, rather than a comprehensive approach to information and understanding. The importance of satellite sources, in particular CNN, as a resource of images for broadcasters around the world who do not have their own capabilities to cover conflicts internationally, is also considered – what might be understood as the real 'CNN effect'.[35] The chapter also includes examination of images of abuse at the Abu Ghraib prison in Baghdad, emerging during continuing US operations in Iraq, and their impact. These clearly had a major impact on political discourse and legitimacy in the US and elsewhere. Other aspects of the conflict are also dealt with here, including the absence of images of 'Weapons of Mass Destruction', which counterfactually it might be argued would have made all the difference to perceptions of the conflict. The chapter overall argues that it is moving images, in both the emotive and physical senses, that determine television news coverage of contemporary conflict, as with other branches of moving-image media.

Chapter 6 considers additional aspects of moving-image media in relation to contemporary armed conflict, themes and issues that provide context building on the foregoing chapters. One of these concerns places, situations, or events, which do not normally register and which it is in the practice and nature of Western media to overlook – notably, as we discuss, the continent of Africa and its security questions. In separate sections, we discuss the changing nature of the moving image – and matters of continuing importance despite change. First, there is discussion regarding the rise of the internet and digital capture as moving-image media and resources, in the context of armed conflict, as well as the atomisation and diversification of output and impact that the World Wide Web makes possible. Then there is consideration of change and stasis institutionally and the impact and importance of 'authorial' voices, whether news anchors and reporters, or, as we discuss in the final section, long-format directors and producers (fiction or factual), who offer different approaches to the moving image representation of modern war.

Chapter 7 explores the nature of contemporary armed conflict, introducing a revised version of the famous Clausewitzian 'trinity', arguing that, contrary to numerous commentators during the 1990s, the trinity remains relevant – but not only this, more important, it needs to be understood as a multifaceted, multivalent phenomenon, what we call the 'Multidimensional Trinity Cubed-plus', or the *Trinity*$^3$*(+)*. Relating this to the key concept of legitimacy, which we argue defines success in contemporary warfare, the chapter identifies the twinned kineses of armed force and moving-image media, and identifies a number of principles for handling moving images as weapons, including the principle of Image Environment Domination. Finally, the conclusion, offered within the chapter, draws together analyses in the remainder of the volume, reinforcing the argument built throughout that moving images themselves determine the nature of representation, interpretation and understanding offered by moving-image media, and that these do not result in a necessarily reliable, comprehensive or even predictable instrument of war. Images are the key weapons of contemporary war.

# 2 Moving images and meaning

## The nature of the weapon

If moving images constitute weapons in contemporary warfare, as was argued in Chapter 1, then it is necessary to understand the nature of moving-image media – in a sense, how the key weapon of contemporary war works and what forms it can take. To understand the effects of an instrument and how it can be used, it is necessary to identify its main elements. This is the purpose of this chapter, which considers the evolution in relations between moving-image media and war, from the first footage of war onward, examining also the different dominant forms which moving-image media can take – notably the major film forms (feature fiction, television news, and current affairs and documentary). The chapter then proceeds to examine the nature of the moving image weapon itself, extending from the understanding of context established into analysis of narrative in the moving image context – the essence of how the media function and how their content is framed. Finally, the chapter explores what can be gained from the study of moving-image media in relation to war, concluding that study of these media enhances examination of war and particular wars, and that the relationship has become central in twenty-first-century warfare.

### Film, television and war

War has been a favourite subject for moving-image media. In the still early days of the cinema, the first actuality film was *The Battle of the Somme*, a remarkable enterprise since it was quite probably the only uncensored, artistically open war reportage ever filmed. Five separate camera crews were dispatched to film the offensive launched on 1 July 1916, with no restrictions whatsoever on what they filmed (somewhat naively). The film, edited and rushed into theatres within a week, managed for the most part to draw on the few positive features of that offensive, rather than the culturally more familiar heavy losses, although some of these were honestly admitted. It also included the curiosity of the first occasion of soldiers performing for the camera, although the prominent example is one prisoner of war noticing the camera as they are being marched along, looking into the camera as he notices it, then running round again to be further back in the line so as to appear again. That initial actuality film, more actual and open than much of what would follow in the next century, still held the basic elements that would inform all moving-image media in their treatment of warfare, whether feature fiction film, actuality or documentary film – and whether for theatrical release, or later for television and the twenty-first-century multi-media environment made possible by digitisation and the internet. These included the focus on individuals or small groups, the inevitable dominance of the striking image over information of other kinds, the emphasis on action and emotion, rather than reflection and reasoning, that derives from the nature of the medium, all of which constitute the shared demands of narrative within the moving-image medium, with only minor differences between fiction and the various types of actuality moving-image representation of war.

Since the advent of film, an extensive relationship between moving images and war has emerged, whichever is the precise medium in which they are rendered – celluloid, analogue television or some form of digital media. Despite this relationship, and despite the enormous growth of interest in communications media studies at school level and above, in the UK, at least, and commensurate expansion of provision, there has been little serious attempt to bring the two together. Where there has been specific attention to war and film, aside from the occasional coffee table book, there have been some studies of specific types of film in relation to specific wars, for example, the Second World War,[1] or the Vietnam War broadly.[2] However, even these areas of coverage are limited and often uneven collections, or weak and descriptive studies (though not quite wholly – the studies just referenced on war and society in the Second World War and American combat films are about the only serious and systematic studies thus far). Generally studies pay attention either to the relationship of film with changing social context, or the curiosities of production history. Yet, there is increasing attention to film in most fields, including international relations and the study of war and peace. The theoretically oriented journal *Millennium* began an interesting film section in 2006, carrying short interpretations of individual films and their relationship to international issues.[3] In 2000, King's College London's Department of War Studies introduced a revised core course for the MA War Studies programme, framed around 15 key texts, one of which was consciously selected as fiction feature film text, as a way of showing that investigation of the nature and character of war need not be restricted to written sources, nor purely academic and analytical.[4] However, despite these trends, there has been very little real focus on how filmic sources can assist the understanding of war and peace (despite the analogous long-standing relevance also of literary classics, such as Shakespeare's *Henry V* and Lev Tolstoy's *War and Peace*).

Moving-image media contain a variety of types and forms. The term 'moving-image media' is intentionally generic. It includes objects made using different formats, such as varieties of traditional celluloid negative film, varieties of magnetic videotape, and the growing wealth of digital means for capturing, editing, framing – and so on – moving images. The format used, however, is not of particular concern here – although we do consider the impact of the digital revolution in relation to war, in certain respects, in Chapter 6. Rather, our focus is on types of object within the domain of moving-image media.

There are three main types that concern the present study. These are feature fiction, current affairs and documentary, and television news – a typology that structures the book through Chapters 3 to 5. The distinctions between these types and the elements that feed into them, of course, require further explanation and contextualisation. The differences between the categories may appear obvious to some observers, but will raise questions for others – for example, we treat current affairs and documentaries together, as a type (as explained below), where some practitioners and analysts would draw a sharp distinction between them.[5] Equally, as we note below, distinctions occur within the categories we identify as well. We operate at the level of analysis indicated because the typology permits us to explore the common characteristics shared by different types of moving-image media, despite their differences.

The typology used here depends, first, on a distinction between fiction and non-fiction, or actuality. While there are cases and ways in which the lines between the two can become blurred, on the whole, there is a clear, well-established and recognised division between actuality films and their fictional counterparts. The defining aspect here is whether a film purports to present an account of the empirical world, based on evidence of some kind, including observation of phenomena from the 'real' world, or whether it is an invention of creative imagination, not intended to represent the 'real' world of empirical detail and experience. Of course, there is creative imagination in actuality filmmaking, just as there can be references to the empirical world in fictional work. However, the fundamental difference still applies, creating a necessary boundary between that which aims to mediate information to present some aspect of the empirical world as it is, or whether elements are clearly removed from that world in order to convey meaning through imagination. The key difference is really whether all the events, or detail, depicted have an authentic existence outside the process of moving image creation: if they do, this should be seen as an actuality film; if they do not, even if some elements fit this standard, then they are part of fiction's realm.[6]

Actuality treatments may be divided into two broad categories – short-format and long-format. One of these is television news, which relies on moving images, but is also composed of a series of short-format 'mini-movies',[7] such as package reports, perhaps lasting no more than 1 minute 33 seconds. The purpose of short-format 'mini-film' in a news environment is to capture the important detail and development concerning a subject, to show this in pictures and to support the pictures with verbal narrative and explanation (ideally, that is – of course, there are all too many news reports where the verbal dominates and the graphic dimension is little more than wallpaper pasted weakly to the sound). The short-format film tends to be event driven and will be forgotten and replaced by the next day's or week's 'news', just as a daily newspaper's reports end up in the rubbish bin the following day. Short news reports tend to be ephemeral, although there is an increasing trend for some of them, at least, to be preserved – for example, that great news corporation, the BBC, began to make packages of this kind available indefinitely by linking them to script reports on events published by BBC Online, the web-based version of BBC News.[8] A similar spirit appears to have inspired CBS News in the US, but the material appears to be more selective in the first place, and less likely to be kept (for example, much of the 9/11 material that was available at one stage was inaccessible by summer 2006). However, the CBS policy deserved credit, despite its comparative limitations vis-à-vis the BBC, given a commitment to making material available free of charge, like the BBC. These are important resources for the curious and, above all, for anyone interested in serious research into topics themselves, where they may be used referentially for the information they contain, or, more interestingly, for anyone engaged in the study of moving-image media.

The long-format actuality film, by contrast, may be used to create a fuller narrative and deeper, more reflective understanding of issues and events. The long-format can give context and perspective, getting away from the day-to-day detail and investigation of the short-format film, exploring different dimensions that would not be covered by the main news coverage. The long-format allows for greater depth in treating a topic, sometimes permitting the films to be foci for significant attention to, discussion of and engagement with issues. The long-format may be divided into two subcategories in the contemporary era – current affairs and documentary. This reflects a growing division between the two, with the former increasingly appearing to chase the coat-tails of the daily news,[9] offering fuller versions of shorter reports included in the news (this trend could be seen most evidently in the way BBC News included parts of *Panorama* films, or CBS News used reduced *60 Minutes* reports – in both cases serving also to trail the long-format programming as well). The link to the news agenda means that, as a trend, documentary films are increasingly transient, with their significance not in longer term or inherent value, but in addressing passing issues more fully than the news format permits. Current affairs films are 'documentaries' in the traditional sense of being actuality, or factually based, films. However, they are treated separately from films categorised as documentaries because of the increasing short-term focus they have – even if this cannot be an absolute division, as some short-term focused films could, despite their origin and intention, have longevity (whether in terms of the topic covered, or the intrinsic role of the films themselves). Documentaries, by contrast, are made for their inherent qualities, the intrinsic merit of the stories to be told and what the filmmakers have to say about them, and, to reach a wider audience and, if successful and fortunate, to have a longer shelf-life – increasingly, for example, the educational benefits of documentaries, in terms of their shelf-life, are seen as a factor separating this form from the long-format current affairs film.[10]

Although there can sometimes be a naive tendency to assume that documentary films, broadly, are either 'documents' themselves, or based on documents, and in either case representing somehow scientifically objective attempts to purvey 'the truth', in practice this is not necessarily the case, a position recognised by those involved in making such films, and, as far as it is possible, there is conscious acknowledgement of the limits of the medium. In saying this, it is important to recognise that documentaries come in different forms and types. While all, including current affairs films, are examples of actuality film rather than feature fiction film, the ways in which they can differ are numerous and of some magnitude.[11]

The world of actuality filmmaking has been transformed in the course of its history. From the early 'documents' on film – graphically recorded fragments of something happening, whether a train running or someone riding a bicycle, with no further contextualisation and no editing involved to structure narrative – to the advent of drama documentary and highly stylised presentational structure of a film such as Kevin MacDonald's seminal *One Day in September* (which caused consternation in some circles that its flashy narrative style was a betrayal of the documentary tradition by those who did not recognise that innovation and engagement were valuable tools when seeking to connect with a wider audience).[12] The crucial point, whatever the style or type of documentary, is to recall the vision of Dziga Vertov, the great early Soviet documentary filmmaker: his ethos was to point the camera and record reality, yet in his seminal *Man With a Movie Camera* (*Chelovek s kinoapparatom*) he showed reflexively that the filmmaker's conscious intervention was always present, behind the camera and, eventually, in the editing suite. Documentaries, no matter how much they are founded in empirical reality and documentation of the world as it is, are creations, depending on the filmmaker's human agency and decision making, as well as the availability of visual information, all woven into narrative texture to tell a story.[13] Whatever type of documentary – some of the types identified by scholars and practitioners include expository (the most common form, involving a narrative voiceover and emphasis on description and information), observational (where the camera follows what happens to present a 'slice of life' – the 'fly-on-the-wall' approach, for example, without pre-determination of the events and information that would make a film interesting, only the decision that to film a subject in this way would in itself be interesting – the departure point of reality television), interactive (where the filmmakers consciously become part of the film, whether through interviews or appearance in situations, creating a dynamic in events), and reflexive (such as Vertov's, which consciously finds ways to identify the process involved in making a film and so how issues of availability and selection influence outcome).[14]

These types of documentary do not include some of the more radical and challenging types, where elements of the world of fiction overlap. This realm may include the innovation of drama documentary, where elements are re-created, in place of genuine 'actuality' footage, as well as films, where the high style of the film overrides its fundamentally empirical character, in order to emphasise mood and reality, not in terms of physical depiction but atmosphere, or the unreliability of testimony and witnesses, using approaches more familiar in feature fiction. MacDonald's approach in *One Day in September* is an arch example of the film's qualities – fast-cutting, jump-editing and so on – taking the documentary away from the dusty idea of the document as empirical evidence from the archive of life. Both stylised, more subjective, actuality films and those including dramatic re-creation can be controversial among practitioners, but drama documentary has also excited concern beyond the world of the practitioners themselves.

The use of facsimile actors is confirmation of the vital requirement for pictures – the moving-image media are nothing without them. Drama documentaries were pioneered precisely as a way of making visible that which was otherwise unshowable. The technique was pioneered by Leslie Woodhead and the team working at Granada's *World in Action* in the 1960s and 1970s in order to be able to show things which they knew about communist Eastern Europe and were unable to film (in contrast, as Woodhead openly confesses, to the easy targets they were constantly striking against the US, where they were free to travel and film[15]). This innovative use would appear to be the measure for when and how the technique should be used – when a film is worthwhile enough and there is no other way reasonably to show something; but concerns about 'fakery', a lack of authenticity, the undermining of the ethics of factually based filmmaking, and, worst of all by far, laziness, filling gaps with re-creations rather than seeking out alternatives, are valid.

Another distinction within the family of actuality films involves the divide between one-off, self-standing documentaries, which is what most films of the kind are, and the documentary series. The documentary series differs from the single documentary in two crucial ways. The first is the obvious difference between a one-off and a multi-instalment, or chapter format, where a set of related films examine a topic in different stages and degrees of detail. The second is that the documentary series is sold as a whole on credibility and quality, not on novelty. This contrasts with the self-standing, single documentary, which generally needs to be pitched on grounds of novelty – which untold story will emerge?

Among the prominent examples of documentary series are several major works related to war, such as *The Great War*, the major 1960s undertaking to remember and understand the First World War, the pioneering documentary series, followed by the *World at War*, about the Second World War; since then, documentary film series relating to war have flourished, with examples ranging from the memorial collection of early colour film curiosities, *The Second World War in Colour*, and weighty, historically based series, such as Richard Holmes' *Wellington*, the more general histories in which war features are strongly fronted by a great communicator, such as Simon Schama. However, key examples of the documentary series are related specifically to contemporary war, such as *Fighting the War* and *The Death of Yugoslavia*, both discussed in Chapter 4 (with *The Death of Yugoslavia* known as *Yugoslavia: Death of a Nation* in the United States).

*The Death of Yugoslavia* sits at the pinnacle of at least one strand of documentary filmmaking made by Brook-Lapping, a dedicated company headed by Brian Lapping with Norma Percy as producer, responsible for a stream of films, including *The Fifty Years War* documentary film series. The Lapping approach is distinctive, telling the stories through the protagonists' mouths, thereby generating the feel of a firsthand, authentic document, or set of documents, woven into an authoritative whole. That whole stands or falls by the credibility of each of its parts, but the credibility of those parts works in light of the whole and the track record of the production teams. The approach works where all the interviews they film with the protagonists add up and when they get all the actors relevant to an event participating. The subject matter is contemporary and, despite the research and depth involved, including the quasi-documental character of the films, the character of the enterprise is journalism not academic.

This six-part documentary series is a treasure trove. Much of the history of the Yugoslav dissolution and the war that accompanied it is revealed from the proverbial horses' mouths. The method used in research, filming and production, of juxtaposing the version of one protagonist with that of another, creates a narrative flow in which detail that would not otherwise be available appears. However, as much as this film (or set of films) can be used to establish a more or less reliable picture of that which happened, it is not beyond question. The documentary, whether series or individual, for theatre release or television, is just as much driven by the demands of image and emotion as is fiction. The following section, therefore, will consider the nature of the moving image medium and the notion of moving-image narratives.

## Moving images: the nature of narratives

Narrative languages in different media hold a variety of possibilities for creating syntheses of form and content. There are, however, clear differences between those languages and the ways in which they work. It is the narrative nature of film, the means available to it and the demands it makes and satisfies, that are crucial to this study – understanding the nature of the media, and what moving-image media narratives can and cannot do. This will be explored in this section by reference to written texts and the inherent differences generated by the discrete forms. Film adaptation of literature is where analysis of the differences between the media is focused. As will be seen, the emphasis on the nature of film and the importance of being 'true' to it, as advocated by many film theorists including, notably, the early Soviet contributors to the field, may be misguided. Likewise the limited idea that a 'true' adaptation is impossible because the qualities of literature do not translate may be equally misguided. Another approach recognising the differences of medium is Iurii Lotman's concept of equivalence, whereby the filmmaker who aims to 'transcode' a literary text clearly must find filmic equivalents for the meanings expressed in the literary text.[16]

From its inception, film theory, as with film itself, has naturally tended to emphasise the visual qualities of film. This approach to film analysis has valued the technical and cinematographic aspects of cinema over other features, such as composition, drama, acting and, later, sound. The trend seems to have developed from the early years of cinema due to a desire to establish the medium as an art form in its own right. Doubts had been expressed that 'anything which could, by the wildest stretch of the imagination, be called art' might emerge from cinema.[17] The essence of this view was that film should be regarded as no more than recorded drama: film merely mechanically reproduces that which occurs in front of the camera.[18] This idea was rejected by film theorists, in particular the Hungarian Béla Balázs (who was also a script writer, poet and film critic), and some of the great early Soviet film specialists such as Lev Kuleshov, Vsevolod Pudovkin, Dziga Vertov and Sergei Eizenshtein.

Balázs specifically argued that film was a new art which produced rather than reproduced.[19] To reinforce this concept Balázs discussed the visual side of cinema. Seeking to put distance between cinema and the notion that it was no more than a recording of a dramatic performance, Balázs drew on fine art theory to promote the notion that it was not the internal content that mattered for artistic purpose, but the way in which it was formed in the given material, whether paint, marble or celluloid. The most important aspect of cinema was the way in which the means of filmmaking could be used to impose a particular design on the reality of whatever was placed in front of the camera. In all of this, the art form is determined to a considerable extent by the technical materials involved: the camera and the celluloid which runs through it, traditionally, and more recently, acetate and digital analogues – all of which, by their nature, demand and provide motion and image. It is the motion of the film and the movement in the images it uses that define 'film' as a creative, representational or observational medium. Meaning in film, more than anything else, is shaped by movement (including, at times, the absence of motion).

Lev Kuleshov, in 1917, was the first film director and theorist to use the term 'montage'. By this he was referring to the principle of composing a film by editing together various fragments to create a series of united images.[20] He saw this process of composition as forming the essence of cinema, and as a technique for imparting clarity and emotional impact to a narrative.[21] He used the technique to wonderful effect in his 1924 satire *The Extraordinary Adventures of Mr. West in the Land of the Bolsheviks* (*Neobychainye prikliucheniia Mistera Vesta v strane bol'shevikov*). Kuleshov proved to be a great influence on many other great Soviet and non-Soviet filmmakers, including Vsevolod Pudovkin.

Pudovkin used his own style of montage, a technique of dynamic and often discontinuous editing.[22] In his films he fused his innovative methods with literary and stage tradition, in particular realist style and elements from the psychological school of acting.[23] As in his famous Gor'kii adaptation of 1926, *Mother* (*Mat'*), Pudovkin takes individual heroes and puts them in historical, mass contexts, but with little reference to historical figures.[24] In complete contrast the experimental director Dziga Vertov, a committed Constructivist, hated all fiction film. He believed, instead, in 'catching life unawares' through a documentary approach, as exemplified in *Man with a Movie Camera* of 1929.[25] Vertov emphasised the social utility of film, believing that cinema was an autonomous art and one that everyone could understand. He saw it as a means of educating the masses away from 'bourgeois' melodramas and towards non-acted films, which would reveal revolutionary truths.[26]

Today, however, Sergei Eizenshtein is the director most readily evoked by the word 'montage', although he was neither the inventor of the concept nor the first to use it. Eizenshtein saw montage not as something exclusive to film, but as a technique already existing in other arts, particularly painting (for example, Leonardo da Vinci's planned *The Deluge*) and literature (for instance, Milton's *Paradise Lost*).[27] The technique is evident in his films of the 1920s, *Strike* (*Stachka*) (1924), *Battleship Potemkin* (*Bronenosets Potemkin*) (1925), *October* (*Oktiabr'*) (1928) and *The General Line* (or *The Old and the New*) (*Staroe i novoe*) (1929). Eizenshtein's ideas of montage treat it not as a series of logically connected shots, but as a *juxtaposition* of shots.[28] Eizenshtein referred to this kind of film as 'intellectual cinema', intending it to convey abstract ideas rather than a narrative.[29] For Eizenshtein the strength of montage lies in the fact that 'it includes in the creative process the emotions and mind of the spectator'.[30] For Eizenshtein, it is the 'kinetic' aspect of cinema that drives narrative – the movement from one image to another.[31]

The advent of sound altered the movie-making equation by creating a whole new dimension. However, the appearance of sound to accompany moving images did not remove the essential and necessary importance of the image as the defining element. The great Soviet film theorists and filmmakers were so adamantly committed to their visual art with its rapidly developed array of techniques that they took a stand against the misuse of sound technique in 1928. They were concerned that its advent might detract from the artistic character claimed for film and return it to the apparently barren lands of drama. Eizenshtein, Pudovkin and Aleksandrov called for the 'contrapuntal' use of sound in which the desired effect would be achieved through a sharp discord between the audible and the visual, rather than simplistic equivalence.[32] However, even though the role of sound is important, where present, inevitably, the visual tends to be elevated over other dimensions in the study of moving images precisely because they define the medium – there is nothing without them. This is why those who have described television as a 'talking' medium, where familiarity and sociability override visual aesthetics (for example, when compared with cinema, particularly of the artistic variety), may miss the point if they overlook the necessary condition of moving images for the medium.[33]

It is the visual that makes television's familiarity, talk and sociability distinct from, say, radio or other oral traditions. There will always be relationships between the forms, including those of heritage, just as there are between written forms and other media. But the visual creates a clear distinction between oral, aural and written media, generating a need to understand the impact of images on creation, structure and narrative, in contrast to other media. Images are the media's 'essence'; its 'primary content lies in the visual images that unfold'.[34]

One of the most influential figures in critical literature on moving-image media, George Bluestone, wrote in this vein. He followed in the footsteps of Balázs in particular, but departed from him by placing emphasis on the viewer's reaction. Bluestone argued that the difference between film and literature, induced, for example, by the different physical and technical means involved in their creation, is compounded by the distinction between the viewer's perception of the film's image and the reader's conceptualisation of the written text's words in a 'mental image'.[35] However, this study is not concerned with investigating audiences.

The prime theoreticians of film include André Bazin and Christian Metz.[36] Metz provided the first attempt to establish an analytical approach to narrative, which was specific to cinema. The result was a codification of the 'specific signifying procedures' which constitute the 'syntagma' of cinematic narrative.[37] However, the particular signifiers identified for this cinema-specific approach and the analytical framework to which they are essential have been found to be confusing, unclear and inadequate.[38] Within all of this, it is the visual dimension, which counts in defining narrative in moving-image media as a set of signs. Bazin recognises a distinction between films in which the director imposes order through montage and those in which the director allows 'reality' to emerge through the use of long, continuous shots which would permit 'pre-existing structures' to be revealed.[39] This is, however, no more than a distinction between two approaches to editing and use of the camera, both founded on the assumption that image constitutes film. Such a view is taken to its extreme by Siegfried Kracauer, whose phenomenological approach equates the qualities of cinema entirely with those of photography and centres on the 'material phenomena' from which its emotional and intellectual content emerge (in contrast to the 'mental continuum' derived from literature).[40]

As Victor Perkins suggests, this is a strain of criticism which threatens to exclude, for example, even D.W. Griffith, the director credited with inventing the vocabulary of cinema.[41] Yet it is clear that such a vocabulary does exist, and it includes the use of the close-up, extreme long shots, panning shots, split screens, and parallel editing, montage and masking techniques (such as the iris and the dissolve). It was the Soviet directors and theorists who then gave it grammar, as Boris Eikhenbaum shows in his discussion of film-phrase as the elementary unit of film articulation. Synthesizing the contributions of the great practitioners from Kuleshov to Eizenshtein, Eikhenbaum demonstrates how the progressive use of film-phrase resembles literary narration.[42]

Literature provided source material for cinema from its outset. This gave rise to critical assessments that the latter diminished the former in adaptations. Cinematic versions of works of literature were found to be guilty of a number of crimes against the original, including omission, simplification, exaggeration, destruction and lack of originality.[43] Aside from the very literal comparative approach, which simply points out the differences between a film adaptation and the book upon which it is based, the essence of the charges against adaptations is found in discussion of storytelling or narrative.

At the heart of this discussion is the distinction between concept and percept, noted above, with reference to the work of Bluestone. The difference between literature and film is that the former can 'tell' things while the latter can 'show' them. Seymour Chatman gives the following example: the author can write, 'A woman entered the room'. At this point, stripped of adjectives and other detail, the reader will conceive of an image of a woman to whom he or she attributes unstated characteristics. The filmmaker, in contrast, must inevitably show the woman entering the room and supply full description and detail – as Chatman puts it, the equivalent of a 'potentially unlimited verbal paraphrase: 'A woman entered a room with a Roman nose, high cheekbones, and blond hair piled elaborately on her head (etc., etc.).'[44] Conversely, the written word cannot dictate images no matter how much detail is provided in description.[45] Each medium has intrinsic qualities which separate it from the other.

These inherent differences led many, such as David Bordwell, to infer that film can have no narrator, even where, as with Bordwell, they concede that film can have narration (in that the viewer constructs something akin to a narrated understanding by watching the film).[46] However, while the essential differences of form cannot be denied, the suggestion that film is without narration or narrator because of its visual character has been challenged since the 1970s. In 1972, for example, Perkins criticised the emphasis on the visual and on technique in film analysis, which led 'the orthodoxy' to present narrative as 'an alien form' which film could 'translate and annotate but not absorb as part of its creative mechanism'.[47] He argued that film criticism would have to take into account the film as a whole, recognizing that story-telling informed 'the character of the medium used in the telling' rather as differences in form and medium did not exclude narrative from 'poetry, novel, strip-cartoon, or theatre, [and] it cannot reasonably be seen as hostile or irrelevant to cinema'.[48] The film is the sum of the decisions taken by the maker, or makers, regarding what to include and what to exclude, in which way, for how long and so forth.

Since Perkins there have been serious efforts to address the question of narrative in film. Avrom Fleishman, for example, notes that even where form, in his view, still precludes true narration, there is a 'set of film practices' which 'produce the impression of narration, the narration-effect', while certain films make explicit use of narration either on screen or only on the soundtrack (with a voiceover).[49] Seymour Chatman has gone further than this, arguing that alongside other forms of discourse often not considered, such as argumentation and description, narration occurs in film and, above all, derives from a narrator. Taking as his starting points criticism of Bordwell's position of constructed narration without a narrator, as well as Wayne C. Booth's discussion of the implied author, Chatman argues for recognition of implied and 'reconstructed' narration.[50] From this he recommends that a distinction be made between the presenter and the inventor of a story. He explicitly takes the idea of narrator beyond the 'recorded human voice "over" the visual image track' treated by Fleishman (although voiceover can be one component of film narration).[51] The implied author, in Chatman's terms, presents the story, whether by use of one specific 'teller' or many of them, or in combination with other parts of the 'composite', which is the 'cinematic narrator'.[52] However, this composite is actually more the sum of narratorial devices and options than an actual narrator.

Following from Chatman, again in the wake of Booth, James Griffith has put forward a 'neo-Aristotelean' approach.[53] Whereas Chatman has an abstract narrator, Griffith, criticising the former, takes the inventor dimension of the narrator and sees both film and literature as capable of narration and, indeed, of being faithful to each other in terms of meaning and effect. The key lies in assessing the relevance and coherence of the narrative devices chosen by the creator of a film or novel (or a poem) from the range of available possibilities. The medium may be different, but the question of choices remains the same: 'according to the material, technical, and formal choices the artist has made, what effects are necessary and what peculiar powers are possible?'[54] Film and literature, alike, draw on a set of instruments available to the medium in order to create the combination of form and content which most effectively achieve the desired artistic outcome.[55] Thus, a proper understanding of narratives will recognise that different media possess different means for achieving the same, or similar, ends.

This approach from the 1990s, and the critical canon from which it emerges, focuses on the possibility of harmonious blending and on the inherent differences which the two material forms necessarily create.[56] In terms of adaptation these include 'film's traditional difficulties' with time and space, abstraction and representation of the interior dimension of thought and emotion.[57] In adaptation there are selections which determine the way in which the film represents the source novel and maintains its 'story' and supporting narrative; key issues may involve selection of plot lines and sub-plots, characterisation and compression of characters as well as structure and sequence.[58]

Very often, despite the best intentions of those involved in making moving-image media, elements of the output and especially its meaning may be distorted by the shift in medium. The restricted notion that faithful adaptation is precluded by the inherent qualities of literature is mistaken. Both media are narrative means, which use a range of possibilities for melding content with form. However, the clear differences between them present difficulties when moving between one form and the other.[59]

Understanding the issues involved in translating from one medium to another, or in adapting narratives from other forms of text to the visual moving image medium, is a crucial step towards understanding the nature of moving-image media, and hence the characteristics of the crucial weapon in contemporary warfare. Whether the issue is the relationship between the text, or texture of events, and how the empirical detail involved in these is adapted to the screen, or understanding the way in which image-hungry screens will tend to use images kinetically, blending the kinesis of cinema-plus with the kinesis of weaponry used in a strategic context. If narratives are essential, either to understanding conflict, or to defining success – who wins – in contemporary warfare, then understanding the nature of moving-image narratives through predominant types of film theory, and the innate differences of form by reference to critical discussion of adaptation and narrative, we are in a position to move to consideration of the relationship between war, in particular strategy, and moving-image narratives.

## Strategies of understanding

The nature of the medium, with its thirst for images, action and emotional engagement, can significantly limit the ability of film to capture or convey war on screen. Similarly, the scale and scope of war means that it cannot be reflected as a whole. These two features taken together mean that certain aspects of war are better suited than others to filmic treatment: the experience of warfare, whether in combat or away from it, as known and shown with reference to an individual or an identifiable small group of them offers far easier and more compelling material for the moving-image medium than, say, strategy, which is, in its essence, a reflective and conceptual field, and in its practice, usually so broad that depicting the elements at work is likely to be unwieldy or incoherent as such. But treating strategy, as with any other aspect of warfare, is not impossible – it just presents particular challenges.

Strategy concerns the relationship between means and ends. It is the way in which force is created and applied for political purpose. This is the area of war studies in which there is little in the cinema that either captures or enhances the subject, certainly in terms of the intellectual and pragmatic interaction that is involved in reality. While numerous films of the Second World War, such as *The Battle of Britain* and *The Longest Day* did their best to describe some of the strategic thinking that went on through dialogue on screen, they do not convey a sense of strategy. Far more, they reveal the problems of cinematic treatment of thought and its application, offering scenes constrained by stilted set-piece discussion. While some of the discussion and action in Michael Powell's classic *The Life and Death of Colonel Blimp* reflects and conveys change in strategic thought, this is limited both in itself and in context of the film as a whole. Perhaps the only place in which strategy has met with sustained success in cinematic presentation is the first hour of *Independence Day* by Roland Emmerich, which then proceeds to be incoherent and preposterous. The presentation in the opening part of this film shows the interaction of intelligence, planning, preparation and deployment, revealed in verbal terms only through the slow realisation of the American human race under attack that it has been utterly outmanoeuvred – and even then, it is the visual aspect that predominates. The trick Emmerich pulls off (to a limited extent following the dramatic-narrative method used by H.G. Wells and the adapters of his *The War of the Worlds*) is to show strategy by revelation: the brilliance and completeness of the aliens' relationship of ends to means emerges through the gradual processes of realisation and understanding, which depict alien actions and events arising from them, and the developing understanding of what has happened by key characters, such as the US President, played by Bill Pullman, or the wizard cyber-expert, played by Jeff Goldblum. Strategy is unveiled through surprise and revelation.

*Colonel Blimp,* aside from its sense of history, friendship and romance, is also a quintessential treatment of war's social impact. It achieves this on two levels. The first is the impact of change in warfare on civil–military relations – regarding both politics and society as a whole. Changes in the social organisation and culture of the armed forces are reflected in the shift from the chivalric code of the beginning of the twentieth century to the ungentlemanly necessity of the Second World War, if contemporary enemies are to be measured. The second form of impact is on society as a whole. This is seen, for example, in the transformation of 'the female character' (in fact, three separate characters, played by Deborah Kerr in each of the three wars covered in the film). She goes from pure romantic interest in 1900, to nurse behind the front lines in the First World War, to driver in uniform in the Second World War. This reflects the way in which twentieth-century warfare has come to be a matter involving the whole of society.

The area in which war film has been most successful and has most often been treated concerns the experience of war. Whether this experience is that of troops in battle, of troops away from battle, of societies under occupation, of societies under attack, or of societies mobilised for war, this has been the aspect of war that has most often worked on screen. Whether the experience concerns the awfulness, lunacy and humour of war, as reflected in many films about the Vietnam War, or the heroism that gave tone to many American and British films about the Second World War during the 1950s and 1960s, or the longing, lust and loss of those waiting at home for soldiers, or enduring bombardment, it is how war affects individuals that most often appears on screen and which most often works well. This is a function of the needs for character and identification, and narrative and structure, which drive the making of film.

Examination of the potential impact of screen narratives of war on understanding of both war generally and particular conflicts is important, the latter especially regarding regions directly affected by a conflict and outside it. In carrying out an examination of this kind, there are various aspects which can be investigated: the extent to which screen narratives can contribute to processes, such as peace building and pedagogy, or strategy and research on conflict and conflicts through their impact on legitimacy and understanding. To examine the relevance and role of moving-image media in researching and teaching war is, to a large extent, to open up new avenues of exploration – even where there has been treatment, whatever that treatment, it has largely been produced by authors whose backgrounds lie in cultural studies or related fields, rather than strategic studies. This statement stands even where there has been considerable public discussion regarding both the impact of television news, and current affairs films and documentary series usually (although not exclusively) shown on television, which are of relevance to this study.[60]

Television news as a type of screen narrative is distinct from more reflective approaches taken either in documentary or feature fiction films. Each separate narrative in a news broadcast is usually of only three or four minutes' duration, or quite likely as little as one and a half minutes, and is intended to be viewed immediately, whereas the types of screen narrative covered are of longer duration and seek a deeper and more reflective response from an audience. This is the case whether the films are fictional or factual. However, there is a grey area regarding the incorporation of news footage and reporting when used in documentary films, as noted below. The only real focus given to such study for the most part is in the domain of propaganda, where the work of Philip Taylor, a communications media scholar, stands out.[61] This field is important, but reflects only a limited part of the prism – even in terms of strategy and operations, in the contemporary era, it is of limited relevance.[62] However, aside from this particular focus, and despite the increasing tendency to note and include film within the scope of research and teaching at the margins, there is still scepticism that somehow watching films offers little more than distraction.

Indeed, given the contested nature of war – it is, after all the means to which politically motivated groups turn when other avenues for making decisions and settling issues run out – there is good reason to wonder why and how film might offer any useful routes to analysis and understanding. It is clear that there have been many views regarding the nature of war, its causes and conduct, and the locus of responsibility for it. There have been many disputes over who did what to whom, when, for what reason and with however many long-standing grievances to be taken into consideration. In this context, can there be any purpose in seeking to analyse films relating to war? After all, film itself cannot be seen as providing a necessarily reliable version of life. The purpose of this section is to address this and identify the potential use of film beyond the intrinsic confines of studying films in their own right. As has long been recognised, there are important ways in which film can enhance understanding of their social and historical context – although rich disputes reflect the degree to which there could be debate about what understanding can be gained.

Much analysis has concerned the way in which moving image narratives create the conditions for a conflict or shape understanding of it while war is being fought, or has an impact on its character. In particular, there has been emphasis on the way in which simplification and distortion combined with repetition create a strong sense of both national and public memory and of 'the Other'.[63] While national and public memories can usually be regarded as discrete phenomena,[64] in the case of the former Yugoslav countries it has been argued that these have been fused,[65] in large part due to the media processes identified above. However, while these strategies leading to fusion and consolidation of understanding of the causes and conduct of the conflict can be identified *ex post facto*, it is a major challenge to identify the means by which to address this outcome.

In part, this is because no media output, or systematic programme of media representation, can guarantee to have any desired impact. Many political, educational or marketing media campaigns have been failures,[66] while research on audience engagement with television news and security indicates a commensurate pattern.[67] The difficulties in guaranteeing that a receptor audience will understand and accept the meaning intended by authors is also linked to findings concerning the impact on contemporary Western societies of representations of violence in various mass media, primarily in screen narratives. While content analysis has demonstrated increasing incidence of portraying acts of violence in certain areas, such as children's television,[68] it has been more difficult to demonstrate the consequences of this conclusively. On the one hand, research based on the notion that representations of violence in screen narratives provide 'aggressive cues' has shown that violent behaviour observed may also be learned and imitated.[69] On the other hand, studies using notions of reinforcement, which suggest all things can happen, argue that portrayal of screen violence reinforces those things to which the receiver is predisposed, meaning that an individual with violent tendencies might be encouraged by viewing violence to act violently, while an individual lacking those tendencies will not be prompted to act in this way.[70]

In addition to the contentions of these different perspectives, there is a long tradition, dating back to Aristotle, which holds that narrative (and symbolic) representation, including treatment concerning acts of violence, can be cathartic and even therapeutic. In this context, difficult emotions find an outlet, cleansing the impulse to be violent as a result of viewing screen narratives.[71] It is on conclusions of this kind that some researchers in media studies, as well as some in peace and security studies, advance the proposition that the media can have positive effects and play a role in the prevention and management of conflict. The key elements of this have been theorised as providing channels of communication, offering opportunities for education, opening up possibilities for confidence building and mutual understanding, framing and defining the conflict and analysing it, and providing an emotional outlet;[72] that is, catharsis.[73]

The problem, in reality, is that the most that might be said with confidence is that some individuals might be affected in one way, others in an opposite way and yet others might not be significantly affected at all. However, while a particular interpretation might not be received, one area in which research appears conclusive is that screen narratives, of whatever type and with whatever intention and interpretation, can set agendas and highlight issues to be considered, even though they cannot necessarily generate any particular interpretation.[74] The twin departure points that emerge from this for research are that screen narratives will raise issues for discussion and that they can have some impact regarding interpretation. However, assessing interpretation is made difficult by complexity in the subject matter, as well as by the potential variety in reactions. Although the twin reasons noted above offer evidence to investigate the impact of screen narratives on interpretation of conflict, there is a research problem in gauging the impact of a narrative text, as with any other form of communication, on its audience.

The third way in which moving-image media can be related to the study of war is its utility as a tool of investigation and interpretation. One of the key issues for many observers of conflicts on screen is whether they constitute a faithful rendition of actual events, or a distortion of them. Given the wealth of literature and analysis on problems of interpretation and the nature and conditions of 'reality' (debates rage over whether there is an empirical reality that might be conveyed, whole or only partial realities, or essential realities that depart from the restrictions of the purely empirical and stretch into the realms of figuration and metaphor), this might almost seem to be an issue not worth pursuing in an empirical manner.[75] It may be that discussion of news and current affairs coverage, or war films in terms of their accuracy in representing the war, is futile and banal at the same time. In and of itself, analysis of this kind may offer little in terms of salient inference, or satisfaction. However, if it is supposed that investigation of the war is valuable, on its own merit for academic purposes, or for broader understanding of the phenomenon, then accuracy of detail is important. Examination of accuracy in detail, as well as in overall interpretation, might be an effective instrument for investigating the character and conduct of the war itself. In order to consider this, the remainder of this section will consider the character of the war itself, followed by consideration of examples of discrepancy and accuracy.

Aside from the merit of analysing screen narratives in their own right, it is clear that such analysis can be a useful device for teaching and researching particular conflicts and war in general. While the phenomenon of screened war has limitations, it has a particular role in treating the phenomenon of conflict. It offers possibilities for question and enquiry, as well as for explanation and understanding. That it might also, on occasion, offer the chance of contributing to catharsis and reconciliation only adds to this. However, whether through fiction feature films, or documentary films, or television news and current affairs, or digital communications, examination of moving-image media enhances study and understanding of conflict, in terms of the character, conduct and detail of particular conflicts and their political and social contexts. Beyond this, however, the relationship between moving images and war became a crucial part of conflicts themselves in the twentieth and into the twenty-first century, making study of the relationship between war and moving images, and the role of images as weapons, a crucial area of study.

# 3 Feature fiction film

The form of moving-image media objects is primarily established in the domain of feature fiction film. This is the area in which the main elements of narrative have been most strongly developed historically. Although some of the early theorists and practitioners of this kinetic art form pinned their colours to the quest to capture reality and to make faithful and realistic films, most attention went into developing the filming, compositional, editing and creative features that drive narrative in the domain of fiction. This is the idiom in which the three elements identified in the introduction as constituting the scope of interpretation and the drivers of narrative form are most evident initially – interpretation, image and experience. While later chapters will develop understanding of these elements regarding different types of actuality moving-image media, this chapter examines feature fiction approaches to contemporary warfare. The chapter considers analysis of fictional (or fictionalised) treatments of post-Cold War armed conflict in three cases – the Yugoslav War of the 1990s, the conflict over Chechnya in Russia, and the Gulf Conflict of the early 1990s (albeit with implications continuing into the new century), as well as offering specific interpretation of two particularly successful and prominent films, both easily available on DVD enabling critical study: *No Man's Land* by Danis Tanović, set in Bosnia, and *Black Hawk Down* by Ridley Scott, set in Somalia. The chapter as a whole will demonstrate that moving-image media, by their nature, focus on personal experience and the emotional, as well as on the visual – which defines representation on screen, rather than any other factor.

## Interpreting the Yugoslav war on screen

The Yugoslav War of the 1990s provides a strong and coherent example of the way in which feature fiction film operates around human experience and the image, while being unable seriously to capture strategy.[1] It also constitutes a vehicle for instrumentalising film heuristically and pedagogically to investigate the realities and contemporary history of conflicts. In saying this, we are not presuming that only one interpretation of events is possible, nor that feature fiction film itself is sufficient to offer a reliable historical interpretation. But we are confident in pointing to feature fiction film as a device through which to explore the conflicts. At the same time, returning to the main theme of the book, by relating a set of films to the realities of the war and showing what film can and cannot do in terms of investigating and understanding war, the salience of image and experience to the understanding of war in the contemporary age are confirmed.

This section discusses four films with different approaches to the war in Bosnia.[2] Some of them, most notably *Underground* directed by Emir Kusturica, have attracted considerable debate in this context. All, however, reflect a particular perspective and convey a different experience of the war. While *Underground* has appeal for those who would see the war as the incomprehensible and chaotic eruption of Balkan character, *Welcome to Sarajevo*, directed by Michael Winterbottom, identifies a brutal war of aggression – as seen by outsiders and requiring attention. These impressions of character and experience are echoed in the other films, Srdjan Dragojević's strong but stylised *Pretty Village, Pretty Flame*, and Ademir Kenović's simple and sublime *Perfect Circle*.

Perhaps the most controversial film of the Yugoslav War is *Underground* by Emir Kusturica. *Underground*, which won the Palme d'Or at the 1995 Cannes Film Festival, was the subject of fierce debate at the Festival and elsewhere. Some regarded the victory of Kusturica's film as a sentimental reaction to a mediocre film:[3] it had been chosen not on its merits, but because the director was originally from Sarajevo, and to award a major prize would be to show solidarity with the citizens of that beleaguered town. Critics of Kusturica pointed out that he had opposed the Sarajevo government and, in addition, had made the film with Belgrade involvement. Not only was the film tainted by involvement with Belgrade, according to these critics, but by its content.

The starting point for this discussion is the combined use of archive footage and fake old footage, which could be said to reinforce subliminally the sense that the Serbs are victims. Early in the film, Belgrade Zoo has been bombed and the town is destroyed and occupied, while the Nazis are seen to be welcomed in Maribor in Slovenia, and in Zagreb in Croatia. The deployment of archive footage in this way is at once accurate and disingenuous. It is accurate because the footage is authentic, whereas other pieces of archive footage are faked, or computer enhanced. In terms of detail, however, it does not allow understanding that Maribor was a predominantly German town in Slovenia, nor that the Slav population elsewhere in Slovenia did not welcome the occupation. Nor does it illuminate the areas of Serbian collaboration with the German powers.

In itself, this might seem a pedantic and obscure issue for Yugoslav experts, as Dina Iordanova has suggested, which renders accusations that the film is propaganda redundant, as it may only be discerned by those with relevant knowledge.[4] However, it is significant in three ways. First, it clearly marks the film as being favourable to Belgrade. Second, it feeds an interpretation of the conflict as being a backlash of history. Third, by doing so, it effectively serves the purpose of the Belgrade regime, as propaganda. Because it contributes, overall, to a film that emphasises history, culture and chaotic relations, it helps to reinforce confusion among observers in the outside world. It works as propaganda, as far as this charge is relevant to the film, not because it glorifies the Serbian cause in the war, but because the version offered prevents a clear vision of the war's actual causes and conduct. From the perspective of Belgrade, the film works because it will be read in the right way by audiences at home and will prevent clear understanding in the outside world. The usefulness of *Underground* pedagogically, therefore, is to be the tool for unpacking these points and the related sets of issues.

These elements from the past – most likely only to be noticed by those with a sense of Second World War events – were reinforced with the depiction in the 1990s of a war dominated by corruption and criminality, as much as by chaos and small, random, armed forces. In *Underground*, one of the key protagonists, Brzi (meaning Speedy) appears in the final section as a paramilitary leader running his own operation with the war.

The characterisation of the war overlaps, inevitably, with the experience it reflects and absorbs. The protagonists, both in the Second World War and in the war of the 1990s, inhabit a world epitomised by chaos, madness and colour, suffused with the association of sex and violence – most graphically demonstrated in two scenes. In the first, this is shown by Marko's dull sexual experience with a prostitute at the beginning of the film becoming a frenzy of self-satisfaction as she abandons him following the onset of the bombing of Belgrade in 1941. In the second, it may be seen in Natalija's erotic dance involving a tank canon.

This world, and the people who inhabit and take part in war in it, are part of what the director regards as a circus.[5] The understanding of the war offered is the circus of madmen meeting history, since the thread stringing the three parts of the film together and infusing the madness is history: the war of the 1990s is a product of intractable differences, demented individuals and the ineluctable course of history. In short, the people are crazy and the situation is irredeemable.

This interpretation of the conflict is favourable to Belgrade and to the Serbian side. In this view, everyone and no one is responsible, the war reflects the character of the society, and the past is to blame. The war is not a design of political leaders, generals and security service chiefs, according to the Kusturica view. Rather, it is a spontaneous phenomenon, stemming from the nature of the people.

This is an interpretation, especially with its manipulation of archive footage, which seems geared towards an audience which would prefer to be absolved of particular responsibility, rather than one seeking to attribute responsibility. Thus, while the film was received enthusiastically and with packed houses for weeks in Belgrade, it has not been shown in Bosnia, where Kusturica is vilified, nor in Croatia (so far as we are aware). It has been shown in Slovenia, but only as special showings – and the critical reception was hostile. This split in the response was echoed at Cannes and in the UK, where audience and critical reaction tended to reflect background and understanding of the conflict. The split could be simply defined: those for whom the war was one of rational, strategic action, regarded the film as propaganda; those who did not, or preferred not, to see the war in this way, enjoyed the circus.

The allegation of bias and playing a quasi-propagandistic role was also made against Srdjan Dragojević's *Pretty Village, Pretty Flame*. The title itself, with its flagrant exultation, could be felt to reflect the same judgement of the culturally specific gratification of violence found in Kusturica's work. There were two main reasons for the allegations. The first was that, like *Underground*, the film was made with Belgrade backing. The second was that, to some minds perversely, the film took a Serbian platoon, trapped by Muslims in a tunnel, as its focus – turning the attackers into victims, according to these views.[6] However, while a superficial reading would not refute this view, there are important details which suggest that another interpretation should be considered.

It is true that by placing a Serbian platoon in the tunnel as victims, the film will automatically have an audience in Serbia and in Serbian communities: there will be a point of identification. However, by using the conventional device of two friends who find themselves on opposite sides of the conflict and tracing the transformation of the Serbian central character, Milan, from being childhood and adult friends with Halil, the Muslim central character, to being a monster engulfed with hatred and killing a Muslim victim in the military hospital at the end of the film, it shows how people get drawn into events and are changed by them. The salience of this transmutation is reinforced by the simple exchange between the two friends repeated at the end of the film:

*Halil:*   'Do you think there'll be a war?''
*Milan:*   'What war?'

The relationship and Milan's transformation surely gives a potentially authentic depiction of the way, at the local level and through interpersonal relations, the war in Bosnia developed. The conflict, or at least this part of it, is nothing to do with ancient, or ethnic hatreds. However, the conflict transforms individuals and hatred appears as a function of the experience of war.

Within that experience, some of the elements in the Kusturica view may be observed. There is apparently sadistic brutality, both committed by Serbs – resulting in Milan's shooting two Chetniks – and by the Muslims who taunt the platoon in the tunnel. There is the link between sex and violence again, as Velja, an apparent womaniser, places a pistol against his head, then asks the American journalist, who has joined the Serbian platoon and has lost some of her initial hostility towards them as she has shared their experience in the tunnel, for a kiss. At the moment when it seems the kiss might have stopped him committing suicide, he declares, 'Just kidding', and pulls the trigger.

There is also the sense of circus – or at least peculiar fun – among the people, wrapped up with the mutual animosity. So it is that, despite the horrors of the tunnel, there is still singing, dancing and joking to be done. However, while these elements are present in certain situations, or embodied in individual characters, they are parts of the scene, rather than the whole, as in *Underground.*

The use of Milan as a central character offers the possibility of a reading of the conflict in which the involvement of individuals is for a variety of reasons. It is not simply due to visceral blood-lust. The use of a Serbian central character and a Serbian platoon trapped in the tunnel, in fact, it may be presumed, were what made it possible for the film to be made, distributed and well received by the public in Serbia. However, the treatment of Milan's character and his transformation demonstrate the way in which individuals can be susceptible to the worst in certain circumstances – created not so much by locals, as by others in different places.

Where the focus in *Pretty Village* is on a military detachment trapped in a tunnel and is one of the 'insider' perspectives on the war, *Welcome to Sarajevo* is, at its core, about the outsider's experience. It is about a troop of international journalists caught up in the siege of Sarajevo and, understandably, losing journalistic detachment along the way. This reflects the source book for the film – Michael Nicholson's *Natasha's Story*. Nicholson, a veteran war reporter for the British TV news broadcaster ITN, commented on the impact of the Sarajevo experience on the ethics of hardened professional journalists.[7]

This reaction gave rise to the theme of Nicholson's book, expressed in its title – his decision to smuggle one girl from an orphanage out of Sarajevo to the UK. This was an act of commitment that provides the basic story for the book and the film, but is not the central element in either. This is, in part, because the actual act of smuggling, nerve-wracking though it must have been, is accomplished with little incident (indeed, the introduction of incident is one of the ways in which the film reveals its interpretation of the war, as discussed below).

The journalist in the film, Michael Henderson, undergoes a small conversion in the course of the film. This is experienced through juxtaposition with a mysterious Altar Boy, whose red tunic seems symbolically to emphasise the bloody experience of Sarajevo. Henderson's professionalism is shown in the treatment of a street massacre – reminiscent of the actual, infamous bread queue massacre of May 1992. This challenge to

Henderson's professionalism is prefigured by an earlier incident. A Catholic wedding at the beginning of the film turns into tragedy when a sniper shoots the bride's mother.[8]

While his American counterpart, Flynn, combines professionalism with heroism, marching down the street to give assistance – and giving his producers a great story, one captured by every other crew but Henderson's – Henderson and his cameraman have followed the Altar Boy instead. They end up in a blind alley with the boy turning to them, staring at them, swearing and asking repeatedly 'What do you want?'[9] This is a test of Henderson's conscience: what is he doing? What does he want? In a sense, Henderson seems to be confronting himself in the blind ally of professionalism: it cannot be enough to be another spectator of Sarajevo's suffering.[10]

As if to cement his transformation, he catches sight of the Altar Boy in a crowd. Finally, Henderson follows the crowd to find them all watching a lone cellist playing Albinoni's *Adagio in G*.[11] In this moment, Henderson has become part of the crowd: looking up, as does the Altar Boy, he has become one of the people.

*Welcome to Sarajevo* has this focus in spite of conscious efforts to get away from its source material, in which the story itself is not terribly dramatic and the experience of being a war correspondent shines more strongly than it does in the film. The filmmakers' intention was to avoid the essentially non-dramatic story and the temptation to join a well-established genre of war film. In this genre, the central character is a journalist who goes into a conflict zone and becomes the focus of interpretation for the audience – which is an audience outside the former Yugoslav lands.[12] Rather, the aim was to make Sarajevo itself and its people the focus of the film.[13]

While Henderson is the focus, his presence is not necessarily obtrusive. However, as the film shifts back to its basic story and focuses on Henderson's taking the girl from Sarajevo, it inevitably draws the attention firmly to the journalist (and, in our judgement, makes for a less satisfying film). In the end, the attempt to represent Sarajevo and its people succumbs to that which it sought to avoid and becomes the journalist's story. However, as in other cases, the device helps to draw in the outside audience and, perhaps, to achieve the filmmaker's aim – to make sure that audience did not ignore the war.[14]

However, in seeking to provoke an audience not to ignore Bosnia, issues of accurate portrayal cannot be overlooked, and, indeed, can be useful and interesting for introducing and investigating the war. For example, does it make a difference that the name of the girl at the centre of *Welcome to Sarajevo* has been changed from real life and the autobiographical book that is its source? The Muslim girl Emira who is smuggled out of Sarajevo by a journalist making the transition from the equivalence of professional objectivity to personal commitment is no longer the real

Serbian girl who provides the title of Nicholson's *Natasha's Story*. It is clear that this change reflects the aims of the filmmakers both to focus on the plight of the Muslims in the face of the Serbian campaign in the war, and to make the material accessible to the type of Western audience the film was supposed to mobilise. At the same time, it serves to simplify the reality that there were Serb and other children, as well as adults, trapped in the experience of Sarajevo. The clear use of the film in a study of the Yugoslav War, in this context, is to identify the potential for simplification and bias, on the one hand, and to highlight the more complex and accurate reality involved, on the other.

When *Welcome to Sarajevo* was shown at the Sarajevo Film Festival after the end of armed hostilities it was reportedly received well, but more in terms of politeness than out of genuine affection. Its attempt to show the city and its people, while worthy, was still lost to the story of the outsiders. Ademir Kenović's *Perfect Circle*, by contrast, was rapturously received. This film, made by a director from Sarajevo who had, in contrast to Kusturica, remained in the besieged town during the war and, even, had shot some of the material while there was a war, captured the experience of those who had endured. For those who had the fortune not to be captive in Sarajevo, it is an equally astonishing film in which the city, the victims in it and the spirit of life and human endurance prevail. It can have few points of comparison in its depiction of the experience of war by civilians.

The perspective is clear in the film. There are those inside the city who are ordinary people and there are those outside who are anonymous, although dubbed Chetniks. This is the one film accurately to depict the practice of ethnic cleansing. At the beginning, a small squad of Serbian soldiers wearing balaclavas is seen attacking a village. This is perhaps as faithful a rendition of the terror induced by such attacks as might be possible. While the violence and murder associated with attacks of this kind are not shown directly, the experience of two small boys who survive the raid, and who observe dead adults and animals outside the house in which they hide under a bed, is sufficient to ensure a chilling depiction. In a more philosophical film that contrives to represent the brutal nature of cleansing with sterile, almost abstract distance, *Forever Mozart* by Jean-Luc Godard, determined to make a connection with the 1930s and 1940s, shows those about to be shot (not limited to Bosnians) digging their own graves. The anonymity of the undoubted villains of the war is confirmed by the experience of the two young boys around whose developing relationship with a de facto foster parent, Hamza, the film revolves. The two boys, Adis and Kerim, come to Sarajevo after witnessing this 'cleansing operation'. However, those troops are not seen clearly, and Adis, recalling the boys' experience of the attack, later tells a girl that Chetniks have 'no heads … only legs'. This is the boy's eye-level view, but it serves to separate the inhumanity of the city's anonymous attackers from the great humanity found within the town.

The insider's experience and spirit of simple, ingenious defiance is also captured when a sniper wounds a dog. Having failed in an attempt to find the boys' aunt, Hamza and the boys are returning across Sarajevo when they run into a sniper trap. The trio move behind a disabled tram to a point where it is necessary to cross a small road, but there is a break in the protective wall of vehicles against the snipers (so as to let vehicles use the road at other times). First, a woman is shot and dragged out of the road by some men. Then the snipers' pattern of shooting is noted, before a dog gets shot crossing the road. Kerim runs out to the dog and the others follow, concerned for Kerim. All make it to safety, but Adis asks why the dog was shot. Hamza's somewhat phlegmatic answer is to wonder if the sniper actually made a deliberate decision. When Kerim then asks, 'Is he happy now?' his reply is, 'Probably'. This reveals the resigned sense of the inevitable, as well as offering a measured reflection on the nature of those causing the city such misery.

If this day-to-day experience captures one of the contingencies of life in Sarajevo, what happens to the dog after this goes some way towards giving testimony to the character and ingenuity of the people of the city. Hamza, Adis and Kerim, along with the wounded dog, head for Hamza's flat, where a grumpy old man wonders why the dog is not put down. Instead of curtailing the animal's life, however, the dog is given a new existence, with a wheelchair arrangement for its hindquarters.

The rather bizarre phenomenon of a dog half-dressed like a Roman chariot has two dimensions. First, it is an image for Hamza, the old dog of a poet who imagines himself hanging in the first scene of the film and several times thereafter. The futile existence of the poet who has remained while his wife and daughter have left Sarajevo, and who clearly thinks in terms of putting an end to his own misery, is transformed by the two boys. They are to him what the wheels are to the dog – the means to continue. (The allusion between the invalid dog and Hamza is confirmed when both follow the boys and Marko, Hamza's friend, at the end of the film, in an attempt to escape the doomed city.) Second, perhaps most significantly, it shows the ingenuity of the people in overcoming adversity and making defiant gestures of the human spirit.[15] The character of life in the besieged town and the experience of its inhabitants provide a strong context for the story of Hamza and the boys.

The still simplicity of the film is captured in its title. The perfect circle is what Hamza draws when he becomes 'tense'. This almost meditative reaction to pressure may also be connected with his thoughts of hanging himself – another response to pressure (albeit one which the ghostly voice of conscience from his wife identifies as pretence). It could also serve as a generous implicit explanation for the situation in which Sarajevo finds itself: faced with tension, its besiegers have drawn a perfect circle around it. However, those anonymous besiegers are not all Serbs – as is shown through Hamza's friend Marko, who assists at various stages in the film, including attempting to help the boys escape the town. However, this proves to be fatal for him and for Adis as they try to cross the wrecked part of town where Marko's flat had been.

This all too real outcome, followed by the attempt to find somewhere to bury Adis, confirms the film's wholly authentic touch. There is no sentimentality about the scene: the events have sufficient power to shock and move with only modest treatment by Kenović. The film, created in a direct and simple fashion, captures the experience of Sarajevo and, in many ways, the meaning of the war to many of its victims. That the film is set in Sarajevo is testimony to the people and the city. However, it is only detail that sets the film apart from other places and times where there are innocent victims of war. The film's strength is in stylistic and emotional simplicity, capturing the essence of the human spirit in adverse conditions and its capacity to endure.

Films of the Yugoslav war genre offer mostly limited, though useful, material which reinforces the assessment made that strategy is not easily susceptible to cinematic treatment, whereas experience offers the most fertile ground, and that images are essential. Although the opening scenes of *Perfect Circle* suggest, in line with the comment made about *Independence Day*, in Chapter 2, that the best way to treat such matters is from the perspective of the victims, the presentation of the tactical-level application of a compressed strategic-operational-tactical approach remains limited. None of the other films to appear, so far, even begins to come to terms with questions of strategy.

It is in the domain of experience, however, that the Yugoslav War, as with others, gains most resonance on the screen. *Welcome to Sarajevo* follows the well-established convention of the outsider journalist as a vehicle for approaching the war. For all its sense of commitment and its desire to focus on the people of Sarajevo, the film bears little comparison with contributions to the genre such as Alfred Hitchcock's *Foreign Correspondent*, Peter Weir's *The Year of Living Dangerously*, or Roland Joffe's *The Killing Fields*. Dragojević, in *Pretty Village, Pretty Flame*, on the other hand, has made one of the truly great war films. The film, based on a true situation, and taking the stock convention of a platoon under attack (as well as making references to the genre), uses the situation and technique to unpack the way in which the members of the Serbian platoon, trapped in a tunnel besieged by their Muslim counterparts, came to be part of the war. Implicitly, along the way, some of the threads by which the war was woven are also revealed and, with no more than a nod to the knowing, they are seen to be spun from Belgrade.

The four films analysed here reveal different aspects of the Yugoslav war and varied approaches to it. While *Underground* has met with both international fame and acclaim, and with international hostility, its interpretation of the war is one that has some resonance with certain audiences. The reality is that the celebratory circus of people and culture offered by Kusturica, however superficially (or super-profoundly) attractive and enjoyable, is a film where the interpretation on offer is either made in bad faith, or is misguided.

While Dragojević's *Pretty Village* might seem susceptible to some charges similar to Kusturica's film, there are clear elements which show that these cannot, in fact, be upheld. These include its focus on the character and motivation of those involved in the Serbian platoon, notably the central character Milan who is transformed from an ordinary guy whose best friend is a Muslim to manic Muslim murderer in the Belgrade military hospital. Beyond its structurally complex and powerful investigation of the platoon and its predicament, the Dragojević film in understated ways subverts any charges of being a pro-Serbian misrepresentation of the reality of war.

Both *Underground* and *Pretty Village* have raised questions about interpretation and objectivity. This emerges more directly as a problem in *Welcome to Sarajevo*. Here, the commitment and objectivity of the outsider, coming to Sarajevo in a professional role, is put to the test of experience and conscience. In the course of the film, the hardened war reporter assumes a role in seeking to take one girl out of Sarajevo and to adopt her. By the end of the film, the brutality of an absolutely black-and-white war has softened the journalist and made him one of the people. Yet, in depicting this outsider's transformation, the film misses its target – the attempt to put Sarajevo and its people at the centre of attention and to make it impossible to ignore their fate.

Where the people of the city do shine through, coping with adversity and enduring with humour and ingenuity, is in Kenović's *Perfect Circle*. Through simple and affective story-telling, Kenović's film makes the strength of character of the victims clear, but leaves the predators broadly anonymous. Similarly, simplistic and easy criticism of the international presence is avoided, with reasoned assessment of both the realistic limits of that effort and the character of the people in their desires, offered in its place. Yet, the overwhelming strength of *Perfect Circle* lies in the strength and endurance of the human spirit – a message which is not specific to Sarajevo, but is universal. While the interpretation of the conflict in the other three films might be in some way unreliable, that in *Perfect Circle* is sterling.

## No Man's Land

The film about the Yugoslav conflict, which had most international impact and significance – successful both at Cannes and the Academy Awards (best foreign language Oscar) – is *No Man's Land* by Danis Tanović. This is essentially a dark situation comedy – and the situation is Bosnian Army and Bosnian Serb soldiers trapped in a trench in no man's land, with one wounded Bosnian Muslim, Cera (played by Filip Šovagović) having been placed on a pressure-release projectile mine by a devious Serbian soldier (killed in a fire-fight by Čiki – played by Branko Djurić – the other Muslim), unable to move, because once his weight is removed the mine will detonate in the air; a tragic farce ensues with the UN force attempting to solve an impossible situation, and in the end failing; the Muslim is left on the mine while the UN commander pretends that every-thing has been sorted, and Čiki has shot Nino (played by Rene Bitorajac), the Serb, in front of live TV cameras after they have been escorted from the trench.

The characterisation of the conflict and its presentation both around the trench and in it, especially in the childish discussions between Čiki and Nino, is spiced with humour. This begins with the first scene, where joking and ironic dialogue contribute to the farce of a Bosnian Army relief squad's getting lost in the fog. The humour is darkened when the bright sunshine of morning reveals that they have found their way to just beneath the Serbian Command Post. They have been obviously identified and Serbian forces open fire on them. This sequence includes one sharply shot and swift element where the Serbian soldier's sight is seen to target the Muslim running away, lying on the ground, his back to the Serbian soldier, and then a flash of the bullet hitting the Muslim soldier in the back. This serves as a small reminder of the cruel character of the Serbian approach in the war. It is as a result of this that Čiki is blown into the middle trench in no man's land, wounded and apparently alone – although later the apparently wounded Cera is also discovered to be there, believed to be dead by two Serbian soldiers who then place him on the pressure-release projective mine. The Serbian soldiers are sent there by the commanding officer to check the trench. Both sides have been mys-tified initially, believing that there is no one in the trench. When the two Serbs reach the trench, after spending some time checking it out and then placing what they believe is a dead body (Cera's) on the mine, they are surprised by Čiki, who kills the older of them in a fire-fight and inflicts a flesh wound on Nino, the other, with whom he then comes to share the trench (along with Cera, of course). Nino is a novice soldier, who ends up in a childish argument over who started the war, with Čiki reeling off a list of general and particular accusations, and Nino being forced to concede at gunpoint that the Serbs did. But later, when he gains the advantage after seizing a rifle against Čiki, it is Čiki who has to concede that his side started the war.

Both admissions are made at gunpoint, undermining any validity, of course. But it is the opportunity the second of these exchanges provides for Cera that indicates the interpretation of affairs at the heart of the film: Cera, a metaphor for Bosnia, says that he is fed up with war and who cares who started it. This image of Cera as Bosnia indeterminately, but fatally, with a mine underneath it waiting to explode, is compounded when, at the end of the film, the UNPROFOR (UN Protection Force – the name for the UN mission in the country) mine expert declares that he cannot deal with the mine. This leaves Čiki as the war-weary Bosnia, unable to be helped by the UN – the violence suppressed while ever things remain that way, but unable actually to move or do anything. This is Bosnia at the end of armed hostilities and following the Dayton peace accords, which peace arrangement put in place, *inter alia*, a constitutional framework that was almost designed to prevent positive government action unless there was complete agreement on it.[16]

Beyond the overarching interpretation of the conflict offered by the film, there are two key themes that are treated, both reflecting on the outside world: the UN force deployed by the international community to Bosnia and the international broadcast news media. The first of these concerns UNPROFOR, the UN military force intended to foster peace and security with a primary mission to secure the delivery of humanitarian assistance to the country's beleaguered communities. UNPROFOR had the formal authority to use armed force, if necessary, to help complete its mission, and also played a wider role in protecting six 'safe areas' declared by the UN Security Council. However, the nature of the deployment itself, as well as the politics surrounding it, made it hard to contemplate any major use of force. The complexities of this operation are not, of course, treated in the film, aside from the evident complexity of the situation in the trench itself. There are somewhat ironic statements from UNPROFOR characters saying that things are 'complicated'. The perception of UNPROFOR offered in the film is very much Bosnian.

This can be seen in various aspects of the treatment of UNPROFOR. For example, the vision of HQ UNPROFOR in the Croatian capital of Zagreb as a fine, almost palatial, grand house does not tally with the realities of the less than splendid former military barracks that, in fact, served as UN Headquarters in Zagreb. The lack of real understanding of UNPROFOR is compounded by the presentation of Colonel Soft, the Briton ostensibly in charge of the mission – in reality, however, the officers commanding in both Zagreb and Sarajevo were generals. This figure is played by Simon Callow with splendid cotton-wool effeteness, and there appears to be a suggestion of General Sir Michael Rose, the Briton who commanded UNPROFOR in Bosnia during 1994 – the year in which the action is set. He is seen to be not only ineffectual, but also sly in his scheming either to avoid action or to cover up the failure to save the Bosnian balanced on the mine. In the former case, for example, Soft is seen on screen explaining that there is no way action can be taken over the men in the trench unless there is a resolution of the UN General Assembly. (This is another example of the Bosnian perspective on events and the world, out of line with realities – which were that the UN Security Council, not the General Assembly, gave the authority for the mission in Bosnia, and that the authority to tackle a situation like this existed anyway.) The latter is shown at the end, when, with Čiki and Nino dead, and unable to deal with the man on the mine, he announces that the man on the mine has been evacuated and orders a withdrawal; he then quietly tells his aide to inform both sides that UNPROFOR has information that the other side plans to take the middle trench that night. The implication here is that each side will shell the trench that night, blowing away the evidence that the Bosnian soldier had been left behind and providing cover for the mine's detonation. This reflects the Bosnian view of what were believed to be nefarious British approaches to the conflict – views shared by critics of British and international policy, even if these somewhat unfairly reflected conspiracy theory over cowardly conservatism.[17]

However, while the Bosnian perception of the British is unfair, and the ground-level sense of wanting to take the initiative and make a difference embodied in the French Sergeant Marchand in the film (who makes the point that to do nothing in face of mass murder is to take sides with those murdering) could be found among all the Western troops in the country, some of whom, including the British, Swedish and Danes, engaged robustly, stretching the limits of their mandates in the effort to make a difference. If the soldier's sense of honour and responsibility in the face of events is faithful to reality (and the frustration with the weakness and vacillation of their political masters), so too is the sense of differences between the various national contingents, with national characteristics marking those differences (the French, for example, comment playfully that the German mine specialist arrives 'on the dot'). The reality, as with the impossibility of deactivating the mine, is that sometimes it is not possible to make a difference, or perhaps more accurately, enough of one.

The desire to make a difference is shared in the film's worldview by the international television journalists, characterised by the fictitious correspondent Jane Livingstone from the fictitious broadcaster Global News. The desire to make a difference is evident in the critical approach to the UN, both at a distance and on the ground in Bosnia. This becomes evident when Livingstone reveals to Sgt. Marchand that she has been listening to UN communications and knows that he wants to make a difference, effectively putting him in a position where he is both forced, and has the opportunity, to, make a difference. He and Livingstone make an impact because both he and she tell his command that she will be reporting on the incident in half an hour one way or the other. This spurs attention from the caricature Zagreb command of Colonel Soft, who takes a helicopter to be at the scene, while the French contingent seeks to help out at the trench. Thus, the military on the ground, in the person of Sgt. Marchand, can use the media in order to make an impact. But the news media also impact on him independently.

The military and the media have different agendas. The elements on the media agenda are clear both in the attitude of Livingstone, seen competitively trying to be ahead of her international rivals and wanting to have some material that will get her live on air, and in the attitude of her editors, who are seen pressing her to get interviews with the men in the trench. In the latter case she has already tried and both, in their different and rude ways, have rebuffed her. She therefore responds to the pressure by saying that UNPROFOR will not allow access to the trench because it is too dangerous, but that she will do so when she can. The desire of the interview is the desire to fill the screen with images and novelty, transient though that novelty will inevitably be.

The lust for novelty and image – and indeed, kinetic action and visceral emotion – is satisfied in the end when Čiki shoots Nino dead, in revenge for the latter's attempt earlier to stab the former by using his own knife against him, and UN soldiers shoot Čiki dead in their attempt to prevent his shooting Nino. This carefully choreographed disaster is not only captured by the filmmakers, but is also viewed through the images of the diegetic TV camera, which captures the events directly for live TV, as Livingstone reports on the two soldiers from different sides being saved from the trench by UNPROFOR. This event is such that even the editors back in the Global News studio are stunned into drop-jawed silence. The appetite for image has been satiated. However, there is an irony at work, privy to the film's viewers, which is that, satisfied by the images and drama of the shootings, and accepting Col. Soft's manipulation, the body on the mine remains in the trench, a time bomb waiting to explode, but this goes unreported. The irony is strong because Livingstone's cameraman checks if she wants to get images of the trench, but she rejects the idea, saying that one trench is just like another. Thus, by missing out on the image, she – and the world – misses out on the real story. That remains the privilege of the filmmaker and his audience.

This absent image confirms the vital importance of images, and the way in which it is presented confirms the significance of visual texture in moving-image media. As with other films treated in this chapter, the overlap and interplay of television or video textures with those of the film constitute a key theme, both as a comment on the importance and presence of broadcast news and visual image media in contemporary conflict, and, perhaps more saliently, reflecting an increasing trend for feature fiction film and actuality moving images to overlap and share visual textures. Feature fiction film increasingly has the form of actuality coverage in its attempts to make drama realistic, while actuality moving image output increasingly uses the more dramatic modes of fiction to stimulate and provoke audiences (as discussed in the previous and following chapters). The nature of moving image narrative, whether fictional or actuality, from the outset, has set the boundaries and demands for any finished item. The basic demand for the dynamic of human interest and images is there, as in *No Man's Land*, where the Global News studio's desire to interview the soldiers from the trench is because their experience would meet the demand for interest and their interviews would be talking heads, and so images. Thus, interpretation in and of the film results from the kinetic overlap of experience and image.

In *No Man's Land* the image of the man on the mine, as the camera spirals up and away from him in the closing frames of the film, confirms the dominant interpretation at work metaphorically: that there is no escape, whether from implicit conflict and its legacy in an internationally underpinned peace implementation process, or from the intertwined fates of the country's ethnic communities and their militaries. The way in which the two sides are locked, or even trapped together in no man's land, and the way in which Nino and Čiki argue about who started the war, as well as Cera's weariness with it all, confirm that, as the title implies metaphorically, Bosnia itself is 'No Man's Land' – it cannot belong to one or the other exclusively.

## Prisoners of the Caucasus

Although the conflict in Chechnya is central to the Chechens themselves, it is largely a background matter for Russia. That is how the authorities under President Vladimir Putin wanted it – ensuring that legitimacy was not challenged. As discussed more specifically in Chapter 4, Russia has attempted to prevent almost all reporting from the region, and certainly independent coverage, by declaring it a closed area during what is called the Second Chechen War, the one started by Putin putatively to resolve the issue for good, rather than the earlier campaign under President Boris Yeltsin, which began as a limited security operation and slid into something far more extensive. Putin needs Chechnya to be a background issue because he declared the war to be 'over', yet it continues at the time of writing and can be expected to do so for years ahead. In this context, the focus on Chechnya was blurred by extension into a conflict labelled 'North Caucasus', a label which came to have substance as events spilled over to places like Beslan in North Ossetia and Nalchik in Dagestan. However, the terror in those places and the blurring only meant that something had to be said about war in the region, confirming that trouble there was far from over. Despite Putin's declaration the conflict was over, despite creating a closed area, and despite the blurring of the label for the conflict, the war in Chechnya was still a matter of sensitivity in Russia.

Russia is metaphorically a 'prisoner' of its presence in the Caucasian mountains of Chechnya and neighbouring territories – a metaphor handed down historically from the work of Lev Tolstoy and picked up in late twentieth-century filmic exploration (including actuality film, considered in Chapter 4). One of the two films we consider in this section, by Sergei Bodrov, indeed, echoes the title of Tolstoy's original. Aleksei Balabanov's *Voina* (*War*) provides a complement, which exemplifies the tropes of both contemporary conflict generally, and the Chechen conflict in particular, as we show below, where again, interpretation, experience and image are reflected in the analysis.

In Sergei Bodrov's *Prisoner of the Mountains*, we hear the garrison commander declaring that 'this is not war'. Whether or not we take this view, there can be little doubt that, on screen, in fiction film (and actuality film, alike), the experience of being taken hostage is the dominant feature, with the trope of throat slitting also notable. These quite peculiar characteristics of the conflict are offset by distance in time or location, which marks the incomprehensible from the normal. The focus on hostage taking in both *Prisoner* and Aleksei Balabanov's *Voina* either marks the way in which the garrison commander is right – this is not war – or, more likely, it pinpoints a heightened, intense experience that is salient to the conflict. Hostage taking backed by potential throat slitting and decapitation constitute the marker of the Chechen War, the signifier of the essence of the conflict – and indeed, perhaps, a trend in conflict around the globe. This is the defining experience of the Chechen War, its horrifying human core that provides the main channel of connection with potential audiences.

*Prisoner of the Mountains* appeared in the mid-1990s, built on the image of, and inspired by, Tolstoy's story *Prisoner of the Caucasus*.[18] That title, in itself, renders clearly the situation, not only for the poor individuals in the film, especially the main character, Ivan, who are held prisoner, kept hostage, but also for Russia, as it seeks to subdue Chechnya after two centuries or more of trying to do so, and Chechnya and its people themselves, who cannot escape their landscape and fate. All are prisoners of these mountains one way or another. This title suggests that, while Russia's fate is to be engaged in the Caucasus – it cannot escape – and yet, perhaps because it cannot escape, it cannot win. Therefore, albeit with the ambiguities appropriate to a fine work of fiction, Bodrov's film, from its title onward, questions the legitimacy of Russian commitment in the region.

The doubts over Russia's role in Chechnya are mostly plainly shown in Ivan's commentary to an unseen interviewer, speaking to the camera as though to the viewer, and in the relationships he formed while a prisoner. It is clear that Ivan forms an affectionate bond with Dina, one of his keepers. She is the daughter of Abdul, who has followed a Chechen raiding party who, disguised as peasants on the road, ambush the armoured vehicle in which Ivan and his comrades are travelling, killing all but Ivan, a complete novice, and one other, the confident and experienced Sasha. Abdul's aim is to gain one Russian hostage whom he might exchange for his captured son, held prisoner at the Russian garrison. The father is allowed by the bandit-warriors to keep the two Russians still alive, rather than just one, as both appear as though they might not survive. The two both recover and are kept in relatively comfortable accommodation for hostages, shackled in a barn with straw on which to sleep. This contrasts with the pit into which Ivan will later be cast, a phenomenon that reappears more gruesomely in *Voina* and other films (see below). The two are guarded when allowed out either to work or exercise by rifle-bearing Hasan, whose tongue we learn was cut out by Russian captors at one point, but with whom the two form an amicable and humorous relationship, until, when they try to escape and he tries to stop them, they knock him over the edge of a sharp ravine and, despite efforts to save him from the drop, he falls to his death. Although their roles are prisoners and guard, they have formed a human relationship – a relationship, it is felt, that extends significantly beyond the mere tactical deployment of 'human' approaches that any captive would be advised to generate. Although Sasha knows that, if they get out, they can never come back, despite the bonds that appear to be forming, Ivan believes at one stage that he will. At the human level, despite the animosity of their sides in war, and the bitter, brutal, ugly character of action by each side in the war, these are human beings who could get along well. But, in another play on the film's title, they are prisoners of the situation.

Ivan's affection for the people he has known there is explicitly stated at the film's end, when he speaks of the love he has for them, as their ghostly visages are superimposed on the screen, Russians and Chechens, alike. But, whether dead, like Sasha and Hasan, or presumably alive, like the others, he knows that he will never see any of them again. Ivan's memories and attachment are reinforced by the romance of the mountains them-selves and Chechen culture, emphasised by the elegant, poetic cinematog-raphy. And long before his explicit statement of the affections he formed for the people and the place, it is evident to the viewer that Ivan has a particular affection for Dina, which she shares. This is made most explicit when she is taunted by local children, who proclaim that she will never have a suitor because she will never have a dowry, but Ivan says that he would marry her. She, of course, notes that this would be impossible. But this confirms the bond between the two of them, which then becomes a vital element, we must presume, in Ivan's eventual survival. That relation-ship and the romance of the Chechen mountain culture, as depicted in fabulous images, generate ambiguities in the text, which can only add to gentle questioning of Russia's part in the war, and perhaps in the bizarre and unnecessary character of the war itself.

Ivan survives, ultimately, to tell the tale to the camera and to pass comment, but Sasha does not. As the two Russians try to make their escape, they come across a shepherd with his flock, sitting against a tree, holding a rifle. Sasha approaches the shepherd in a friendly manner, talking to him, but, crouching down, stabs him fatally in order to take his rifle. This is a small, but key moment. First, it reveals the underlying 'us' versus 'them' situation of war. Sasha has never had any doubt while held captive that there is no real possibility of bridging the divide – including telling Ivan that they will have their throats slit, and that Ivan will probably have his testicles cut off if not, and that, even if they do manage to get out, they can never return. Sasha, an experienced soldier, kills the shepherd in cold blood, clearly as a necessary act in the battle for their survival, even though the shepherd appears harmless and innocent. This is a fateful moment, the second way in which it is a key event, as the escape goes wrong from that point, and both the rifle and killing the shepherd crucially feature in their undoing. The rifle, almost a museum model, it turns out, contains only one round, which Ivan manages to discharge accidentally, despite Sasha's urging him not to handle the weapon. The discharge echoes in the mountains and draws the attention of nearby Chechens hunting the fugitives. After a chase and a scramble, the two are caught and Sasha confesses to killing the shepherd. While Ivan is sent back to Abdul, to be placed in the pit and kept as collateral for the Chechen's son, Sasha is taken in the opposite direction. This is the third way in which the stabbing incident is significant: it cues not only Ivan's separation from Sasha, but also the scene in which the latter has his throat slit.

Throat slitting is a part of the Chechen war's mythology. It is a major trope in the depiction of the conflict. Given the nuances and balance otherwise evident in Bodrov's film, showing the possibility of human connection between Russians and Chechens, as well as the futility of the conflict, the almost obligatory throat slit could not simply be an arbitrary move. Sasha has to give the Chechens reason to carry out this brutal act, affording the act itself a sense of inevitable justification, while ensuring the film's legitimacy – a Chechen war film could not be such without a throat's being cut. However, the scene itself is shot primarily at mid-distance. This offers a rather modest presentation of the act, avoiding the temptation to maximise the visual aspect. Bodrov shows Sasha's head being pulled back by the hair and a knife move across his throat, with a line of blood confirming the score that has been made. But this close-up is not developed. Sasha's body is seen from the mid-distance above to have collapsed on the ground beneath the tree and his death squad walks away. Given the nature of the medium – and the tendency to be lured by the greatest spectacle available – this depiction is almost more in line with the restrictions imposed by guidelines and self-censorship in television news, where the truly gruesome is deemed to be too much for the audience.

The seriousness of Bodrov's film is confirmed by the decision to mute the scope of visual stimulation and excitation through more extended and detailed portrayal of the incident. The throat-cutting moment has to be shown – it is part of the expected interpretive scheme with reference to Chechnya. Yet, this dampened approach to visualisation of this phenomenon, using simplicity and restraint, gives backward confirmation to the importance of the image, as much as a highly emphasised, screen-reddening exploration of the act of death would have done so more directly. This visual treatment is, itself, an affirmation of the importance of the image, as well as a visual complement to the human experience revealed in the film.

*Prisoner* is not the only film treating the Chechen War that refrains from exploiting the visual potential of throat cutting to the full. *Voina*, directed by Aleksei Balabanov,[19] is more extensive in the handling of throats being cut and extends its coverage to beheading. Shocking and sickening as this might be, to the extent that it is shown, the portrayal remains limited. However, that portrayal, along with other aspects of the hostage-focused subject matter, is presented with nods to authenticity by the cross-textural use of video within the film. This not only adds an element of visual texture – in line with a trend, generally, in feature fiction treatment of contemporary conflict – but also captures the way in which those using terrorist and insurgent techniques increasingly include making moving images of their gruesome deeds as one of those techniques.

The film begins with a mixture of fake and genuine actuality images, setting the scene among the Chechen people, with bearded militiamen and both urban and rural landscapes of destruction. As the opening titles are still appearing on screen, superimposed on scenes of a Chechen group's camp, two Russian conscript prisoners are seen sawing wood, one of whom is Ivan. He will be the primary on-screen narrator, as he is later shown responding intermittently to questions, telling what happened to camera and offering reflection on both character and issues in a prison interview room; Ivan is Balabanov's dominant narrative vehicle within the director's own piece of visual story-telling (a third level of narrative is mentioned below). As the titles run the two new Russian soldiers are brought into the camp on a truck, along with the two British hostages, and stood in the open, surrounded by Chechen fighters. The frightened, cow-ering British hostages are John and Margaret, kidnapped while part of a Shakespearean theatre tour in neighbouring Georgia. This is shot mainly from the mid-distance. The first of the soldiers admits to having killed the brother of Chechen leader Aslan Gugayev, and has his throat slit while standing; the other falls to his knees, begging to be spared, is seen to have his throat slit while on his knees, then his head is hacked off and held aloft to a cheer by Aslan. All the while, this is being filmed, and parts of the scene are then seen being replayed in near close-up on a television screen by Aslan once the film's title has been shown and the credits have finished. In this brief view, the images, which include the repeated sawing strokes required to slit the throats and a soundtrack of deathly sounds, gurgles and would-be squeals, are embedded as a textural layer on the screen, at once bringing the awful act closer and making it clearly visible, while giving it the distance of being seen on a small screen within the screen. That small screen, physically, symbolically and verbally, is juxta-posed with the internet. Aslan watches his deeds on tape with Ivan and the computer Ivan uses sitting in-between; the latter is a trained computer expert who operates the computer (in return for slightly better treatment) so as to give the Chechen leader a virtual bridge to the world, with Ivan's commenting for the audience via his off-screen interviewer that the videos would be posted on the web.

The handheld camera and issues associated with it return in four differ-ent ways throughout the film. The first of these concerns use of the medium for direct messages, made in images, of terror. The terrorist and insurgent habit of recording atrocity to form a message, here played out by the Chechens, is evident in a tape Aslan gives to Ivan to give to a British hostage John, as they are both released ostensibly to allow John to return to Britain to raise the ransom money for his fiancée Margaret, who remains in the pit. The video, although we do not see it played, is of Semyon, the Jew held with them in the pit, having his finger chopped off – a scene that we have witnessed in Balabanov's film and watched being filmed within it by the Chechen 'cameraman-of blood'. At that stage, the screen shifts from the pit to the interview room and back, while Ivan explains that the finger severance was for John's benefit, while recounting also Aslan's reading a supposed instrument of Islamic law that permits taking money from Jews for the purpose of armed struggle (making finger chopping in the absence of ransom payment somehow justifiable). Ivan reports how John did not really understand the situation and how he simply told him that Aslan did not like Jews. But Ivan does understand clearly, as he tells us in the reliable terms of a straightforward, solid and ordinary Russian, that the de-digitisation performance and its semi-professional recording (including use of lighting) are really for John's benefit. As Aslan allows John to return to Britain in search of the ransom for Margaret, the cassette, though never viewed by the audience as such, is visual confirmation that Aslan's threats are all too credible.

The second strand of camera use interior to the film is the way in which we are shown the interaction of events with television news activity. Ivan and John are interviewed aboard a military transport plane as they are flown out of the war zone.[20] The interviewees – who include Ivan's woodcutting companion – give snippets of experience and comment. While these offer little of significance, the moments on the flight reflect the way in which hostage freedom is met as soon as possible with television news coverage, part excited celebration and part intrusive exploration of experience, as far as that experience can be conveyed through words and detail. The comments on the Chechens as gangsters and ordinary soldiers not being worth much in trade reinforce or feed potential prejudices in the audience. They also lead to passing celebrity, as we see when Ivan, having made his way to his native Tobolsk in Siberia, visits his father in hospital and the doctor is more interested and excited to see him because she saw him on television a few evenings before, than in showing concern for Ivan, or giving any sense of interest in his father's condition. The omnipresence of television news also sees the narrative of John's arrival at London Heathrow covered by the cameras, as well as his publicising the case via a press conference. That press conference cues a plot development which generates a further role for diegetic camera use that also leads to an additional narrative level.

The press conference concludes with John's being approached by a UK Channel 4 television representative who offers a small amount of the money to cover the ransom if John will film everything on his trip back and give it to Channel 4. This link with television provides the third element of conscious camera use within the film itself. Of course, the initial encounter is a little unrealistic, given that it is independent production companies who make films for Channel 4 and so a commission would not occur in this way; but dramatic efficiency, perhaps, excuses the device. The dramatic device allows the plot to take John back to Russia in search of Margaret, camera in hand, shooting himself at arm's length as he goes, failing to get help at the British Embassy in Moscow, the Russian Ministry of Foreign Affairs and Ministry of Defence, but meeting up with Ivan again for the two of them to return to Chechnya. John's filming within the action serves to give a third level of narrative and additional visual texture. As narrative, in addition to Balabanov's overarching view and Ivan's interview version of events, we see and hear John addressing his camera, all the while taking the plot forward and explaining what is happening, as he provides updates on their progress for the visual diary. At the same time, John's pieces to self and to camera provide a further level of visual texture, the bright monochrome images in the viewfinder with recording information imposed on them, contrasting with the clear colour of Balabanov's top-level texture.

Finally, as John, Ivan and their captive guide Ruslan (who volunteers to join forces with them because of old feuds between his own family and Aslan's) prepare to assault the Chechen base and liberate Margaret, having made contact with the leader and told him to expect them two days later to make the deal, the Briton fixes his camera to his helmet, like a miner's lamp. The camera has clearly become part of the arsenal at this stage, as well as opening the way to a form of 'reality TV war', as the attack is captured as it happens. Balabanov allows this device at once to sharpen the intensity and create a layer of distance in those climactic scenes, as the visual texture shifts to the monochrome recording image for key moments. As they enter Aslan's camp, the viewer is offered the viewfinder image – as Margaret is found, this is how she is seen lying, unresponsive next to Captain Medvedev in the pit, and, as John, whose voice is heard calling out to her, turns away, a detonation is captured, rocking the human rostrum to the ground. The combined intensity and distance of John's finding Margaret is repeated in the pit, as she is revealed naked and John infers to Ivan that 'they raped her'. This conclusion incenses John, who loses control. After the naked Margaret, now above ground, is seen in viewfinder mode from behind stumbling away, Aslan, hands bound behind his back, is seen with fright in his eyes trying to run away, as the viewfinder image closes on him a little and then witnesses his being shot dead by John. Thus, the most intense moments are viewed through John's camera, augmenting them at the same time as generating distance from them, making them simultaneously more 'real' because the hand-held camera conveys something that viewers might recognise as part of their own world more than the finely crafted images of Balabanov and his cameraman, and yet less 'real' both because it is monochrome and a different texture to the 'normal' world within the film constituted by Balabanov's composition.

The final issue of visual mediation, one offered at face value, is Ivan's to-camera conversation with the implicit interviewer and the viewer who faces Ivan on screen as though accompanying the interviewer (the viewer is not intended to be one with the interviewer, as Ivan's gaze engages an imagined figure past the camera, just as would be the case in a genuine filmed interview, the camera viewing the subject over the interviewer's shoulder). While the viewer might initially suspect that Ivan is being questioned by an off-screen police officer, or a lawyer, given that he is in prison, Ivan makes a clear reference to the interviewer's being a journalist while recounting John's and his train journey back to the Russian south – and as we see the former, shot from above, trying to record his diary in the person-sized confinement of the train's toilet. While the interview with Ivan does not have a separate visual texture, as a part of the film's normality, it does provide a mechanism not only for the direct narrative of events offered by Ivan, at times, but also for a commentary on the ethics of filmmaking and action in war and peace, some of which might reflect back on Balabanov's film itself.

Ivan's prison engagement with an implicit interviewer and John's egocentric to-camera action and diary allow an ethical commentary to emerge on Russian and Western culture, as well as the very practice of filmmaking vis-à-vis the subject matter. The dual visual texture provided by John's filming helps to illustrate character: John's Western ego is wrapped up in his own recording, while Ivan gets on with business, noticing that John is filming and 'muttering away' beyond Ivan's comprehension, but 'would not guess' that he is actually making a film, while Ivan refuses to be filmed when the moment comes and tells John not to film anyone else who helps them. Ivan, in his interview to camera, finds it 'strange' that '[t]hey're going to kill his girl and he's making a film', while reflecting curiously that 'shoot' has a dual meaning in English, used both to shoot a film and shoot a gun. The honest Russian is contrasted with the vanity and distance of his Western companion.

The contrast between the straightforward Russian and his Western counterpart – who is, of course 'OK' while different – is emphasised by their behaviour at other points. John's untrammelled murder of Aslan – uncompromising killing varies sharply with the qualms he shows about killing after their first fire-fight earlier, after which, Ivan, solid character and feet on the ground, spells out to John that it his 'war' not Ivan's own, and that 'war is blood', as John whimpers over a bloodied garment. Ivan, the honest Russian – who also uses, or is a vehicle for the director to use, the interview to comment on corruption in Russian politics and the misguided war – goes to visit Captain Medvedev's family and ultimately gives them the money that he makes from his adventure with John – although the Captain, as an equally 'good' Russian, did not want to take the money, the viewer is told, as Ivan also comments that he knew better than the Captain what civilian life was like; Ivan also relates that the Captain's wife had written to say the money had enabled the Captain to have necessary, expensive medical treatment, given effective betrayal by the army and the state. In contrast to this humility, John is reported to have become successful and famous through the film (which Ivan has not seen, but says would be fun to view, in his final words) and a companion book, while never marrying Margaret; reasons are not given for this, but the impression might be left that John's vanity, career and success in undertaking the mission to rescue her and record the rescue were more important than human loyalty and taking the time and care needed to be with a recovering victim of the twin traumas of hostage taking and rape. The loyalty-versus-filmmaker issue is certainly contrasted in Ivan's reporting that the Captain was the only one to stand up for Ivan while in prison and on trial, while John did not return to Moscow for the trial, although he did give evidence in London.

The noble, ordinary Russian soldier's fate is that of Ivan, left in prison, having faced murder charges because he was, of course, a civilian at the time he and John undertook their paramilitary mission to Chechnya – meaning that the deaths they caused were not justifiable at all as military action, so criminal. So too were Ivan's actions against Ruslan the shepherd, who reported how Ivan had tortured him and killed Chechen women and children, who, of course, profited with the money Ivan gave him for his role in the action, as well as having claimed Aslan's scalp for his local purposes and ended up living in Moscow with his son at university there, nonetheless. While, in an aside on Russian politics and justice under Vladimir Putin, Ivan says that he does not think he will be given a prison sentence, it depends – televisual mediation determinant, once again – on what Putin will say on TV about legal reforms, and no one can know, for sure, what will happen to him.

In the end, following a story framed around hostage taking, Ivan is left hostage to the political mood surrounding not only legal reform, but also the conflict in Chechnya itself, where the overriding impression from the two films – reinforced by actuality film, as we shall see in Chapter 4 – is that Russia itself is held hostage by its commitment to keep the rebellious republic and its reluctant people as part of the Russian Federation. Bodrov's film clearly seeks to humanise relations between Russians and Chechens, while recognising the structural antipathy and how this makes any Romeo and Juliet wholly impossible, and captures the romance of the landscape. Balabanov's film is starker, leaving no real prospect of greater humanity in relations, something that the director believed could be rendered on screen, in part, by actually filming one scene in Chechnya itself, aspiring to greater authenticity.

Of course, there's a different smell there ... a different energy in the air. I have no doubt that the energy of a place, of a landscape, of people and attitudes is always captured forever on the tape. Otherwise cinema couldn't exist.[21]

Despite the contrasting tones between the films, there is common ground on the hostage theme, both as subject matter and as metaphor, and, in the end, even the more muted sense of eternal irreconcilability in *Prisoner*, still a sense of the inevitable. The 'hostage' is intrinsic to the experience of the Chechen conflict, and the hostage experience offers a good opportunity to exploit the multi-textured visual phenomenon that is moving-image representation of contemporary warfare.

## Kings in the desert

*Jarhead* is directed by Sam Mendes and stars Jake Gyllenhaal as the central character, Tony Swofford, the real-life US Marine, on whose autobiographical account of life in the Marines in the build-up to, and during, the 1990 to 1991 US-led, UN-authorised operations to remove Iraqi forces from Kuwait, the film is based.[22] Mendes, a Briton, who had made the move from acclaimed and innovative theatre director to big screen direction with the enormously successful *American Beauty* in 1999, had picked up a book that conveyed much of the banal, real experience of military life. He seems to have been set on creating as realistic a picture of Marine life and experience as possible. At the same time, the attempt to capture the 'real' experience, including the waiting – uncommon in film, which normally seeks out action whenever it can – and the frustration,[23] as well as the behaviour during training of the Marines themselves, makes *Jarhead* an intriguing and unusual film about war.[24] Mendes presents an honest portrait, derived from the book, which could be disturbing in its approach to waiting and the quest to understand men's motivation in joining the military and, in Mendes' words, 'why men want to go to war'.[25] Thematically, the film addresses the frustration of those recruited to do a job, which they understand as killing, at not being able to be part of the action. The desire to shoot and kill, and the frustration at missing out on the action and the chance to do so is a theme shared with *Three Kings*, by David O. Russell, but handled in very different ways – as we shall show, Mendes tends to accept this frustration, while Russell uses it as a prompt to undermine it.

The title *Jarhead* refers to the nickname applied to themselves by the US Marines, a label owing ostensibly to the supposed resemblance between the Marines' haircut and a jar, but also connoting an empty vessel with a hard outside that can be filled – Marines do not, in this sense, think for themselves; they receive instructions and follow them. This meaning is made clear in the early stages of the film, when Tony Swofford arrives for

induction and the voice-over explanation is followed by examples of interaction with the Staff Sergeant, in which the point of having an empty
vessel and only acting on instruction is shown. However, it is clear that
there is a little more to the experience than this, as Mendes takes us into
the grainy reality of experience.

Mendes' intention appears clearly to involve authenticity of experience,
although, as with Steven Spielberg's *Saving Private Ryan*, for example, he
uses hyper-stylised cinematic technique at times to render experience as
rudely and grittily as he can, using the intense sunshine of the desert and
the pallid, unstructured landscape to compose pale, washed-out pictures.[26]
Nor does he forget the moments of digital chemistry that can convey the
absurd, which, when deployed sparingly to represent moments of subcon-
sciousness, can be highly effective, as in *American Beauty*'s rose-petal
fantasy. In *Jarhead*, the use of digital play conveys Swofford's disturbed
dreaming, starting with his ostensibly realistic getting up to go the bath-
room in the night, and ending with his vomiting sand into a sink, before
we see him waking, choking on the imaginary sand, while his fellow
Marines are all wide awake and alert, and one of them comments on the
strange noises he had been making.

The attempt to capture the reality of war has three principal strands.
The first of these concerns fog and fear, and death and destruction. This
aspect emerges strongly during the four-and-a-half days the Marines are
deployed on combat duty. During that period, the fog of war – a
metaphor generally for the way in which those at the tactical level in the
field, engaged in combat, cannot know about the war as a whole – engulfs
them. It is impossible for them to have a sense of the big picture. (In addition, of course, it is not necessarily easy for those in the rear, at higher
levels, whose role it is to command the overall picture, to form a full
understanding of what is happening by piecing together fragments of
information gathered from the multitude of tactical points on the
ground.)

The fog of battle, as well as the fear and loss of any control over events
that can accompany it, is depicted in one sequence with heavy fire incoming, but not knowing where that fire will land or whom it will hit. This
sequence borrows heavily stylistically from Steven Spielberg's *Saving
Private Ryan*, as the screen is shaken and chaos is conveyed, using grainy
images of bodies moving quickly, matter being thrown around, and fear of
the incoming fire, which explodes from nowhere, with no idea of where
or whom it will hit, is manifest. The fog of war also includes incidents such
as friendly fire, where some of the Marines are shot up by American A-10
ground attack aircraft, or discovering nomadic tribesmen in the desert,
which is the fate of the five who continue after the others who were
subject to friendly fire and wounded remain behind to be medically evacuated. But it is under a vast cloud that the fog of war emerges.

In *Jarhead*, the fog of battle is given visual presence by the thick, unpleasant cloud that rains oil and refracts the distant orange of the sun and the earthly oranges of the oilfields set ablaze by retreating Iraqi forces. Eerily, this group of Marines wanders, somewhat lost, in the desert. In a fairly visually surreal – although actually quite realistic – sequence, the Marines find themselves spotted and then covered with oil, raining like heavy drizzle from low cloud or dew from morning mist.[27] They make camp under the cloud. Then, wandering like phantoms themselves in a foggy atmosphere appropriate to any horror movie, they accidentally stumble across the charred, ghostly presence of vehicles and bodies on what became known as the 'Highway of Death'. This was the road to Basra, on which civilians, as well as military, were fleeing in the final phases of US-led operations in 1991, where the entire column of traffic was shot up and burned out. The Marines wander among the remains of vehicles, aghast with wonder at the discovery. Then they see the charred remains of human beings, frozen by flame and death in momentary poses in their vehicles, or spread on the ground.

After wandering among this motorists' graveyard, the Marines make their hole-in-the-ground beds for the night. As the squad begins to settle, the focus shifts to Swofford, who is clearly disoriented and disturbed by this direct experience of death and destruction. He wanders over a dune, presumably to be alone to try to adjust to what he has seen. There he discovers what looks like a military vehicle and position, with the frozen, charred remains of a soldier sitting on a box. He too sits on a box and contemplates his new friend. He then vomits between his boots, the physical expurgation of psychological turmoil. He returns to the others, assuring the staff sergeant that he is all right and saying that he has seen nothing over the dune. But, even more disturbingly than the sight of Swofford's spewing, another member of the squad has a reaction of a completely different kind.

One of his colleagues has decided to take one of the charred corpses with him to the other side of a sand ridge, a sleeping companion-cum-trophy – this is his dead Iraqi, and he is going to claim the body as one that he killed. This somewhat sick moment highlights, however, the growing frustration among the Marines that they are not getting the chance to apply their skills, above all, to open fire against opponents and kill them. The stark, shocking reality is that these are young men who are not only trained to kill, but who are desperate to have the chance to do so. Thus, some of the stark realities of combat experience are revealed starkly, albeit on a highly stylised screen – but it is the stylisation that helps render the reality that much more starkly.

The second way in which the reality of war is addressed emerges through the different visual textures used – moving images within the moving-image creation itself. The film uses different visual textures to convey important elements of interpretation and understanding. First, as became almost compulsory – and certainly habitual – in the war films of the 1990s, if not earlier, televisual material is used within the film, creating different visual textures (as already noted in the discussion of Yugoslav War films, such as *Welcome to Sarajevo*, above). So it is that the Marines learn of the situation that will mean their deployment to the Middle East from the *CBS Evening News with Dan Rather*, where a still quite youthful-looking Rather announces portentously that Saddam Hussein's Iraq has invaded Kuwait, declared that country to be its nineteenth province, and provoked a major international crisis that will result in America's taking a stand. The televisual dimension, here, as in other cases, represents both a reinforcement of the overall attempt at authenticity – the real Dan Rather, from the real *CBS Evening News*, even more than the invented, fictional television reporting in films such as *Welcome to Sarajevo* and *No Man's Land*, confirms the grainy reality of that which is shown on screen. The televisual aspect also serves to confirm the distance between the Marines and both the political world in which the major decisions affecting them and their deployment are made (this is reinforced by the comments of their Colonel commanding once they arrive in the desert) and the world outside, the normal, non-military viewers whom Rather must be presumed to be addressing – those normal, non-military viewers who are likely to form the major audience for *Jarhead*, but whose viewing of the film thus far has enabled them also to enter into the world apart of the Marines.

The second key aspect of visual layering concerns the intertextual use of *Apocalypse Now*. Coppola's supreme visual-philosophical exploration of the nature of war appears on screen, being shown to a large audience of Marines. The young Marines' mode of watching far more resembles that of a football crowd than the reflective audience which Coppola, it might be speculated, sought for the film. The Marines loudly chorus the Wagnerian anthem adopted by Colonel Kilgore's air cavalry in the film, as ground attack helicopters sweep across the sea, over the coast to attack a Vietnamese village.[28] The strong melody of the *Walküre* ride is chanted, interrupted by loud and raucous cheers, accompanied by jumping up and down, and punching the air at such moments as the first appearance of the helicopters on screen, or their unleashing of their payload on the villagers below. This is not an enquiring audience, examining the character of warfare. It is an audience that is instructed to understand war as personal survival in a context of 'us' or 'them' – it is a football match in which, perhaps childishly, the Marines cheer on their team. This experience, thanks to use of the original film, outstrips any scripted rendering of the moment from the book due to its utterly visual nature, with the diegetic screen sometimes seen only through the crowd of leaping, cheering Marines, who offer a different level of visual texture on the screen which *Jarhead's* viewers watch. The double-visual texture, as well as confirming the essential nature of image in terms of moving pictures, also ensures that through the admixture of significant vision with reinforcing sound, the quite possibly disturbing character and experience of those recruited into, and readied by, the Marines is revealed. These are men who know that war is about having and taking sides. Beyond this, however, they revel in their side's taking destructive action against opponents. This representation also implies that they are gung-ho and keen to do their bit of killing for their side – an implication taken up explicitly later in the film. This is their job: it is what they have trained to do. And this, their jarheads filled with the mission to pull the trigger and kill, or building on a predisposition to that mission, with the knowledge and skills with which to accomplish it with excellence, is what Swofford and his comrades want. It is not what they get, however, which results in a great deal of frustration.

The third way in which the film really succeeds in addressing the realities of combat concerns the long, long periods of waiting and the frustration both of waiting and of not being able to do what the Marines themselves think they are there to do. This is one of the features that makes *Jarhead* distinctive as a war film, and is made clear during the long phase of build-up in the film, where camp life is shown, and the commentary reveals that masturbation alternates with some other activity as a means of occupying the time – other activities including training for chemical or biological attack, gambling on scorpion fights, playing football and being forced to present a limited and happy face to television news media. It is also shown by the use of script on screen, where particular numbers of days, hours and minutes appear as titles at the bottom of the screen. This is the arithmetic of deployment – more than six months deployed to the desert, and only four-and-a-half days engaged in the field.[29]

The culminating point in the film confirms the frustration theme. It occurs when Swofford and his companion are finally given a mission that will mean the latter's pulling the trigger: as trained scout snipers they are given the mission to kill two Iraqi generals who have been observed in a control tower. However, just at the moment where, targets located and locked on, the sniper team is given the order to fire, a superior officer charges into the position that the two have taken, tells them to watch, since as he has called in air power to take out the whole position rather than just the generals commanding it, and countermands their order. At that point, fellow sniper Allen Troy (played by Peter Sarsgaard) goes berserk, challenging the officer and demanding that they be allowed to fire; in any case, demanding that they be allowed to fire at something, someone, anyone. Aside from personal aspects that show him disposed to wanting the chance to kill earlier in the film, this outburst is symbolic of Swofford's and all the Marines' frustration that the nature of contemporary warfare, with the US emphasis on high-power technical means – air assets and sophisticated artillery – results in those whose feet were on the ground appearing almost redundant. Troops who had been trained to cope with the intensity of action, and, above all else, to be machines that would kill or be killed in combat, spend over six months deployed to the desert in Saudi Arabia waiting for action, and then four-and-a-half days in the field on active mission, and do not get to fire a shot in hostility. The only shots fired, albeit perhaps a little in anger at not having the chance to pull the trigger in combat, are celebratory ones, as firearms are discharged into the air (an action, incidentally, prohibited during the US-led operations against Iraq in 2003 and after). The film, in the end, addresses the question the Marines implicitly pose to themselves and the audience in the film: What is the point of being a Marine if you do not get to open fire?

A similar sense of the reality of the 1990 to 1991 Iraq expedition for US ground forces emerges in *Three Kings* by David O. Russell, which is, even so, a less conventional film. Until the appearance of *Jarhead*, this was the only major film to use Iraq 1990 to 1991 as the setting or to address that situation. Despite the similarity of theme, all the action in *Three Kings* is set immediately after the end of hostilities (just before the first scene begins, a title card proclaims that the war has just finished), not in the long run-up to Operation Desert Storm's starting. That is, in itself, a commentary on the very short period in which ground forces were deployed in action. As in *Jarhead*, there is a sense of the great frustration felt at not having seen battle – the impression is given that these troops have not even endured friendly fire or bombardment by Iraqi artillery. However, while dealing with the same sense of frustration and desire to see action, Russell's highly intelligent film goes beyond description and explanation of the war-in-waiting phenomenon. This involves raising issues, as discussed in this section: first, frustration, as noted; second, violence and the treatment of violence in war – or even action – cinema; third, the relationship and relevance of television news media; and finally, issues of ethics, morality and responsibility. Ostensibly an action war movie with four soldiers undertaking a gold heist in the wake of American ground operations against Iraq, the film is really about information, ideas and interpretation.

The sense of frustration at missing out on the chance for action is established in the opening scene. One of the 'Three Kings' of the title, a reservist new father, Troy Barlow (played by Mark Wahlberg), is heard running, kit rattling, as the white desert landscape is broken up by his helmet appearing from the bottom of the screen, before he stops, stands, asks if they are still firing and, following no conclusive answer, fires a single shot over several hundred metres at an Iraqi soldier standing atop a bunker and apparently raising his rifle. Troy and the others in his detachment run forward to the bunker and the fallen soldier, where Troy, the first there, reveals the blood-spewing neck wound of the Iraqi, before his colleague arrives to declare that Troy has 'got himself a rag head' with a strong blend of excitement and jealousy, before continuing to declare ingenuously that he thought he was 'never going to see anyone shot in this war'. Of course, it is possible that the soldier was preparing to surrender but did not know how, given a later scene in which authentic cartoon cards explaining in pictures how to surrender are shown – and that the Iraqi was standing on the bunker making himself a target rather than hiding in or behind it. This reinforces the clear revulsion and discomfort, frozen briefly on screen, that Troy experiences on witnessing the consequence of his decision to fire. That revulsion contrasts, of course, with the immature keenness of his young colleague Conrad Vig (played by Spike Jonze), or another who just wants to photograph the dying corpse.

The frustration felt by the soldiers is archetypal in the Vig character. He exemplifies it in different ways. He wears night-vision equipment during the day because he had no opportunity to wear it while not seeing action. This provides the visual opportunity to create the night-vision effect in daytime – achieved by squirting washing-up liquid on to the camera lens – as the viewer sees another principal character, the former Delta Force Major Archie Gates (played by George Clooney), approach the tent (for which Vig is supposed to watch out) through a liqueous green gel, distorted by the plasmatic effect, with visual perspective clearly lost as Gates pushes Vig – who is trying to block him, but is evidently unable to gauge his own spatial relationship to the purposeful officer. It has already been established in Gates' tense exchanges with his superior officer, questioning why they were there and stating that he does not understand what the war was about – though it is clear, even at this stage, that he does really; the statement is not about his incomprehension, it is about his frustration at the situation. This depression and frustration is reinforced visually by the use of disorienting cinematography – a brief sequence at the end of this exchange as his superior's ascending helicopter throws up dust, filmed at six frames per minute but printed at 36, which gives a jogging, smearing effect. This effect dramatises Archie's disappointment. His bewilderment is echoed also by another main character, TV reporter Adriana Cruz (played by Nora Dunn), who declares that the 'war is over and I don't fucking know what it was about?' – a journalistic echo of the experience of the military who 'managed' her.

The frustration at the lack of action is also shown when the four main military characters (Troy, Archie and Chief Elgin (played by Ice Cube), the Three Kings of the title, along with Conrad – this potential fourth king is killed by an Iraqi sniper's bullet in the desert later in the film) all head off through the desert by Jeep. Until one transitional point, the four wear darker chemical protection outfits, reflecting the anticipation – rather than actual action – that prevailed in the run-up to operations in 1990 to 1991. Archie, the officer in the group, allows the others to fire a few rounds at American footballs thrown into the air as targets by Chief, already established as a fine quarterback player. However, Conrad, whose disappointment at the lack of booms and bangs during his time in Iraq, decides to strap an explosive to the side of one ball before it is thrown, meaning that a large explosion occurs when the ball is hit by Troy. When Archie stops the vehicle and challenges his junior partners in prospective crime, Conrad's response is to bleat, 'We didn't get to see any action, sir'. That response is the cue for one of the key scenes in the film – visually and philosophically – to occur, as Archie, a special forces veteran with deep knowledge and experience of combat, sets out to educate his reservist juniors. This is also a cue to heightened imagery.

Archie shows his team the charcoal remains of incinerated Iraqis half-buried in the sand. He is effectively questioning whether or not they really would have wanted action, as he notes that these petrified volcanic remains are action. This is also the cue for Gates to explain to the others what happens when a bullet enters the body. The ghostly bodies in the desert give way visually to high-luminosity, vibrant colour. This is the remarkable digital re-creation of the wound, tracing what happens from penetration to infection. This gruesome CGI approach – amplified by the non-digital effects that appear to blow up a cow and the vision of a charred, petrified body in the sand (like a Pompei sculpture rendered in volcanic lava), in terms of educating both characters and viewers about the effects of munitions – is repeated later when the camera takes the viewer inside Troy's chest when he receives a lung wound. The depiction is based on serious medical understanding, which Russell found while he was writing the film in New York City. Russell tempered the loneliness of writing by sharing what he was doing with friends, one of whom was an accident and emergency doctor, who discussed with the director the trauma caused by a bullet wound and introduced him to medical journal articles on the processes that occurred in void of the wound, with flesh convulsing involuntarily (an aspect which the director failed to render completely) repeatedly in a manner all but invisible to the human eye.[30] This inspired the detail in the scene, but also met the director's desire to engender a sense of responsibility by recognising what destructive violence really meant. This scene became a vehicle for re-inventing what he saw as the war or combat movie by focusing on one or a handful of bullets in detail, where the viewer can 'feel the impact of every single one', rather than have hailstorms of hundreds of bullets at any one time – the shoot-out with Iraqi forces about to murder Shi'a rebels in the village is presented with slowed motion and heightened sound, so as to capture the issue and impact of each round. This is a comment on violence in action feature fiction films and on violence and the physical damage caused by war. Archie's expertise both in explaining what happens and later in treating Troy's wound operates on both levels, stirring reflection both on the moving-image media depiction of violence in war and on the realities of that violence and war themselves.

The bold colour and lighting stands in stark contrast to the pallid effect deliberately used prior to this in the film. That colour tone, also reflected in Mendes' later approach in *Jarhead*, was intended to drain everything of colour, reflecting the 'moral blankness' of the soldiers. The first half of the film was made using a risky and expensive technique, bleach bypassing, where the silver is washed off the film. The only exception in this first part of the film is the baby on Troy's hat, which, along with a scene where he calls home on his cell phone, are the only links to the comfort of home and the almost complete disconnection, in Russell's eyes, between consciousness in the US and the realities of the troops deployed in the desert and their mission. The baby and the home scenes, in themselves, suggest that strong colour connotes real value or meaning. This was Russell's intention and is confirmed by his shift to using Ektachrome film stock as the narrative develops when the three reach the village where their destiny turns. The change of stock alters the visual tone and quality of the film, bringing out the stark, startling and vibrant colour shocks of the desert, as he came to see them. The shift in stock and image reflects the character shift in the film, both in terms of its characters' development and the interpretation itself.

Instead of being a dubious heist film, driven by material greed as three soldiers set off in search of gold, this becomes a film about taking responsibility and coming to terms with the ethical challenges presented by the situation in Iraq. The director judged the Iraq military action as 'unexamined ... strange, morally complicated ... and morally compromised'. Colour gives meaning and its scope grows as the narrative develops and Archie and his companions take responsibility. They take responsibility for the fate of the Iraqis whom they encounter, initially trying to avoid them, but then assisting them – most of them are eventually able to escape Saddamite retribution, but only because the Three Kings give each one of them a solid gold bar from the bullion haul, using it otherwise to influence colleagues to bend (or break) operational rules to permit their escape to Iran; at the same time, a few, also boosted by gold and assistance, remain behind, honourable, inevitable martyrs in the Shi'a resistance to Saddam's rule.[31]

The Three Kings are helped to translate their epiphany into effect thanks to the presence of the television news. In *Three Kings* it is only the assistance, in the end, of Adiana Cruz, the famous female correspondent for an unnamed news outfit, with the presence of cameras and the threat to show the world US troops effectively condemning Iraqi Shi'a rebels and civilians to murder by Saddam's thugs. When Archie Gates summons help, he says to make sure to bring a reporter – who turns out to be Cruz. The presence of TV news is essential for protecting the moral legitimacy of the Three Kings' action. It is this reporting, we are informed in a telegraphic coda, which also ensured that each of the Three Kings was honourably discharged, rather than facing court martial for their unauthorised actions, both in intending to steal gold bullion, initially, and in breaking rules to aid the Shi'a rebels and their civilians, because they could make a difference, even if they were not authorised to do so. The US, it is evident, has adopted a morally bankrupt approach in evicting Iraqi forces from Kuwait, encouraging an uprising but failing to support it.

The Cruz character may well be derived from CNN's Christiane Amanpour, who built an international reputation during the 1990 to 1991 Iraq intervention. Certainly, Russell, as well as basing the look of the film on the photojournalism of Gilles Perez in the *Los Angeles Times*, also based the style and look of the film on studies of CNN's coverage, which involved a 'panning and zooming style' that gave an 'out of control and real feel' to the film. Certainly, the scenes in which she, or a competitor, Nora from NBS, appear, confirm the realities of almost ever-present news media in contemporary conflict, certainly, involving major Western forces. This is seen in the early scenes where Archie is supposed to be looking after Cruz, but is reprimanded by a superior for not carrying out his mission to 'make her feel good about stories that we want, not push the stories that we don't want', to say nothing of walking away from her to 'screw another journalist'. This conveys both the realities and the tensions of media management in contemporary operations – albeit that, in reality, many military personnel build good relations with their journalistic counterparts, even if the latter do not understand military affairs and are, at best, never on board. This is an inevitable outcome of the conflicting military and media agendas.

The frustration is shown the other way around later in the film, when Cruz opens her heart to her military driver while chasing Archie and his colleagues in the desert: 'The war is over and I don't fucking know what it was about. What was this war about? I was managed by the military.' 'Me too', responds the driver with innocent irony, who then complements her style, as she explains that she seeks to be 'substance based not style based', thereby showing the military–media misunderstanding on a different level. He then complements her appearance, which is a cue for Cruz to offer a pointed commentary on gender and the nature of US television news:

> there's a sexual politics that says it's about looks, it's about sex, it's about style. Believe me, many an anchorman came onto me and I didn't go for it, I didn't play that game. I never dropped to my knees for an assignment. Christ! I came out to the desert because nobody else had the fucking balls to do it!

In presenting Cruz this way, and in giving her the role of moral protector to Gates and the others, Russell is offering perhaps a sympathetic and, in some regards, authentic approach to television news and its journalists. Although he shows the multi-layered visuals of the other reporter, Nora, having sexual intercourse with Gates while her broadcast from the previous day is on screen, or the soldier's comment on how much shorter she seems than on screen (a common observation regarding film and television faces). But it is the serious and authentic approach of the Cruz character, rather than frivolity and friction, taking responsibility alongside the soldiers with souls, that stands out. Despite the professional pressures and the sexual politics she bemoans, in the end, the success and legitimacy of the Three Kings' mission as saviours would not be assured, and might not even be possible.

This is the key to understanding the relationship between moving-image media, especially regarding actuality material, and contemporary warfare: legitimacy is the key to success – even if, in the case of *Three Kings* the success in question is that of an ad hoc semi-criminal group, which takes responsibility where political superiors have not, saving a little of America's honour; and it is the right images that are decisive in securing the legitimacy of what Archie Gates and his team have done. *Three Kings*, in the end, is about taking responsibility for situations. It is about what the director and many of the military personnel who informed his research for the film deemed to be America's moral failure, celebrating victory while Iraqi rebellion in perhaps 16 of Iraq's 18 provinces was being brutally suppressed by Baghdad; for those on the US side who noticed, not supporting the rebels was a failure. Of course, the ethics of this situation were more complicated, as both UN authority and the politics of the coalition joining forces to evict Iraq from Kuwait meant abiding by the limits of the mandate and political realities. And, ironically, the corollary of the view that the job was not done regarding Saddam and that the rebels rising up had been betrayed was the view of warfare based on brute force and victory that perhaps underpinned the 2003 American-led campaign to change the Iraqi regime, while claiming to enforce UN Security Council authority by securing Iraqi compliance with both Security Council mandatory conditions and the terms of ceasefire agreed in 1991. It is hard to believe, however, that Russell would be a supporter of the 2003 action. It is more likely that he would see the common elements in Mendes' *Jarhead* and the dissenting comment on Iraq 2003 implicit in that account. While *Three Kings* confirmed the relationship between image and legitimacy within its action, the overriding interpretation present in the film narrative itself questions the moral legitimacy. Ostensibly about the same conflict and also the same side in that conflict, and shadowing many of its predecessor's qualities, including both theme and visual style, *Jarhead* is implicitly a negative comment on Iraq 2003, despite its faithfulness to the original book and event on which it was based as an experience of war. In either case, the key element is the dynamic of image, experience and legitimacy.

## Black Hawks downed

If the relationship between image and legitimacy was sharply focused anywhere in the early post-Cold War world, it was in Somalia, where the pictures of two American Rangers' corpses being dragged naked behind trucks driven by 'technicals' critically damaged the legitimacy of US involvement and were generally seen to have prompted Washington's withdrawal of its troops in the country. The circumstances in which those images appeared formed the basis for a best-selling book by journalist Mark Bowden, *Black Hawk Down*, which is a detailed account of the events in the Somali capital. Mogadishu, on 3 October 1993, formed the basis for Ridley Scott's eponymous film. Scott's *Black Hawk Down*, winner of two Oscars and by an Oscar-winning director, one of the most commercially successful war-related films ever, on US operations in Somalia in the early 1990s, is the quintessential contemporary war film and a *locus classicus* for understanding the issues involved in representing combat through moving images. The film provides a solid foundation for studying both the interaction between fictional and non-fictional modes – and, indeed, their conflation, and the salience of moving images regarding legitimacy in armed conflict.

*Black Hawk Down* portrays in unprecedented detail one combat mission, which in reality lasted 18 hours, but is condensed into 144 minutes on screen, including time taken for swift and efficient contextualisation and introduction of characters. The title refers to the two Black Hawk helicopters shot down during a US Ranger raid to capture Somali warlord Mohammed Farrah Aidid and his top leadership team, in Mogadishu, the Somali capital – a mission that went painfully wrong, leaving 19 US personnel dead and America's military reputation badly damaged. Overall, although Aidid was killed several months later, this event spelled failure. It was riddled with confusion because US forces had been operating on a discrete mission, separate from the main UN peace force (which the US had initially spearheaded alone), which created confusion and resentment – evident in the film when the Pakistani command contingent has to assist in the rescue of the US personnel trapped by Aidid's forces in central Mogadishu (although the US operation to target Aidid was a response to Aidid's ambushing and killing Pakistani forces). The effect of the failed operation was to undo the good work that the first US force had done in stabilising the Mogadishu area, turning broader success into dismal failure focused on one operation. The legitimacy of US engagement in Somalia was destroyed and the perception formed both around the world and in US circles that America would run the moment anyone managed to kill a few of its soldiers.

If the situation depicted in *Black Hawk Down* can be quickly summarised – US raid attempts to catch warlord, goes wrong, troops are trapped and a dramatic rescue and extraction operation takes place – then the realities of depicting it are riddled with the complexity that represents the fog and friction of real combat. The early stages of the film depict the friction in relations between different components of US Special Operations Forces – in this case Delta Force and the US Rangers, where vanities and sensibilities show in the mess tent as the US Ranger officer commanding tells Hoot, the arrogant composite Delta Force character (played by Eric

Bana), that he is going to need the officer's Rangers. Of course, these forces are all on the same side, as events turn out the other way round and it is Hoot and the Delta Force who rescue the Rangers in the final stages. As noted already, the friction between the Pakistani-led UN Forces and the US contingent is also clear, both in terms of operational (non-)communication and the politics of operating in the same theatre alongside one another, ostensibly in partnership, as well as the issues of jurisdiction and Rules of Engagement (early in the film, a Black Hawk is denied permission to intervene to stop Aidid's technicals from shooting civilians at a UN food distribution point because of these factors). The fog and friction of combat are also to be seen in last-minute substitutions, such as that of Grimes, played by Ewan MacGregor, whom we see initially as a clerk registering Blackburn (played by Orlando Bloom) as a new arrival at the camp. Grimes says that he has found a way to avoid combat and when he is thrust into the front line by necessity it is clearly not with the enthusiasm he professes to the experienced Sizemore, immediately before the latter informs Grimes that he is to go as Sizemore's own replacement. In that ironic moment, Grimes affects to complain about his lot as a clerk and coffee maker of some reputation, saying that he believed the advertisements 'to be all you can be', but ended up making coffee through US operations in Iraq and Panama. Grimes' 'Hell Yeah' emerges from MacGregor's mouth with just the right blend of gulping-while-expressing evident lack of confidence while trying to express that quality. The last-minute substitutions – things that just happen – can make a difference: Grimes performs well, but the implication is that things might have been different if some of the 'first team' had been available in other respects.

The film focuses on the operations themselves, capturing the reality of the operational military environment almost hermetically sealed from the outside world, with virtually no sense of that world or contact with it. The depiction of Somalis' different ways offers some perspective beyond that of the troops – the starving, frail bodies and the corpses of the opening sequence as the setting of famine caused by civil war and international engagement is quickly established, the goatherd boy with the mobile telephone who exposes it to the sky and the sound of the Black Hawks and their smaller Little Bird companions racing towards Mogadishu, and relays it to one of Aidid's commanding thugs, the ferocious Aidid warriors and supporters in Mogadishu, or the celebrating, cheering Somalis who act like a crowd cheering on Olympic marathon runners on the final approach to the Stadium, which in this case is the Pakistani-UN base. The discussions among the troops in the mess tent allow a reflection of both the outside world and the realities of different perspectives among the soldiers, as Sgt. Eversmann (played by Josh Hartnett), the everyman central figure in the film, indicates real humanity and a desire to help the Somalis, disparagingly dubbed 'skinnies' by the troops, while others cannot see the point of their being in the country. There are glimpses of the outside world in a failed last phone call before setting off, the photos that one of the helicopter pilots tries to hang on to as members of Aidid's gang beat him and drag him off, or the connection with the outside world in Ruiz's letter to his family, to be passed on in the event of his death, which event occurs. There is only one reference to the broadcast news media, quite unusually for the contemporary war film – and that is in Eversmann's discussion with others about helping the Somalis, or not doing so, when he tells his colleagues, 'We can help, or watch the country destroy itself on CNN.' But these miniscule fragments of connection with an outside world only strengthen the sense that the film is intrinsically concerned with the military, their culture, their world, their experience.

This internal, military operational world is reflected in discussions between Eversmann and Hoot. The focus on the realities of combat and loss is confirmed in exchanges between them at the end of the narrative, where the arrogance and friction of the food tent scene early in the field is contrasted with a more modest food tent scene towards the end, where Hoot exudes modesty rather than arrogance, confirming the emphasis on combat and experience, something that, despite the best efforts of Ridley Scott and other directors in the history of war and moving-image media, only those who have really experienced it can truly understand. Hoot says that people outside will say that he is a 'war junkie', but that he will not say anything to anyone: 'They won't understand.... It's about the men next to you. And that's it. It's all it is.' This reflects the truism that, in combat, soldiers fight for their buddies, not political leaders, political purpose, or even country. However, despite the loyalty to comrades in arms, Hoot still reveals the individualistic streak in him, ironically, when he rejects Eversmann's offer to go back out with the former to search for the US personnel still missing. 'Don't even think about it,' he says, 'I'm better on my own.'

This imperfect sense of the 'Band of Brothers' in arms brings the two together, following earlier exchanges on the nature of their business. Eversmann asserts that Hoot does not believe they should be in Somalia. The latter responds by removing the politics and purpose implicit in Eversmann's statement from the equation – turning the situation into one where soldiers have to do what soldiers have to do, a world of combat where the original political purpose is lost in the totality of combat. 'It don't matter what I think,' Hoot tells his counterpart: 'Once that first bullet goes past your head, politics and all that shit just goes right out the window.' This reflects a view of the war–politics connect, which predominated in the US military into the twenty-first century, and reflected the nineteenth-century perversion by Herman von Molkte and the Prussian General Staff as that which distorted the vision of Carl von Clausewitz, the doyen of writers on war, and whose genius insights included the recognition that war is a continuation of normal politics – it is part of the political spectrum, but a particular means for pursuing political objectives.

The crucial element here is that the use of armed force only makes sense if it is aimed at achieving political objectives. The disconnect Hoot expresses is of course indisputable: combat is an experience apart and the political purpose of the overall mission lies on the dark side of the operational-tactical moon once the fray is entered. But that experience and the way it obscures the political should not mean that the latter is deemed not to count at all. As we shall see in the final chapter, keeping the political in mind and closely aligned with the operational is vital in contemporary warfare.

Above all, however, it is in the superbly rendered depiction of combat, in all its chaos, that Scott's film excels. As one commentator noted, this chaos is depicted with precision-guided clarity of camerawork and direction.[32] One of the things that art and craft also make clear is how far creating the sense of visual reality on which this project depended actually requires manipulation that exceeds reality. Put another way, reality does not look very 'real' on screen. The artefact of reality is the filmmaker's creative accomplishment. It was, of course, also Scott's intention in making the film. The aim was to create the most realistic depiction of modern warfare possible. In effect, the approach taken is quasi-drama-documentary, but using actors with recognisable Hollywood names, and fictionalising elements of the story by combing characters or events for dramatic efficiency (for example, there was no actual Grimes, and Hoot was a super-Delta Force creation from bits of several real Delta Force characters) while keeping faith with both Bowden's famous book and the actual events on which the film is based, themselves. Digital effects and 3-D graphics were used, therefore, to make key scenes 'real' because live action was simply not real enough. There was a need to give the film more realism.

The film is, as the director himself acknowledged, 'stressful' because it depicts difficult and grim realities of war – death, damage and destruction. This includes the blown-off hand and watchband-bound wrist of a Ranger that is picked up and put in a pocket, so as to keep the US military's emotional ethos 'no one gets left behind'. It also includes the remarkably rendered loss of legs and lower body, as a still living, conscious and suffering torso is dragged away by soldiers seeking to evacuate the wounded man from the open; there is a strange, though wholly realistic, juxtaposition between the uniformed upper body and grimacing face under a helmet, and the meat carcass on display beneath it, where legs and genitalia would have been. The depiction of the awful physical damage that can be caused by combat is capped by the bloody depiction of Ruiz's arterial wound, when the severed main artery is described as having recoiled into the chest cavity and there is a rough-and-ready field-surgery attempt to tug it back so that it can be joined to its lower part again. The site of this action, inside the soldier's body with the medic pulling on the tough, rubbery, grey body matter of the blood channel, is a realistic cavity, which, in this moment of crisis, compares strongly with the surreal educational wound cavity described in *Three Kings*. The latter has the shock of process and analysis; the former, literally, has visceral impact.

However, the depiction of the arterial wound, strong though this is, is dwarfed by the effects work in the film to achieve the realities of action. Special CGI work was done to create 'photo-realistic' dust, for example, as the helicopters swirl in dust clouds as the Rangers descend on a rope at the onset of their operation. Digital dust was needed to generate reality, while reality itself generated relatively little dust while filming – and could not be allowed to do so due to the need to coordinate the different elements of action and filming.[33] Similarly, when the Little Birds strafe the rooftop full of Aidid warriors on the building where some of the rescue targets are located, although the helicopters fired blanks as they swept over, this real fire could not appear 'real'. In part, this was because tracer bullets, so familiar from any moving-image account of modern warfare, streaking across the skyline of cities in television news coverage, could not be used in filming due to the serious risk to the rooftop full of actors playing the Somali fighters. With the actors' firing up, the sequence using Little Birds and blanks was judged to be 'tame'.[34] This is because the impact of real fire does not show well on screen – rather as rainfall on screen generally needs to be three times stronger than genuine rain to appear 'real'. Therefore, the air artillery impact was filmed separately from the actors. The makers invented a computer game to get the strafing effect, as well as to find the lines of fire randomly across the set of weapons discharge on the ground (which were then layered with a collection of filmed images of destroyed objects, mostly masonry, already made by the effects team). When the Little Birds fire 4,000 rounds per minute, it is not possible to simulate this fully on set and it does not impress visually. So, tracers and other effects were added using CGI to make 'reality' more 'real'. The challenge of showing how war really is, in particular, how dangerous it is, ironically requires significant additional work; reality does not appear real on screen.

The biggest challenge of all in making the film realistic was to crash the Black Hawk helicopters of the title, which were at the hub of events. While the filmmakers had four real Black Hawks and four real Little Birds, courtesy of US military cooperation and paying $6 million for that cooperation, there was, of course, no possibility of actually crashing one of them – even if cinematically there could be a guarantee to get the one shot right. Because the title and the actual event demanded it, the Hawk has to go down on screen. Because a real crash was impossible, a mock-up was made on set with a scale model also created. Then, CGI was used to provide spin and slide – that is, to capture the effect of the wounded Black Hawk turning out of control in the air and then hitting the ground, carried along by momentum. The virtual helicopter had to be able to interact with the real ground. The combination of genuine, mock and miniature works so effectively that it is impossible to know that there is a real Hawk and a CGI Hawk in the end. The importance of understanding how effective this is correlates with the need to comprehend the salience of the visual in moving-image media. This is something of which Ridley Scott has supreme understanding, with a background in art which means that he very carefully conceives of, and draws for the storyboard for the film, almost every frame in detail;[35] Scott's visual acuity and skilled hand, allied to a command of the industrial side of filmmaking, are the essence of what makes *Black Hawk Down* rich in images and so striking and apparently realistic overall, although, of course, that apparent reality, in its close-ups and face shots, as well as in the significant exaggeration-through-effect to create the semblance of reality, is, in truth, quite unlike reality (as may be seen in our discussion of Dodge Billingsley's actuality film *Virgin Soldiers* in Chapter 4). Self-evident as it might, or ought, to seem, the visual is so important that it dictates how objects must be rendered and what will constitute success in moving-image media.

Although the scenes of Rangers' corpses being dragged behind vehicles through the streets of Mogadishu, famous from television news coverage, appear only fleetingly in the film, they confirm the whole incident as a US failure strategically, and an event that generated a legitimacy deficit. However, while the film totemises the legitimacy link on one level, there are two further dimensions to this issue. The first of these is that both book and film place emphasis not on the failure of the snatch operation and the overall impact of that failure, but on the heroism and relative success of the rescue mission. Thus, while the film cannot undo the overall impression of deficit created by the Mogadishu debacle, it can provide a more positive and upbeat image of the US military – there were things about which to feel proud, things that had been lost in the overall mist of failure. Second, and crucially, given the effort to create a more positive image of the US military's performance that day, the film was rushed through post-production in the last months of 2001, following the September 11 attacks on America. The events of that day had initially prompted Scott and others to wonder about delaying the film (shooting was already completed),[36] but it was swiftly decided to bring it forward and to show it as soon as possible. The film's positive tone against a background of disaster was probably right for release on the American market – the market is the crucial factor in considering any commercial film. The film, indeed, performed well at the US box-office and, because more than three prints were able to be shown before the December cut-off date for the Academy Awards, the film was nominated for a string of Oscars, including best director and best film, where it failed, and special effects and sound, where it won. However, what was positive in the US meant that the film had a considerably more mixed response around the world, particularly in Europe, where the director believed it 'rattled … cages' and was seen as a jingoistic American film, almost as though it had actually been made prior to September 11 and not made by a Briton. In the end, while not a significant factor, *Black Hawk Down* occupied an ambiguous position, part affirming the legitimacy of America's response to the

September attacks, but also, overall, presenting a courageous interpretation of overall failure and legitimacy deficit.

The interpretations of feature fiction movies depicting contemporary conflict in this chapter permit us to draw out themes that percolate through them. The first of these is that frustration and futility are prominent features in the representation of contemporary conflict, at times set against one of the hallmarks of contemporary conflict, atrocity, in the context of wars 'among the people' or featuring some form of external actor. Second, experience emerges strongly, as suggested at the outset, as key to narrative representation – the personal interest; the emotional or psychological testing of individual figures made familiar by the films is, at a minimum, the vehicle for presenting other issues or aspects of conflict, but much of the time this is the core of narrative interest.

Third, the image is, by definition, central to the medium. Narrative is predominantly, though not exclusively, a particular sequence of images. Some of those images will have a particular quality, giving them a status on their own, whether these are the archive and fake old film that provoked controversy around Kusturica's *Underground*, the missed image that means missed understanding at the end of *No Man's Land*, the throat-slitting trope of the Chechen war, or the high-tech rendering of every aspect of an urban combat incident in *Black Hawk Down*. It is this last example, with its classic standing and in its visual richness, that confirms the vital nature of the image to the medium – and how the quest for reality requires images sometimes to be wholly unreal in their construction. However, the effort devoted to securing the authenticity of the image, in itself, also confirms the vital importance of the image. Without the right image, there is, in effect, nothing in scope of the medium – certainly, there is nothing if there is no image at all. Understanding this is to begin to understand the mechanics of the medium. That has implications for understanding moving images, or images in the moving-image environment, as weapons in modern warfare.

Fourth, the importance of the image is also confirmed by the interplay and overlap of actuality means and images in the feature fiction domain, and the relationship between actuality moving images and modern warfare. In almost every case there is some presence of television news, at times the centre of the action, at others tangential and in the background. Even where the latter is the case, in *Black Hawk Down*, the very nature of the film as fictionalised account of a real event made as though a highly stylised docudrama account emphasises the increasing crossover between, or fusion of, feature fiction and actuality moving image forms. This is important in understanding the kinetic elements of narrative in moving-image media – even in supposedly non-narrative objects. Finally, it also begins to exemplify, as is implicit in the case of Chechnya and explicit in those of Bosnia and Iraq, the weapon-grade potential of moving images in securing legitimacy.

# 4  Documentary and current affairs

Although there can sometimes be a naive tendency to assume that documentary films, broadly, are either 'documents' themselves or based on documents, and in either case represent somehow scientifically objective attempts to purvey 'the truth', in practice this is not necessarily the case, as noted in Chapter 1. However, whether *parti pris* or academic, and whether current affairs or documentary, or one-off, or series, the actuality form, despite its differences from fictional cousins, is underpinned by the triangulation of interpretation with images and experience. Indeed, film's strongest role in terms of registering and analyzing detail and events lies beyond the sphere of the fiction film treated thus far. Actuality films, whether individual films or series, may be more important in this respect, even if they do not gain the size of audience that mass entertainment ventures might achieve. Despite the apparent emphasis on reporting 'factual' matters, it is the necessary blend of image and experience that defines interpretation in these films. This chapter demonstrates this by reference to various types of actuality film in relation to particular conflicts, starting (in roughly chronological perspective of the conflicts themselves) with documentary series related to the Yugoslav War, followed by treatment of the conflict in Chechnya, and then its extension into North Ossetia and other neighbouring regions – handled specifically in relation to the Beslan incident. Both the events of September 11 and their aftermath are covered in the subsequent section, which includes the highly polemical approach of Michael Moore's *Fahrenheit 9/11*, contrasted with the reverential *9/11* by Jules and Gédéon Naudet. The final section looks at documentary work emerging from the 'embed' scheme established by the military for the 2003 Iraq enterprise. This confirms the trinity of image, experience and interpretation (and, hence, legitimacy) – argued by reference to feature fiction films in Chapter 3, and the variation of form and style between films, with the brash and the humble, and the conventional and the unconventional appraised by reference to particular moving image texts, as in the previous chapter.

## *The Fall of Milošević*: the final *Death of Yugoslavia?*

Overshadowed by looming war over Iraq, in January 2003, BBC television broadcast a three-part documentary series, *The Fall of Milošević*.[1] Produced by Brian Lapping Associates, the three one-and-a-half hour films charted the final phases of the Yugoslav War, culminating with the man widely credited as the chief architect of that war, Slobodan Milošević, boarding the helicopter that would fly him to The Hague to become the first former head of state to appear before an international tribunal. Covering the run-up to the Kosovo campaigns of 1997 to 1999, those campaigns themselves and the aftermath, including Milošević's ouster, the films are remarkable texts that at times almost convey the sense of being documents as much as documentaries. The films use the same primary approach that producers Norma Percy and Brian Lapping had used to excellent effect in earlier work of this kind, including *Reykjavik*, *The Second Russian Revolution*, *Watergate* and, most notably, *The Death of Yugoslavia*, which won a string of awards after its initial broadcast in autumn 1995, including two BAFTAs: a narrative that is delivered primarily from the horses' mouths of the actors in these events, as intercut extracts of film interviews with the protagonists carry the story, with each voice appearing to continue where the previous one had finished. This fascinating approach and the sometimes truly remarkable material that it contains generate a series of questions regarding the nature and status of the documentary series, in particular, the apparent completeness and authority that mark these series.

While the achievement in these series is quite remarkable, closer inspection reveals that both completeness and authority are less than may at first seem to be the case – as will be discussed below. In this sense, it is also worth posing a question about the links between *The Death of Yugoslavia* and *The Fall of Milošević*: given that the two series emerge from the same stable, using the same principal technique, and focus on the earlier and later periods of the same war, to what extent is the latter a continuation of the former, albeit with a new director and a different series structure, and, whether or not the *The Fall of Milošević* should be seen as a continuation of the earlier series or a sequel to it, how does it compare with *The Death of Yugoslavia*? As we shall argue, there are clear ways in which the *The Fall of Milošević* undoubtedly constitutes a continuation of *The Death of Yugoslavia*, but, despite being an important and vital source of information and access to the personalities, it is not the equal of its predecessor in terms of visual mediation and texture, source material and truly outstanding detail, and overall significance.

*The Fall of Milošević* began life as the end of *The Death of Yugoslavia*. The original idea appears to have been to finish off the story begun – and apparently ended – in the original series. That series itself had two endings. The original showing finished with Part 5 of the series. However, no sooner had the events in that hastily re-edited programme been broadcast in the UK, than the war came to an end in Bosnia, accompanied by the peace talks at Dayton, Ohio and the agreement that emerged from those talks. The end to active armed hostilities in Bosnia meant that the series needed another programme to be complete. While Part 5 had covered the fall of the UN-designated 'Safe Area' in eastern Bosnia and how this had sparked NATO-led international action, it required Part 6, originally not a part of the plan (it therefore required additional funding), to complete the Bosnian story. 'Pax Americana' picked up events and took them through to the agreement of the peace accords at Dayton. The series was then rebroadcast, parading its awards, with Part 6 in place. This appeared to have finished the story. However, that was not the case. In 1999, there was scope for further instalments. This was the working idea when Lappings decided to take on the post-Dayton events, focused around Kosovo.

Thematically, *The Fall of Milošević* (hereafter, '*Fall*') is the continuation of *The Death of Yugoslavia* (hereafter, '*Death*') in three important and overlapping senses. The first is that the two series together chart the rise and fall of Slobodan Milošević as the chief political figure in Serbian politics. The second is that the two series cover the whole of the Yugoslav War, of which 'Slobo' was the principal architect (although the two series make perfectly clear that it would be simplistic to allocate all responsibility to him). Finally, the focus on Kosovo, which prompted the final three films, to a large extent, completes a circle, given that Part 1 of *Death* opens in Kosovo and devotes much of its length to the situation there in the 1990s and to Milošević's rise to power on the back of that issue.

After Part 1 of *Death,* Kosovo was forgotten. This reflected the background status of the province through the early and mid-1990s in terms of the main story and international attention: the focus was on the war zones in Slovenia, Croatia and Bosnia – because armed hostilities had not emerged there, the story, under time, space and resource pressures, did not need to revisit the province. However, the early material on Kosovo and Milošević's rise to power is among the most important and striking throughout the two series. The original series was generally at its strongest in the earlier parts, charting the road to Yugoslav disintegration. Kosovo and Milošević, as a case, exemplifies this. One of the early jewels in the Lapping crown was to establish that Milošević's rule was 'founded on a lie'. Through filmed interviews with Miroslav Šolević, a Kosovo Serb political activist and Dušan Mitević, head of Serbian Television news, as well as archive news footage, it was apparent that Milošević made two visits to the troubled province in the same week in April 1988. This is vital to understanding the subsequent events and, perhaps even more so, to understanding the nature of the Serbian leader's rule.

The founding myth of the Milošević story is his spontaneous response to the pressure of a Kosovo Serb crowd, complaining generally of their treatment in the province and, in particular, about being beaten by the Kosovo police seeking to control the crowd. The Serbian leader's apparently spontaneous response – 'no one shall beat you again' – became legendary. Broadcast that same evening on Serbian TV news, his reputation was made and his populist-nationalist ascent to power was almost cemented as it began. However, this received version, which has made its way into most accounts of anything relevant, was not faithful to the events that had actually occurred. Milošević, deputy head of the League of Communists of Serbia, had been dispatched to temper the pressures emerging from that province. He had been sent by his mentor, the leader of the Serbian Party, Ivan Stambolić (the latter clearly seeing that some response was necessary, but that a positive outcome was unlikely).[2] The success for *Death* was to find the film of Milošević's Monday visit to the province, as well as the more famous appearance the following Friday. The Monday Milošević bears all the characteristics of the *apparatchik* doing his duty, using the stodgy, formalistic language of communist Yugoslavia, intoning the mantras of brotherhood and unity. Clearly under pressure and apparently intimidated and possibly a little scared, Milošević responds to calls for him to take action and to return to the province, by asking if Friday would be all right. The crowd assent, Milošević is off the hook for the moment – and the embryo of a new political era is embedded.

When Milošević returns on the Friday, everything is ready. This includes preparations engineered between Kosovo Serb activists and the Serbian Security Service to provoke the Kosovo police into action against them. As Šolević explains, trucks full of stones were parked around the corner to ensure that there would be ammunition with which to pelt – and so provoke – the police. The police duly responded at the time by using batons. The roaring crowd complained as Milošević emerged from the meeting in which representatives had been making their fervent petitions, to be met with complaints of being beaten. Mitević's news team captured the response (without showing any of the context) on Serbian TV news that night: Milošević telling the crowd that no one would beat them again – and addressing them in a very different manner from Monday's statements. This time, Milošević was confident and eloquent, having dropped all party-speak – favouring, instead, straightforward, direct, accessible speech. As that moment of apparent authenticity and loyalty to the Serb cause was broadcast, Milošević's rise to power was as good as sealed. Yet it was a moment of orchestrated artifice, not the spontaneous moment it appeared. The impact was such that, even after *Death* had shown the evidence firsthand, the story did not change.[3]

A similar example of the tremendous, revelatory strength of the earlier parts of *Death* is the treatment of the arrest of Janez Janša in 1988 (a Slovenian journalist, at the time, who later became the country's defence minister) and the discussion surrounding the possible declaration of a state of emergency throughout the Socialist Federative Republic of

Yugoslavia in March 1991. Each of these, unbelievably, draws on secret film from Yugoslav military intelligence. The first of these shows film of the interview carried out by Colonel (later General) Aleksandar Vasiljević of the Yugoslav People's Army (JNA) Military Counter Intelligence Service (KOS). While the content of the interview adds little substantively to the Janša story, the inclusion of this material adds enormously to the visual texture and the general sense of impressive evidence found in the film. The quality of the camera-in-the-corner footage adds atmosphere, while the matter-of-fact voiceover narrative at that point reveals that the footage is from Yugoslav military intelligence. The understated tone is in stark contrast to that which might be expected in more conventional TV news journalism, or even in the self-standing TV documentary, where much is made usually of the slightest 'new' or 'secret' evidence (both as part of the pitching and commissioning process, and within the particular films). The viewer, if attentive, is left to marvel that the film contains footage from KOS – and to reflect on the utterly amazing feat of the series makers' having access to this material.[4] While the material adds nothing immediate and substantive, it (and its presentation) adds enormously to the credibility of the film series as a whole, as well as this particular part of it.

A similar, even more remarkable use of KOS footage is made in Part 2 of *Death*. This involves the attempt by Serbia and the leadership of the JNA to win agreement to declare a state of emergency throughout the SFRY in March 1991. The film shows the tense meeting at which the top general in the JNA, Defence Secretary Veljko Kadijević, warns of an alleged plot to break up the SFRY and to provoke civil war; the only responsible action, in the circumstances, according to the general, would be to declare a state of emergency. The meeting had been called at 24 hours' notice by Borisav Jović, the Serbian representative to the State Council (aka the Collective Federal Presidency), at that point holding the presidency of the Council – and the other members of the State Council had learned of it only on TV, as the Macedonian representative, Vasil Tuporkovski, reveals in the film. The film shows the tension in a chilly room as Jović goes round to each of the eight members of the council, asking for their vote. There is great attention to the hesitant decision of the Kosovo representative (Jović impatiently snarls that he will take the rambling response as a 'yes' to the state of emergency) and on the reflective approach of the Bosnian representative, Bogić Bogićević. The latter was a Serb from Bosnia and appears to have been assumed to be an automatic ally of the Serbian cause in promoting a state of emergency. However, Bogićević weighs the issues carefully, to the obvious frustration of Jović, who, in the end, barks at his Bosnian counterpart to vote – 'vote yes, vote no, just vote!' Bogićević votes 'no', to the cold, resentful acknowledgement of Jović. At this point in the film, the voiceover narrative announces that the vote was a tie. As a narrative, the story is brought to its dramatic point of conclusion and the viewer is left ready to move on to the next part of the story, having witnessed one of the more remarkable moments of history as it is made. This is first-rate drama and first-rate filmmaking.

However, it is at this zenith that questions might be posed in terms of journalism and certainly of scholarship. While the film is honest in the sense that the viewer sees that which happened actually happening, and not through reconstruction or dramatisation, there is a fallacy in the way in which the drama is presented. The viewer is unlikely to take a wrong, false or skewed interpretation from the film. However, the informed viewer, paying close attention, will realise the fallacy: that which is presented as one meeting on 12 March was, in fact, two meetings.

The real meetings were held on successive days. The main clues lie in the voiceover commentary, in recognising those attending the meeting and in considering the four–four split decision in the vote. Given that the sequence begins with the voiceover narrative stating that the Slovenian representative did not attend for fear of being arrested, the four–four split vote should have been impossible – without the Slovene, there could not have been more that seven votes in total. The visual giveaway is that, for those who recognise him, the Slovenian representative Janez Drnovšek (later to be Prime Minister and eventually President of Slovenia), can be identified in the scenes around the vote. The voiceover narration is not mistaken, but the overall impression left is not wholly faithful. In fact, there were two meetings held over the two days. The Slovene, indeed, did not attend on the first day, wary of what might happen. However, once the gravity of the issue and the potential damage to Slovenia had become apparent after the first day, he took the risk of attending. The impression of one meeting on one day is, then, a visual-verbal sleight of hand.

This betrays the degree to which the documentary series is not the same as scholarship or even conventional journalism. The detail is not quite right – the two meetings are elided into one. As a device to keep the story flowing and to maintain the drama (as well as to fit the time constraints imposed by the structure of the series), the elision is justified. However, in terms of overall credibility, at least a small shadow is cast by the failure to identify clearly that there were two meetings. If there is a question of this kind at this point, the sceptical viewer might wonder if there were similar moments at other parts of the series – perhaps where harm might be done. While the series appears at times almost to have the status of a primary document, constructed as it is to such a great extent from primary interviews and primary visual material, minimising voiceover narration and verbally imposed interpretation, the elision of the two meetings is a reminder of the degree to which the films cannot be taken as 'documents'.[5]

There is no real equivalent of this type of material in *Fall*. While the quality is certainly high, there is no equivalent of the meeting, or the Janša footage, or the real story of Milošević's visit to Kosovo. There are unknown stories – the Niš town hall clerk who helped to steal forged voting slips, the tractor driver and his comrades rolling in from the Serbian provinces, evading roadblocks and impediments, to help force the removal of Milošević, the meeting between Zoran Djindjić (later to become Serbian Prime Minister, once the Milošević regime had gone, before being shot dead by an assassin in March 2003). But, there is nothing to compete with the revelations to be found in *Death*. Even as far as the 'new' stories in *Fall* offer detailed insights, they emerge from the talking heads, not the richness of the visual material or the overall texture. In this sense, *Fall* does not really live up to the precedent set by *Death*.

In general, the visual texture in *Fall* is thinner than that of its forerunner. While *Death* has quite possibly the richest visual texture of any documentary series ever, *Fall* struggles by comparison. There is one moment in Part 2 of *Death* where the visit of General Kadijević to Moscow is covered briefly by a panning shot across the Kremlin wall and voiceover narrative. While this is not quite the only panning shot-visual filler in the series, it is rare enough to place a spotlight on the truly remarkable extent to which the remainder of the series comprises the talking heads of the protagonists and, even more than this, a rich variety of images – from home movies to tourism commercials to cartoons to TV news – that maintain the narrative flow. *Fall* has its share of varied images and image sources, as well as a good range of talking heads. However, there is a far greater sense of filler material being used, evidenced by the considerably greater use of the voiceover commentary: used sparingly in *Death*, this is far more prominent in *Fall*.[6]

There is a valiant attempt to cover one of the most significant holes in *Fall* – the absence of an interview with Milošević by the filmmakers. This is a significant weakness, given the degree to which the strength and texture of the approach is predicated on getting the protagonists to tell the story themselves. A film series about the fall of Milošević, based on direct testimony from those involved, is at a disadvantage if the central figure is not available. In other cases, treatment of events might be left out or overlooked because one or more protagonists is not available, but the main actor cannot be ignored – and because he is central to all events, there is little scope to leave anything out. According to the philosophy by which the programmes are made – interviews with the key actors on all sides and intercutting them to create a narrative – the absence of Milošević could be a blow to sink the series. The production team get around this by making use of three sources: their own old interview footage, a curious interview carried out by a Texan academic during the course of the Kosovo campaign in 1999, and archive material of the Serbian leader making statements (primarily, it appears, from RTS). These sources are cleverly deployed to make sure that Milošević and his words appear at relevant points in the narrative. However, they are no substitute for an interview in which he had been specifically asked about points that had emerged in interviews with others.

By contrast, *Death* had been suffused with valuable – sometimes humorous – Milošević interview material. While *Death* was strengthened by this, it would have been feasible without it. Indeed, it was only at the very last moment, when Part 1 was already just about at its final cut and soon to be broadcast, that the Serbian strongman finally agreed to an interview. The interview was on condition that all the material in the interview should be broadcast – an apparent attempt to make the directors' and producers' jobs impossible at this late stage, as to include the whole of the interview somewhere in the series would mean undoing much of that which was already in place and, quite possibly, distorting the series. However, producer Norma Percy played Milošević at his own game, competing in the slyness stakes by agreeing to use all of the material in the interview, but not including all of it directly in the series. Rather, with the agreement of the BBC schedulers, the interview was shown in its entirety as a relatively late addition to the BBC2 schedule at 2 a.m. on a Sunday morning. With little prior announcement, only assiduous readers of the TV listings with an interest in the subject would have been likely to notice *The Milošević Interview*, without any additional explanation of what the broadcast was. This smart response to Milošević's attempt to wreck the series meant that the terms of the agreement for the interview had been met – the whole of it had been used – but that the Serbian leader's ploy had not worked.

Instead, *Death* benefited from the chance to intercut Milošević and Slovenian leader Milan Kučan in such a way as to suggest clearly that Milošević had indicated his effective assent to Slovenia's leaving the SFRY, but seeking agreement on a reinterpretation of key terms in the 1974 Constitution. While Kučan did not agree to the terms, this seems to confirm two things: that the Slovenian leader understood that he and his country would not significantly need to contend with Serbia in the breakup, as Milošević's interests lay elsewhere; and that there was some kind of understanding between the two states and their leaders prior to the declarations of independence and the onset of war that would make Slovenia's route easier and leave Croatia and Bosnia more vulnerable to Serbia's ambitions. Once again, this is one the ways in which the approach taken in these series, and the value of *Death* in particular, lies in quietly uncovering the elements of the real political record.

The presence or absence of one part of a story can be definitive not only in terms of comprehension of what happened, but also of the extent to which the whole story is comprehensively addressed. If one set of voices is not available, then it becomes difficult, perhaps even impossible, to cover a topic. A key example of this is the virtual excision of the Vance Owen Peace Plan (VOPP) and the 'lift and strike' debate that dominated attention to Bosnia during 1993. Together, these constituted one of the biggest issues of the war, yet they are passed over in a few moments of voiceover commentary in Part 4 of *Death*. Instead, there is a sequence taking up around one-third of the whole film, devoted to the kidnapping of Bosnian President Alija Izetbegović by the JNA at Sarajevo airport in April 1992, as armed hostilities in Bosnia are beginning in earnest. The emphasis on an event that, while dramatic at the time, is a very minor moment distorts the overall treatment, especially as the twinned issues that, perhaps more than anything else, dominated discussion of war in the Bosnian theatre are more or less omitted.

The explanation for this lies in the availability of material – interviews and contemporary footage. Much of the Izetbegović kidnapping was played out on Sarajevo TV, leaving a reservoir of material. Supplemented with interviews, this meant that there was a wealth of material to use concerning a relatively dramatic incident. The extended treatment in the film already seems to be on the verge of diminishing the drama of the incident as a story, although it retains value in terms of capturing the experiences of those involved in the incident (see below). The kidnap sequence is one of the weakest across the two series in terms of its real significance and contribution to a depiction of Yugoslavia's demise.

Another example of the availability of visual material driving production is the story of the Otpor rock concert – a cultural resistance moment. Why tell this story? Because the production team had talking heads rehearsing it and film of the drummer keeping the crowd going until midnight, when the concert was supposed to begin. However, at that point, someone began to read out lists of names of those killed, or abused by the regime for their resistance. This was followed by images of the silent, stunned crowd in darkness at the end, when no concert followed the reading of names. The incident, in itself, was not one of great salience – and it was certainly no more important than other moments that might well have been incorporated. Yet it was a story where there was visual material available, footage that had a minor dramatic moment in its ending, which was enough to justify inclusion.

*Fall* gives attention to an amusing and entertaining 'digger man', who blamed the Milošević regime for the collapse of his business. This attention comes in the context of the Otpor March on Belgrade, which protests would lead directly to Milošević's fall that day. Why does he receive attention? Because he is endearing and the makers have both the talking head and images of the digger itself at the time. This is an image-driven, human element. The digger and the 'digger man' arguably do not deserve the attention they receive. While the digger was significant in the images of the approach to Parliament and, in practice, in getting the protesters into the Parliament building – he used his digger to lift the first ones in up to the first floor – this is a minor detail in the scheme of events. The tide of people entering the Parliament, or on its steps, and the images of flames leaping out of the windows as curtains inside burned, provide the main story.

On the surface, to favour such extensive attention to relatively minor events, such as the Izetbegović kidnapping, while passing swiftly over the intense international debates of 1993 to 1995, appears to show a want of judgement. However, it is the availability of material that drives these choices in the context of the techniques used in making the films. The VOPP, with the potential for tellingly bitter inside stories, was barely touched on because the interviews were not available. While the filmmakers had been able to carry out research interviews with the major US Administration figures regarding that period of the war, they were unable to secure film interviews that could be used on screen.[7] As a result, in terms of their own philosophy, they could not tackle that part of events: if both, or all sides, were not there to tell the story from their own mouths, then the issue could not be addressed. To do so would be to lose the perspective of objectivity sought through the intercutting, intersubjective use of the protagonists, making the story appear to be telling only one side. It could also serve to undermine the credibility of the series as a whole if one part were seen to be imbalanced. The omission can be entirely justified on the terms the filmmakers set themselves. However, in terms of the apparently comprehensive treatment that *Death* offers, it is a significant flaw in the fabric, patched over by the voiceover. In terms of the credibility and quality that the documentary series makes possible, the knowledgeable viewer will notice the weakness here, however understandable. Part 4 shows the real vulnerabilities of the series.

In some cases, the absence of particular interviewees can be accommodated. For example, although there were preliminary contacts, it proved impossible to film an interview with General Kadijević. This might have made telling certain parts of the story impossible. The texture of the relevant parts of Parts 1 and 2 of *Death* might well be weaker than they would have been had there been an interview with the general. However, the one key moment where an explanation for his actions is required is covered by an interview with his mentor, Admiral Branko Mamula. The latter supposes that the general's failure to go through with a plot hatched with the Serbian political leadership to declare a *coup d'état* is to be explained by a prick of conscience. While this is not Kadijević's voice, and so there might still be reason to wonder about his motives, the explanation given certainly seems plausible – and, in terms of making the film work, there is a voice there to round off that particular passage in the story.

Equally, and perhaps more significantly, the absence of an interview with Milošević for the three *Fall* films presents a potential gap. This is covered, as noted above, by the use of the earlier interview he gave for *Death* at one point. At others, it is covered most significantly by the interview he gave to a Texan academic otherwise unknown in the field. This is the closest that the filmmakers can get to an interview that covers the *Fall* period. However, while it can offer useful material, it cannot be an adequate substitute for that which might have been possible if a purpose-filmed interview with Milošević had been available. There are two reasons for this. The first is that the interview is clearly a propaganda activity from Milošević's point of view. The reliability of what he says in it must be questioned. The second is that the filmmakers cannot cross-reference and test his version and those of others using their normal methodology. For example, in Part 1 of *Fall*, that interview is used to introduce Milošević's voice on the talks at Rambouillet in France, shortly before the NATO action over Kosovo began, in 1999. The view he offers in it regarding the purpose of the agreement being proposed – Kosovo's independence, he says – might well have been one that he would have sustained in a new interview. However, that position could have been tested against what others said. With no such interview, of course, there can be no certainty on this. And without that interview, there is no chance of hearing from the man's own mouth exactly what he thought he and others were doing throughout the whole period. However, the missing interview is not an impediment to making the film – the key requisites are there for making the film: the actors saying relevant things on film and additional visual material to enrich the texture. In the end, while a documentary series, such as *Fall*, might be gauged on credibility and quality, above all, in the Brook-Lapping canon, the vital element to make the film viable, or not, is the voices and faces on film, to make the intercutting story-telling possible. Without the visual reinforcement of the face, the narrative is not possible – and so it is overlooked. *Fall* falls down, in the end, because *Death* was too good.

## Chechnya and media management: prisoners of the Caucasus

The war in Chechnya was declared by Russia's President, Vladimir Putin, to have been successfully completed. Therefore, while military operations continue and the conflict is not at an end, no one is allowed to, or dares to try, to report on it or to make documentary films about it. These would not be broadcast. Only a bomb incident at the 2004 '9 May' parade, marking the anniversary of victory in the Second World War, in Grozny, opened up the possibility of reporting on Chechnya – and in some respects that situation appeared staged (including Putin's declaring the President dead from Moscow, when the early local reports had announced only light wounds). In a sense, the puppeteers (or should that be software designers?) of virtual democracy[8] confirm what one interviewee said regarding the impossibility of making films on Chechnya in Putin's Russia – 'Once a Chekist, always a Chekist.'[9] This means that the conditions for reporting from Chechnya, and media standards in Russia more generally, were increasingly those of the Soviet Union, under a leader who bore the hallmarks of a surface-modernised Soviet leader.

In this section, we examine documentary treatment of the Chechen conflict in two ways. First, in line with the feature fiction treatment by

Sergei Bodrov, discussed in the previous chapter, we examine Tolstoy's image of Russia as a 'prisoner of the Caucasus' through one film with that title. Second, we consider the issues that arise in terms of potential presumed impact of any film covering the conflict against the background of official and 'self-' censorship, resulting in difficulties even making or showing films, as well as those of personal commitment, responsibility and subjectivity that arise in the context.

*Prisoner of the Caucasus*, directed by Yuri Khashchavatski (Germany/ Poland 2002), is a minor film, but one that draws on literature and history to give context and to move beyond the immediate events of the post-Soviet Chechen conflict, even though that is its focus. The formal voiceover narrator – taken to be the director's voice – makes the comment that we normally only see short, edited extracts on our TV screens. We do not see the whole of a situation. This might be because of time constraints, self-censorship on the part of those producing the images or even imposed censorship.

The wedding scenes might put the viewer familiar with Michael Cimino's *The Deerhunter* in mind of the wedding and send-off scenes there, in particular, as they are set among a Ukrainian émigré community in industrial Pennsylvania. The feeling of swirling celebration is similar. This ending to Khashchavatski's film in some ways confirms the degree to which it is a strong, authorial film in the Soviet and Russian tradition, as Ian Christie has pointed out.[10] It is very literary in both its content and style and has almost the structure and character of fiction. It is very much in the tradition of Soviet-Russian documentary in which the director is taking command of the film and communicating in strong, direct terms. Although different in structure, the purpose, and perhaps even the tone, is that of the early Soviet documentarists and re-creators of revolutionary events, such as Medvedkin or Eizenshtein.[11] As Christie again has observed, the filmmaker's voice is clearly expressed in the film – quite literally, given the verbal commentary.[12]

The images of fire in the opening scenes are stylishly – and no doubt symbolically – reflected in the spectacles of a filmmaker. This is the reflected image, through the lens in the eye of the beholder – in one image, the different levels and prisms of capturing the destruction of war (and even its aesthetics) are folded together. Luscious images of tomatoes and other fruits and vegetables in the Grozny market in 1991 complement the commentary, which refers to the bright colours that could be found in the province prior to the onset of armed hostilities. There is an image of a little girl standing on a tank. She is clearly happy with this and enthusiastic to continue playing. Her innocence and eagerness is contrasted with that of what is presumably her mother, who is clearly aware of the danger and is trying to persuade and physically to get the child down from the tank. The mother's anxiety is sharply distinguished from the girl's happiness. This reflects the difference between consciousness of that which is taking place and naive adventure.

Another striking image is that of a woman in what appears to be (and is described as) her dressing-gown holding an AK47. This embeds the sense that the Chechen rebellion is a people's cause and conflict. All are part of it. The voiceover narration emphasises that people knew and expected that there would be war in 1991, although other, unidentified commentators had later suggested that no one expected that the war would or could happen. Across images of armoured personnel vehicles the commentary also states that, following Tolstoy, generals always need a little war to win.

Shots of the charred bodies of soldiers beneath the tanks, with crowing Chechen spectators, are displayed in black and white, although the original footage was clearly coloured. The commentary notes that these are 'distressing images' and say that this is why 'I' – the filmmaker – did not show them in colour. However, it could be that by casting the images in black and white, the director has not saved the viewer from an awful scene by mitigating its effects in some way. Rather, the monochrome view, consolidating as it does to some extent the tones of the charcoal corpses, draws out and emphasises exactly what has happened.

The commentary observes that when the cameramen have time they film things for themselves, not simply to report the conflict. Sparrows in a tree are framed to back this statement. There is a focus on one in particular that has an oversized piece of food in its beak – a piece that it cannot consume as it is, but cannot handle without letting go of it. This bird is said to be symbolic – though of what, the viewer is left to calculate. Is it a symbol of a Russia that cannot gobble up Chechnya but cannot let it go? Or is it a symbol of a cameraman filmmaker who doesn't want to let the unseen images go? The commentary drives home its point – this image would not be seen on the television news, which has no interest in irony or time for peaceful contrast to violence and conflict, or, perhaps, even for symbols.

'Nobody likes looking at a wounded soldier, that's why I ordered him to be taken to a first aid post.' The Lev Tolstoy quotation is used over the image of a wounded soldier – initially as though original commentary, but the reference to Tolstoy's writing over 100 years ago reinforces the sense of futility and inevitability of history's repeating itself. It also prefigures the graphic presentation of war itself. Images that capture the flashes of MLRSs, tank canons, and helicopter gunships firing rockets are sequenced, suggesting power and disproportion against a weaker opponent. We see sniper fire emitting from the top-floor window of an apartment block immediately before the tank round flashes from the canon and explodes precisely on that window. We also see a completely destroyed one-level building, presumably an ammunition store, which has bullets leaping out of it and spitting and splitting visually and aurally in the air like firecrackers. A scene of torment, of throats being cut and heads cut off, is punctuated visually by slightly delayed fades in and out of black, as well as slightly dulled sound. This both breaks up the horrific image but also draws out and reinforces the sense of horror. The structure and delay in this scene makes sure that the viewer cannot blink and miss it. It makes sure that the message gets through, while at the same time being palliated. The commentary also seeks to reinforce a sense of revulsion by pointing out that the viewer should look again and look closely: these are not barbarian Chechen rebels committing atrocities against poor Russian soldiers, but Russian soldiers using knives to score and score again the flesh of what are presumed to be Chechens, before finally slitting their throats as the victims squeal and scream protests that they do not want to die. In the end, although we are told that the heads are severed, we do not appear to be shown this explicitly.

These images of the scoring and slaughter were not restricted to appearing in films of this kind. The phenomenon of modern electronic communication meant that digital images such as this could be circulated as MPeg attachments to email messages, or posted on internet websites. These images could be circulated – and ostensibly were – to create awareness of atrocities. However, this was also clearly a potential instrument of misinformation. In an age where images made messages, such an image offered powerful evidence. However, most potential viewers would not know whether the victims were Russians or Chechens – apart from what they were told in accompanying verbal or written text. Khashchavatski's express comment that the perpetrators and victims are Russians and Chechens, respectively, is made to counter either assumption and pre-judgement that the roles were reversed, or more probably, the reality that images such as these had been in circulation, but asserting that the Russians were the victims. The author of this film, *inter alia*, sought to make his point about responsibility while also challenging other interpretations. This move in itself confirms the competition for image and interpretation. Even if we are inclined to take the director's version as authoritative, we are still reflexively confronted with the possibility that his version may just be another salvo in the battle for our hearts and minds.[13]

Edik Dzhafarmov, one of the freelance, or stringer, cameramen whose footage is used in the film, is the only one named in the text. We are told that he has been filming in various theatres for over a decade. He is given a name-check early in the film because he becomes part of it in one of the most striking and worrying scenes in the film, called 'Soap and Water'. The soap refers to bars of soap that are delivered as humanitarian aid to disappointed recipients, some of whom tell the camera that they had been waiting all night in the hope of getting some kind of food. The voiceover then tells us that what happened next would have killed Edik, had he not moved away to take a panorama shot of the crowd outside the shop that has been serving as a humanitarian aid distribution point. The film shows the shop exploding, with the crowd around it. Khashchavatski then tells us that he has added the image of the explosion using 'post-production techniques.' He reveals the original footage, which begins only after the explosion has occurred and there is already disarray in the crowd, with some fallen and others staggering shocked, if not wounded. These pictures of the aftermath are used consciously to confirm the reality that only most rarely are images of incidents of destruction – the action of armed conflict – captured as they happen – the way that they are in fiction, for example. Khashchavatski fictionalises the actual footage here in order to render the truth of destruction, while at the same time using the reflexive commentary to address the tension between authenticity and truth, between drama and that which is normally possible to capture on film.[14] It is also possible, of course, that the director is playing a double-bluff with the viewers here, apparently bolstering his reliability and authority by revealing his cinematic trick, thereby gaining authority for his voice.

The film is unified by an interview with a lieutenant in a railway carriage, sharing experiences of loss – soldiers who are missing, or buried – and the effect of confronting death and destruction. As the film moves into its latter stages, he talks about corpses and charred, mutilated bodies – supplemented by the comment: 'Only they understood what war is.' The images are of wooden boxes that serve as coffins being loaded on to heavy lift aircraft to be transported back to their families. This is a precursor to the final scenes of the film, which focus on loss and death. This is marked by the sickening and almost comic scene of soldiers attempting to deliver one of these basic box coffins, struggling to get it through the door to the small house, bumping it on the door frame, turning it on edge and tipping it up, like a sofa or wardrobe too large to fit. There is no laughter, however, as the woman inside weeps.

Before Khashchavatski returns us to the family, he introduces us to a Chechen teenage boy, who is manning a checkpoint with a machine-gun. This young boy, who has not been to school for a year, has both a smile and eyes that are sweet and charming. He wears a blue bandana, which he explains is the symbol that he is prepared to die for his homeland. Even given this strong-yet-gentle showing and the boy's bright defiance, as the image is held, it captures his bold smile giving way to an expression of uncertainty.

After meeting this gentle yet fearsome and ultimately slightly scared child, we return to the family of A.A. Volkov, the soldier whose death box we have seen being returned to them. The father reads out a last letter sent by the son, while the family, including his wife, of course, watch the video-recording of his wedding. The pathos of the father's reading the letter while the happy scenes of the video play is strong. It would be hard not to be moved by such a scene. This is a strongly rendered moment, in many ways simple, yet playing on the layering of images, with the video on the television screen within the film offering one texture, while the family gathered around sets another level. Either would be affective on its own, but the two together, with the video providing a different visual fabric, are chillingly evocative. There can be no real thought at this moment.

The potential damage that referential or documentary moving images might have on Russia's campaign in Chechnya was confirmed by the direct and indirect censorship imposed by the government. In terms of direct censorship, the territory itself was a closed area, where journalists and others who might report were officially forbidden to go. This meant that those who went there could only get to report or film there by, effectively, smuggling themselves in. The official ban, of course, meant that national output within Russia of whatever those who had smuggled themselves in might find was just about impossible, as state-controlled or dominated broadcasters would not show material from the closed zone. But, this direct attempted control over journalism and photography, whether moving or still, had a wider indirect component. There was an effective ban, not only on filming in the war-torn region, but also on even raising the topic and considering making a documentary film of any kind that addressed the conflict.

*Prisoner of the Caucasus* is a minor, elegiac documentary only ever destined to be seen by a relatively small audience. Even more direct documentaries, however, would not easily be shown in Putin's Russia, if at all, because all such material has a potential to detract from the legitimacy of Russian operations in Russia itself. In an atmosphere where it was virtually impossible to show films or reports about Chechnya and the awful features, notably abuses of human rights, associated with conflict, the opportunities for films to be shown were limited to film or human rights activist festivals. The latter, supported by bodies such as the International Helsinki Federation,[15] however, could only reach limited audiences, usually of those who were already aware of issues and needed little persuasion. However, the human rights NGOs could attempt a very limited, subversive version of the famous propaganda, or educational trains, used to spread the Leninist message throughout Russia in the early years of the Revolution. This meant the production of VHS cassettes for distribution throughout Russia. One compilation tape of this kind, produced by the International Helsinki Federation for Human Rights, Amnesty International and ARTE (the Franco-German arts and cultural broadcaster), contained five documentary films from the selection shown at the 'Chechnya' International Festival.[16] This reel included one film made by NTV, before the government circumscribed the scope of that Russian TV station's independence, and four films made outside Russia.

One of the films on the festival cassette is *Il était une fois la Tchétchénie* (Chechenskaia kolybel'naia) by Nino Kirtadze.[17] The film starts by using early Soviet archive footage about Chechnya. This is important visually as it gives the film a striking opening, which also establishes an historical frame for the problem. While the slightly comical figures who worship Allah – represented by an inter-title abbreviated version of their repeating that name for God as half understood by Russians, perhaps – are shown with the ugly scars of debilitating illnesses, such as tuberculosis, and the implicit suggestion that these primitives can be redeemed by Stalin's Soviet Union, there is a sense of implacable, unbridgeable eternal distance. The striking old images preface a strong film that blends the personal experience and material of three journalists who had ventured as explorers into the closed region, to capture images of, and report on, what was happening there. The first is Robert Parsons, a freelancer who made reports for the BBC, who shares his library of footage and views on the situation with the camera. The second is the celebrated Russian journalist Andrei Babitsky, who was detained by his own Russian side, eventually, and after a period of protests, released as a prisoner to the Chechens, as though he was to be regarded as a Chechen himself. The third is Petra Prokhatskova, whose harrowing images and tale highlight not only the nature and important of images, but also issues of professional and personal character, and the ethics of both working with people in conflict zones and capturing images of them professionally.

As the final segment of this picture-journalistic triptych begins, Prokhatskova is seen phoning a report to her editor at the *Chersk Gazette*, her hometown local paper. She now lives in Grozny, the Chechen capital, and has bought a house there that she has turned into an orphanage. Her purchasing the property is an act of personal transformation and responsibility. She owns the place so as to be there, having known Grozny already in the old days, when she could travel freely, before devastating warfare struck it, as well as the ban on access to the so-called Autonomous Republic. Prokhatskova reports to the camera under Kirtadze's direction that there are problems, obviously, in Grozny, with utility supplies, but that, despite this, she can sense 'togetherness' by living there. This is something that would be impossible as a journalist who comes and goes. She confesses that for most of her war experience, from 1994 to the present day, there was a sense of the more blood, the greater the number of corpses, then, so much the better. Kirtadze makes extensive use of Prokhatskova's personal archive, including the raw images of corpses she filmed after exhumation. 'It was awful', she self-evidently comments, before noting something perhaps so much more awful – that 'today no one is even looking for them'. As Kirtadze's film uses Prokhatskova's footage to trace the ruins of human bodies, illustrating the latter's reflective commentary, the screen finds boots left on the end of bones. The personal commentary regards the boots, left solid on fleshless bodies, as deeply symbolic. There is irony in the endurance of the material meant to assist and complement human existence, keeping their feet on the earth, surviving the loss of spirit and corporeal degradation and disintegration. The boots are all that remain.

The personal examination continues as Prokhatskova tells how she did not feel sorry for any of those people at the time, and suggests a strong, and likely sound, view: 'I doubt that any journalist feels sorry. You take pictures, you write something. Maybe you feel sorry later! I was like that.' The locals, who would always help her in taking pictures and filming, were nonetheless a little bemused, asking what it was for, perhaps slightly disbelieving that anyone could be interested enough 'over there in Europe' or, indeed, anywhere else, to look at the horrible human detritus and devastated physical environment. These comments on the helpfulness, but the incomprehension of the locals neatly throw into relief the confessional aspect of the camerawoman's professionalism, as well as the personal transformation and development of responsibility that her take reveal.

The real turning point in Prokhatskova's experience came in Dagestan, the year before the interview for Kirtadze's film. She was travelling with Russian forces when the Armoured Personnel Carrier she was in hit a mine. In professional terms this was a great moment, since the camera was turning as it happened. Of course, this means only that the sound of the explosion, rocking and a burst of dust are captured, rather than a carefully framed moment. However, one of the troops was fatally wounded by the blast. She recalls his being dragged from the vehicle after the noise, and that he had trousers with no legs inside them. And we see her film of him on the ground and hear her describe his breathing as an 'awful sound, like dragging out a fish' and watch, informed by Prokhatskova, that he filmed his last breath. The detonation and the dying soldier were the rare images capturing something as it happened. On the professional level this was a great moment, confirmed by her calling in to her editor, but personally it was a moment of distaste and rejection.

The telling images were, indeed, exciting for professionals. The conversation with her editor, decisively etched on her memory, prompted the change. Once he knew that they had hit a mine and that the camera had been rolling, so the moment had been captured, in true professional style, he said, 'That's excellent!' His reaction confirmed the centrality and excitement of key, action images. But for the woman in the field with the troops, it also challenged any sense of humanity. She had expected him to ask if she was all right and if anyone else was hurt. But his focus was on the images. This was clearly the cue for her to withdraw from that kind of frontline professionalism, as she recognises how the professional might feel pity if someone dies in front of their very eyes, but is likely also to rationalise the moment with 'a voice that says "he would have died anyway, and it's good that he died right here, now, in front of my camera"'. She adds: 'That's when you have to stop.' Professionalism had brought her to that point, but it was also a point where perspective could be lost.

Prokhatskova had begun to see the war as her own; she had realised the extent to which, as a responsible human being, she was a part of it. She was no longer, in her words, 'a person who is standing by it, recording it. You are a participant.' Work had only become a means of getting to the place where she had formed personal relations over the years, even though she did not know where some of the people she had known had gone, or what had happened to them. But her growing qualms over the professional capturing of images of suffering led her, little by little, to find something that she could do to be in Grozny with those people. This led to her purchasing the property and running it as an orphanage. She acknowledges that this is only a small contribution, but is convinced that 'it is better to do something for those fifty children than to let the world know that there is a war going on'. It is clear that there is a greater responsibility, to paraphrase Voltaire, in cultivating a *Kindergarten*, of a kind, than in capturing images of devastation, destruction and death for a wider world. The delusion, for her, of believing that she was performing some great role in helping to make information and images available to people about what she terms a 'cruel and unjust war' was removed by filming not only the booted remains of the dead, but by death itself, and the hard, inhumane professional response of her editor. Prokhaskova's experience and her film are used effectively by Kirtadze, in a way that confirms the salience of both experience and image where film is concerned. In this case, the two are tightly intertwined. It is one filmmaker's own experience of capturing those vital images that is used both to reveal the importance of image itself, as well as issues of professionalism, ethics and social responsibility. And it is that same experience that offers insight into the personal and human levels of warfare, giving some access to understanding, even if, inevitably, the whole conflict cannot be captured, but confirming that experience is the key aspect of war, rather than strategy or conduct, in terms of moving images and modern war – while the appearance of Kirtadze's film on the human rights' lobby VHS cassette confirms the significance of images, or their control and suppression where possible; and Russia is a place where the vast size of the country, covering one-sixth of the Earth, and the nature of the polity make this easier.

## From prisoners to hostages: Chechen terrorism and the Beslan siege

*Il était une fois la Tchétchénie* in one way confirms personal commitment and the virtual impossibility of being somewhere and not taking sides. But the Chechen context illustrates wider questions about professionalism and personal commitment. *Immortal Fortress* by Dodge Billingsley, made in the interval between the so-called First and Second Chechen Wars, highlights the essential issues of image, access and objectivity that emerge in filmic documentation of contemporary conflict. War is about sides. Gaining access to, and capturing images, on one side, means working with people and getting to know them – and, quite likely, convincing them that the person with the camera is not working for their opponents, in some way. There is no way to gain access and not, in some sense, to forge bonds of identity. Just as Prokhatskova's personal links, which eventually led to her rejection of professional photography to inform the world (although this does not necessarily mean the end of her filming to document the predicament in Grozny, of course), were what gave her access in Grozny, Billingsley cannot gain access both to the Chechen warlord leader Shamil Basayev and to the Russians – contact with one precludes association with the other (as Babitsky's being detained by Russians and then released as a prisoner to Chechens confirms).

In the end, the view presented is inevitably and openly one that is more sympathetic to the Chechen perspective than the Russian, including how Chechen tactics outwitted Russian military might at times in the first conflict and, due to the contact and filming of Basayev, gives a human face to one of the 'warlord' leaders of a hydra-independence movement. It is significant, however, that the film was shot just after the end of the first war, in the interregnum. The sympathetic frame around Basayev (in part, because his human face is presented) is at odds with the Russian, and later, general, image of Basayev as not only a separatist insurgent, already responsible for harsh acts in the name of that cause, but also an agent of the militant Islamist agenda promoted by Usama bin Ladin among others. During that interregnum, Basayev clearly came under the influence of violent Islamists, who clearly saw Basayev and his Chechen brothers as ripe material for their international avant garde. Billingsley reports Basayev's transformation in *Chechnya: Separatism or Jihad?* – a generally less interesting film on Chechnya than *Immortal Fortress*, made for Combat Films and Research's 'Beyond the Border' series, an educational package made in association with Brigham Young University for use in university education on international affairs, and also shown by the PBS network in the US. This largely balanced and information-driven film, including a voiceover commentary, which Billingsley eschews in more personal pieces, and interviews with expert, or former participant, 'talking heads', making it more conventional as a documentary film, extends the Basayev story, as well as briefly considering some of the other Chechen 'warlords', into the twenty-first century, where he and his followers have given real material to support Russian allegations of their being Islamist terrorists. As that film shows, Basayev was responsible for a string of nasty terrorist incidents in the southern Russian North Caucasus region, beginning with a hospital attack where hostages were taken in 2000, the Moscow theatre siege of 2002, and continuing until the seizure of hostages at Nalchik, in Dagestan, in 2005. Each of these events involved the taking of innocent hostages by a team of suicide operatives orchestrated by Basayev; and each ended with the Russian security forces launching, and effectively bungling, an extraction operation. The most notorious of these incidents occurred at Beslan, in North Ossetia, on 1–3 September 2004, the siege of School no. 1 on the first day of the new school year, where over 1,200 people, 70 per cent of whom were children,[18] were kept at gunpoint and surrounded by booby-trap bombs in conditions calculated to provoke distress, and which ended with 350 people dead, over half of those children from the school. While *Chechnya: Separatism or Jihad?* gives a summary narrative description of the horrific developments there, another film, on a different plane altogether, captures the horror itself. This is Kevin Sim's film *Beslan: Siege of School No. 1*, as it was shown in the Wide Angle strand on PBS in the US in July 2005, otherwise called simply *Beslan* when originally shown just before that in the UK, as part of Channel 4's Dispatches season, which commissioned the film.[19]

*Beslan: Siege of School No. 1* was 'a shocking film to make', according to its director.[20] He wrestled with dilemmas making a film on a subject of this kind raises, knowing that those responsible for keeping the schoolchildren, their parents and their teachers hostage were out to make a mark and, precisely, to grab the attention of televisions news and documentary-makers, and who, he says, have made it clear are already prepared to do worse in order to make sure of getting noticed by the right people: 'If we following [*sic*] the law of diminishing returns, terrorists must try harder and harder to catch the eye of the news editor and the commissioner of documentaries.' Thus, the ethics of filmmaking in cases such as these (including others treated below) are acutely demanding, negotiating the intricate pathways between wrong and right, seeking to diminish what is still some inevitable publicity for, and benefit to, the terrorists, while showing what happened and, in some sense, being true to the victims and allowing their story to be known. In this sense, Sim's accomplishment is excellent.

*Beslan* benefits from two particular sources that allow it to combine experience and image into a remarkable film account of the siege. The first of these is the film the captors themselves took inside the school, primarily inside the gymnasium, where most of the hostages were held. The second is a set of remarkable film interviews with some of the survivors, particularly those with Larisa Kudzieva and Zarina Dzampaeva. The film benefits from other material, such as film of the celebrations surrounding the first day of school the previous year, and original footage, it must be presumed, of the religious event marking the passing of souls 40 days after their death, which structurally complement each other, the former while setting the scene, the latter towards the end of the film, as well as strong interviews with victims and others. There is also news footage shot outside the school. This includes footage showing the naked and near-naked girls as they escape the school after the siege is broken. It also reveals the confusing circumstances of the assault in the school by the Russian military. It is said that the military had been ordered not to attack, but that local vigilantes panicked about the situation, opening fire, and forcing the security forces into a position where they had to act.[21] But, the two contributing elements that make the film outstanding are the hostage interviews and the terrorists' own film.

The quality of the talking head interviews, relating their experience, is admirable in its sensitivity. In particular, Kudzieva presents a remarkable image. Evincing shaken composure, already some time after the event, with great calm, she recounts what happened to camera, while sitting on her hospital bed, her right cheek heavily dressed where, we learn, a bone had been jutting out completely. Her wound and her dignity make her a mesmerising image that encapsulates the emotional and physical torture of what has happened. Her damaged face and gentle, haunted eyes are visually magnetic as she recalls what happened: the man bleeding to death in front of her and her blood-soaked dress, unable to imagine that blood could ever be so heavy; being made an impossible offer by one of the terrorists, in which her children and anyone else she wanted could go free if she were to wear an explosive belt – an offer she rejected; and the terrorist who had to keep his foot on the pressure bomb apparently singing, but then explaining that this moaning was his soul, as he clearly wanted to lift his foot but could not do so, and relating to her fatalistically that his leader's talks with the Russian authorities are not going to work, with the implication that this means the end for all of them. This is powerful and moving material. Another woman, Nadia Totiev, who lost a son and a daughter, relates how red tears in the latter's eyes confirmed her death. But the most telling of all is the Vermeer-like image of Dzampaeva, whose only child died of a heart attack in front of her during the siege. It is she, who with impeccable stillness and no sentimentality, gets to utter the words that must have been on the tongues of all the parents. Why their child? What could they have done to deserve their fate? Uttered as the film moves towards its close, the camera's pause on the bereaved mother's face weighs heavily, conveying the dignified emptiness of these rhetorical questions and of the mother's soul, where she has lost her 'sunshine', her reason for living. Together, these are moving and powerful talking heads, which represent considerably more in the way of presenting images than the run-of-the-mill talking head used to fill a pictorial gap in the absence of stronger images, or a limited visual support to verbal information. This is a transcendent blending of experience and portrait image, infusing interpretation overall.

The primary source of image and experience that makes *Beslan* such a strong film is the footage taken inside the school by the terrorists themselves. This is astonishing footage, which confirms the conscious use of images as weapons by those involved in actions such as these. They film themselves and their prisoners, happy mostly to reveal their faces, as well as the network of explosive tripwires they have arranged, whether belt-bombs strapped around the torsos of so-called 'Black Widow' female suicide operatives (one of whom, in this case, is reported to have told a hostage, that she and her colleagues had come to the school to die), or the arrangement of bombs like Christmas decorations (as one interviewee puts it) strung across the room between light fittings, or the terrorist with his foot on a pressure pad, boldly pointing at his foot on the pad for the camera to make sure that, cartoon-style, almost, the point cannot be missed – although there can be none of the humour associated with that style.

Similar material filmed by the hostage-takers in the Moscow siege of 2002 has been decisive in another fine film, Dan Reed's *Terror in Moscow*. However, while there are similar features in events filmed – the common appearance of 'Black Widow' female suicide operatives on camera, booby-trapped human bombs, tired and frightened hostages inside the building and something akin to holiday pictures of the terrorists themselves as one of their number films the others as they sometimes smile, or pose for the camera – the footage in *Beslan* stands out because of the children. This terrorist home movie is extensive, not only in its fetishistic delineation of the bombs, but also in its presentation of the child hostages themselves. This exceptional and authentic film from inside the school makes the whole documentary possible. It is not appropriate to call this 'serendipity', but it is a matter of remarkable chance that the hostage-takers wanted not only to shoot a few images clearly for propaganda purposes, but turned out an inside visual account of a terrible event itself. Footage of this kind is rare, but it makes for singularly riveting film when it is available and well used. It is authentic footage of this kind that also made 9/11 such an un-imitable event and, in particular, resulted in one of the most intimate and compelling accounts of that day, *9/11*, by two young French filmmaker brothers, Jules and Gédéon Naudet, which is discussed in the following section, along with another film rooted in that day, Michael Moore's *Fahrenheit 9/11*.

## Turning up the heat: fire-fighters and *Fahrenheit 9/11*

*9/11* and *Fahrenheit 9/11* are two radically different actuality films, both widely seen and available, which incorporate the blending of the date on which commercial passenger aircraft were transformed into cruise missiles to strike New York and Washington, DC with the 'epo-numerous' tele-phone access code for the emergency services in the United States. Each relied on dreadful serendipity of images and the essence of experience for its impact. And each, in its own way, could be regarded as relevant to the issue of legitimacy in America's Global War on Terror, the latter con-sciously so, the former more contingently.[22]

The Naudet Brothers' film was changed from a potentially worthy doc-umentary on a 'probie' – a probationary fireman – and the work of the Fire Department of New York, Engine Company 7, Ladder 1, based in Duane Street, lower Manhattan, into a graphic record of the September 11 experience from inside the dust clouds of destruction. It is a film in which the brothers are true to their word to the fire-fighters only to make a film that 'would be made with the original spirit still intact'.[23] One image, in particular, guaranteed that the brothers and their film work would have a place in history: the only film that captures the first plane flying into the north tower. Jules Naudet was filming a routine incident with the fire chief on a corner 14 blocks up from the World Trade Center when the roar of the plane overhead led him to look up and follow the last few seconds of American Airlines Flight 11. That unique piece of film confirmed the brothers' date with destiny.

Beyond that unbelievable moment, unbelievably captured on film, the brothers, working independently with different parts of the fire department battalion, were in a position to film from inside the storm. While Jules captured the one and only image of the first plane, something unique, much of the dramatic film from inside the disaster scene was filmed by Gédéon, who also filmed the impact of the second plane, after setting off separately with the novice fire-fighter and some others in response to the emergency, and made a documentary record of the scenes inside the collapse. Between them, the brothers registered on film the character of the fire-fighters and others caught inside the event and the experiences of surviving the collapse of what had once been the tallest constructions in the world. One unit was beneath ground level at the first tower, with the thunder and thud of the building beginning to collapse above them, and they and their attached cameraman ran to climb the escalators out towards safety. One of those fire-fighters smothers the brother under his body protectively. Initially, this seems like he is being crushed to death by the force of the other body. Everything goes black with bits of rock across the camera lens, as the tower comes down above and around them; only later, via accounts of television news, do they realise that the other tower had already collapsed first. This is both image and experience from the core of the collapse.

The subsequent images of bewildered figures, coated in fine white dust, wandering like ghosts through a devastated landscape, and with a storm of dust, debris and paper swirling all around go beyond description. But they make clear that the clouds of collapse were filled with furniture, computers, stone and ash, but also body parts – perhaps the most awful aspect of the experience, as marked by fire-fighters' comments when the battalion has regrouped back at the station. The film also embraces the brothers' sense of potential loss, not knowing what had happened to the other. And, amid the awfulness, the Naudets' encounter with fate also leaves them with a relatively happy ending to their particular story about one team of fire-fighters. In the end even Tony, the probationer they had set out to film, the only one unaccounted for, wanders into the fire-house, having more than satisfied his colleagues that he merits full membership of their ranks.

The Naudets captured much of the raw experience of being inside this calamity. This appears foolhardy on one level – a far from unreasonable policeman tells one of them, when shown the brother's letter of credentials attaching him to the FDNY, to take his camera and his letter and to get out of the area. It is peculiar to be filming in such an environment. Yet the tension between opportunism and responsibility in such a moment almost certainly dissolves, with each leading to the conclusion that a record of this phenomenon and experience needs to be created. Certainly, the sober treatment given to the events in their film indicates that the Naudets not only realise that they had a lucky escape while inheriting one part of the burden of historical record, but that they know their real place. Their work with the modest heroes of the fire department has certainly left them with a sense of what really counts: that sense of the fire-fighters' courage in face of unimaginable chaos, destruction and death, and their evidently continuing to regard the brothers as part of the team, despite not being so, and, not even being American.

The authenticity of the film is the authenticity of both the filmmakers', but more significantly, the fire-fighters' experience. The sense of honest heroism in face of adversity makes the film a strong reminder of why America's response to the attacks was free from any significant challenge regarding legitimacy in the first months after the attacks, both in the US and around most of the world. While the same images, notably that of the successful strike using aircraft, also served the competing legitimacy purposes of al-Qa'ida, the detail amid the ruins of the twin towers without any sentimentality or embellishment and the feats of the emergency services are powerfully affective. The film initially courted controversy when shown in March 2003 in a TV version on CBS Television with an introduction and interventions from Robert de Niro.[24] It was thought by some – including CBS executives and the Federal Communications Commission – that it might be too soon to show something of this kind and that it might be offensive to some viewers.[25] However, the film, which deliberately eschews the goriest and gloomiest images available for the sake of good taste, defied those worries. In its straightforward, honest approach, using its dark jewel images, it is far more effective than any more manipulative effort would be.

In many respects, *Fahrenheit 9/11* could not provide a bigger contrast, as director Michael Moore takes a very deliberate swipe at the George W. Bush Administration regarding September 11 and surrounding and subsequent events. There is no doubt that the film is intended to bolster the ranks of those challenging the legitimacy of Washington's Global War on Terror and, in particular, of its engagement in Iraq. Whether or not it manages this, it certainly appears to have given strength and succour to those already subscribing to an anti-Bush, anti-Iraq war agenda.[26] This is polemical filmmaking, a world away from the authenticity of the Naudet Brothers' film in its attempt to remain entirely faithful to powerful material. Moore takes disparate material and welds it into a remarkable, telling film, albeit one that is, in many respects, open to accusations of being disingenuous and manipulative. Yet, despite the gulf in tone, purpose and message between the two films, the strength of *Fahrenheit 9/11* depends on the black serendipity of images depicting one particular experience of war.

*Fahrenheit 9/11* is a political film. It is not an object of traditional documentary-making, which cherishes the academic virtues of objectivity in gathering evidence and presenting an argument. It is an example of what has been labelled 'docutainment', or 'rhetorical' documentary.[27] Some, however, have said that it is an 'obscene' film, if there can be such a thing, describing Moore as 'the Road Runner of manipulation ... removing all avenues of thought through over-determination ... leaving no room for the viewer's own judgement', and reported the view that it is not a film at all but 'images serving a discourse', an *oeuvre* that 'declares war on cinema as a means to knowledge, memorialisation, reflection, historical lesson'.[28] It is intended as a treatise that will have political impact, ideally. It follows in the wake of Moore's other campaigning films, notably *Bowling for Columbine*. That film took a 1999 incident at a school in Colorado as the trigger for a campaign against firearms and a condemnation of American society, simplistically attributing the significantly greater incidence of murder and violent crime in the US to the right to bear arms.

The errors and false reasoning which marked that film are matched in *Fahrenheit 9/11*. The errors and the perspective in the film attracted, among other ardent critical challenges, a counter film, *Fahrenhype 9/11* (directed by Alan Petersen), made in the same style, but by no means as successful, of course, putting alternative perspectives and correcting errors of detail in the Moore film. The false reasoning in *Fahrenheit 9/11* is evident to anyone applying basic on-off logic empirically to the material on offer. For example, Moore, in best conspiracy theory fashion, reasons with syllogistic logic, somehow, that there is a connection between Bush and bin Ladin, making the latter's actions somehow the responsibility of the former. While Moore's version is not quite so crude as this rendering indicates, he does try to create an impression of something akin to this. As one far from antagonistic commentator has noted, his approach to relations between the Bush family and the Saudi Royal Family and others is 'loose, circumstantial argument that relies heavily on the weak suggestion that association equals influence and collaboration'.[29] He takes as evidence business associations between Bush's father, President George Bush Sr., and members of the Saudi Royal Family, notably Bush Father and Prince Bandar, and their large entourage and business contacts, including 24 members of the large bin Ladin family, noting that various Saudis, possibly including a bin Ladin, were given special permission and protection to fly out of the US even after the September 11 attacks had closed down US airspace. The notion that the Saudis might have been helped to leave for their own protection against a potential backlash enter into the Moore worldview. The Saudis who left clearly benefited from having money and connections to the Bushes in their escape, which, Moore is right, would have been almost impossible otherwise at that stage. But even though there is something in most of his claims, there is also always something doubtful.[30] Moreover, the alleged implication of a bin Ladin family member (whom Moore cannot confirm concretely attended a meeting of the Carlyle investment group immediately prior to the attacks,[31] as his cautious language in comparison to strong and certain language regarding others at the meeting, including Bush Sr., underscore) ignores the fact that UBL and his family had largely disowned each other over the years and the probability that the family members were as despising of his actions as the Bushes. The director is misleading to juxtapose pieces of information about the connections and the exit to an implied desire to protect UBL himself, somehow. And while he cites mid-level security officials offering opinions about normal procedures and seeking to interview the bin Ladins, in normal investigations, and while this is undoubtedly a sound judgement about those normal circumstances, these circumstances were different. Any favourable treatment to the bin Ladin family, given their connections to America's number one enemy, it has to be presumed, came after the CIA had investigated them and found out as much as they could already about this black sheep of the family. A normal police investigative approach would not be necessary.

The key visual moments in the film occur early and late in it. The humorous clips of Bush as a president permanently on vacation stand out in setting the tone, although, not without reason, they have been described as 'cheap'.[32] He is apparently not on top of policy detail (although it may well be with Bush's cultivated 'folksy' approach that this was not always a reflection of the real picture – even if sometimes the image and reality might coincide). This implication is stretched into the key moments during which the attacks take place, while Bush is on a routine trip to Florida to promote his education policy, by making a speech at school, accompanied by photo opportunities. Bush is presented as though not knowing what to do, after having been informed of the first plane's hitting the World Trade Center and suspected terrorist hijackings in addition to this just before starting his visit to the school. But an equally valid reading of this situation might be a form of presidential strength, not showing initial panic, waiting to hear more and not wishing to spoil the schoolchildren's experience of having the President visit them and hear them read – and it might be noted that Bush was hearing them read, not reading to them, and, in his brief time with them, showed what could be seen as calm and strength, still able to engage in questions or discussion with the children in a warm, friendly manner.[33] It is hard to imagine what else Bush might have done at that particular moment. Had he immediately departed, it would have sent negative signals to all those around him, particularly when confirmation was still awaited of what exactly was happening – which confirmation came effectively with an official's whispering in his ear about the subsequent attack, informing him that America was at war, under terrorist attack. Bush, despite his apparent failings, had been patient and respectful before taking his leave in a dignified manner, explaining to the children and the gathered press what had happened.

Moore's scattergun and scrap-book collage approach to filmmaking emphasises the relevance of strong visual material at almost every point, as he meshes his original footage with a large amount of 'found' film, edited together in an effective manner,[34] whether the blend is old TV titles and themes, or military recruitment films, or pre-broadcast rolling film of Bush and other political figures readying themselves to perform on screen. The way in which Moore moulds these pieces of film shot by others is a 'bewildering accumulation' that draws out the vivid imagery with which he puts his case,[35] although he is sometimes prone to what has been dubbed a 'triumph of sledgehammer editing'.[36]

The opening sequence in which Moore relates the events surrounding Bush's election and the electoral outcome in Florida is a fluent, elegant piece of filmmaking. But perhaps his treatment of 9/11 is the greatest stroke of cinematic insight and confirmation of the image imperative. In a *coup de cinema*, Moore chooses to have a black, otherwise blank screen, relying on his audiences' familiarity with the images of the planes striking the towers. The soundtrack has sounds of aircraft and explosion, as well as a range of sounds from emergency sirens and general background hubber-bubber to very clear and specific statements. The black screen dissolves into a scene on the street below and a woman saying 'God! Save their souls!' The sounds are apparently those of 9/11, although they could equally have been the work of sound experts (and of course, this flash of film genius could always have been forced on the director by finding himself unable to secure use of footage – although only a lack of funds for, or access to, the Naudet Brothers' shot of the first plane striking the tower could explain this, given the familiarity and almost saturation use of those images since the event). The decision to use sound to let audiences who could, hardly, not be aware of what was signalled by this sequence of blank screen, in itself is the greatest confirmation of the value of the image. The absence of the actual image, in this case, only served to focus its vital essence.

However, what makes *Fahrenheit 9/11* an undoubted success both as a film and polemic, despite its failings, and beyond the skill, bluster and bravura of its director, is the blind chance that he is able to show the personal transformation of one mother. Lila Lipscomb is seen to make the revolutionary transition from military cheerleader to bereaved mother of a son, Sgt. Michael Pederson, killed at Karbala in Iraq. This is the visual and emotional linchpin of the film.

She is first encountered as an executive assistant in a military recruitment agency, in both her and Moore's hometown of Flint, Michigan. Following a sequence in which the density of US troops in Iraq is shown to be profoundly inadequate and shortfalls in American military recruitment are reported, she is filmed proclaiming the virtues of military life and the benefit of recruitment to a poor, high unemployment area such as Flint; she is from a family with military experience, including her father and two of her children, a daughter and a son, who sees herself as more patriotic than the average American and a 'conservative Democrat'. Moore was seeking to draw out the irony that military recruitment and support is strongest in the poorest areas of the US, such as Flint, who pay the price for what he seeks as a war for the rich and their interests embedded in the Bush Administration in their 'wrong address' campaign in Iraq. Lipscomb originally beats the military drum and asserts support for both what the military does socially and economically, recruiting in poor communities such as hers, and for US engagement in Iraq, where her daughter served in 1991 and her son is serving a dozen or more years later.

However, in a way that could never be planned, Lipscomb is seen experiencing a complete reversal and emotionally battling to make sense, where none is really available to her, of losing her precious son. This is a sensation to which anyone with a heart, let alone a parent, could not avoid an emotional, sympathetic reaction. Moore must be eternally grateful to Lipscomb for involving him in her grief and the response to it, and allowing him to film those phenomena. Without this element the film would lose much of its power. She is seen visiting outside the heavily guarded White House, where she tries to comprehend how decisions about the lives and deaths of boys such as hers and others are made. She is also seen talking to activist anti-war protesters and defending them against accusations by a counter-protest that the events they describe were staged by asking if the death of her own son was staged. This is a stunning moment, confirming her transformation from drum major for the recruitment bandwagon to wounded woman taking up the cause of other mothers and trying to ensure that their still living sons do not end up the same way. It is in the wake of this encounter that Lipscomb breaks down, crying, and, with bitter honesty only possible in a mother, declares harrowingly that she 'needs' her son. The power of Moore's film comes from the human interest and emotion found in Lipscomb's dreadful experience and the remarkable way in which he is able to capture her before the loss, in order to have 'before and after' images with which to concoct his powerful moving image brew, in both senses of the word 'moving'.

## 'Real war movies' and embed specials

If films such as *9/11* provide a contrast in nature and authenticity to the highly constructed and didactic approach of *Fahrenheit 9/11*, they still use their material in ways that structure and evoke the pinnacles of visual drama and personal, emotional experience, then there is yet another approach to authenticity altogether. This is a form of *cinéma vérité*, or realism, that, while never able completely to escape the demands of formal narrative structure, seeks to minimise this and to create a form of 'authentic' war film, modest in its approach and seeking to minimise anything that appears to be an attempt to dramatise war beyond its realities by relying on conventional narrative heightening. This approach is used in *Virgin Soldiers* by Dodge Billingsley, discussed in the final section of this chapter, who shot the film as an embedded journalist during the 2003 US-led Iraq campaign. This film was one of a host of 'special' films, including seasons of them on television and DVD packages, that emerged following the end of major combat operations, mostly a contingency of the arrangements made to embed – that is, formally attach – hundreds of journalists to military units, giving them complete access to whatever they could capture, although, as we discuss below regarding the BBC documentary series *Fighting the War*, Billingsley was not the only one whose mission was purely to make an actuality film after the event, even if the styles involved were markedly different.

Although war reporters had travelled with armed forces in the past, and the concept of 'embedding' was not new, there was a new and particular approach to embedding by the US-led Coalition in the context of Iraq 2003. The perceived importance of television news, in particular, meant that the US-led operations in Iraq would need a major information operation. Extensive embedding was seen to be the answer to this, creating over 600 opportunities for journalists and cameramen to be associated with a particular unit, to travel with it and to make reports 'from the front', wherever they happened to be. The terms of this arrangement appeared attractive at face value: the news and communications media representatives were to be given complete access, allowed to talk to any member of the unit to which they were assigned and military personnel were instructed to talk freely. The only restrictions were not to reveal specifics of location or operations, by any means not an unreasonable request. The negative side of this arrangement concerned those who were not embedded: the US military made it clear that any transmissions from the theatre of operations not from accredited and recognised positions or operators might be treated as hostile. From an operational perspective this could be seen as a reasonable precaution, given that, in the fog of war, there might not be time to verify who or what was emitting a transmission before a decision to act had to be taken as a precaution. However, this also appeared as a form of threat, intended to ensure that no uncontrolled news media reports were possible – or at least, not safely so.

The issue of embedded journalists could not be avoided. Leaving aside the tensions between official – political and military – perspectives on the responsibilities and roles of the press, there were other points of strain. Being embedded was a test of journalistic ethics in some cases. There was a need to observe terms – as there was on the other side, taking into account Iraqi monitoring and restrictions (although, in this conflict, the Iraqis had understood that they would do better by allowing as much reporting as was feasible, since this would better serve their strategic purpose). The issues of journalistic ethics and press freedom were compounded by warnings from the Pentagon that any journalists not accredited, but using satellite communications, should be wary, as any satellite transmissions not recognised (and to be recognised they would have to be officially sanctioned and embedded) would be treated as hostile and open to attack from coalition forces.

This reinforced the sense that, although the embeds would not be subject to censorship and formal control, de facto, this is the situation in which they found themselves, as what they could report was no more than a letter-box impression gained from one part of the theatre.[37] This meant that whatever could be reported was never more than an atomised fragment of what was happening. It might be open and full coverage, but only of one small, tactical-level situation. There was no overall perspective. In effect, this allowed the military a degree of control at the operational and strategic levels because the open reporting either lacked perspective or relied on briefings at the media control centre in Doha, which meant the wider perspective could be more easily established on military terms. The alternative, or complement (depending on perspective), to this was for editors in newsrooms, or producers away from the scene, to piece together a bigger picture from the various facets of the fly vision the embedding arrangements provided. The potential downside of this, however, was that, given the strategic-tactical compression characteristic of contemporary warfare, combined with the importance of images and information, if something went wrong in one particular letter-box frame, there could be a tendency to telescope this into an impression of the whole (rather than understanding it to be something viewed only under a microscope in reality). However, this depended on any particular incident involving an image or outcome that would make an impression and capture the imagination of news producers and their various publics, and, on balance, the arrangements worked in the military's favour, even if there were occasional distortions, as noted below.

The overall effect of the embed arrangements appeared to leave some elements of the broadcast news media with a sense of having been outmanoeuvred by the military, and disappointed at what they were actually able to produce in terms of output. Moreover, this frustration with the letter-box perspective was also a result of the embeds' being dependent on what they actually knew or understood about where they were and what was happening, and, indeed, just how close they were to any particular action. There was frustration that embeds had to be left behind the pace of the advance into Iraq in some cases, as noted in the discussion of *Fighting the War* below, which created personal disappointment. That sense of disappointment, on the personal level, was amplified at the organisational level. The embed arrangements were a major commitment for the companies getting involved with the embed system, in terms of the human and technical resource costs involved. Embedding was an offer that those able to secure slots could not afford to reject, but, at the same time, could hardly afford to sustain.

The scale of investment meant that embeds had to be on air as much as possible. The impression was that no one could afford to risk missing out on the key story – the big breaking news. Breaking news on-screen labels might better have been cast as 'breaking rumour' or 'breaking news – don't believe this, it will be changed later', or 'breaking news – it will be eventually'. The desperation to get breaking news, not to miss out on something and to justify the massive investment and the number of journalists present meant that anything could end up reported as 'breaking news' and making headlines that would then need revision. This was unfortunate for the governments in London and D.C., especially, as the reductio-excitable versions of the news producers meant that news reports were taken as being that which the Coalition claimed. In reality, the Coalition had expressed caution. 'There appears to be something going on in Basra, some kind of disturbance' became an excitable 'Basra uprising begins' in the news coverage. The British troops outside Basra were reported to have identified an uprising inside the town and to be moving in when, in fact, this was quite different from the real position, in which the British were uncertain about the position inside Basra and were cautiously waiting outside the town (as they did for some time, until it was clear that conditions were propitious for entry). Similarly, 'troops are securing Umm Qasr' became 'Umm Qasr is in coalition hands'. Examples such as these then led to the criticism and sometimes jokes focused on the Coalition and the governments, in which the port was said to fall for the fifth time, or the uprising begins for the nth time. The ticker-tape coverage across the bottom of the screen meant even more that rumour was being reported in a way that was taken to be 'truth'. There were many things to be said, but little sense.

Ironically, the best account of British operations in southern Iraq came from a non-embedded current affairs team for the BBC's *Panorama*. Jane Corbin's *Panorama* film 'The Battle for Basra' made a lasting impact on one level, with research showing that it still featured in the consciousness of military personnel involved three years later, as an example of how the presence of cameras might give pause for thought and affect, or not, difficult operational decisions.[38] Corbin's report begins with British troops on security patrol in Basra using night vision. Close to the end it returns to night vision – this is almost an introduction and conclusion. It is the equivalent of a cinematic return to the same scene and conventions at the end of a film, which there had been at the beginning. This is a convention to indicate the film's structure and to suggest to the viewer that the story is being drawn to a conclusion. But Corbin extends this with a coda, having returned there. However, the strength of the film rests on the presentation of one incident: an American air attack coordinated by the British force on the ground.

Corbin's film is very good in capturing the British troops' side, but also in presenting the horror of a family in the house next to the targeted building, a Ba'ath Party centre, where one of the most notorious figures of the Saddamite regime in Iraq, Ali al Majid – 'Chemical Ali' – was reliably reported to be, along with Ba'ath Party command cronies, when the attack came. While the strike took out its target, it also killed ten members across three generations of the neighbouring family. Although many of the Ba'ath Party leadership were killed, Chemical Ali, in all probability, was wounded and made his escape – he certainly was not killed there, as he was to be detained for genocide and put on trial later, alongside his cousin, Saddam Hussein.[39] Corbin, however, seems to take the position that he was probably not even there. Corbin confronts Brigadier Graham Binns about the incident. Binns handles the questioning very well – but cannot really say much. However, in acknowledging that he still gets five reports a day about Ali's whereabouts, he cannot exclude the possibility that the latter escaped somehow, while the family was devastated. Corbin handles both sides of this extremely well. She is sympathetic to the family, but does not challenge Binns in a simplistic, confrontational manner.

Corbin's film is one of many, many special reports that emerged after main combat operations in Iraq were over, but it is unusual in that she and her crew were not embedded. There was a reason for the emergence of so many embed 'specials'. The cost of sending embeds, already noted above, emerged as a particularly acute issue, when major combat operations were accomplished relatively swiftly, and, for the most part, without significant and striking events emerging from the embed system. This led to a rush to create 'specials' of different kinds. This was a move to get something out of the major investment made. The resulting 'specials' were mostly personal stories compiled from reports and experiences, turned into current affairs and documentary form. In addition to this, a small number among those embedded were there specifically to make longer duration actuality films, as were some non-embedded teams. A device that was intended to fuel the rolling news industry, and which, in truth, produced a process of 'breaking rumour' in search of news, gained its greatest value in the non-fiction film form of documentary and current affairs.

In the UK, one of the BBC's senior news correspondents, Ben Brown, set the pace, with his being the first 'special', recounting his experience of the advance of the unit to which he was attached, broadcast on the major domestic channel, BBC1, almost as soon as major combat operations were over. This meant that the hurried film must have been prepared, as such, before those operations were over, and with a view to being the first in the field, revealing the clear sense that, with moderately weak material, in normal televisual terms, it was important to make some sense and use of it, and that meant novelty – making a mark before others did the same thing. The spate of 'specials' that emerged included composite DVDs produced by some of the major American news organisations seeking to make something out of the commitment they had made, where the major combat operations themselves had failed to produce an outcome that clearly justified the outlays made. *CNN Presents – War in Iraq – The Road to Baghdad* (2003) (following the model of *CNN Tribute – America Remembers – The Events of September 11th* (Commemorative Edition) (2002)) and *ABC News Presents War with Iraq – Stories from the Front* (2004) led, inevitably, by Peter Jennings, were composites of the news producers' experiences and examples of their footage and films (revealing the necessary role of experience and image in moving-image presentation of war). These were films about the news producers themselves and their experience, including that of embedded reporters, and, as such, provide interesting material on the values of the news producers themselves and their work processes. However, in many respects, these specials offered little real insight into the campaign and the military operations themselves, or the context in which they occurred.

Filmmakers who focused on current affairs and documentary films, in the end, produced more interesting moving image output than the news-turned-documentary cash-in creations of the disappointed news producers. Two particularly interesting examples of this work were *Fighting the War*, a documentary series filmed for the BBC by Neil Hunt (director) and Simon Ford (executive producer), and *Virgin Soldiers*, a film made by Combat Films and Research, written, produced and directed by Dodge Billingsley, originally for a season called 'Real War Movies' on Channel 4 in the UK, but commercially available. Both presented 'inside' views of the military in the buildup to operations in Iraq, the former filmed with British troops, the latter with US Marines. However, as much as *Fighting the War* is an interesting account of the British military, with different units at work across the different points of the UK operation, its intermittent presentation of embedded media representatives is perhaps of equal interest in terms of content and insight. *Virgin Soldiers*, by contrast, is entirely focused on and devoted to the troops and their experiences of the campaign. However, its unusual authenticity and faithfulness to the troops, including its depiction of the fog and friction that mark war, as well as the waiting and boredom involved, make it a brave and distinct piece of filmmaking, and, in itself, a commentary on the conventional nature of war films, whether fictional or actuality.

*Fighting the War* presented the buildup to the Iraq operations, with troops deploying to the region, and what is described with some distancing as the 'so-called coalition of the willing' coming together, and then the operations themselves, through to their end. The film series benefited from unique access not only in the field, with embeds filming but their footage being 'ring-fenced' for use in this film and not available to news agencies, ensuring that its makers could claim its images as 'never seen before',[40] but also to the UK Permanent Joint Headquarters (abbreviated as 'PJHQ') at Northwood and the Ministry of Defence in London, offering the chance to depict the Iraq operations at all levels of command and control. This clearly offers some insight, and the discomfort of Secretary of State for Defence Geoff Hoon is evident in the images at times. However, it is still the work of the embedded teams with British Marines and others in the field that provides the main material for the film, and which generates interest.

The depiction of civilians at a checkpoint and crossing a bridge as they leave Basra, at the start of Part 3, is great in presenting the chaos and atmosphere that mark this experience of war. However, the strongest aspect over the series as a whole in military terms was its treatment of 'blue-on-blue' incidents. That is, the embedded proximity of the BBC teams meant that moments where forces fired on their own side, which might normally have been played down or covered up to a large degree, were caught in the raw reactions of the troops – or in one case could be identified and the official version of events challenged by the images captured by the filmmakers. Already, early in the series, incidents of friendly fire are treated (more British soldiers were killed by their own side in the 2003 Iraq operations than by their enemies), where a civil servant at the PJHQ at Northwood is heard explaining friendly fire and commenting that 'it doesn't help that this kind of thing' had 'happened three nights in a row, now'. The unit in the field in Iraq, a voiceover commentary notes, had been asked to stop filming because two members of 9 Squadron were not coming back, both killed by American air action. This request is consistent with the policy of checking all information and getting it right and contacting the families in question before allowing anything to be published – although, especially with broadcast media around, even if not filming, rumours circulate, and it is noted that TV News and other press outlets speculated on what had happened, putting pressure on military families, especially those affected by the losses.

However, the major moment in the series is the identification of a friendly-fire incident by the filmmakers themselves, working with their own images and discussion with colleagues of one member of 9 Squadron Royal Marines, Chris Madison, who was killed as a result of a missile fired by another British unit. Madison's colleagues were evidently suspicious about the circumstances of his death, which had been recorded as resulting from enemy action. The film is excellent in the way it presents this case, clearly working with the sympathy of the troops and using their images effectively to challenge the official version of events produced by the UK Ministry of Defence (MoD) and its Special Investigations Branch (SIB). That version was eventually overturned, as the Ministry of Defence's agreeing to cooperate with a coroner's enquiry in the wake of the film attested, which the filmmakers announced at the end of Part 4 of the series, when originally broadcast. The original investigation had concluded that British forces at Checkpoint Anna on the Great Delta could not have fired the MILAN rocket involved because the MILAN has a range of 2 km, but Madison and his colleagues, who survived the hit on their river boat, were said to be 2.8 km away from the checkpoint. However, *Fighting the War* asserts that the SIB failed to take account of all the relevant evidence. The film itself is a vital part of this evidence. The images filmed at the scene include one of the squadron, Kevin Jones, seen as he is pulled from the river, with three mud huts clearly in the background. However, eyewitnesses and those familiar with the local geography could pinpoint the position as being only 1.6 km from Checkpoint Anna, and so within the MILAN's range. The images of Jones and the huts, marking a specific point on the river, confirmed the possibility that a British MILAN could have been responsible. Backed up by strong visuals of 9 Squadron on the river, a map of the Great Delta, laying out the positions clearly, and complementary graphics, these images of Jones' being dragged from the river with the mud huts in the background were decisive in reopening the investigation into the circumstances of Madison's death and getting the verdict out.

Away from the *coup d'image* and the serious achievement which that treatment of Madison's death represents, in some respects, *Fighting the War* offers, perhaps contingently, a leitmotiv on the news embeds themselves. In Part 2, Alex Thomson of Channel 4 News in the UK, sitting with other journalists, can be seen and heard complaining that the embeds are some distance behind the advance as it moves forward into Iraq. He and the BBC's Ben Brown want to get across the border into Iraq, but have to stay with the convoy. Had they been independent, they might have tried to move forward anyway. But under the terms of their arrangement they were not allowed to do so, if the officer commanding did not approve.[41] The sense gained from Thompson's comments is one of considerable disappointment with the arrangement overall. Specifically, there is a complaint that a promised helicopter ride to the port of Umm Qasr has not materialised. That ride eventually materialises on the third day, but following a two-hour round trip, at the end of the day, back at base in Kuwait, the correspondents are even further behind the front line. By Part 3, however, the first aid deliveries are seen arriving at the Umm Qasr port. This is essentially a 'propaganda' event, one designed to be a media opportunity, as Col. Steve Cox suggests. Col. Cox, accompanied by a female aide, describes handling their charges as 'herding cats' and asserting somewhat dismissively, if not necessarily inaccurately, that there is 'not an original idea among 'em'. As an implicit counter to this, Ben Brown arrogantly rejects what is being offered in terms of assistance, saying sneeringly that 'these facilities are not what I am really interested in doing'. This is another passing example of, and insight into, the reporters' evident disappointment at the embed condition. There is little understanding of the military in the attitude of the embeds presented in the film; and there is only a little more understanding in the frame set by the film itself.

*Fighting the War* is a developed film series that seeks to portray the real experience of UK troops as they prepare for and undertake action against Iraq. However, its form, style and spirit are solidly within the conventional approaches to war on film. There is an attempt to shape and structure the film series, in line with the feature fiction form, around individuals and their experiences, while seeking out novelty and drama (if sometimes forced), and in constructing and arranging images creatively, as a means of attracting audiences and involving them. Of course, on one level, these same things apply to Dodge Billingsley's *Virgin Soldiers*. Any moving image format depends on pictures – there is no film without them. And any film, in some sense, intends to find an audience of some kind – it is meant to be of interest, especially if it is made for, or introduced into, the market-place of mass audiences in the theatre or on television. Yet, *Virgin Soldiers* is a very different kind of film, which seeks closely to reflect the real experiences of the young squad of Marines it follows from 29 Palms, their base in Arizona, USA, to the streets of Baghdad. While there are moments of some dramatic effect, or at least potential, these are all accurately depicted as damp squibs.

*Virgin Soldiers* was originally commissioned for and presented as part of a season called 'Real War Movies' for Channel 4 in the UK. Whereas the last film in that season, presented by *Channel 4 News* anchor Jon Snow, offered a collage of images and ideas where 'real war' was about showing the consequences of war, in terms of death and damage, blood and burning, this was, essentially, a conventional film from a liberal-left, more or less 'anti-war' viewpoint (as though anyone normal could be 'pro-war', where they perceive any choice), following from the consolidated image of loss and futility that formed, in the 1960s and after, of the First World War – the experience and interpretation of war coined by the Great War's poets such as Wilfred Owen, Rupert Brooke and Siegfried Sassoon, and reified by artefacts such as *Oh! What a Lovely War* and *Blackadder Goes Forth*.[42] No one can afford to forget that war can mean loss. However, Billingsley's film is radically different and brave in the way it seeks to eschew, or play down, the conventions of the 'war film', as well as any sentimentality, presenting 'war' as mostly dull and undramatic, punctuated by moments of tension, fear and, most of all, confusion and frustration.

Benefiting from unprecedented access, Billingsley, a winner of the Rory Peck Award for earlier work and a nominee again for this film, *Virgin Soldiers* does what a film should, in many respects: it shows. What is shown is 2nd Squad 1st Platoon India Company 3rd Battalion, 7th Marine Regiment, crack US frontline troops in Iraq. Aged 19 to 23, Iraq was the first time any of them had actually been sent into combat. Billingsley had built up good relations with the Marines already, as well as having experience of working with other military units, including the US Army's 101st Airborne and the Australian SAS, the platoon with which he was to work two months before they deployed to Iraq. He filmed their preparations for deployment, the process of deployment itself, their waiting in the desert, and their eventual going into action. Billingsley's experience was almost entirely that of the Marines – including the 'trench' humour that often keeps troops going and the frustration and boredom of waiting around, punctuated only by the physical training and exercises invented for the ordinary ranks by their superiors, just to puncture the tedium at times – qualities reflected and depicted also in Sam Mendes' fact-based fictional film *Jarhead*, discussed in Chapter 2.[43] Ironically, the blurb for the film on its DVD packaging and on the Combat Films and Research website attempts to make the film sound like a more conventional, and indeed unusually exciting account of troops in combat, which includes their 'occasionally humdrum day-to-day life'. The reality of both their experience and the film runs counter to this, however, as discussed in the remainder of this section.

While the focus on a squad, in this case 11 individuals who live and work together, fits the stock framing of combat movies (they are seen discussing motivations and wider political aspects of the operation from their diverse, if limited, views, much as happens with Ridley Scott's US Rangers in *Black Hawk Down*, as noted in Chapter 2), with small portraits established of different characters – although all are taken as they are found, with no significant effort to fill in any personal background. And, in the end, there are 'big' moments where the squad moves forward, albeit ones that never result in serious fire-fights – thus the dramatic high spots of feature fiction films are not found here. The lack of action and the frustration it brings that David O. Russell and Mendes sketch in the fiction films *Three Kings* and *Jarhead*, respectively, are shown here, but without any set-piece detonations. The soldiers' experience is ultimately edited into a finished form. However, as far as might be reasonably possible, it is simply shown, without a voiceover commentary and with only minimal and basic referential information filled in by an on-screen script (for example, indicating a name, or offering coordinates of time and place). Their experience is shown with no neat, tied-up ends.

In a sense, *Virgin Soldiers* is a film in which nothing happens. The squad is seen doing physical exercises in the desert, sitting around discussing each others' views, practising Arabic phrases and using cartoon surrender cards, joking and waiting. Individual to-camera interviews focus on their frailties, fears and concerns. One member of the squad, Velasquez, reflects on what they might have to do, saying that he never thought he would kill someone and questioning by what right he can take a life that is 'God-given' – clearly troubled by a possible act against God in his mind, and, yet, facing the reality that when combat begins, the opponent has assumed the right to take his life; neither side has a choice once it becomes kill or be killed. Yet, Velasquez still wonders if he can pull the trigger when it comes to it. This simple portrait is free from posturing, either by Velasquez himself or the director. It is the quiet tug of the soul that any person of conscience might recognise, irrespective of their god, or views of God. Velasquez's comments are quietly underscored by Hart-mann's recognition a little later that those on the other side are in the same position and are 'the same kind of people as us', who, he remarks, 'do the dirty work' when they are ordered to kill.

The non-events in the film, once the campaign has begun and the waiting in the desert is over, start with a military store at al-Zubyr. Exempli-fying the confusion and 'fog' that characterises combat, this objective turns out to have no one left there, meaning, as one of the Marines puts it, they have done nothing more than 'waste ten rounds on nothing'. And yet, it is clear that the experience even of capturing an undefended non-target has been 'kinda stressful'. It is far from easy, this simple presenta-tion of not knowing where they are going exactly (and even less what they will encounter there). 2nd Squad and their companions have been fortu-nate, as Velasquez notes, in only getting to know the real anxiety of preparing possibly to die, while trying to avoid that outcome. As the film and the Marines progress, the stress of combat, even where the soldiers encounter no significant opposition in the end, is evident. Muniz, famed among his colleagues for his capacity to sleep, complains that he has not 'really slept', only having 'naps', which are 'not really sleeping'. Of course, Muniz is not alone; as the on-screen script information reports later in the films, the members of the squad averaged three hours' sleep per night over 16 days on operations.

Similar situations emerge as the Marines are set subsequent targets: the Salman Pak military complex 15 km east of Baghdad which again turns out to be deserted with no opposition shown, and Fedayeen Headquarters in Baghdad itself, where a little resistance is encountered initially, but, amid the fog and friction of combat, neither the troops nor the camera see the enemy, only their own troops in ragged lines, running and hiding against a background of gunfire and other noise. Of course, if the camera does not see the enemy, then neither does the viewer – in sharp contrast to the feature fiction form, there are no close-ups of the enemy,[44] nor of the Marines themselves even, only side and rear views of these troops advanc-ing. It is not clear what is happening and where exactly, as the Marines advance. The troops go to ground, the air is filled with smoke, there is a complete lack of any pattern or structure; there is no battlefield aesthetic (except, perhaps, the cameraman's framing). By the time the Marines take charge of the empty Headquarters, such little resistance as there had been has been removed because the handful of presumed Fedayeen hiding behind a wall are judged to have fled once they caught sight of the vast M1-A1 Abrams tank which had been called in. Following this intense highlight, the squad, which remains in Iraq for a further four-and-a-half months, is assigned to a security role, looking after one particular cross-roads, at times seeking shelter from sniper fire, with no sense of from where this faceless fire comes.

All of this is faithful to the reality of much of combat, even if the blurb for film is not true to this reality when it claims that these actions 'played a vital role in the liberation of Iraq', and exaggerate the 'action' parts of the films, no doubt with good marketing reason (in a world where Discovery Channel documentaries on armed forces, weapons and war are expected to have 60 detonations an hour).[45] While the footage in *Virgin Soldiers* is, indeed, 'remarkable' if realities of events are that, whatever the tension for the Marines, the 'battles with the Iraqi 32nd Mechanized Infantry Brigade and the destruction of the Fedayeen Headquarters' are barely anything warranting that term. The blurb is accurate in suggesting that '*Virgin Soldiers* reveals the true story' (again, always a good marketing claim it must be presumed) of these Marines. But the claim that they 'fought their way into the heart of Baghdad', just about technically true, given the small amount of resistance at Fedayeen Headquarters, is, in the final analysis, unfair to the film. This is both because it represents an exaggeration of the actual fighting required and shown and because it does not reflect well on the true merit of the film as something approaching an antithesis of the conventional combat, or war, film, whether feature fiction or documentary. It creates this antithesis through an honest and faithful presentation of the Marines and true character of most combat, even for most frontline troops.

The real character of combat, notwithstanding that there could be moments of real intensity and bitter fire-fights that could occur, is summarised by Diaz, who relates the reality of their experience (and that of many others) to film in a wry comment, looking mostly up and away blankly from the camera at this point in his interview:

> Hollywood has like really messed us up. 'Cos if you think 'war', it's like John Rambo running in there, Schwarzenegger killing people, you know how it is in movies.... They should make war movies six hours long with like fifteen minutes of fighting scenes, and the rest just sitting around, throwing rocks [as he throws a stone at the ground]. That's what war is.

This is true to their experience, but it is not the one that Diaz wants; as he later depicts the more Hollywood-style 'pretend stories', perhaps part jokingly, he says he will tell his friends and grandchildren about 'The Great American Iraq War', in which he will have, Rambo-style, grabbed the '50 cal' – the machine-gun atop an armoured vehicle – and 'fired it by the hip' and other *bello*-centric fantasies. However, despite this playful bravado, Muniz gives the more authentic summary of the Marines' experience after the Salman Pak operation which, he also notes, owes a lot to the work of prior air action: 'I'm happy. They [the air force] did my work for me.' That view is echoed by Thompson close to the end of the film, when he says he does not feel like he is being done out of anything; rather, he is 'happy the enemy didn't want to face us'. The best experience of war, in this sense, is to have survived unscarred. This is unsentimental, as is the rest of the film, in truly documenting the Marines and their story such as it is – but, in a conventional sense of narrative, there is no story, just a record. However, there is experience and there are images, all serving to construct a novel, but more authentic interpretation of combat troops doing their job.

As we have seen in this chapter, different types and styles of actuality film, whether current affairs or documentary, in relation to different examples of contemporary conflict, share common features with feature fiction films.[46] They are narratively driven by the need for images, which, blended with incidents of human experience, form the core dynamic of interpretation. In the two documentary series covered regarding the Yugoslav War, the vital importance of both talking heads as images for carrying the 'story' from the mouth of one protagonist to another was evident. So too was the significance of both unusual, novel film images, such as those originating with Yugoslav military intelligence, which is not only crucial to the construction of the film and the account of events given, but also to our identifying the sleights-of-production-hand used by the filmmakers to fuse material and technically falsify in their efforts to present what might be termed the 'essential' truth of events, if not the actual detail, as such. This confirms that, even where a creation is as monumentally authoritative and quasi-primary documental as *Death of Yugoslavia*, it can still be prone to the demands of the general film form. And comparison of *Death* with the subsequent *Fall of Milošević* also confirms that it can be hard to create anything like a sequel, where the strength of the first produced is its original material, while the latter also confirms the tendency of availability of images, even if these are stronger as visual material than the actual contribution they make to the historical or analytical narrative the film purports to cover – as with the inclusion of the sequences with the tractor driver, for example. Of course, the attraction to structuring films around available images is in the nature of the medium.

The salience of images is also clear in the treatment of post-Soviet conflict in Chechnya. This can include the part-entertaining, part-contextualising use of archive footage of Soviet-imperialist propaganda regarding the Chechens in *Il était une fois la Tchétchénie*, or the attempt by the Moscow authorities completely to eradicate the conflict by removing visual presentation of it, other than at great personal risk to those involved in penetrating the closed zone, as also shown in that film. *Il était une fois la Tchétchénie*, in its presentation and discussion of Prokhatskova's experience of capturing and disseminating images of the conflict, and her eventual epiphany and rejection of filming and the filmmaking form to take personal responsibility, also shows not only the power of images, but that there are significant ethical dimensions to the process of capturing them. It reveals the blind importance of getting the image over human realities, in a world where the image is all – or at least, it appears to be all, when immersed in a mission and a medium dependent on the visual. That importance is also validated by *Prisoner of the Caucasus*, which not only uses the metaphor handed down from Tolstoy to set its tone, but also exploits images and reflexive honesty about using post-production enhancement to get the right impact of images, as well as including straightforward images of the dead returned home and the experience of loss among the family to make its gentle case.

It is with the images of children and terrorists inside the school at Beslan, filmed by the perpetrators of the deed for their own political purposes, as tools of war, that the vital importance of images is established. Those images, along with the striking on-camera interviews in the film, offer not only visual stimulation, but also reveal harrowing experience. The blend of image and experience in the film combine to render a devastating account of the school siege which, in itself, at least potentially, might serve the terrorists' purpose, but which also confirms the devastation caused not so much by the detonations as such as by the unbearable consequence of parents having to bury their children. This evades alternative interpretations, where, perhaps, some of the parents involved might bear an element of responsibility for precipitating the violent unravelling as it happened – even if ultimate responsibility would always rest with the terrorist child snatchers. But the terrorists' filming themselves and their victims, even if no throats are seen to be slit, matches the visual snapshots and monuments to the actions of Chechen fighters captured in feature fiction films treating this conflict – as seen in Chapter 2. However, this real-world snuff movie goes beyond earlier Chechen activity from the 1990s and marks the emergence of Islamist influence and, in the vein of Usama bin Ladin and his acolytes, the use of video diaries as an essential component of their strategy; that is, as weapons of war designed to bolster legitimacy among supporters and those who can be swayed, and to undermine legitimacy, morale and spirit among their opponents.

Filmed images recorded 'inside' an event also generate the authenticity of *9/11*, which encapsulates the horror experienced interior to another major terrorist act – this time not inspired by a violent Islamist approach, but by al Qa'ida, the corporate brand leader in the field. The startling images from within the crumbling towers and, especially, the unique footage of the first plane strike serve the purposes of the terrorists, of course – as does *Beslan*: in the end, they gain something of what they want from the visual translation of the event to the rest of the world, it is part of their strategy. However, the awfulness of these events and, in particular, the honesty of the Naudet Brothers' depiction of the ordinary heroics of the New York fire-fighters, undoubtedly also underpins the legitimacy of the response, both immediate and longer term. This is in well-defined contrast to the polemical bad faith of Michael Moore's *Fahrenheit 9/11*. Yet, that film is certainly a success as an inventive and effective piece of filmmaking, and as a challenge to the legitimacy of the US response to the September 11 attacks. Of all the films considered, this is the one that most obviously and decidedly may be said to reflect on legitimacy in contemporary armed conflict – in part, because it consciously intends to do this, but also because it is the one film that clearly engaged a mass audience on the political plane.

The promiscuity of Moore's visual tirade, made after the fact and primarily from film research rather than original camerawork, potentially had a greater impact on issues of legitimacy than the work of embeds, whose arrangements with the military were meant to contribute to legitimacy, at least, by minimising the chance of a sufficiently coherent perspective from which to be responsible for a critical challenge (although, as noted, the compression of strategic, operational and tactical levels of war meant that even one snapshot might have a widely disproportionate negative impact). *Fahrenheit 9/11* also stands apart from the documentary films deliberately resulting from the embed system in terms of style and impact – although some current affairs and documentary work, in a limited sense, also raised issues of legitimacy in a significant way, as seen regarding the *Panorama* film 'The Battle for Basra', or, perhaps, also *Fighting the War,* with its filmic evidence on friendly fire. Moore's film, with its bravura and bombast, is barely comparable with the latter as moving-image creation, since the latter takes a conventional approach and relies almost entirely on original footage. *Fahrenheit 9/11* is also far away from the modest authenticity of *Virgin Soldiers;* the artifice in the former contrasts radically with the more referential approach in the latter, using entirely original footage. The former has no real sympathy for those engaged in Iraq, while the latter clearly works because it is sympathetic to its subjects, who are presented in the most ordinary manner possible. Yet, as noted above, this unconventional style and philosophy of filmmaking, which is dull and undramatic by normal film standards, still relies on the same basic elements as any other film, feature fiction or actuality: images which are essential, and experience, which are combined to present a 'real' interpretation that spiritually counters not only the more conventional filmmaking of *Fighting the War,* but that of the markedly 'unreal' *Fahrenheit 9/11.* In the end, despite the differences between all of these films and the relatively diverse approaches to direct reflection on legitimacy, in every case interpretation is the product of experience and images. Having established how these elements, which drive feature fiction film narrative, also determine actuality films no matter what the format (and despite common assumptions), the next step is to move to an analysis of television news, to explore how the same factors, once again, are decisive, even though the medium is distinguished sharply by temporal issues. This is the subject of the following chapter.

# 5   Television news

There has been notable attention paid to the relationship between television news and war, with a significant literature emerging. The main focus in such work has been the degree to which television news coverage of armed conflicts is accurate, and, whatever the degree of its accuracy, whether or not it forms part of a propaganda or media conspiracy to manipulate information, one way or another, in order to shape opinions, one way or another.[1] However, these approaches have generally shared two serious flaws. The first of these concerns the assumptions often made about both the nature of political power behind broadcast news and its ability to manipulate what is presented and the presumed impact on an audience, which seems to be assumed to be homogeneous and susceptible to a simple impression phenomenon, where whatever is transmitted is absorbed, unfiltered and accepted in full by the viewer. Research indicates that this is not the case,[2] as might well be assumed by anyone reflecting in a rational and sensible way. The second big flaw, it seems to us, is that the overriding importance of moving-image narrative in television news does not appear to have been addressed, perhaps because the visual aspect is too obvious, or perhaps because the focus on politics has obscured it. Whatever the explanation, as the foregoing chapters have made clear, the nature of medium means that human experience and images determine moving-image narratives and the interpretations they offer or invite.

This chapter builds on the attention to interpretation, experience and image developed in previous chapters concerning feature fiction and actuality moving image-objects, focusing on television news. There are important differences between the forms discussed in previous chapters and that of television news – most notably immediacy of production, transmission and reception, as well as the potential size of audiences and scope of impact. However, the basic elements of moving-image narration remain – the vitality of images, the desire for human interest and emotion, and interpretation dependent largely on those two qualities. The issues of immediacy and potential impact, however, give television news additional saliency in the realm of contemporary warfare, where images are key weapons, and television news, by its presence and nature, is the prime vehicle for delivering them. To explore this, we consider a range of examples, in broadly chronological fashion, in the remainder of this chapter, starting with the impact of images in the Yugoslav War. We then consider the relationship between the unprecedented images of September 11 and the potential experience of that event and presentation and interpretation of it, both in live transmission and as newsrooms took stock of what had happened later in the day, looking at both American and British coverage. The treatment of 9/11 includes readings of CNN and CBS live coverage of that day, both related to available DVDs including that coverage. The former considers that broadcaster's essentially local coverage of the event, including the moment in which image overwhelms words, and relates it to CNN's de facto role as a provider for most of the world in situations such as this. The latter explores the difficulties of matching understanding and interpretation to such powerful images as they happen. CBS News features in this case due to the availability of its live coverage on DVD – in some ways making it a target where others' output that day is no longer easily available. But CBS also features strongly later in the chapter, following discussion of how Washington's engagement in Afghanistan was treated, because it is uniquely responsible for aspects of covering the Global War on Terror, or the Battle for Iraq – its Fallen Heroes segment, 'honouring' America's dead servicemen and servicewomen, and the publication of images of abuse by US military personnel at the Abu Ghraib, which, more than any other incident, demonstrates the vital importance of images as weapons and their power when presented via television news, to present a critically damaging challenge to legitimacy, and so the prospect of success, in contemporary warfare.

## Bosnia by television[3]

Vietnam was said to be the first 'television war'. However, although television impact was significantly registered for the first time – this was the first major war affecting an advanced industrial society in the television age – the sense in which it was televisual remained quite limited. Although, by the end of the war, same-day film reports had become possible, for most of the war, film reports could take perhaps a week to find their way back to news headquarters to be broadcast. Moreover, those reports were limited and isolated. By contrast, the Gulf Conflict of 1990 to 1991 had a different claim to being the first television war. This was the presence of CNN and 'real-time' television, broadcasting images instantly via satellite around the world, on the one hand, and the fabric of US satellite, cockpit and weapon-head images of destruction, on the other. However, perhaps the first truly 'television war' was the Yugoslav War of the 1990s. This was the first war in which television was everywhere, a prefiguration of the twenty-first century phenomenon of an image-dense digital age, where almost anyone, anywhere, could capture images with handheld devices and these would then form part of the visual tapestry depicting the war and shaping the battle for retinas, the principal route to winning hearts and minds. It was also the first war in which images, and particularly those presented in a moving-image environment, became central to the conflict itself – at the heart of strategy, rather than contingencies of it.

This was clear from the outset, when armed hostilities began in Slovenia in late June 1991. The documentary series *Death of Yugoslavia* depicts the first day of major armed hostilities in Slovenia, at the beginning of the war, and uses a selection of images and excerpts from the television news of that day, notably the opening sequence of BBC 2's *Newsnight*, supplemented by talking head interviews with participants explaining their perspectives. While the film itself does not reveal or depict strategy per se, it shows the importance of media management as part of Slovenia's integrated strategy. The film makes clear the assumptions of the Yugoslav People's Army (JNA) commanders dealing with Slovenia that there would be no armed conflict. It also describes what appears to have been the first opening of fire in the war (although this point is not made in the film).[4] That incident concerned the shooting down of a JNA helicopter (carrying bread) over the Slovenian capital, Ljubljana, in the early evening of 27 June 1991. The film then shows the way in which this was presented on news broadcasts across Europe: the message was that plucky little Slovenia was defending itself against the communist Serbian JNA. The reality was that the downing of the helicopter at a moment where the event would make the headlines of main evening news broadcasts across Europe was consistent with Slovenian strategy.

This was to provoke armed clashes in favourable situations, then to convey messages of struggle and success through the well-run media management centre established in the Cankarjev Dom, the Slovenian equivalent of the Lincoln Center or Carnegie Hall in New York City, or of the Royal Festival Hall in London. There, the Minister for Information, Jelko Kacin, had no need to do more than report part of the truth to his audience of journalists who would then relay the message, often embellishing it, or presuming that Kacin had said things which he had, in fact, not said. For example, he informed reporters about the location of a burned-out JNA armoured personnel carrier. The reporters hurried to capture images of it, believing it to have been destroyed by Slovenian anti-armour fire. However, the reality was that logs on the road laid by Slovenian defence forces had trapped it, the crew had abandoned it, and then children had burned it. The story presented, however, was one of success, contributing to the overall success of Slovenian strategy.

Television news and images also became an issue at the end of the decade when the focus of conflict was on Kosovo. Images of displaced persons and refugees – the victims of ethnic cleansing – were an important factor in mobilising support for the NATO air action aimed at stopping Serbian tactical-level ethnic cleansing through strategic level application of force. The decision to intervene on humanitarian grounds had been deeply contested. However, once the images of trains transporting the victims of ethnic cleansing towards the border with Macedonia had spun around the Western world, the doubts in many cases were removed (although some observers alleged – wrongly – that the NATO action itself had provoked Belgrade into this action). Strategy and images interacted to bolster the legitimacy of NATO action.

NATO attacks on Radio Television Serbia (RTS) headquarters in Belgrade also constituted a significant aspect of the television news and image nexus with strategy. These attacks outraged Western journalists, with many of those involved in reporting from the region angry that friends and colleagues appeared to have been targeted. The bombing of the TV tower also drew the initial interest of the Office of the Prosecutor at the International Criminal Tribunal for the former Yugoslavia in The Hague. However, a preliminary report into this and other suspected incidents concluded that there was no criminal case to pursue. It was noted that, if the attack had been intended purely to impede Serbian propaganda, legality may have been doubtful. However, the evidence suggested that NATO's aim was clearly because the RTS formed part of Belgrade's military command and communications structure. The RTS building was a legitimate target because of its military communications' role. However, disrupting Belgrade's broadcast news media was also an important aspect of strategy, given the nature of Belgrade's domination and control of its own environment

The situation in Serbia under Slobodan Milošević was such that he was able to dominate the information available to the vast majority of Serbia's inhabitants. This was in marked contrast to the position in which Western political leaders find themselves and illustrates both the utility of action in the case of Kosovo, but also how the difference in Serbia illustrates the issues that confront Western governments. The difficulties confronted by modern liberal democratic political leaders can be placed in context by understanding the situation in Serbia. Two factors were significant. The first was that the Belgrade authorities' continuous polling included samples of 10,000 or 20,000, which meant, in terms of opinion polling, an almost infallible grasp of views, attitudes and beliefs in Serbian society. This meant that the audience, its concerns and the stories that it was ready to absorb and which would reinforce its prejudices and understandings was well known; as a consequence, it was possible to provide the audience with that which would satisfy it. This was facilitated by the second factor involved – control of the TV news reaching that audience. The reality in Serbia was that the state controlled RTS 1 and 2, from which 80 per cent of the Serbian population gained its news. Newspapers were a limited source of information, given that their cost meant that many would not buy – and in any case, these were also largely controlled or dominated by the Milošević regime. In addition, while there was a variety of TV stations available in the Belgrade area, including at least one that was genuinely independent (B-92), these were only available in the Belgrade area, meaning that even those who might want to seek different sources to RTS could not do so. So, for many years, Milošević was able to convey messages, stories and images to the vast majority of the Serbian audience while in a position to know what would, or did, register with that audience. This dominance was in the end broken not only by weariness during and in the wake of the Kosovo engagement in 1999, but by word of mouth and informal organisation.

Despite the vital significance of the television news–strategy link regarding both Slovenia and Kosovo, it was Bosnia which ensured that the combination of television news and war reached a new pitch. This was true in various senses. First, this was the first war where locals had personal video cameras, making them potential reporters. Second, it was the first war in which new satellite technology was widespread. The reality of independent satellite news dishes in theatre (going well beyond the clunking and military-dependent equipment of the 1990 to 1991 Coalition operations against Iraq) providing genuine and pluralistic 'real-time' transmission, combined with the near universal presence of the handheld camcorder, made the Yugoslav War the most comprehensively media-documented ever. It was the true television war.

The war in Bosnia was also the first significant example of contemporary warfare where the competition for 'truth' and for decisive images lay at the heart of legitimacy and, so, success – and some of the parties to the conflict were well aware of the need to compete and win psychologically.[5] While war has always had some element of competition for 'truth', which is often, as Sen. Hiram Johnson has frequently been quoted, 'the first casualty', and the truth recorded for history has often been that of the victors on the battlefield, the shape of contemporary warfare, as noted in Chapter 1, is such that victory – and so the definition of 'truth' – is no longer a matter of decisive victory, but of winning the battle of wills by establishing one's own 'truth' in order to secure victory. In the case of Bosnia, images were deeply contested. Croatian and Serbian broadcasters each used exactly the same images of old women and families, and claimed that the individuals pictured were Croat and Serb victims, respectively. There was strong contestation over responsibility for major incidents, such as attacks on the Markale marketplace in Sarajevo, each time with images of victims and damage to the core of the contestation, with stronger and more forceful international action likely if the Serbian side was believed to have been responsible, but less likely if the Bosnian Army was. In May 1992, there was an attack known as the 'bread queue' massacre, in February 1994, and again at the end of August 1995, with images of death and destruction in the Sarajevo marketplace. In each case, these images preceded stronger international action than had been the case previously. While the Sarajevo marketplace incidents were almost certainly the work of the Bosnian Serb force, as verified by UN military and additional governmental sources outside Bosnia, the May 1992 incident almost certainly was not. The wounds evident in the images of the scene were consistent with an anti-personnel mine rather than a mortar detonation (feet blown off and lower body injuries, rather than chest and head impacts); there was no mortar crater impact; and although a camera was immediately on the scene which was said to be television news coverage from Sarajevo TV, based very close to the site of the incident, this was not a broadcast quality recording; rather a non-professional handheld device was used. Yet, that incident led to significantly greater international involvement, including the decision at the UN Security Council to impose sanctions against Serbia and Montenegro. There was the possibility that in situations such as these, immediate images could create immediate action, but the images could be misleading.

It was images that made the impact on the legitimacy of international inertia regarding Bosnia. In particular, one set of images shifted international policy. While print journalist Ed Vulliamy of the *Guardian* joined Independent Television News journalists in discovering and reporting on the camps run by the Bosnian Serbs, there can be no doubt that it was the television pictures of the camps, particularly the emaciated individuals against barbed wire, that made the real difference when they were transmitted around the world. As Nik Gowing has demonstrated conclusively, this was one of very few clear instances where government policy was changed and shaped by television news images.[6] The reason for that, Gowing correctly judges, is 'policy panic'. Where there is no real governmental policy, only, at best, a desire to pretend that a problem is not there, but images then appear, this generates a knee-jerk, rapid creation of policy. That is what happened when the ITN pictures of the Bosnian Serb concentration camps at Omarska and Trnopolje were broadcast. While there had undoubtedly been some knowledge about the existence of such camps, governments had not had to confront the issue and had apparently chosen to avoid it. The immanence of these images, particularly that of Fikret Alić, the emaciated figure at the camp wire, whose withered body and face appeared on the front page of newspapers around the world the following day, meant it could not be ignored. The resulting policy was to hold a conference in London in August 1992 initially, and what emerged from that conference was a rolling international conference and the decision to deploy armed forces to Bosnia authorised to use 'all necessary means' to assist in humanitarian relief. This was the starting point of a policy of military engagement that, after moments of dithering, confusion, complexity and change, resulted in the decisive use of armed force in 1995, which was the precursor to ending the war in Bosnia.[7] While there were twists and turns to come, and still much pain, as well as further salvoes from the image arsenal, the ITN images from northern Bosnia made a difference, modifying international policy considerably – and with that, contributing significantly also to the cause of the Bosnian government.

The Yugoslav War was, in many respects, the epitome of contemporary conflict. This included the way in which the importance of images as weapons in a quite new way began to emerge, not as a support to strategy but as an object of strategy itself. While governments are unlikely to turn the ship of policy around in face of images where it is already at sea, when the ship has not sailed – or perhaps does not yet even exist – then the right salvo of images, as Bosnia showed, could alter the balance and prompt policy. Bosnia was the first war where competition was conducted by television and alternative means of image delivery. Subsequently this was to be the norm, with the impact of images, the experience of immediate interpretation and the array of images and means for capturing and transmitting them, which had emerged extensively regarding the Yugoslav War, developing intensively in other contexts, notably that of the 'Global War on Terror' and the events of 11 September 2001, which catalysed it.

## September 11 live and reflected – the ABC of coverage

The events summarised by 'September 11' are among the most significant ever in terms of TV news coverage, as well as for international relations generally.[8] The event is significant for TV news coverage because many of the key early moments in the unfolding history were caught live and raw on television, most notably the second aircraft hitting the World Trade Center. Within minutes of the first attack, ABC television in New York, with others quickly following the lead, had cameras trained on the site of the incident. This made for remarkable images that not only defined the story, but also fell neatly into complementing the 'terrorist' strategy of the attackers: maximum visibility and coverage (Table 5.1).

*Table 5.1* September 11, 2001 – live coverage

| Event (actual timing, EST-New York Time) | ABC | BBC24/BBC1 | BBC World |
|---|---|---|---|
| Live on air | 0851 | 0853.30 | 0900* |
| Image of 2nd plane hitting tower | 0902.58 | 0902.58 | 0908.16 |
| Recognition of 2nd plane strike | 0903.02 | 0904.37 | 0908.16 |
| Recognition of terrorist attack | 0903.21 | 0908.12 | 0909.13 |
| Link to 1993 WTC attack and other al-Qa'ida attacks | 0857.53/ 0908.50 | 0907.36 | 0909.13 |
| Naming of UBL | 1010.12 | 0907.39 | 0948.40 |

Note
* Timing from available material, presumed to be start of coverage.

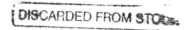

There are two notable features of the live coverage. The first is the (perhaps inevitable) dominance of fairly static images of the World Trade Center, or repeated images of the attack or the collapse of the towers, with considerably less attention given to images of the Pentagon. The stunning and dramatic nature of the New York images is the most likely explanation for this, whereas images of the Pentagon were nearly always from a distance and of the *ex post facto* situation (although, at another time, the Pentagon images would no doubt have been dramatic enough). This confirms how TV news is dominated by key images.

The second issue is the difference in types of professionalism and the speed with which the heart of the story of the unfolding events is identified – and so the experience offered to the viewer. Three channels that offered immediate live coverage were analysed: ABC in the US, BBC News 24 (quickly carried also by BBC1) in the UK, and BBC World broadcasting internationally. ABC's coverage emerges strongly in this context – their studio anchor immediately saw the second plane coming in from the right (although asked for a replay to check), whereas BBC News 24, taking exactly the same feed from ABC, showed the plane striking the south tower, but the anchors did not register what had happened verbally for over a minute and a half – although they did note a 'second explosion' and the presence of a helicopter (in fact, the Boeing 767 – but the connection was not made in any case); BBC World took longer still – not showing the plane hitting the tower until eight minutes after it had happened. In terms of what exactly was happening and identifying the connection with Usama bin Ladin (UBL)[9] (albeit as a probability) there was a broadly similar pattern – although ABC was last (by some margin) to name UBL, having been the first to identify any possibility of a connection with the group (i.e. al-Qa'ida) that had carried out the 1993 attack on the WTC, as well as other attacks on US targets. BBC World only after some time raised the hesitant question of a terrorist attack, given the second plane crash; once the second attack had been registered, News 24's Foreign Affairs Correspondent David Loyn offered a sharp, accurate and full interpretation – including naming UBL, in effect, as prime suspect (Loyn's strength was later complemented by strong analysis from Diplomatic Correspondent Brian Hanrahan). In this particular instance, viewers of News 24 had the opportunity very quickly to have as good and as clear an assessment of what was really happening as could be in the circumstances. In all cases, assessments were offered with great caution – ABC recalled the jumping to false conclusions initially over the Oklahoma bombing.

The images that defined the early coverage also dominated more reflective reporting later in the day at a few hours' remove. However, the relative simplicity of more or less static live images had become considerably more textured, with a variety of other images of the WTC attack and collapse, notably from different angles, including from ground level. In addition, there was considerable additional visual texture provided by ground-level images of the collapse and, importantly, of the human dimension – New Yorkers coping with and escaping the scene. This aspect was noticeably missing from the immediate coverage.

The degree to which UK News bulletins focused on the human tragedy angle, the American political and security implications, varied considerably. *BBC 10 O'Clock News* (hereafter *BBC 10*) was more immediately dramatic, showing footage of the south tower collapsing in the background as one of its reporters was recounting how he had been inside the entrance of the north tower when the first attack had occurred. He then has to flee, along with the cameraman and everyone else in the street, while the camera continues running, picking up the screams of people around them as the tower collapses. It is striking, however, that none of the UK terrestrial broadcasters in their main news coverage appear to have used the images of individuals leaping from the WTC to escape whatever was inside, but to certain death. However, *BBC 10* showed the footage of people waving from the north tower for 14 seconds having seen the south tower collapse, but, as the reporter states, 'it was already too late' for them, as this tower also collapsed seconds later.

Each channel covered the human dimension, albeit in very different ways. In contrast, the implications for the US security community were not covered at all by Channel 4 or Channel 5.[10] However, ITV's anchor Trevor McDonald stated ten minutes into the programme that the event was an 'operational disaster' for the FBI and CIA, and discussed with ITN's diplomatic editor the likely political and security forces fall-out from the day's events. *BBC 10* also picked up on this topic, echoing McDonald's assumption that this represented some kind of failure for the FBI and the CIA – declaring it 'remarkable' that the attacks had not been foiled by US intelligence. This strong feeling of expectation and failure was not significantly mitigated by any sense that the intelligence agencies were not omniscient or omnipotent and would have had to be very lucky to have foiled such attacks in the circumstances.

Despite the fact that UBL had clearly emerged as the prime suspect, there was considerable attention paid to the situation in the Middle East, particularly Palestine, and to the repercussions of the events there. In general, there appear to have been considerable attempts to give a context in which there is implicitly assumed to be a connection between the attacks and the Israel–Palestine situation in particular, yet there is distance noted between the attacks and material which suggests that the attacks are in some way 'understandable', given resentments towards the US in many parts of the world.

One key item concerned reaction among Palestinians. All channels showed images of Palestinians celebrating, although the images were not exactly the same. All three ITN channels showed a short sequence of images of Palestinian boys dancing around and smiling in front of a café, holding the Palestinian flag. These images were shown on ITV's *News at Ten*, contributing to a running news special on ITV, using these images in its summary of reaction around the world around two-thirds of the way through the normal bulletin's length, although the commentary sought almost immediately to establish distance over them: 'In Arab East Jerusalem, some Palestinians reacted to the news with street celebrations, though Palestinian leader Yasir Arafat later ordered them to be curtailed, and expressed his shock and sorrow at the attacks.'[11] The BBC also reported that its images were of the Arab Quarter in Jerusalem, but also included scenes of men firing rifles into the air as part of perhaps more extensive shots of celebration – making it almost impossible that these images emanated from Jerusalem and far more likely that they came from the West Bank. While there is some possibility that this was a mistake, it could also give the appearance of seeking in part to mask the extent to which many Palestinians may have been jubilant. The BBC's Orla Guerin stressed that Arafat had been genuinely shocked, that there had been some celebrations (which were 'horrific') but sought to play them down, suggesting that most people had stayed at home in fear and in awe watching TV, and emphasising the need to put the matter 'in context'.

BBC World, despite using many of the same packages as *BBC 10* and covering similar ground, presented a distinct approach nonetheless. One difference was in the use of visual material. The broadcast began, for example, with a dramatic shot of the second plane streaking into the south tower of the WTC, which was embedded in a package on *BBC 10*, and served as the lead in to the anchor's voiceover introduction. This was amateur footage shot from the other side of the Hudson in New Jersey, in which a voice is heard saying, 'there's another one' immediately before the speck of the second plane hurtles into the tower and a vast ball of fire ballooning, as the cameraman zooms in.

Sky News was perhaps even more unusual regarding footage in two respects. The first is that it showed footage from Fox News, the US and US-international network also owned by Sky's proprietor Rupert Murdoch. Although BBC packages included a very brief image shot from a helicopter by the Fox New York affiliate, Fox News was extensively used by Sky – its primary source for material, including a live transfer to Fox News at one stage, as well as using other Fox material and carrying a Fox interview with Shimon Peres. Thus, although the character of Sky News is generally quite distinct from that of its US relative, on this particular day, Sky in some senses became a Fox vessel, carrying its images and messages.

The other distinct footage on Sky News came from Libyan State Television. This showed people celebrating the attacks in the streets of Tripoli, as well as the footage of celebrations said to be in the Gaza strip featuring the little boys and white van (although the same images were reported by the UK terrestrial stations as being in the Arab Quarter of Jerusalem). There was, however, no sense in covering this, or in assessing the source of responsibility for the attacks, of concern for how those in the region, or their kin elsewhere, might react to the presentation of jubilant Arabs, or to the suggestion that UBL's terrorists might be responsible. While there is presentation of a denial of UBL's responsibility offered by a Taliban spokesman, as well as caution that the finger had been wrongly pointed too quickly over the Oklahoma bombing, this did not strongly temper the presentation of UBL's training camps.

BBC World pointed out that suspicion fell on Islamic extremist groups, but John Simpson stressed the importance of drawing a distinction between UBL, the leading suspect, himself (explaining that his organisation would indeed be capable of carrying out such an attack, with discussion of training camps), and the Taliban government. Tom Carver's report names UBL too, and includes an expert saying on film (Paul Beaver of *Jane's Defence Weekly*) that 'American pilots would not do this', pointing out that 'Arab fundamentalists', on the other hand, might. This reference to 'Arab' extremists is quite unusual and goes against much of the grain of UK terrestrial reporting. The BBC World News anchor reports that 'according to Islamic Jihad the attacks were a consequence of US policy in the Middle East'. The general concern for Arab (as opposed to other Muslim) communities is further developed in BBC World coverage, which includes tape of a 'Middle East expert' expressing the hope that the whole of the Arab world 'will not be stigmatised' – reflecting the apparent fears of Arabs that collectively they could be held responsible by the US and subject to punitive measures.

BBC World again demonstrated even greater attention to the Arab angle – especially in light of its global mission, no doubt. A special assessment of 'Arab reaction' was given by Frank Gardner, reporting from Cairo. His report makes clear the degree to which the attacks had brought some satisfaction among many Arabs. His assessment was quite blunt:

> It may come as shock, but on the streets, certainly in the Palestinian refugee camps all across the Middle East there has been jubilation – chanting, cheering, celebratory gunfire, people have been handing out sweets; they're ecstatically happy. They are saying, now, at last, America is having a taste of the same sort of suffering that we, the Palestinians, have had.

The report moves on immediately to stress how this reaction is at odds with the official one of Yasir Arafat and the Palestinian Authority, as well as to suggest that the jubilation is not shared by Arabs across the Middle East generally (who are regarded as having sympathy for the human losses, even if there is still a sense of quieter satisfaction at America's getting its come-uppance while they sit at home glued to their TVs).

This is in marked contrast to the more circumspect and even apologetic interpretation offered by *BBC 10* to its domestic audience – there is no mitigating 'context' explained. Gardner also reports the clear feeling abroad among certain Arabs in the region (he carefully distinguishes between those of different backgrounds) as reflected in the morning papers in Egypt, which at the time of the broadcast have just emerged with headlines holding Israel responsible for the attacks. The raw character of some Arab reaction is captured in this way by BBC World and is not tempered by any suggestion of needing to 'understand' the feelings among Palestinians or other Arabs – in marked contrast to *BBC 10* (and, indeed, other UK terrestrial channels). While BBC World clearly demonstrated some concern for Arab and Middle Eastern sensibilities (it also broadcast a tape interview with Shimon Peres), it was prepared to report them seemingly as they were to be found – possibly as a means of seeking to earn the respect of its audience in the region.

BBC World also had a package in which not only images of people in distress at the windows of the north tower were shown, as on *BBC 10*, but also comment was made on the fact that there were people leaping to 'certain death' to escape the horror high up in the tower. Thus while some UK terrestrial channels did not even cover the people at the windows waving for help, only BBC World made any comment on those leaping to their deaths. This strong approach was echoed in the use of images from street level, which showed scenes of disaster, including the shocked and distracted walking wounded, and an interview with a man who had blood pouring from his head. The scenes were rightly described as 'eerie'.

### The real 'CNN effect': the epicentre of the storm – local news for the world

Since the 1990 to 1991 Gulf Conflict, CNN International has been recognised as the international brand leader for immediate news coverage of major, unfolding stories.[12] This reputation has been established in part because of the network's permanent news mandate – it is always available; however, it has had some company in this context, most notably Sky TV in Europe and latterly BBC World. CNN's reputation has also been established because of its immanence to stories and its immediacy – it was CNN that left a reporter in Baghdad during the 1991 Coalition air campaign against Iraq, and it is usually CNN that is first (or seen to be first) with major breaking news stories; however, while this has been true some of the time, at others, the extensive BBC network of reporters, the enterprise of Sky or the daring of others has, in fact, been ahead of CNN. Yet the brand's reputation has endured and, despite research findings generally to the contrary, the much-vaunted 'CNN effect' – that is, media influence on Western, especially US, policy – persists as a fallacy of common wisdom. That fallacy is that international news coverage of crises around the world shapes policy – as seen above already regarding Bosnia, that case proved how exceptional influence of that kind could be. In reality, the 'CNN effect' is not really about making policy, nor is it even the more accurate judgement that international coverage places pressure on policy makers, even if it does not, in the end, influence policy – although this could be deemed a 'CNN effect'. The real 'CNN effect' is to shape reporting and understanding around the world of major international issues simply by being the source of most coverage in those counties, as CNN International's broadcasts tend to be the source upon which domestic broadcasters around the world tend to rely (even if this might be despite themselves in some cases).

Real-time and near-time coverage of the September 11 attacks on New York and Virginia may well be an example of this: even though CNN was probably not the original source for much of the material it broadcast, it was the vehicle by which that material was largely transmitted to the world. The curious thing, it emerges from analysis of the network's coverage that day, is the manner in which this major international brand leader, right at the heart of the biggest international news story of the year, in effect operated more like a local TV news station in much of its coverage. Thus, both the events at the centre of international crisis and conflict and the reporting of them were treated in a manner that was in many respects, though certainly not entirely, oblivious to shockwave impact in the global context. At the same time, as noted below in the case of one example drawn from Croatia which reflects the situation across many parts of the world, CNN, in the case of September 11,[13] was the dominant source of coverage, streamed and then repeated in an unadulterated form. Thus, CNN's parochial coverage at the heart of the crisis was at the same time a global phenomenon.

One way in which CNN's coverage of September 11 was fairly consistent with its conventional approach to emerging international crises was in the overall format of its reporting. This constituted a series of rolling reports, coordinated by studio anchors, with an open time frame, no breaks, and no beginnings and ends. The closest to any sense of normal scheduling was an 'update' from the Atlanta Headquarters just after the 'top of the hour', when the anchor there explained that this summary update of the events (of which it is hard to believe that anyone not watching, even, was unaware) for those who might have tuned in at something like a normal start time. Otherwise, the one significant difference was the use of three anchors in three locations, operating in relay to keep the news rolling. Thus, the headquarters' anchor, Carol Yin, formed a team with Judy Woodruff in Washington DC and Aaron Brown in New York City. This was also a reflection of combined CNN International and CNN Headline operation at work.

The three presenters conveyed three distinct images. Yin, wearing an open-collar black shirt in Atlanta, was standing, mostly in front of a graphic and otherwise a studio wall, sometimes inclining to give emphasis to the material. Woodruff in DC was more formal, seated behind a desk, with banks of TV monitors and the newsroom behind her – and wearing standard newsreader formal wear, including a smart jacket. This suggests that she was the duty front person as coverage began. The most distinctive of the three was Brown, whose anchoring (if the verbal metaphor stands) came from the roof of an 8th Avenue Manhattan skyscraper, looking downtown to the vast, billowing column of smoke rising from the site of the destroyed World Trade Center. While this was an anchor role, it also conveyed much of the immediacy of the events and the proximity of coverage that might normally be expected to emerge with a correspondent at the location of a major event. However, Brown's role was clearly to lead reporting rather than to do it.

The most salient moments of the live coverage available on CNN's commemoration DVD of the account belong to Brown. It is he who has the stock, almost local news-style interview with a survivor of the Twin Towers, alongside Brown, on camera, on a rooftop in Midtown Manhattan, with the dust cloud of the collapsed building at the end of the island some way behind them. But it is perhaps the moment when the second tower crumbles that most demonstrates the power of image in the medium. Great swathes of CNN's commemoration of its coverage do not relate the actual coverage on the day itself: there are the reporters' accounts of their experiences and events, and there is a rich tapestry of images of the day, many courtesy of sources such as the Fire Department of New York or the Federal Emergency Management Agency, as well as at least one quite shocking clip of the second plane hitting the tower, not widely shown elsewhere. This suggests a certain lack of confidence in the coverage on the day itself, as well as a desire to be reflective. (This stands in contrast to the CBS example, discussed in the following section.) However, in the moment of the second tower's collapse, Brown recognises that the image says it all. 'Oh! Lord!', he softly exclaims (and, according to the evidence of the recording, in contrast to his recollection of saying 'Oh! My God!'), continuing that sometimes there are simply no words, and urging his audience simply to watch.

The three leads roughly equally shared time, announcing packages and interviews, although the dominant image was clearly that of Brown against the bright blue sky, Manhattan and the tower of smoke. The reports and interviews, although generally apparently free form, were also generally four to seven minutes long – the longest of these at seven minutes was the direct transmission of a sequence of rolling amateur footage (see below), while interviews and reports generally took four or five minutes, suggesting either clear management or an inbuilt, ingrained sense of how long parts of the broadcast should be.

For the most part, reinforcing its leading edge on reporting breaking news, CNN had a complex visual approach. Aside from the anchor presentation, much of the time there were five elements on screen. This arrangement was dominated by two frames around talking heads against a background of mid-blue silver-grey. One of these was the presenter, while the other was the person to whom the presenter was talking (a correspondent, or an expert, or occasionally one of the other anchors), or a rolling image (for example, of the Twin Tower collapse). The presenter was to the left in a frame that was lower and considerably smaller than the one embracing his or her interlocutor. This created a stable dynamic on screen and, in terms of the developing content, treated the anchor as precisely that – the point holding everything together – while giving temporary emphasis to the passing interviewee.

The third visual element was the constant banner just over a third of the way up the screen, declaring 'Breaking News' to the left and 'Live' in a red-background, white-bordered box at the right-hand side of the screen. The remaining two elements each involved script. One of these was placed immediately below the 'Breaking News: America Under Attack' banner, giving headline summary points, or explanations and references to support and underline the images above. For example, these flashes, which would stay on screen for some time, might indicate the name of the expert being interviewed. Alternatively, there might be a key point of developing news to underline verbal reporting by the anchor to camera or over-rolling images. For example, the presenter's announcing a statement issued by a political actor would immediately appear in its essence in the script – for example, 'Islamic Jihad: "We are against the killing of innocent people"' (although often there were visual balances or ironies against the script comments) – thus the Islamic Jihad message appeared while the main image was of the ex-Israeli Prime Minister and serving member of the contemporary government Shimon Peres being interviewed.

The final element was the newsbar – a form of script ticker-tape – running across the foot of the screen. This ran for much of the time. There were two modes to the ticker-tape. One began 'Timeline', and gave the times at which incidents occurred and a short statement on each. After each 'Timeline' run, there would then be a period in which elements also identified under the breaking news heading described above would also appear, sometimes with slightly greater detail (permitted by the constant rolling of the tickertape), as well as many other items that were flashes, updates, announcements and so on. Some of these would also be reported verbally by anchors, but not necessarily so, and there was no necessary connection between the script ticker-tape and the anchor presentation.

Perhaps the most striking thing about the CNN coverage, however, with Headline and International fused, was that the essentially 'local' reporting of September 11 was the mainspring of most international reporting. This is because the scales and economies of media operations in the globalised world mean that most broadcasters, in most countries, do not have the resources to run international bureaux or send reporters all over the world. In this situation, while other news organisations, such as BBC World, with the special status and resources of the BBC, also feature alongside CNN, it is the latter which is the dominant source of coverage for the poorer broadcasters of the world. Evidence from other countries, particularly those in Eastern Europe, shows some heavy reliance on CNN.[14] In Hungary and Romania, for instance, news programmes featured their news anchors relaying information from the CNN screen visible in the background.

This effect has been demonstrated in a study on Croatia, which provides a good example of the reliance on CNN, in particular, and BBC World (as well as other international satellite broadcasters to a lesser extent) and their penetration of the television news in the world. Croatia's principal broadcaster, HRT (*Hrvatska Radijo Telvizija* – Croatia Radio Television), was mostly a medium for summarising and relaying agency and CNN material to the Croatian public, without an agenda of its own, and with very little analysis or commentary offered.[15]

The format of the news broadcast on HRT is common across the former Yugoslavia and similar to news broadcasts in many other continental European countries. Bulletins invariably begin with an introductory statement by the presenter, followed by a collated report on the subject. Collation is an important aspect. Most foreign news items comprise collated agency material, foreign TV media broadcasts and other press material. A direct link to reporters on site is very rare, other than a link with a correspondent by phone, which in turn is rarely live. HRT, therefore, depends heavily on material from international broadcasters. This is inevitably due to economic factors – a limited news-gathering budget and logistical difficulties. Hence the majority of items are collated reports relying on a number of sources. Other types of report include reporters on the scene in Croatia (with rare exceptions, there are reporters further afield), studio-based talking heads, interviews with Croatian experts, politicians and US citizens in Croatia, as well as referential accounts read to camera (or even on occasion, eyes to sheets of paper in the hand) by the newsroom presenter, without additional analysis.

On September 11, at the time of the regular evening news programme *Dnevnik*, coverage of the attacks on America totalled just over 30 minutes, which is the normal length of the bulletin. The majority of items lasted between one and three minutes, with in-studio talking heads providing a notable exception as item 16. The use of experts is, nonetheless, rare. Filmed talking head interviews are not interviews as such, however, as only an edited statement by the supposed interviewee appears. All of this is quite consistent with the overall use of visual material in HRT reports, which is restricted to images adopted from other sources, including archive footage. Almost all collated reports rely on images from other stations. This was the essence of reporting on September 11. Moreover, HRT's use of the material it picks up from other sources is not very sophisticated, with the same image sometimes left to run over and over again, or images are used which relate to the overall story, but not to the particular item. For example, item 7 on September 11, 2001 was a collation of reports about reactions from European capitals, but the visual material used was of New York City and the collapsing twin towers. In all of this, material from CNN was crucial. HRT ran coverage live from CNN, accompanied by simultaneous translation. As early as item 4 on September 11, there was an interview with a survivor from the World Trade Center, conducted by CNN and simply run straight by HRT.[16]

Aside from the studio anchor, four categories of speakers appeared on the HRT coverage: in-studio experts who answer questions and offer analysis, out-of-studio interviews, statements by officials, both Croatian and foreign, and the assimilation of interviews originating with CNN or other broadcasters. In-studio experts are scarcely used by HRT, and when they are they tend to be local academics. On September 11, two such experts appeared. One was a retired University Professor and head of the Centre for Defence Studies in Zagreb, and the other was a current Professor of Political Science at the University of Zagreb. Neither made reference to al-Qa'ida or Usama bin Ladin on that first day, even though his name had been mentioned in a news item preceding their analysis, although the Israel–Palestine analysis was given one minute out of almost seven minutes devoted to the two experts. In typical fashion, there was very little interaction either between the presenter and the guests, or between the guests themselves. The presenter would ask one or two questions and the experts would then expound uninterrupted.

HRT relied mainly on material from CNN for most of its eyewitness reaction reporting. The tone of these reports was left as it was in the original, very little being lost in the dull voice of the simultaneous translator (the original sound could still be heard in the background). As no comments were added to any of those items, the tone and message remained the same as that of the original report. Limitations in reporting forced HRT to adopt a distanced approach, relying heavily on footage from other stations, agency material and the comments and reports from its correspondents on the ground, transmitted by phone. The reliance on CNN made HRT a badly edited version of the US network's programming. At the same time, that bad cover version revealed the salience of the CNN model, parochial though it was in merging CNN Headline News with CNN International, and broadcasting in the style of US local TV news. Notwithstanding the unusually hyper-parochial idiom of CNN's September 11 coverage, what emerged was that the real 'CNN effect' is not the shaping of policy – or even creating pressure on policy makers – but its role, along with a small number of other major 24-hour news producers, in providing the coverage that large parts of the world will adopt wholesale, at critical moments, and to a considerable extent at other times.

## CBS news: *What We Saw*

The exceptional images of 9/11, from the static camera shots looking down Manhattan to the wealth of images from different angles that emerged showing the towers being struck and then collapsing, created a jaw-dropping fascination. Initially, a web-based archive was created to give access to comparative coverage of that day's events. The collection in the Television News Archive included the rolling live coverage from broadcasters around the world, starting with ABC in New York, at 0830, and BBC World, at 0900. The archive spanned to Russia and China from later points in the day where, inevitably, perhaps, the degree of attention was not so great. However, after around a year, this open-access web-streaming archive ceased to be available at a click, although the home page remained with its indicative selection. However, links led to a web provider's home page, not to the promised streams. Although these were moving images for posterity, the raw live coverage of them would not remain openly available in this way. Thus what was initially a great research and educational asset ceased to be.

After this resource had disappeared, the principal remaining possibilities were BBC *Online*, the internet arm of that unique broadcaster, and the CBS News website. The former had vast amounts of material available in small packages, meaning that various clips or incidents might be found. However, these were mostly not collected into systematic, or continuous run, packages on the website. CBS had more or less complete and open availability for some years, but eventually that resource also ceased to be available. Nonetheless, CBS maintained its policy of free web access, a great deal of material remained accessible, and web pages indicating the existence of the 9/11 archive were still available.[17] CNN's memorial disc predominantly included recollections of their experiences by journalists spiced with richer material that emerged from other sources at later stages and only brief replays of clips from the day. Despite the significance of the attacks as a live news event – simply as a disaster, let alone as an act of war, 9/11 was unique in that so much of what occurred was watched as it happened – the record of coverage was no longer widely or easily available as the object of interest and inquiry that it was destined to remain. This meant that the only record of that live coverage openly available was the DVD which CBS News had made and packaged with a book commemorating the events themselves and the coverage of them, both titled *What We Saw*.[18]

*What We Saw* extends beyond the live coverage of the day, but the bulk of it concerns that day, with edited passages of coverage introduced by Dan Rather, the long-time anchor of the *CBS Evening News* (discussed below and in Chapter 5). The day's coverage of what CBS labelled the 'Attack on America' on the disk concludes that day's reporting (although snippets from the days and weeks after 9/11 appears as with Byron Pitt's

honest and moving summary, including his and colleague Mika Brzezen-
ski's experience as reporters in Downtown Manhattan, hiding in a school,
the sky turning). The coverage starts at 08.52 with *The Early Show*. Host
Bryant Gumbel welcomes viewers back from a commercial break with the
news that a plane is thought to have crashed into the World Trade Center.
A static-camera live image is shown of the Twin Towers with fires burning
and smoke emerging from windows on two sides high up one of the
towers.

The live coverage segment of this early stage includes three sections of
the coverage, all involving eyewitnesses on the telephone. The first of
these is the immediate attempt to establish anything at all about what had
happened. Unfortunately for Gumbel, the man on the phone is not that
well placed, being located at Thompson Street which is in lower Manhattan, but still some way from the towers themselves, and he does not have a
particularly good vantage point, although he did see 'a small plane' that
appeared to have 'bounced off the building' before a huge ball of fire
appeared at the top of the building. However, he seems to be something
of an unreliable witness, as it is not entirely clear what he saw – certainly,
his judgement of the size and type of the plane is questionable and he says
that it had happened 'ten minutes ago' at only 08.52, in addition to being
so relatively far away. His limited experience adds little to the quest to
know more about what has happened. The second clip, which despite a
smooth edit that shows no clear join has skipped forward a little in time,
has the same image on screen and the witness is far better placed initially
– the doorman at the Marriott Hotel at the World Trade Center, right on
the spot. Although the doorman had rushed inside for cover, as he tells
the host, he could confirm some of what had happened. He had been an
eyewitness at the site, albeit briefly. But the clip makes evident that the
knowledge and experience that could be gained at this stage of what was
happening is not exploited due to an apparent concern to avoid the weakness of the previous eyewitness's location. Much of the call is taken up
with the interviewer's establishing where his witness is and was located,
and concerned less with what he had seen outside, than his present position, taking refuge inside.

With the third witness, the CBS *Early Show* is well placed to get solid eyewitness commentary from a woman, Theresa Renaud, in Chelsea at 8th
and 16th, with a clear view. Her apartment window, she reports, looks
down the island, straight on to the Twin Towers. She reports a 'major
explosion from about the 80th floor', and gives a very clear and precise
account, including a fairly accurate indication that several floors have
been affected by the blow and the flames. More strikingly, she is on air to
Gumbel as the second plane hits the south tower. She exclaims that this
has happened, describes the impact and declares – instantly and accurately – that the impact was deliberate. However, the host appears sceptical, checking with her and asking her why she says it was deliberate –

missing the seemingly obvious point that a second plane has flown straight into the second tower. The anchor then says that they will rerun the tape and augments the tone of sceptical wonder by saying that there is no sign of a plane on the rerun, slow-motion image. The plane, however, is evident to the viewer. After viewers must have registered the explosion caused by the impact already, Gumbel notes the explosion itself.

The immediate live CBS coverage indicates three principal things about television news coverage, particularly over live and breaking news. The first is how the image dominates everything. Because there was such remarkable visual material, the camera is trained on the smoking tower. That image remains on screen almost uninterrupted. However, the priority of the image is such that there is little or no concrete information surrounding it. In the attempt to build up more of a picture of what has happened, the broadcaster uses eyewitnesses on the telephone to give their accounts of what has happened. However, much of this second element focuses on personal experience rather than description of events – and where there is an accurate description of events, this does not emerge clearly. In part, this is due to the attention to personal experience. However, it is also due in part to the presenter's struggling to get both experience and drama, on one hand, and good detail about the situation, on the other. That constitutes the third notable aspect evident in this situation: just how difficult it is quickly to piece things together live on air. Trying to establish what is credible, trying to keep abreast of developments and trying to get the most out of exchanges with eyewitnesses and other reporters, as well as keeping a sharp eye on the pictures themselves and what is in them, is far from easy. It requires particular talent and experience.

Both CBS and Gumbel were brave and proud (or perhaps foolhardy) in leaving their live coverage so firmly on the record and open to scrutiny. The viewer's experience of the CBS coverage meant that a basic sense of what had occurred was on offer, but might have been stronger. Gumbel establishes where he is at 59th and 5th at CBS News headquarters in the attempt to make sure that his eyewitnesses are in a position to offer something useful, but this meant a distraction with location rather than concentration on information. His labelling the World Trade Center towers as east and west, rather than north and south, indicates a relative lack of background and depth, even if there is clearly some knowledge about the towers. In addition, if it were not inappropriate in a moment of great loss, his perfectly human failure to see the second plane looming across the screen might provoke laughter.[19] The comparative experience of a BBC reporter's thinking the second plane was an emergency service helicopter shows that Gumbel was not alone in this predicament. It may well be that the quality of ABC's Hawkeye Charles Gibson, who identified the second plane immediately on his monitor, on the other hand, confirms that in the competitive world of live news coverage, there is no substitute most of the time for real quality and experience. In fairness to Gumbel, of course, his background lay in sports reporting. With no disrespect, he was probably not the man for the moment, but he was the one whom fate favoured with the CBS seat as events unfolded initially.

*What We Saw* includes Gumbel's summarising events just before 10.00, including a reference to reported hijackings out of Boston, and handing over to Dan Rather to lead the CBS News *Special Report*, which would be the coverage for the rest of the day. Rather immediately establishes his authority – and to some extent pomposity – as he appears on screen (which Gumbel has not through the coverage included in *What We Saw*) and pronounces that it is important to understand, first, that 'there is much that is not known about what is happening' and to 'separate the rumour from the facts'. That care sometimes balanced between clarity and appearing not to pay attention to whatever his interlocutors had to say. At one point, Rather is talking by telephone with a veteran correspondent at the World Trade Center's subway station, who thinks that only part of the building is coming down – clearly in the situation, right underneath it, he could not immediately see the whole perspective – and reports this. Rather asks the reporter to confirm that part of the building has collapsed – even though it is evident from the images on screen that this is true and more, and even though his interlocutor has already said so. Rather has this last point sharply reinforced by the reporter, frustrated that he has told Rather this already, and who snaps back, 'that's why we were running'.

However, his presence is meant to lend authority. That authority also comes, at a later stage, from other veteran reporters. Jim Stewart reports from DC that the FBI is working on the assumption that this is an act of terrorism and that it is likely the work of UBL. This is a clear, responsible delivery of information as it is understood, with the correspondent's face the image of serious and authoritative reporting. Another reporter, Carol Martin, appears in the studio with Rather, at 11.48, covered in dust, with a split-screen image showing the fulminating dust clouds from the World Trade Center and connecting her to the disaster; she has survived being in close proximity while trying to find CBS crews in the area and just escaping the second collapse when 'a ball of flame, storeys high' was coming towards her and others, and a fire fighter shouted 'run', and then picked her up as she ran and fell, before throwing her against the wall of a building and covering her, just ahead of the collapse and the burgeoning tide of debris; 'we were both so sure we were going to die', she says. Authority also comes from Washington reporter Bob Schieffer (who was to replace Rather as anchor of the *CBS Evening News* subsequently – see below and Chapter 5). He reports to camera, in white shirtsleeves and tie, from Washington, DC. With almost grandfatherly, genteel authority, he acts as propaganda transmission belt for a joint statement from leaders in Congress (who have been evacuated as a security measure), declaring unity and strength in a message of defiance, clearly intended to rally and boost an audience of the shocked American people. Their familiar on-screen faces might be seen as images of competence and reassurance. However, there is nothing to suppose that these voices of authority and lengthy experience would necessarily have been closer to Gibson than Gumbel in their visual acuity and news acumen, although, of course they may have been, notwithstanding that Rather later fell from grace. It is the character and ability to incorporate the images and to get things right under duress that marks the quality of television news, especially when reporting major incidents of security live. The potential to get things wrong, or, effectively, to do one party or another's propaganda work (unawares) by conveying images and other forms of information without being fully aware, while legitimacy, and so, success, depends on images and information channelled through the broadcast news media, is such that winning and losing wars, at some stage, may depend on whether a Gibson or a Gumbel is at the helm at the crucial moment.

## After September 11 – Afghanistan and the 'war on terror'

In the wake of September 11, the US mobilised troops quickly for action against al-Qa'ida and the Taliban regime that hosted it in Afghanistan, and rallied some international support for the subsequent engagement. Whereas television news had been entirely in reactive mode, inevitably, as the aircraft hit the Twin Towers and the Pentagon, by the time US-led operations in South Asia began on 7 October, television news organisations were ready. Although unable to predict precisely when the campaign would begin, the studios and their reporters and crews were ready.

There were two big stories on that day – the launch of the US-led attacks in Afghanistan and the prompt issuing of a pre-recorded tape message by UBL. Each of these presented considerable difficulties for TV News. The first did so because there was relatively little visual material. In contrast, the second caused problems because Western broadcasters did not know quite how to handle either the UBL film itself, or to treat its source, al Jazeera.

Although there was an expectation that attacks were imminent, reporting of the onset of attacks was limited. Proximity and the visual aspect were important factors in this. There were no reporters actually inside Afghanistan as the military operations began, so to-camera reporting could only come from neighbouring Pakistan, where most of the journalists were based. This meant a lack of immediacy, both in terms of content and image. Package reports on the BBC channels and Sky used archive film of UK cruise missiles being test fired and (BBC only) of B-2 Spirit stealth bombers, as well as studio presentations with computer graphics to explain what was known about the operations. Unlike dominant memories of previous major US–Allied operations since the end of the Cold War, there were no images from cameras at the tip of munitions being sent in as they zoomed in on the target, or from the nose cones of ground-attack aircraft. This was understandable, given that the reports made clear to those who had an understanding of such matters (but certainly not for those without a relevant background) that appropriate weapons systems for providing such images were not being used in the very first states of Operation Enduring Freedom. Because the initial nature of the assault could not produce images and because there was no news reporting presence in Afghanistan equivalent to that which had been in Baghdad in 1991, Sarajevo in 1995 or Kosovo in 1999, there was a paucity of images to be used. The only source of images inside Afghanistan was al Jazeera – and while these were used, the use was not as extensive by the BBC, Sky or CNN as might have been expected, or as might have been the case with images from another source on another occasion. This reflected a notable caution regarding al Jazeera – discussed separately below.

CNN offered a different kind of coverage to other stations analysed for this date, in that its coverage was rolling rather than regular programming. Headline News and International were primarily operating jointly, as they had on September 11. However, whereas September 11 had been completely unified and a joint effort, on 7 October, International was simply taking the Headline News coverage, except for interrupting periodically to offer updates several minutes long of a similar and repetitive nature, reviewing what various international figures had said (rather in the vein of old-style communist broadcasts in the Soviet Union and Eastern Europe), relying mainly on tapes of statements from international figures, or live links with reporters at other locations, such as the White House or Islamabad. The live links were of different types: two-ways with the anchor; to-camera updates; reporter interviews (for example, with the former Pakistani Ambassador to Washington, DC); and a telescoped hybrid of two-way, to-camera and interview. The last of these involved a sequence with a two-way between the studio and Christiane Amanpour in Islamabad, a period entirely with Amanpour to-camera who then began a visually odd interview with Nic Brumsfeld, the CNN correspondent in Afghanistan until a few weeks before, who faced Amanpour for the questions, but then delivered the answer to-camera (with the camera closing in to frame him in a standard to-camera style), but turned to her again at the end of his statement. This well-choreographed to-camera-within-an-interview is a stylistic hallmark of CNN's coverage, which, although visually awkward, gives added authority to the interviewee.

While there was little actually to say about the military operations that had been launched and even less to show, it is notable that all channels gave appropriate attention to two aspects of the operations that met the political needs of the US Administration, in particular, and Western capitals, in general – the involvement of UK forces in the initial attacks (as well as general international support and commitments) and the humanitarian strand to operations. The involvement of the UK was stressed in British sources, but was perhaps more important in the CNN coverage. Aside from undisclosed special forces operations, the only direct UK involvement in the first weeks of the operation came in the very first wave of attacks. A UK role at this stage was important for the UK to show its status and for the US Administration to show – above all to its own public – that Washington was not acting alone, but had the legitimacy of international support. This is important because research in the US had shown that public opinion is supportive of US military action where others are involved, but deeply sceptical if America acts alone. Thus, the presentation of UK involvement was especially important in the US, lending added legitimacy to the action. CNN was clear always to describe US–UK operations, even though the British involvement at that stage was very limited (and would very soon be dormant). Both Headline News and International (where it separated) gave additional emphasis not only to UK involvement, but also to the degree of support for the action from around the world. International's interruptions of the main current of Headline News consisted entirely of rounding up the statements of support from world leaders in a clear hierarchy – despite no footage from Germany – beginning with France's President Chirac, then Canada's Prime Minister Chrétien, Germany's Chancellor Schroeder and so on. The only contrary voice in this current was the Taliban Ambassador to Pakistan, denouncing the attacks as 'terrorism'. The ticker-tape script running across the bottom of the Headline News screen carried almost continual telegraphic messages reinforcing the sense of broad international support, whether bullet points of the same comments in the round-up package, references to US–UK action, or President Bush's having stated that over 40 countries had given assistance, such as use of airspace, to facilitate the operations – all signals of international support lest the doubting American public become concerned.

The humanitarian part of the military mission was also important to the governments involved in terms of the intended message. Although there were certainly other dimensions to this operation, the inclusion of the humanitarian role served the interest of the Western governments, who had deliberately included a humanitarian strand to reinforce the sense that the governments were acting beneficially for Afghanistan as far as possible in launching the operations. Since the Gulf Conflict of 1991, addressing humanitarian issues alongside more conventional military engagement, while genuine in intention and meeting real need, has also been recognised by Western governments as a vital 'legitimating' element. In this context, the BBC channels, Sky and CNN all made reference to the 37,500 ration packs that would be dropped on the first day, as well as bombs. They also generally noted that the attacks were not on cities and people as far as possible, but on air bases and terrorist training camps outside builtup areas. Where CNN's Christiane Amanpour at one point did not express this message accurately – saying attacks were on cities – Retired General Wesley Clark (described as CNN's military analyst) was quick to offer correction before getting into his own two-way with the anchor. Thereafter, all concerned – notably Amanpour in her next intervention – noted that the attacks were on specific targets outside cities, not general and on the cities.

The second big story of the day involved the UBL tape delivered to al Jazeera. The handling of this tape is notable for two reasons. One was the decision of Western news channels not to broadcast the tape extensively; the other was what it revealed about attitudes among news channels in the US and UK, as well as some other Western countries, to al Jazeera itself – in part, reflecting the positions of relevant governments. Because Western governments were concerned that UBL's video message might be a secret coding system sending out a message to al Qa'ida affiliates around the world, they asked news channels not to show the film extensively and not in its entirety. It is highly unlikely that any Western broadcaster would have transmitted the whole message in any case, given the pattern of using sound bites in packages. Certainly none put the tape out in full, thereby complying de facto with government wishes. Sky showed one minute of the tape, but its coverage did not extend beyond this. Ironically, against the grain of most Western broadcasting, indeed, CNN cut into the brief extract of the UBL video it was transmitting as part of its summary to play a tape of Bush's statement on TV for its complete six minutes, before moving on to show a relatively extended clip of Blair 'announcing' that the operations had begun.

Al Jazeera's role in this was of particular interest, as it was the station to which the UBL tape had been delivered. Although all stations used some al Jazeera images of tracers and explosions from Kabul, these images were transmitted quite sparingly on the whole – in contrast to other occasions where, say, BBC or CNN cameras have been in place and the images of flashes in the sky are presented for long periods. CNN was an exception when it chose to interrupt its own material to take a live feed with simultaneous voiceover translation direct from al Jazeera, which was conducting a two-way interview between its anchor and Taliban representatives in Kabul (who were claiming to have shot down a US plane). Otherwise, the relatively limited use of al Jazeera source material was accompanied by presentations of the UBL tape that did not give too great emphasis, or credit, to al Jazeera's role in the matter. For example, *BBC 10* carried a report from Stephen Sackur in Washington, DC that featured al Jazeera footage, but did not give credit in the image and was acknowledged by Sackur only as 'from an Arab station'. Later, further coverage of the tape is clearly labelled as being from ABC with its logo in the bottom right-hand corner – but includes ABC's 'Courtesy of al Jazeera' credit. At another point, the anchor notes the role of 'an Arab TV station' in receiving and initially broadcasting UBL's tape in a two-way with John Simpson. The latter responds that he had been 'at that station – al Jazeera, in Kabul' only 'a couple of weeks' before and points out that 'it has very close links with Usama bin Ladin and they've been careful to foster those links'. He continues to offer an interpretation of al Jazeera's role on UBL's behalf: 'It looks to me very much as though he had supplied them with a pre-recorded message that they were to play directly that they heard the news of the bombing.' Simpson's reference was the only clear 'name-check' for al Jazeera in the BBC coverage, even though its mediation of UBL's message was clearly considered to be an important part of the story.

On 13 November 2001 *BBC 10* featured Rageh Omar expressing his concern that 'it wasn't meant to be like this'. The US and its Allies had spent weeks trying in vain to get the rival anti-Taliban factions to agree on a common future and now the Northern Alliance were already taking revenge on the Taliban. This report was shown on BBC World News too, and both also included a section with graphics entitled 'Filling the Vacuum'. Sky also devoted a substantial part of the broadcast to the future of Afghanistan, with graphics and a correspondent's report from Washington that included the Bush-Putin summit, Jack Straw's making a statement at the UN Security Council and Donald Rumsfeld's giving a briefing at the Pentagon. However, ironically, the future of Afghanistan was a topic that would become less and less 'newsworthy' over the months and years ahead, until it would be rediscovered, at different points, as 'the Forgotten War'.

However, the region was not completely forgotten, with one issue, in particular, ensuring that it would reappear from time to time: the fate of UBL, who remained somewhere in the Pakistan–Afghanistan border areas. From time to time this would be the focus of special reporting. For example, the *NBC Nightly News* with Tom Brokaw on 28 February 2004, fronted by Brian Williams, Brokaw's successor-in-waiting, returned to the issue, following the capture of a senior al Qa'ida figure. The broadcast had a background to Williams with half the screen taken up by an image of UBL, his finger pointing upward, and then a mobile and dissolving set of images, generating a flow. Williams began by announcing, 'News today of a high-level capture. Here's NBC's Jim Maceda from Islamabad.' The latter's report begins with film of a convoy on a road and turns this into evidence:

> Proof that the hunt for Usama bin Ladin and the top al-Qa'ida leadership is intensifying. These pictures emerged today of a house-to-house sweep by Pakistani forces earlier this week in one the lawless tribal areas called South Waziristan, close to the Afghan border.

The report is dominated by images of troops, riding on open-back trucks, with the soldiers wearing turbans as headgear and outfits that, overall, make them look like Khyber rifles of some sort from the nineteenth century getting on to them. There are also images of helicopters in the mountains and valleys of the region and, at one point, a picture of a house. 'Waziristan' is highlighted on a map of the Afghanistan–Pakistan border, with Waziristan named and shown with slight definition and shading. The package cuts from this to images of two men in tribal wear walking carefully down a hillside, apparently in the mist. Maceda's commentary continues by stating that 'US and Pakistani intelligence sources believe that both bin Ladin and right-hand man Ayman al Zawahiri have been hiding here'. This might be a reminder to the audience that UBL and his sidekick give purpose to the operation in Afghanistan and to cooperation with Pakistan in the region. However, the news of the day is not that US forces have found UBL or Zawahiri, but that the Pakistani 'operation netted over two dozen suspected al-Qa'ida fugitives and sympathisers, including NBC News has learned one of bin Ladin's bodyguards in Sudan and Afghanistan is now under interrogation'. While the latter was an important catch on one level, and while the news should generally be seen as positive, the reality was that these captures only reinforced the continuing liberty and so legitimacy of bin Ladin. Against images of 'tribal' figures, and housing in the mountainous region, the talking head of Gen. Barry McCaffrey (Ret.), described as the NBC Military Analyst, says that this means they are 'getting close to pinning the guy down on one side of the border or the other'. However, as time would tell, this was more wishful thinking and talking up the possibility.

Following this, there is a cut to a landscape scene, with mountains in the distance and rocky formations in the close foreground, and some green and flat terrain in between, with military vehicles in the close-middle-ground, stationary, doors open, with soldiers running between vehicles. These images are intended to back up the reporting that the Pakistan Army says that 'its carrot-and-stick approach is paying off: demolishing the houses of tribesmen who harbour al-Qa'ida or Taliban, while building water wells, roads and schools for tribes that co-operate in handing over al-Qa'ida members.' This somewhat primitive approach to the 'hearts and minds' question of contemporary warfare focuses on what is effectively the Mafia's approach – bribery on the basis that if it is not taken, then security might be in question. Images of damaged houses – holes in walls, then rubble in the course of 'demolishing' and water jetting out of a pipe on 'water wells' – provide visual reinforcement of the 'carrot-and-stick' notion.

But buildup of 50,000 troops into the former no-go tribal areas has raised tensions, the package makes clear (backed by further images of nineteenth-century-looking soldiers on the backs of trucks). However, library images of gunmen and gunfire and Maceda's commentary make clear that there had been fighting and that locals were agitated, with some tribesmen saying that they blame the Pakistani military and calling for revenge, declaring that 'The Pakistani soldiers better watch out!', in Maceda's version of events.

However, South Asia was not the only place where the search for al-Qa'ida figures was underway, as an image of an Arabic newspaper, scanned from right to left, and then panning back to the end on a photograph on the page visually supported Maceda's reporting that 'elsewhere today there was also success'. He continued by saying that the Arab newspaper confirmed 'with a photo that Zawahiri's brother Mohammed has been under secret arrest for two years and will be publicly tried', pointing out to anyone who had not paid attention to the earlier part of the report that he was a 'key' al-Qa'ida supporter. While Maceda relates this, a picture of UBL and Zawahiri sitting somewhere in the mountains gives way to an image of the photograph in the newspaper again, this time with jogged rotation from right to left, before closing up. With a cut to a half-body shot of Maceda in Islamabad, the reporter concludes by noting the obvious in all of this – none of it directly concerns the capture of UBL himself, about whom, 'despite the flurry of rumours concerning bin Ladin's whereabouts, US and Pakistani officials admit that they don't know where he is', even if he finishes by relating their talking up the prospect of his detention, by adding that 'intelligence is getting better every day and they are closing in'. The interplay of images and reporting, in the end, does little to support this last assertion. Instead, it conveys the sense of a far less developed world, where the locals helping bin Ladin will always have an advantage, even over their apparently nineteenth-century armed forces.

In the campaign in Afghanistan, aside from any military successes in the early days, the UK media was terribly proud of its journalists' entry into Kabul alongside (and ahead of) the troops, and each channel highlighted the fact. *BBC 10* featured a long report by John Simpson, who entered Kabul ahead of the Northern Alliance. It showed the corpses of the former Northern Alliance supporters who had defected to the Taliban and had been killed by the Northern Alliance, and Simpson reported that the people are friendly but 'chanting, I'm afraid, kill the Taliban'. There is a report by Rageh Omar in Kabul showing the fleeing Taliban, including the moment where he comes across a fighter who had threatened to shoot the crew two days earlier, but was now leaving in fear.

A particular angle on the intrepid nature of journalists concerned the US bombing of the al Jazeera offices in Kabul (an item barely mentioned, if at all, by other UK news broadcasts), close to the BBC's, but it did not include news of a BBC journalist who had been making a video-telephone report when the attack occurred. *BBC 10*, on the other hand, shows BBC reporter William Reeve sitting in his office, then being thrown over as an explosion occurs. The report states that an American missile had completely destroyed 'a building barely 50 metres' away, but does not name al Jazeera. Two levels of reluctance are notable here. One is the clear reluctance of ITN to include the fact that a BBC journalist had been as good as at the scene and visibly thrown by the blast. The other is the general reluctance among British broadcasters to give more than absolutely necessary acknowledgement and recognition of al Jazeera – even to the point of avoiding giving it a name-check (as noted above regarding the 7 October coverage). Other UK news broadcasts gave no, or virtually no, attention to this incident, curiously. This suggested that the importance attached to this story by the BBC, essentially, was the impact on their own correspondent and the image of his being blown over by the blast – other broadcasters, without the immediate focus on experience, or access to the image, found no real interest in the story.

### The WMD phantom and the Law Lord's shadow: 'non-image' images and absent images – Kelly and Kay

Although the issues surrounding the decision by the US and the UK (with others) to launch major military operations against Iraq in March 2003 were more complex and the formal basis for that action was a claim to be acting under UN Security Council legal authority, Iraq's possession of, and attitude to, so-called Weapons of Mass Destruction (or Impact – WMD/I) appeared to dominate public understanding of the motivation for action. However, once the Coalition forces were in Iraq, it began to become clear that Iraq no longer appeared to have even the chemical weapons it had been known to possess when UN Inspectors had last been allowed access in 1998. Saddam Hussein had apparently discarded those weapons while at the same time continuing to give the impression not only of possessing them, but of developing new ones. Once it was clear that this particular emperor had had no clothes, not even old ones, perceptions of the legitimacy of the action against Iraq, already imbued with significant amounts of scepticism, became critically damaging. In the absence of the weapons themselves, all those who believed that the weapons had been the justification for action concluded that the military campaign had been launched with a false prospectus.

In this context, two figures were iconic in the delegitimising discussion. One was the UK government weapons specialist Dr David Kelly; the other was the American in charge of the Iraq Survey Group – which was charged with finding or accounting for Saddam's stockpiles, and a former weapons inspector in Iraq, David Kay. At crucial moments, each of them was significant both in terms of interpreting the Iraq expedition overall and in terms of the media–government security nexus.

David Kelly was a well-respected civil servant who had served as an expert weapons inspector in Iraq, having worked for different UK government departments and was employed by the Ministry of Defence at the time he came to public prominence, shortly before he committed suicide, after having been revealed to have lied to his employers over contacts with the media. The core of the case involved assertions originally made on BBC Radio 4, attributed to 'senior' government sources (an exaggeration of Kelly's position), that the UK government dossiers on Iraq's WMD/I capability had been, in the notorious phrase, 'sexed up'. This was widely taken up as a story in the UK, with both broadcast and print news media chasing the scent of an opportunity to damage a government with which they had come to have a fractious relationship. However, the story was challenged by a government that saw an opportunity in the errors in the original report to land decisive blows against the BBC in their continuing fight. In that process, although Kelly denied being the source for the report to his employers, it turned out that he was, as he came fully into the glare of public scrutiny, both in terms of his being obliged to appear before parliamentary committees, where he also denied being the principal source for the report, although he admitted having had contact with the journalist involved, Andrew Gilligan. Of course, the problem was Gilligan's treatment of the more reserved explanation Kelly had actually given him about what should actually be understood by what was written in some parts of what would become known as Prime Minister Tony Blair's 'dodgy dossier'. Gilligan had gone beyond what Kelly had said. In doing so, he had unleashed a battle between the BBC and the British government, with Kelly caught in the middle and deciding to commit suicide.

In the wake of Kelly's suicide, the bitterness between the BBC and the government and the furore over the infamous, but non-existent, weapons themselves, an enquiry was launched into the circumstances surrounding Kelly's death, led by Lord Hutton, a senior figure with experience of dealing with sensitive, security-related cases concerning Northern Ireland. After holding the enquiry primarily in public, there was great anticipation over the announcement of the findings, with most critics expecting – largely because that is what they wanted, it seemed – the government to be savaged. As it was, while there was criticism of the government, particularly the lack of duty of care found concerning Kelly's employers at the MoD, Hutton, with his experience of government-related security matters, understood how things had been on the government side, but had no similar understanding of journalists and the BBC, who bore the brunt of criticism. Indeed, Sir Christopher Bland, Chairman of the BBC Board of Governors from 1991 to 1996, told *Newsnight* on 28 January 2004, the day the Hutton Report was published, that Hutton used a different measure to gauge the conduct of ministers and officials than he did to judge the BBC and its journalists. He did not seem to take account of the pressure under which Alistair Campbell, the former No. 10 Communications Director, had placed the Corporation, in Sir Christopher's view.

The Hutton Report's outcome presented the BBC as a whole with a challenge, given the criticism levelled at it, of which pressures were greatest in the flagship *BBC 10* reporting of the Hutton enquiry. Greg Dyke, the BBC Director General, was shown accepting that mistakes were made, that Gilligan's report had been mistaken, and apologising. While most of this apology was presented, as would any other statement, directly to-camera, there was an additional shot through the viewfinder lens of a camera focusing closely on Dyke, showing his face as though in the viewfinder for a rifle. This emphasised the close scrutiny on Dyke and the BBC as a whole, the image reinforcing the forensic attention to them, as well as their vulnerability. The BBC was offering visual and so reporting distance on its own boss.

However, in reporting the virtual exoneration of John Scarlett, Chairman of the Joint Intelligence Committee, and Alistair Campbell, the two were shown in a split-screen presentation (from archive film) as though side-by-side. This visual image reinforced the association between them that was, in reality, limited at best. The implication, visually, appeared to be that they were close, had colluded, but had somehow been exonerated.

The BBC's procedures, as well as the accuracy of Gilligan's reporting, were found to be deficient by Lord Hutton. However, perhaps the BBC's biggest deficiency was judgement in its handling of the particular issue – an issue outside the scope of the Hutton Report, but worth making analytically. Had Greg Dyke, or anyone else involved in managing what became a major farrago, had any sense, they would have realised that when Alistair Campbell categorically rejected Gilligan's assertions regarding the embellishment of the dossier, he would not have done so if his position were not 100 per cent certain and solid. Politicians, officials and their professional communicators rarely give categorical statements. Anyone with experience of reading official documents, listening to political statements or hearing the answers to questions knows how to play close attention to the phrasing and use of particular words. These sources and their authors rarely say anything so completely black and white as 'yes' or 'no'. If ever the Pentagon, or the White House, or No. 10 – or any politician or official – says that something is categorically not the case, then it is almost certain that this is the truth. If, by some chance, it is not, then either it is said to be so honestly because the information on which it is based was itself flawed, or, perhaps more likely, because there was something of which the individual involved was ignorant. When a master of phrasing such as Campbell says clearly and directly that something is or is not so unequivocally, then it is pretty certain to be solidly veracious.

It seems likely, therefore, that Campbell, hated by the press and broadcasting journalists generally, constantly subject to attacks, and frustrated with what he perceived to be the BBC's unfair coverage of the government, had spotted his opportunity for revenge and to improve his public reputation. Angry and riled, he saw the chance to get his own back because Gilligan had made claims that were simply false – this was the one hundred per cent solid ground on which he could seek his revenge, probably not believing that the BBC would go to the barricades to defend assertions by a reporter with a questionable record that Campbell – and no doubt his Prime Minister – knew to be what the Hutton Report would term 'unfounded'. Campbell's approach and the BBC's response transformed an important and deeply serious, but potentially little remembered, allegation from the invisibility of radio, into the images of television news. Those images ran from the stride of Alistair Campbell to the country walks of Dr David Kelly, often replayed as though they were the film of him making his last walk to his place of suicide.

However, Campbell somewhat lost the advantage he and the government had briefly gained by heading to the television news studios effectively to gloat and, in a sense, to oblige the BBC to acknowledge that he had told them so. This certainly appeared to be the case when the famously ferocious Jeremy Paxman confronted Alistair Campbell on BBC2's *Newsnight* on 28 January 2004, the day the report was published. Paxman pointed out the 'vehemence' of Campbell's entries in his diary regarding the advantages of getting Kelly's identity into the public sphere – it would famously, as Paxman quoted, 'fuck Gilligan and the BBC'. However, Campbell's assured, calm and confident presentation, firmly grounded in his more or less absolute exoneration by Hutton, led to a unique image for those used to Paxman's own confident, persistent and domineering questioning of his victims: Paxman's face showed worry, his voice and demeanour became defensive and the grand inquisitor was tamed. However, the effect of this calm, forceful, arrogant display was almost to engender sympathy for Paxman along with his various BBC colleagues, and to suggest a fair degree of hubris in Campbell's (perhaps understandable) desire to parade his vindication.

The importance of image could be seen even in the apparent lack of interesting image in Lord Hutton's presentation of his report. He had carefully managed his plans to present the report so as to prevent spin and misrepresentation of it. The static image of the recently retired Law Lord reading the summary of his verdict was crucial, in this context, for seizing the agenda and ensuring that he, in effect, could control the presentational agenda for his report. Although not particularly striking in itself and dull in comparison with most images that occupy nearly one-and-a-half hours of live television – not only on the 24-hour news channels, but also on the main terrestrial channel, BBC1 – this focused image on the Law Lord provided the beast of broadcast news with what it could not ignore, even at its dullest: live news-making images. It was clearly due to the importance of having the television component as part of a delivery and dissemination package that it was vital to have any image at all. The almost non-image of Lord Hutton, dry and wholly undramatic, was nonetheless living testimony to the importance, if not the utter necessity, of having a visual image to manage the message.

The focus of the Hutton Report meant that it did not consider comprehensively or formally the thing which most people seemed to think it should have done – the issues of intelligence and non-existent WMD/I, rather than answering the questions posed to Lord Hutton about the circumstances of Dr Kelly's death. On 10 February 2004, *BBC 10*'s headline report concerned the government's decision to announce an inquiry into the quality of the intelligence on which assessments of Iraq's capabilities had been made. This announcement was made in the wake of the Hutton Report and in the context of a senior US weapons expert's declaration that everyone involved must have been wrong about the scale and scope of the WMD/I question in Iraq. David Kay had resigned the previous week, presenter Huw Edwards told viewers, adding that Kay had said that there were 'no weapons of mass destruction stockpiles'. *BBC 10* carried package reports of Kay's going to the White House for an audience with President Bush. The report says that he resigned, claiming that intelligence was wrong and that no stockpiles would be found.

The coverage of Kay's resignation and his pronouncements had already led the BBC's Washington correspondent, Matt Frei, to conclude that the 'policy of pre-emption is fundamentally undermined' (*BBC 10*, 2 February 2004). Of course, this is not what Kay said. Kay actually said that if the large stockpiles he and others in various governments, European ones included, had believed existed had actually done so, then he and the Iraq Survey Group he led would have found evidence of it by now. He specifically did not exclude the possibility of finding some chemical weapons, confirmed that Saddam had again begun a rudimentary nuclear weapons programme, that he was at an advanced stage of developing Ricin, that interviews had confirmed that some WMD programme material had been transferred to Syria, and that evidence had exceeded expectations in terms of strategic missile development; but he also said that the intelligence that had indicated large-scale chemical and biological capabilities was wrong and concluded that Saddam had still been 'an imminent threat' even if his weapons stockpiles were not as great as was believed by the governmental authorities.

Kay's resignation and announcement (albeit probably also made because it was clear that he was not going to receive the resources, especially time, to complete the WMD/I survey in Iraq) featured prominently in news broadcasts on either side of the Atlantic, but with different emphases. Fox News (at 10 p.m. on 4 February 2004) reported what Kay had said regarding the advanced stage of Ricin development and international terrorists going in and out of Iraq, but, adding a typical hard-line conservative tone to its report, he commented that the 'President mentioned none of that today', as though President Bush was implicated in accepting, wrongly, that there had been no evidence to support the case against Saddam. The package included images of the banks of cameramen and reporters in the White House for the meeting, as well as a clip of Poland's President Aleksander Kwasnievski meeting with Bush at the White House and saying that a top UN inspector had told him that Saddam had weapons or was ready to produce them – as though

Kwasnievski's reported evidence should be sufficient to counter the lack of actual evidence. The report alleged that opponents in Congress did not accept Kay's assertion that intelligence analysts genuinely believed that the evidence indicated WMD/I in Iraq – 'Congressional critics who embraced Kay's other remarks refused to accept that part' – and that there had not been political pressure on him from the White House to skew evidence, while unmarked library footage revealed images of men in white suits with large syringes (apparently looking for biochemical materials). The package continues with images and sound bites from Congressmen Carl Levin (D-MI) and Tom Daschle (D-SD) with the label 'SENATE SELECT INTELL CMTE'. Levin is quoted as saying: 'It is incredible. It cannot be allowed to stand that way without someone looking at the exaggerations of the policy makers'; and Daschle: 'It's not appropriate for us to wash our hands and simply let it go away'. Reporter Jim Angle finishes the report to-camera in the snow outside the White House by reporting Bush's saying that everyone should wait for the inspectors to publish their findings (notwithstanding what the chief inspector had just told him and the world). It also made a point about how this was a political football with significance for the election.

While others carried packages about the White House visit, the *NBC Nightly News* had an interview with Kay himself, conducted by Tom Brokaw and marked 'Exclusive – *Nightly News*'.[20] This begins with Brokaw to-camera, in the studio against a partly moving background image of Kay that emerges top-right above and behind. Then images of Brokaw with Kay in a warehouse in Baghdad 'last summer' and the date 'July 16, 2003' appear on screen (which is when Kay had told Brokaw that all these boxes of documents would show evidence of WMD). Brokaw then proceeds to the interview with Kay in a 'non-studio' location, with library footage of documents and buildings in Iraq as additional visual context and texture, replaced by the CIA seal and an on-screen quote from the report about Iraq's nuclear weapons programme. Archive footage, first in black and white, then in colour, of Saddam and a military parade in Baghdad, rein-force discussion about the 'threat' that Saddam constituted. The visual fabric is maintained with images of protesting crowds and the threat of civil war, scenes of British troops in Iraq in 1918, blending with images of US troops in Baghdad over 'Vietnam' comments by Kay. Thus, while Kay may be thought to be 'telling it like it is' over the weapons, including pointing out what was there or under development and that Saddam was a threat, the visual backdrop contains images that only reinforce a negative perspective.

Presentation of the interview was complemented by an 'In Depth' feature, introduced by Brokaw, in which he reports that British Prime Minister Tony Blair has been forced to do what President Bush had done the previous day – acknowledge that the reports about weapons prior to the engagement were probably wrong. Images of inspectors and troops appear behind Brokaw, followed by pictures of Blair at the House of Commons Liaison Committee in shirtsleeves, one of the key moments in advance of the Iraq expedition, followed by a string of flags underneath – Iraq, UK, US, UN and so on. Further archive footage of Blair (marked 24 September 2003) speaking to Parliament is then soft-edited with overlay-ered images of Blair at the Liaison Committee and Parliament, and then a Kay image, followed by Blair shaking hands with troops and Foreign Secretary Jack Straw in Parliament. The package ends by noting that the inquiry Blair has announced will conclude in July 'before President's'; Blair, it is surmised, can afford to move faster because there is no election this year in the UK, reinforced on-screen by the script message: 'MONTHS BEFORE US EXPECTED TO PUBLISH CONCLUSIONS.' Jim Maceda's report from London concludes, however, that the enquiry 'won't help Blair's plunging poll ratings – only finding the weapons' will do that. This judgement was largely correct – although the British Prime Minister's poll ratings, despite dropping, still kept him well ahead of the opposition. But there could be no doubt that images of real weapons, rather than reports about phantom ones, would have completely changed the political and security landscape.

When the reports in both the UK and the US appeared, their impact was already dulled, as both confirmed significant weaknesses and failures in terms of intelligence, including secret information gathering and assessment. Kelly and Kay had already paved the way for these conclusions, each focused around the icon of respected experts with standing correcting the overriding impression that had guided government policies to some extent. Whatever the narrow detail of the basis for action, the absence of WMD/I left a hole in the heart of US–UK legitimacy, present-ing a critical challenge. In the end, the importance of image linked to legitimacy is confirmed, in this context, by the absence of image. It is hard not to accept the counterfactual supposition that an image confirming some kind of WMD find would have transformed the perceptions of Iraq and, therefore, altered the legitimacy agenda.

## Fallen heroes, flags and faces

The *CBS Evening News* added to its weekday broadcasts a daily initiative to remind viewers of the 'fallen heroes' in Iraq (and in theory Afghanistan, although cases from that theatre were so rare as not to be featured), making sure that individualised sacrifice was noted. Some of these had a wider impact than the daily identification of those who had lost their lives. On 8 November 2005, a year on from the original 'Fallen Heroes' segment on Corporal Shane Colton from Midwest City, Oklahoma,[21] there was a follow-up report to close the broadcast, labelled 'The Kindness of Strangers'. In the original, the personal aspect was a reference to Colton's promise to his son Lance that when he returned from his second tour of duty in Iraq, they would complete their 'project'. That project was to rebuild a wreck of a 1968 sports car, turning the Camaro into a jewel. However, the junk car, unrestored, sat as a reminder after Colton was shot down near Baghdad a month into that second tour. With on-screen labels describing the 'son of fallen hero' and 'widow of fallen hero', reporter Lee Cowan recounted how first local mechanic 'shop' students had offered to take on the project, but who, in a military town, were all quite quickly unable to do it, as they too, in many cases, were on their way to Iraq. Another group of 'shop' students from North Carolina, some 1,200 miles away, stepped in, receiving the original vehicle parts and others from donating suppliers all over the US by Fed Ex, and then rebuilding the car, finishing it in bright banana yellow with two thick black stripes running its length, and giving it a memorial plate that read '*Colton Camaro* Built in Memory of CW2 Shane Colton 10/30/71–4/11/04 "Vampires"'. The vehicle was unveiled to son, widow, cameras and onlookers in Las Vegas, Nevada (no explanation for this location, neither where the car was rebuilt, nor where the family lived, was offered), to be delivered to Lance at home the following day, 9 November. The human side was emphasised by the son's comment that despite the evil and awfulness in the world it was 'amazing' that so many people were 'selfless'.

The Fallen Heroes feature appears to have been spurred originally by an encounter with a bereaved mother in October 2003, Lynn Braddack, whose son Travis Braddack-Nall had been killed in Iraq after volunteering to stay on there for an extra three months.[22] That this was the origin of the Fallen Heroes segment appeared to be confirmed in a Saturday broadcast that met Mrs Braddack once again, this time in the context of the gathering movement of grieving mothers accompanied by a growing band of anti-war protesters who had gathered outside President Bush's Crawford Texas Ranch.[23] Reporter Lee Cowan noted that 'we first met her two years ago ... she told us something back then that has stuck with her, and us, ever since.' The file film of Braddack then has her talking direct to camera, offering a message to the world: 'The whole world's heart should be breaking. If you all could have met all these wonderful boys, they're all not just soldiers, they're wonderful boys.' After that personal seed had been sown, the *CBS Evening News* proceeded to introduce one face of each of those 'wonderful boys' – and occasionally girls – with a brief biographical note that allowed viewers the chance to 'know' those wonderful boys in passing.

That movement, which gathered outside the President's ranch, had been spurred by one individual mother, Cindy Sheehan from California, who had begun a lone vigil there, attempting to meet the President face-to-face. At the time of the report, Mrs Sheehan had returned to California to care for her ailing mother, but she had been the all-important lightning rod for both broadcast news attention and all the others who had made there way to baking Texas to set up camp with her. Cindy Sheehan had provided the icon that could draw in the energy of others – as Braddack put it in a walking interview with reporter Lee Cowan, she had come there because 'I guess this is where the face of the message was'. That face was the image needed at once to make the television news and to focus the legitimacy challenge to US engagement in Iraq.

That the 'face' provided the necessary focus for a challenge to the legitimacy of US engagement in Iraq did not mean that anyone had intended for this to be so. Nor did it mean that anyone intended it to provide the image that would give protest access to television news, although it is likely that to some degree this was part of Sheehan's aim. Irrespective of intention, Sheehan's face was the image at the hub of the message, and the message was opposition to involvement in Iraq. However, as to whether or not there was clear intention is a moot point in considering the television news image environment and the impact of images found there on the legitimacy in war. Just as much as the image has potency in one direction, it has uncontrollable impact in others. Sheehan's face very quickly became the focal point for mobilising an equivalent movement of military families in support of the war. Undoubtedly, just as Sheehan's Camp Casey had become the lodestar for a nebulous cluster of groups that had seized on 'the face' and had activists actively managing support (rather than everything's being a purely spontaneous reaction by those involved), there were managers, perhaps even at some level on behalf of the Administration, organising the counter-movement, the reality was that those managers could do so because there was support for their position – and that support was focused on 'the face', no less than backing for Sheehan's vigil.

The importance of giving, or not giving, recognition to images of the dead was also focused by a US government policy of not providing images of the dead being returned home. On the one side, this could be seen as a measure to protect the privacy of the bereaved, a perfectly reasonable position. On the other, however, it could easily be seen as a clumsy effort to dominate the image environment to the extent that preventing images of coffins returning draped in the stars and stripes was intended to prevent any chance that support for the Iraq campaign might drain away in the face of visible evidence of the price being paid. This was all the more the case, as the move not to show flag-covered coffins could be interpreted as denying respect to those lost and their families. In a sense, the *CBS Evening News*' decision to 'honour Fallen Heroes' filled a gap left by the Pentagon policy.

A Memorial Day feature focused on the importance of images of the returning dead in the coffins – albeit that the report fell fairly quietly at the end of the Saturday broadcast.[24] The report showed several still images that had been obtained by a group using the Freedom of Information Act. Those images were of the flag-draped coffins being carried from planes, or slipped into the sea, or en route to cemeteries. In each of them, as reporter Anthony Mason noted, the faces of the Honor Guard troops carrying the coffins are blacked out. Mason's commentary reinforced the significance of the images lest there be any doubt, noting that everyone was 'familiar with images of war, but these are also images of war', as the montage of pictures of coffins proceeded. The images of coffins also carried an on-screen script version of a statement from the Pentagon read as a voiceover declaring that there was a ban on pictures of the dead returning 'to protect the privacy of families during their times of grief'. Mason prefaced this by noting that the Pentagon had declined to be interviewed on the issue – thereby denying the possibility of visual reinforcement (in itself recognising the saliency of the image and the personal dimension) – and had issued the statement instead, which CBS News had given visual treatment, though of a necessarily limited kind.[25] The report continued by acknowledging the privacy issue and how many families who had lost loved ones had supported this, but that others who had lost people did not agree with it. The balance in the report was clearly towards the second of these positions, using a film interview with Jean Prevette, one of the bereaved who did not agree with the no-show policy. Her visual testimony confirms her support for 'the war' but that 'we need to see all sides of it'. Seeing her in the report pushes the viewer more towards seeing her side of the argument and, indeed, the reality of a bereaved mother whose loss appears to be compounded by the impossibility of her son's and others' coffins being seen generally.

The importance of the visual in this context is further reinforced by reference to a different set of still photographs and the words of the photographer who took them, Nina Berman, responsible for a book called *Purple Hearts*, depicting wounded, permanently damaged soldiers who had returned from Iraq. She, somewhat obviously but also unreflexively for someone involved in photography and the use of images, states the importance of the images: 'Pictures make things real.' Berman supplements this by adding that statistics have little real meaning – hearing that another one or four soldiers died in Iraq on a particular day does not have real impact or resonance. However, in her opinion, it is not possible to 'turn away from images'. It is the images that bring home the realities of mutilation, in the case of Berman's subjects, or death, in the case of Prevette's son and his dead colleagues. Mason's final words underline the image issue: 'They are powerful pictures of the tribute given to fallen soldiers. They are also powerful images of the realities of war.'

The Fallen Heroes segment had impeccable ambiguity. On the one hand, there was a drip-feed of individualisation, which served to bring the campaign in Iraq to those ready to meet each of the wonderful boys or girls. This might contribute, over time, to the slowly forming view in some quarters that the engagement was not worth the death of those whom they could meet on the CBS feature. This was certainly one trend that emerged by the time Braddack found her way to Sheehan's 'Camp Casey' (the name others gave to the camp, that of Sheehan's dead son) in August

2005. That the personalisation might be intended to undermine support for the Iraq engagement was supported by two other pieces of evidence. First, not only those killed in action of some kind or another, or close to it were included, but also those who died in accidents. While these deaths were clearly no lesser losses than those in combat, or related to operations per se, it did seem a little to be straining the 'Fallen Heroes' label. Second, and perhaps more persuasively, the feature only included those who had fallen in Iraq, with no mention ever of the dead from the continuing – and to some extent 'forgotten'[26] – campaign in Afghanistan, something not lost on those appointed by the Bush Administration.[27]

On the other hand, however, the way in which the feature was labelled, introduced and presented could not be deemed anything other than that which it stated. Indeed, it was welcomed in certain quarters, where America's apparent lack of honour for the dead was a matter of shame and the CBS initiative, little as it was seen to be, was at least some acknowledgement of the sacrifices made. It was also seen as a small-scale counter to the general trend towards negative and pessimistic coverage of the war by all the main broadcasters in the US.[28] The ritual introduction 'CBS News honours fallen heroes …' could not be challenged, all the more because the heroes were being honoured on this night-by-night roll-call of the dead. The title 'Fallen Heroes' made no question of the war, or the status of the dead. And the short, sympathetic, sometimes poignant, sketches of the men and women who had lost their lives were human but not mawkish in any way; they were wholly respectful in tone, offering no suggestion of editorial comment – beyond any that might be imagined in the viewer's mind (and that meant multiple points of view, no doubt, depending on the viewer in question).

The impeccably crafted ambiguity in the Fallen Heroes segment, notwithstanding the question marks that could be posed against it, was not quite enough. It apparently became undermined and the doubts of the critics were perhaps confirmed. Changes at CBS News seemed to play a notable role here. Certainly, there were shifts in presentation of the segment in the last part of 2005. First, CBS seemed almost relieved to have an opportunity to stop running the segment. Then, after a short period in which it ran again, the segment was transformed, at once continuing that which had been before while also altering its title and content – crucial differences that produced a completely different tone.

The big change at CBS concerned personnel. Long-time anchor Dan Rather was forced to step aside, following grave errors of judgement as senior editor during the 2004 presidential election campaign. He took personal responsibility for anti-Bush reporting, which had been based on false documentation and, worse, where the decision had been taken editorially not to use expert opinion doubting the documents which CBS News had taped in preparing the reports. This smacked of a significant anti-Bush agenda at CBS News, whether or not that was actually the case.

Rather, in the tradition of US news anchors – not just presenters, not just well-known faces, but senior editors, making decisions and leading news teams[29] – was the main guiding force at the *CBS Evening News*. There could be little doubt that the Fallen Heroes segment had his commitment. However, after his resignation as senior editor, and in light of the apparent anti-Bush agenda, it is hard not to judge that others at CBS must have been unhappy with the feature – and that they were embarrassed by the loss of neutrality and integrity. In this context, whatever the real motivation behind the Fallen Heroes segment, it seemed all the more to be what critics felt it was – anti-war – despite the careful ambiguity.

The segment could not be discontinued, of course. However, as soon as Hurricane Katrina struck, devastating New Orleans and other parts of the American Gulf Coast, in early September 2005, CBS wasted no time in substituting Fallen Heroes with an equivalent package concerning missing persons following the continental US humanitarian disaster that occupied coverage in totality for a short period, where nothing, or almost nothing else, even made it into the evening news reports. The format was very similar. The lead-in 'CBS remembers Fallen Heroes ...' was replaced with 'CBS invites you to help find missing children ...'. However, once the main thrust of Katrina had passed, Fallen Heroes returned, albeit with its hold broken, showing that an alternative could help to ease the *CBS Evening News* away from an innovative device that had become in some ways an albatross, and an item that was not, as such, 'news', but a continuing implicit comment.

The Fallen Heroes segment was to become 'American Heroes' at the end of 2005, having disappeared and reappeared during the American Gulf Coast humanitarian disaster caused by 'Hurricane Katrina' in the previous October. On 5 December, the new approach was announced, with Schieffer introducing it as an 'expanded version of our nightly salute to US servicemen and women', continuing that 'our series "American Heroes" is now going to include not only those killed in the war zones, but also those who displayed exceptional courage on the battlefield and beyond.' The first example in this new format was Melissa Stockwell, an amputee wounded in Iraq who was planning for the 2008 Paralympics, where she hoped to run the marathon. By 19 December, the 'American Hero' was, once again, a 'fallen' hero, killed by a land-mine in Iraq.

The American Heroes segment differed in four notable ways from its Fallen Heroes progenitor. First, it was not solely concerned with the dead – a shift in focus which meant that those not killed in action could be comfortably included without question. Second, both those who had been wounded in action and those who had performed heroically could gain attention; this step maintained the neutral position on the Iraq engagement – and possibly enhanced it – by giving space and credit not only to death, but also to survival and achievement, allowing a more rounded appreciation, whether the viewer's perspective was for or against the deployment. Third, the scope was expanded to include military personnel involved in Afghanistan (for example, Army CWO Clint Prather, a helicopter pilot who had flown Afghan President Hamid Kharzai, but who had been killed on operations when his helicopter was downed in a sandstorm on 18 January 2006). Fourth, the respectful, mournful version of the *CBS Evening News* theme – generally played on occasions of grief – that had accompanied Fallen Heroes gained a brighter, upbeat companion piece; the former continued to accompany features on the fallen, but the latter, with sprightly confidence, accompanied stories of survival and success. Overall, these changes, from the name to the component parts, while maintaining the continuity, removed the grounds for criticism, thereby, however, suggesting that, intentionally or not (and the suspicion had to fall on intention), there had been grounds for that criticism. This inference was supported by the fact that the American Heroes segment was not to be sustained night after night. Before long, it gradually became an occasional feature, slowly eased out but never certainly completely gone, and 'transformed', as an executive put it, into a supposedly more substantial feature, as a two-part report by David Martin on 3–4 August was claimed to exemplify.[30] The criticism of the Fallen Heroes segment, implicitly recognised in the shift to American Heroes and the increasing irregularity with which the feature appeared, all reflected the long-term potential for reminders about the individual human cost of the military commitment to Iraq – showing faces and families and giving identity to statistics, presented in a reverential manner and completely acceptable in itself – to drip-drain legitimacy.

## Occupation preoccupations – America's image problems

A key aspect of the varied and complicated context in which strategic success is sought concerns the moving image environment itself. In this environment, nothing had greater prominence or impact in the years following the 9/11 attacks than the images of abuse from the American-controlled Abu Ghraib prison in Iraq, from which pictures emerged in April 2004 via CBS News, both in a *60 Minutes* special and its refraction on the *CBS Evening News*. Although the abuse had been under investigation for some time by the military and a briefing about it had been given to a largely unresponsive media contingent in Baghdad in January, it was the images that set the issue ablaze.

The images appeared despite efforts by the Pentagon, using friendly relations, to prevent publication because of the very reasonable assumption that they would impact negatively on operations, which for the US at that particular moment, in spring 2004, meant a major assault on the insurgent stronghold of Fallujah. In a Senate hearing in May, broadcast live in its entirety by news channels in the UK and carried extensively in unusual programming in the US, Secretary of Defense Donald Rumsfeld was asked if he had authorised Gen. Richard Myers, Chairman of the Joint Chiefs of Staff, to call CBS to 'suppress' its report and publication of the pictures – Myers had drawn on a long-standing relationship with CBS' Dan Rather, using personal influence, to persuade CBS not to broadcast the images while they could be detrimental to operations and the lives of US military personnel. Myers and Rumsfeld both rejected the use of the word 'suppress'. Myers, in addition, denied that his concern was the impact on the troops at the most difficult moment since the end of major hostilities and that he was only asking CBS to delay its report. He also said that he knew the report would come out anyway, but just to avoid transmission at such a sensitive moment. Rumsfeld underlined that asking CBS to delay the report was the right thing to do, in his view.

The problem, as Rumsfeld so acutely judged, was having to function 'with peacetime restraints, with legal requirements in a war-time situation, in the information age, where people are running around with digital cameras and taking these unbelievable photographs and then passing them off against the law to the media, to our surprise, when they had not even arrived in the Pentagon'. This was a situation in which there was not 'a person at this table, except General Smith, who'd even seen them [the pictures from Abu Ghraib]' – and the General had only seen them because of his role in the investigation into the incidents. It was immediately surprising that the Defense Secretary had not seen the pictures until 7.30 p.m. the previous day, given their political significance (and there was always the possibility that he had preferred, politically for whatever technical reason, not to see them). However, there was the equally reasonable and probably more plausible reality that the importance of the photos had not been registered, so they had not been requested, and, as Rumsfeld stated, they had formally remained part of the criminal investigation, where they were guarded closely and kept confidentially as part of that process, and remained *sub judice*. As a consequence of this, in part, at least, Rumsfeld had not seen the videos either, which he had mentioned in his testimony. He confirmed this in response to questions from Senator Lynsey Graham (Rep. S. Carolina).

Senator Graham asked a series of questions about the photographs. Echoing Rumsfeld's opening remarks, he said that 'worse is yet to come.' He asked Rumsfeld if he had seen the video yet – he had not. (Rumsfeld's answer was curious, rambling over whether there were two separate discs with discrete sets of images, or whether he had simply had a copy that did not contain the video material.) Graham asked Gen. Smith when he first saw the photos and what he then judged might be the implications; he said late March and that it was part of the investigation. He eventually stumbled to the answer that he was aware that the pictures would be explosive. Gen. Myers was asked if he had seen them when he called CBS. He had not, but he had been aware of them, as had many people in the Pentagon, who were aware of the issues and the investigation. Gen. Myers also said that in retrospect it would have been better to brief the White House and Congress fully about what was to come. But the problem was that although those who had seen the photographs and those aware of them knew that it would be a highly sensitive issue if they entered the public domain, the descriptions of the images still did not register quite the impact that the images themselves would have done. In effect, it was never truer that a picture paints a thousand words, or, indeed, many more.

Running somewhat against Gen. Myers' view – and that of the Defense Secretary expressed earlier, Senator Hilary Clinton (Dem. NY) suggested that the abuse was fully and graphically described in the Taguba Report – the internal military investigation into the abuse, which had been completed in March, just before the images emerged. She further concluded, therefore, that the emphasis on the pictures making a difference was wrong. It did not take much imagination, she said, to turn the words into images. She also asked about the Geneva Conventions and Rumsfeld's declaration that they did not apply over Guantanamo detainees. This she said had 'sent a signal' and that the Taguba Report linked the abuse to Camp Buka in Afghanistan. Rumsfeld's response confirmed that the Taguba Report was graphic – and said far more than the earlier press releases and briefings on the investigation. But, crucially, he added, seeing the pictures really did make a difference. Given the difference of coverage and impact between the initial verbal reports about abuse in January and that after publication of the pictures in April, it was hard to avoid the conclusion that Senator Clinton had a less persuasive analysis here than the Defense Secretary. As he opined: 'You read it and it's one thing, you see these pictures and it's another.' Rumsfeld admitted that his error was not to realise what these words meant. He had not seen the pictures until 7.30 p.m. the day before, apart from those which had appeared in the newspapers. He had failed to see the 'gravity' of the case. This point was underscored by Senator Bill Nelson (R) who affirmed: 'You're right when you say there are times when words just simply don't do it. Pictures and perhaps symbols are more important for expressing thoughts or images [*sic*].' In his confused language, Nelson got the point right. What was an internal military criminal investigation, it was evident by the time of the Senate Hearing, Rumsfeld recognised, had the capacity to become strategic dynamite.

The strategic impact of the Abu Ghraib images and the difficulties of managing images strategically in a layered and complex communications media and multi-directional audience environment could be seen in the *CBS Evening News* broadcast of 5 May 2004. That broadcast demonstrated various aspects of this layering and complexity compactly in its first three packages. All three were about the Abu Ghraib prisoner abuse scandal, which CBS has been the leading actor in exposing. The first package report began by announcing that President Bush had appeared on Arabic

Television news stations, and used parallel clips on inset TV screens and a third blank screen to emphasise that Bush had not spoken to what is perceived as the main international Arabic channel, al Jazeera, and making clear that the President had fallen short of a full or unequivocal apology. The second package covered direct, to-camera apologies by Brigadier General Mark Kimmitt and General George Miller from Iraq, but also coverage of the Abu Ghraib prison itself, intended to show the prison in a good light, but undermined by screaming women and preparedness to show other camps but not key compounds at the prison. This package, which also shows Defense Secretary Donald Rumsfeld visiting Abu Ghraib at an earlier moment, undermines the military apologies in the second package by situating General Miller, along with force commander General Ricardo Sanchez, in positions of influence, knowledge and command regarding Abu Ghraib and the abuse occurring there. Taken together, and underscored by newsbars and website references, as well as the interplay of images, these three packages from one broadcast reflect the *visiculture* in which images dominate understanding of war and politics, but overlap and have uncontrollable and unpredictable impact.

The period leading up to CBS' broadcasting the Abu Ghraib images lasted for about one month, when General Richard Myers, Chairman of the Joint Chiefs of Staff, who happened to have a long-standing friendly relationship with Dan Rather, the senior editor and presenter of the *CBS Evening News* at that time, was leaning on Rather, and asking him not to show the images and carry the reports due to the continuing operations in Iraq. Myers stressed awareness of how damaging the images could be in that context, as well as the possible impact on the report into the abuse by General Antonio Taguba, which had just been completed and was being considered internally. Rather agreed to this for one week, then another and another, but finally had to say that he would have to run the images and was going to do so, because others were aware of their existence and it was unavoidable that someone else would use them (the *New Yorker*). Rather emphasised to Myers that it was the journalist's job to do this, even though he personally and CBS were prepared as far as possible to cooperate to minimise the potential risk to troops in the field. However, he underlined that if they could be first with the images and the story, then commercially, CBS had to be first. In the end, whether it emerged via the news media or through political channels, there could be no denying that the public accountability provided by it was both desirable and essential. But the material that makes accountability possible is also potentially damaging strategically.

The three packages, together, introduce four factors that give pause for thought and need to be considered in relating the importance of moving-image media, in particular, but of images, per se, to contemporary armed conflict: intent; nature; diversity; and complexity. The first of these issues is intent. What was President Bush's intention in appearing on al Hurra and al Arabiya – and, indeed, in not appearing on al Jazeera?[31] Was the intended audience in Iraq? Was the intended audience in the United States? Was it in the wider Arab world? Or was it in the world as a whole? While it is impossible to be certain about this on the available evidence, the suspicion has to be that, for Bush, the intended audience was primarily American. But it does not make any difference who the intended audience was, because once this particular talking head image entered the frame, it was going to be received and interpreted in all those other places. Once the image is there, it is uncontrollable. It is impossible to guarantee the impact. It is impossible to control what the response is going to be. It is not necessary to measure particular audiences, in particular ways, to do this. What was the intention of the generals? It would appear that they were more likely trying to address an audience in Iraq, but unlikely to have much impact there. It is quite significant that, whereas Bush could not quite bring himself to apologise directly, the generals were bluntly saying 'I apologise'. In this context it is hard not to feel sorry for Brigadier General Kimmitt, the second one shown apologising, because he was the one who had given a press briefing the previous January to say that this abuse had been identified and that the military was investigating it – but no one paid attention to him. Only when the images emerged did it suddenly become a big story. The images of empty cells in the package suggest a US military clearly trying to say something like, 'look, this is quite nice, it's not that bad, as prisons go', ruined by screaming women from upstairs, because the sound is laid over the image. The intention was to show that Abu Ghraib was not that bad, but the images of the empty cells, with noise from somewhere else, only left a haunting sense that something was wrong. The images of vacant cells filled with off-screen sound make the attempt to create a good image hollow. In terms of intention, there was no way to control what happened; it just went awry.

The absence of images of Abu Ghraib prisoners in the package, explained by reference to the Geneva Conventions, is also counterproductive – not least because there had been plenty of other cases where prisoners had been shown, despite the Geneva Conventions. This does not mean that those occasions were right, nor does it mean that the decision not to show them on this occasion was not right. But previous practice does mean that the absent images create a black hole in credibility. The decision to allow images of other camps, if prisoners were going to be shown at all at that stage, seems like an empty placebo in this context. A positive image would not have made up for all the negative images of abuse, but it might have had a better chance of stealing back some of the ground.

Second, there is the medium. Clearly the first level is television news, with the moving image dominant as the key medium in this example. However, that is supplemented by script newsbars constantly running, whether on the *CBS Evening News* or on the broadcasts on al Hurra and al

Arabiya – and the same would be true on al Jazeera. (And of course, the problem about the President's not going on al Jazeera is that it will still be picked up by that station, only rebroadcast and interpreted in a different way, possibly with only certain issues addressed on the station's terms, rather than on Bush's.) A further level is the importance of digital mobile phones and cameras in generating the images of abuse in the first place, but increasingly also in transmitting images, once again, beyond the control of anyone seeking to manage campaigns.[32] A still further level involves old-fashioned newspapers and cartoons. These take the images and develop them in new ways to satirise and undermine. Given their representation, all together, in one American news package, it is evident that these satirical transformations of the damning images are not just relevant in each of their individual cultural contexts, but also across all the others and, above all, in the American image-legitimacy environment. These satirical cartoons will not in themselves undermine US military legitimacy, but they might contribute to, or mark, the sapping of support in the US, reinforcing tendencies perhaps already emerging in response to the situation. And, of course, yet another level comprises internet websites, to which those interested are guided by messages across the stream, and which viewers will generally know are there anyway.

Diversity constitutes a third major issue. There is diversity in terms of the plurality of different media (remembering that 'media' is a plural) and there is diversity of the sources within each medium. How many websites are there which deal with news and images? How many television stations are there? The packages discussed here from one edition of the *CBS Evening News* provide a small sample of all of them. There is also a diversity of talking heads. These, it should be noted, are always images. Television news does not like a blank space. It will always go with a talking head in order to provide some kind of an image. But this means that there is always a variety of voices. So, President Bush's attempt to present himself as a talking head, to offer that image, is always going to be complemented, nuanced or countered by those of others.

Diversity means complexity, the fourth factor here. In that complexity, it is impossible to control the messages because it is impossible to control images and their impact. This is true of all the images discussed here – the talking heads, the camp prison, the unhappy Iraqis, and above all the abuse. Clearly, any attempts to suppress the images of abuse were not a good idea, because they were always going to get out anyway, somehow, it should be assumed. Would it have been better for Kimmitt to produce one image in January when he gave the original briefing, entirely on US military or government terms? This would not necessarily have been 'good', but the question must be asked as to whether it could have helped. Of course, that one image would still have been entering the diverse and complex environment, where it would have gone in many different directions, but the chances are that it would have been better that way than to wait.

Finally, General Miller appears in both the second and third packages. While he is presented as a positive talking head in package two as he apologises, in package three he is seen as the officer whose words, as head of prisons, set the tone and context on the ground for this policy in the first place.[33] On the one hand, he is seen apologising; on the other, he is apparently the de facto author of the policy. Thus, lack of control over images is reinforced by references to adjacent packages – the image of Miller, the honest soldier apologising, in one package (what the military wanted) is undercut by the image of Miller as inspiration for mayhem and abuse, in the other.

Differences and tensions between politicians and the military can be seen in these same *CBS Evening News* packages from 5 May 2004. Bush cannot bring himself clearly to say 'I apologise' or 'I am sorry', or whatever might be appropriate. The military, by contrast, know that the thing to do is to be straight, up front, and say it directly. It might have been better if Bush had not said anything at all and they had just had the military saying 'sorry'. That still would not have altered, let alone transformed, the situation, but, it might have been that little bit better. As it was, the outcome was that even the American television news was commenting that the President could not properly apologise, that he was trying to give the impression of apologising without actually doing so.[34] The Abu Ghraib incident was described by CBS as 'a crisis'. It was a critical challenge to what the US was doing. It did more to undermine the US campaign in Iraq and more broadly in the Global War on Terror than any other single battle, blow or belligerent image.

Television news is notably different from feature fiction or documentary and current affairs films, which constitute moving-image projects carefully constructed, crafted and completed over time. Television news is more immediately produced and available to its audience. However, like those other forms, as a moving-image medium, it produces material that is open to, invites and offers interpretation of armed conflict. It also focuses on human experience in its attempt to develop understanding and to connect to an audience. Most of all, despite being a medium sometimes dismissed as a realm for talk rather than vision, or for glancing rather than viewing, it is nonetheless a medium that depends on narratives based on images. This is the nature of the medium – it is visual; therefore it craves images. Images make news. The stronger the image, the better, within the bounds of accepted taste in any given context. Where strong and telling images are not available, then there will always be a weaker image, whether a stock still photograph, rambling library footage or a talking head. There is no television news without the visual. However, the more visual the material, the more it is likely to be registered as 'news' on television.

War, in some senses, has an inevitable mutual relationship with television news, where images of conflict are captured. The human suffering and the pictures of explosive blasts, flaming property or military equipment, or target-finder lenses trained on their targets, all constitute the ideal material for television news. This gives television news particular standing in war, built, as it is, on the same narrative-image foundations as other moving-image media, but with a generally wider potential set of audiences. In some respects it makes it a chief battleground in any contemporary armed conflict. As seen in the course of this chapter, the flow and outcome of contemporary warfare depends on the winning delivery of images and image narratives. While these will always be more likely to be coherently developed in the more studied and longer forms of feature fiction and documentary and current affairs, it is in the dominant realm of television news that the real potential to use images as weapons with immediate effect will be found.

Bosnia, September 11 and the Abu Ghraib scandals in Iraq all confirm the way in which images can affect policy, strategy and success. While television news has great limitations, even in the face of the most powerful of images such as the 9/11 attacks, where different levels of familiarity, competence and chance combine to offer different audiences different experiences and interpretations of the event, it also has enormous potential. As the images of the collapsing Twin Towers made clear, whatever the specific interpretation immediately or over time, a strong image of this kind will break through. That image strike, or the incidental emergence of the pictures of abuse from the Abu Ghraib prison in Iraq, the revelation of camps in Bosnia or the drip-feed of individual faces of the dead, all have an impact on legitimacy – even if the precise impact of these unguided weapons cannot necessarily be judged in advance, or even particularly clearly, after the event. And if anything confirms the importance of images in fostering legitimacy – or more important, neutralising and accommodating critical challenges to it – then it is the absence of images of WMD/I following the US-led engagement in Iraq. In the context of contemporary warfare, television news is the dominant means of delivering images as weapons. And those images, or their absence, in some cases, are the key to success.

# 6 The alphabet of images

So far in this book, we have taken examples from different types of traditional moving-image media in order to examine the nature of moving-
image media and their relationship to contemporary war. Having
established that moving-image media are driven by their thirst for the
images that define them, complemented by salient human experience, it
is appropriate to consider other significant aspects relating to the nature
of the medium. These include the 'holes' in the moving-image media
approaches to war – understanding why certain images, let alone other
pieces of information, find little place in the dynamic frame of moving-
image media. It also means considering the advent of significant new elements of the moving-image world, most notably the diverse manifestations
of the digital revolution, even if, as we note, this tends to confirm the
continuing importance of traditional media, as well as the dependency of
new media on the same elements that determine conventional texts. In
this chapter, what is 'missing' is discussed with respect to African security,
which receives less attention in the mainstream Western environment
than other conflict zones, despite its being a whole continent, many parts
of which are riddled with stories and images of peace and war. Following
this, new developments are considered in three sections, covering digital
impact, change and continuity in the world of television news, and finally,
change and continuity in the different approaches to representing war on
screen taken by individuals, incorporating, or despite, digital change.

## Africa, image, war: the black hole

On the morning of September 11, 2001, in the segment after 0830, ABC's
*Good Morning America* had covered the impending launch of a new sitcom,
including a studio interview with its lead, and had interviewed Sarah,
Duchess of York, about what she would be doing for the Weight Watchers
people of Wisconsin at the weekend, before breaking for commercials
around the quarter hour. The round of commercials (in New York, at
least) finished with a sexually implicit piece involving a station wagon
bouncing up and down, on behalf of a European carmaker, following a

trailer for that evening's *Nightline* with Ted Koppel. Koppel's rich voice intoned 'Three years, three million lives ...' over images of emaciated, damaged and dying black African people, before identifying the place as the Democratic Republic of Congo, insisting 'we thought you should know', and confessing that he and ABC were 'ashamed' at not having covered this before, but that that night they were going to 'put this right'. A blank, black screen followed, a solemn, highly unusual moment of mainstream American television, seemingly allowing a reverential pause for contemplation about the sombre trailer. However, those solemn seconds, which could equally have been a small transmission fault, were also moments of still and silence before *Good Morning America* returned at 08.49 with the equally grave news of reports that an aeroplane had crashed into the World Trade Center. The overwhelming images of destruction and death in New York were more immediate, more dramatic, more extensive and closer to home for the ABC news and current affairs producers and their audience. In a moment, after three years of neglect, Africa was forgotten again. From that moment, TV schedules were thrown out. The juxtaposition of Koppel's trailer for a forgotten topic that he and his colleagues were ashamed had been ignored and the return to the news which meant that this particular attempt to make amends would be swept aside was full of irony and pathos. This sequence was a metaphor for the way in which other events tend almost always to sweep Africa off the agenda of both governments and the moving-image media.[1]

The lesser attention to Africa is also measured by an ironic reference in Danis Tanović's *No Man's Land*, where one Bosnian Muslim reading the newspaper comments on the awful things happening in Rwanda. This is both humorous juxtaposition – the Bosnian predicament is comparable if not, in retrospect, quite so terrible as that in Rwanda, signalling that things can always be worse – and an indication of the extent to which Rwanda itself, at that same point in 1994, gained little more attention, most of the time, in comparison with Bosnia, than it does in the film. This is par for the African media-security course. Indeed, this is an attempt not to fall foul of the same tendency completely – although the scope here is less than we intended originally, when we hoped to structure the volume empirically around conflicts, rather than thematically around types and aspects of moving-image media. While the approach taken makes far more sense in light of the mission to investigate the nature of moving images as weapons, the decision not to pursue a conflicts-based approach was influenced by some friendly criticism, which rightly noted that Africa was a whole continent, while other conflict areas were regions, or even just countries, raising doubts about treating the continent as a whole. Despite Africa's being a continent, however, it should be noted that, for the most part, students of Africa and conflicts on the continent, whatever regional specialisations they may have, almost ideologically, tend to view the continent as a whole – or certainly, the Sub-Saharan mass of it.

This would have been enough justification for treating it as a 'case' of conflict and moving-image interaction. However, as argued here, the important aspect of study is to recognise that the entire continent of Africa, riddled by questions of security, forms a whole not only in the consciousness of those who study it, or who are activists related to it, but also in terms of what it offers to illustrate the nature of the relationship between armed hostilities and moving images in the contests of legitimacy that mark contemporary conflict. As noted in some of the research findings indicated below, specialists see Africa as a whole – and they see that vast whole reduced to the negligible in terms of broadcast media and security concerns.

There is, then, a broad principle that 'Africa does not count' – or at least, the exchange rate at which it does come to count is enormously high and painful in terms of human cost. There are of course occasional historic exceptions to this. For example, somewhat ironically, the global era of television formed above all around an African problem: the famine resulting from civil war in Ethiopia. Yet, ironically, it is conflict in Africa that is least understood, least reported and shown, but where the global effect most swiftly wipes that vast continent and its troubles from the news and current affairs screen, as will be shown below. It was Michael Buerk's celebrated reports for the BBC in 1984 that brought the famine to the attention of the world, particularly to that of Bob Geldof. Geldof, often portrayed as a medium-calibre rock star in decline, saw the reports and was motivated to mobilise the music industry, along with another music contemporary, Midge Ure, the front man of a different group, with whom Geldof worked (although this was often overlooked, even by Geldof, it seemed) to create what eventually became Live Aid – the biggest ever media event, linking two charity concerts, one in London, one in Philadelphia, via satellite and broadcasting to the largest ever audience: one-third of the world's population watched Live Aid, which raised enormous amounts of money to relieve the famine in Ethiopia, as well as prompting international attention to that disaster. However, even when Buerk made a twentieth anniversary film, revisiting the locations and people he had encountered in those historic reports (as well as featuring Geldolf along the way), the war was largely missing. As James Walton, reviewing the film's broadcast on BBC1 for the *Daily Telegraph*, noted:

> the closing sections were Buerk's own – as he gave his assessment of Ethiopia in the years since. Any viewers a little rusty on their African politics might have liked more details of who precisely was fighting whom and for what in the country's civil wars.[2]

African security issues, even those of a humanitarian dimension, struggle to register on the Western news organisations' agendas, as is also the case with Western governments, in most cases, most of the time.

The claimed failure in Buerk's reports is par for the African course, in the view of specialists.[3] They regard coverage of the conflict in the Darfur region of Sudan, for example, as oversimplified and decontextualised in terms of the conflict itself. In terms of detail in reports, the general perception is that with a Western story of conflict, such as the London bombs, great attention is paid to empirical detail, such as the precise number of dead, whereas in Africa, even the same report contained completely different figures for the dead, both large, speculative totals[4] – a complete, recurring distinction between places that are 'near' and those that are 'far'.[5] The realities of government, public and, so, broadcaster interest, were such that, in the summer of 2006, with Darfur once again becoming a prominent news topic (the result of a pincer movement created by the looming end of the African Union tiny military peace operation and a publicity drive by celebrities such as Hollywood star and director George Clooney), the images of destruction and damaged human beings from Lebanon took precedence over Darfur. The images were particularly important in this context, with the devastation from Lebanon contrasted with pictures from Sudan that appeared to be no more than standard images of Africa, perhaps with famine present, but with no evidence of the ethnic cleansing that occurred, including murder and burning people out of their homes: the visual evidence was not present.[6]

Images of Africa take something extra to register on Western screens. It is, therefore, notable if African security stories are covered at all. One respondent in focus group research with broadcast journalists noted how in the 1970s and earlier, it seemed as though 'everyone' was in Angola, or Rhodesia, 'week after week' – it was possible, for example, to do a film on one side in Angola one week, and then to go 'straight back' to do an entire [film] from the other side. However, it was not possible to 'imagine that happening now'.[7] The reason for this lies in the news producers' understanding of their imagined audience, which is in some cases well founded on their own organisations' audience research: 'we know it's an audience killer.' This understandably leads to commissioning editors' posing the robust question: 'do we have to do it?' Their reluctance is understandable, of course: 'it's incredibly hard to commission ... because your audience will halve at the end of the day.'[8] As if the less than enthusiastic approach of the commissioning editors is not enough, other difficulties, such as access – getting Sudanese visas to cover Darfur, for example, was cited as a big problem, and the cost of covering stories in Africa, such as Darfur, also contribute. 'It's a multiple whammy. You've got commissioners of TV ... it's incredibly difficult to do and, sort of, it's expensive, it's dangerous, so many issues, you know, safety issues and stuff that it's just not worth the candle.'[9] This was a view strongly echoed in terms of the potential dangers by others: 'is it worth risking a life for half an hour on a Saturday evening?'[10] While there is a sense that there will always be some coverage on the 24-hour news channels, particularly the

BBC and CNN, even this is often limited and obscure, and rarely translates into mainstream terrestrial coverage, where audience volume is so much greater. ABC News' treatment of the Congo conflict, noted at the start of this section, was not unique: 'the Congo war hardly got any coverage in Britain at all and three million people died.' Similarly, when Human Rights Watch, the American-based NGO, first produced a major report about the situation there in an attempt to spur action, 'it was completely ignored by everybody'. Only after another couple of months did any sense of outrage emerge, with coverage in the UK increasing on ITV news and Sky News, with the stalwart BBC able to 'put their hand up' to say 'we've been there five times'. But even that BBC coverage by 'a very good correspondent' might only be shown 'at three o'clock in the afternoon on BBC World ... and I think just occasionally some of those pictures had crept onto the second half of the *6 O'Clock News*, very short and sort of weird and exotic' but nothing 'to go somewhere and actually make an impact, make a policy impact ... to make people realise there's something going on' and to consider 'whether they want to try and put something in an Oxfam box, or they want to write to their MP, or whatever'.[11] All of this stems from the changing character of television, whether long or short format moving-image-making, where the focus is on the audience – everything increasingly needs to be domestic, or with a domestic link. This is a problem identified by journalists, who fear that those who commission are chasing audiences too much, or, in a contrary view expressed by one respondent, the commissioning editors 'rip the audience off'. All of this, in the UK context, is about the UK contact and connection[12] – 'you've got to have a British spin to get it through, rather than it being able to justify itself in its own right'. Or, as another respondent in the same group of journalists put it, 'the sense of actually putting those things that matter on television has completely gone'.[13]

Even atrocity needs to have an extra dimension if it is to generate significant interest, as the foregoing discussion of Darfur makes clear. A specialist focus group noted that two specific examples viewed each cued coverage by establishing other contexts for bothering to treat Africa, in one instance, protests in London (which gave Darfur its relevance for a British audience), in the other, the International Criminal Court (making it an 'international' rather than African issue).[14] Where a wider African context is given for Darfur, the frame used is the 1994 genocide in Rwanda, which may be held to serve a dual purpose. On the one hand, it is used to prompt discussion of Western governments' relative inattention and, certainly, unwillingness to intervene to prevent atrocities in Africa. On the other, it is a comparative point; the icon of genocide becomes an indicator by which to relativise the situation in Darfur and almost suggests that international intervention might not even be needed, because the images were not as bad. However, there was a strong view among activists that Darfur deserved intervention as much as Rwanda had, even if the situations were not exactly the same.

This was a message taken up by Clooney and others using their commercial and cultural profiles to draw attention to the conflict, including Don Cheadle, the lead actor in one of the few, but excellent, feature fiction films addressing the 1994 genocide, *Hotel Rwanda*, directed by Terry George.[15] The trailer running before the film on its DVD release carried a personal plea by Cheadle[16] on behalf of Amnesty International, noting that he played a character amid the Rwandan genocide and claiming that the same was now happening again in Darfur. While the shared continent and the commission of atrocity gave the two cases a link, they were quite distinct: given that Rwanda experienced genocide in the narrow legal sense, without doubt, the events in Darfur were of a different character – atrocities that were clearly international crimes against humanity, but not a clear, undoubted, systematic programme of extermination as such – the definition of genocide.[17]

It is perhaps also a mark of Africa's relative insignificance that, despite the magnitude of the genocide, it took a full decade before it gained the attention of feature fiction filmmaking – unlike, for example, the conflict in Bosnia and Hercegovina, characterised by ethnic cleansing, which had caught the imagination of Western media and cultural figures, and which had films, such as *Welcome to Sarajevo*, being made about it, even as it occurred. When films did appear, two came close together: first, *Hotel Rwanda*, and then, Michael Caton Jones' *Shooting Dogs*, both based on real stories of survival. The former, perhaps because it was the first film, took the lion's share of the attention, but both were high-calibre films which sought ways in which to make treating genocide attractive enough to engage an audience, while not cheapening it.[18]

*Hotel Rwanda* used the true-life story of Paul Rusesabagina (played by Cheadle), the manager of the luxury Milles Collines Hotel, in Rwanda's capital, Kigali, run by Belgian airline Sabena. Paul takes responsibility ethically and then formally (after persuading the Sabena bosses in Belgium to put him in charge) and shelters 1,268 people, both Tutsi and Hutu, from the genocide. Paul is Hutu, but in a mixed marriage with his Tutsi 'cockroach' wife Tatiana (played by Sophie Okonedo) and their four children. The mixed marriage, while a fairly standard device in films tackling topics such as this, is effective, showing that not all Hutus were *genocidaires*, as well as allowing a more subtle presentation of the social processes by which ordinary people come under pressure to participate in the madness of mass murder, as well as the use of the radio for transmitting instructions, and the dangers of swimming against the tide. Paul is on friendly terms with General Augustin Bizimongu (played by Fana Mokoena), who, the closing credits remind the viewer, was eventually to end up appearing before the International Criminal Tribunal for Rwanda in 2002, charged with genocide and crimes against humanity.

This relationship reveals the different aspects of intra-Hutu relations, with the friendship allowing Paul the chance to use money and material goods to bribe the general so as to protect his flock in the hotel, until Paul reaches a point where he temporarily has nothing left in the locker, and the general withdraws protection. The general shows ambiguity within the Hutu community – he is clearly not above participation in the genocide and profiting from it in either direction, but he evidently lacks the ideology or manic passion that gripped so many of his kinsmen. That passion among others is seen to grow frighteningly, surrounding Paul at various points when outside the hotel, and engulfing the hotel itself eventually, as the machete-wielding mob gathers outside the hotel compound and eventually enters it, only to be stopped by the army under General Bizimongu's corrupt command. However, the real horror of the genocide, despite the fortune in commercial cinema terms of finding a hero who swims against the tide and survives to offer something of a happy ending (as well as the clear good fortune for the real Paul and his protected persons), is revealed. The trauma is captured brilliantly by Okenedo as Tatiana, both when cowering and hiding, or blaming Paul for lying to her as he sought to protect the family and the others, and in reacting to the presumed murder of her brother and his wife in adopting their two children, after searching for them among the refugees being bussed out under UN auspices and getting off the bus already leaving when a Red Cross worker stops them, and she find them among the many, and they all walk together down a road in the closing shots, thus conveying the relief of survival and escape. The distress of the events is also harrowingly evident when Paul visits another friendly contact in search of supplies for the hotel. He notices the trail of blood from butchered bodies across the wholesaler's yard, before being advised tellingly to take a particular road home because it is 'clear'. 'Clear' turns out to mean clear only in the sense that the 'cockroaches' – the derogatory term used by the Hutu for the Tutsis – along it have all been 'cleared', as, in the early morning mist, Paul thumps into and over one mutilated dead body after another strewn along the road. Paul's confronting the reality of the genocide in this way is also the moment at which the viewer is invited to confront it directly too, if only relatively briefly.

The film also captures the strains and frustrations experienced by outsiders on the ground. This includes the role of broadcast news reporters, who tussle with their rules, safety and attitudes over how to cover events, and then over the importance of the images they have of genocide outside the gates of the UN compound – confirming the urgent and vital significance of images for the screen, while also confirming that even the most outrageous examples of mass murder do not register so strongly if they are found in an African setting. The Canadian Colonel Oliver (played by Nick Nolte) echoes the reality of the gravelly Canadian commander of the UN force deployed to oversee implementation of the doomed peace agreement, General Romeo Dallaire. His experience was translated into both a book and wrenching eponymous documentary by Peter Raymont,

*Shake Hands with the Devil: The Journey of Romeo Dallaire* – that rare thing, a documentary on African security issues that registered with more than groups of narrow specialists, while winning awards – although the personality of Dallaire himself has something to do with that success, as he revisits Rwanda and what he sees as the UN hierarchy's shameful failure, a decade on from the genocide, scenes of which are shown raw, as machete mutilations and murders are witnessed by cameras.[19] As with Dallaire's reality, the Canadian officer in *Hotel Rwanda* struggles, first, to use information that the Hutu Interahamwe political movement is preparing to destroy the peace settlement, and then, with the limited authority of the UN force to act. In the end, he is seen to assist Paul and his family, as well as thousands of others, but this is nothing compared to that which he might have been able to achieve with greater authority to act and more troops.

The opening scenes of *Shooting Dogs* feature Marie (played by Clare-Hope Ashitey) running: first just legs and skirt, a prefiguration of what the viewer will be shown at the end of the film, as she runs and runs and runs to save her life; then around a track, inside the Belgian UN compound. As he races round the track, Joe Connor (played by Hugh Dancy), a White Christian non-governmental activist, yells a mock-commentary as though she is running in the Olympics, urging the crowd of children to cheer her on as though in a televised competitive race, while a Belgian soldier sits in the middle and does nothing. This is a metaphor for what we see played out later. Later, there is a murderous context as the crowds are mobilised – but in a form of mass madness, which results in machete-led industrial butchery – and Marie runs for her life, while the Belgians as the face of the UN are seen to do nothing but abandon Tutsis to mob massacre, inhibited by the limitations of their formal mandate and mission from the UN Security Council. These are scenes that directly raise the political level of analysis in the film, albeit failing to take account of the genuine difficulties in which the so-called peacekeepers found themselves.

Difficulties are not peculiar to the UN soldiers. Joe and a BBC journalist Rachel (played by Nicola Walter) discuss getting the genocide on television – the only thing that will make a difference, the viewer is told, reflecting a received (and false) understanding of the 'CNN effect' and the presumed capacity to influence policy. They film mutilated bodies, a few among the hundreds of thousands, but the impact is not the same in terms of both coverage and experience. Rachel captures the White European Western outsider's position: 'Last year in Bosnia … cried every day; strangely over here not a tear. No. It was worse than that. Any time I saw a dead Bosnian woman I thought "that could be my mum". Over here they are just dead Africans. What a thing to say.' This recognition of her reality reflects that of many others. The reality, in some way, is that Africans are less 'People Like Us' to those who can do something to make a difference than were Bosnians in a European context.

Caton Jones has made a film that, despite strong shared features with *Hotel Rwanda* – the roles played by images and outside broadcast news organisations, the UN force, the outside world (in particular, the authentic film of a US State Department spokeswoman's sinking, tongue-tied attempts to avoid openly, clearly or directly using the word 'genocide' appears in each of the films), and awareness of the building evidence of preparation for genocide – is distinctly more political.[20] In the film, all the outsiders, bar one, eventually take the chance to save themselves and get out. The one who stays is the missionary, Father Christopher (played by John Hurt), who takes clear responsibility for the situation, sacrificing himself to save Marie and others. The film is also political as a production. First, it was made on location in Rwanda, where the actual incidents depicted in the film occurred – this is a clear political statement concerning the film's commitment. Second, a number of victim-survivors of the genocide are featured in the closing credits, all of whom are survivors, seen to be engaged in making the film – again, a sign of political engagement.[21]

*Shooting Dogs* engages the issue of the relationship between legitimacy and communications media in the complex environment of contemporary conflict. The US Somalia experience, where the US was perceived to have withdrawn because it had taken a small number of deaths, is suggested to have informed the Hutu in Rwanda, capturing and killing UN peacekeepers, so as to force the UN – or at least its Belgian contingent – to cut and run and induce flight by the internationals broadly, who might make a difference. There can be little doubt that the film's reflection of the read across from one conflict to the other is accurate, reflecting the ways in which images of loss, whether incidental or deliberately generated, affect the legitimacy of military operations in conflict zones. Rwanda in this context, however, is the measure of how Somalia condenses the issues of legitimacy and success in contemporary warfare.

From the perspective of outside responsibility and intervention, it is the downed Black Hawk in Mogadishu that defines both Africa and legitimacy in contemporary conflict. In terms of television news coverage and actuality treatment, this means the bodies of rangers being dragged through the streets of Mogadishu and apparently leading to a US withdrawal. In terms of the feature fiction version of that event, Ridley Scott's landmark film appears to stand way beyond any other source in terms of its actual and potential power to shape understanding of the events in Somalia specifically and in Africa more generally. The strength of both the actuality and fiction moving-image treatment of the Black Hawk story is that it combines experience – the horror of the American soldiers dragged through the streets – with the image that conveys this experience.

Africa is defined by image. Just as much as *Black Hawk Down*'s images of the devastated bird and the mutilated corpses of the US Rangers epitomise the fragility of external intervention, its early scene-setting also captures the essence of Africa as found in the stockroom of moving images, the kinds of 'wallpaper' images of desert landscapes, with straw housing and emaciated bodies noted above regarding television news pictures – typical images that could make scenes of ethnic cleansing in Darfur not immediately distinguishable from these standard views of the continent and its people. The scenes of famine, the Somali landscape and so on are depicted in a respectful elegiac manner by the visually sensitive Scott, an approach supported by the simple typographical comment at the end of the film that 1,000 Somalis and 19 US personnel died in the course of the 18-hour operation shown in the film. That simple comment reflects the imbalance in attention, treatment and meaning. The comment, especially alongside the consideration and honour shown in the images of Africa, appears almost to suggest that the 1,000 Somalis should not be forgotten. The suggestion, however, following the images of famine and the icon of the downed Black Hawk is almost confirmation, in itself, of the way in which conflict and death in Africa are way behind those same phenomena in the US or Europe on the scale of broadcast news media or Western governmental importance. As with the mixed-up numbering of deaths in Darfur and the precision over the London bomb victims, the specific number of identified US personnel in this case is measured against the rounded approximation of Somali deaths. Numbers and images both indicate that African security counts less than that of other continents or regions, which, quite probably, means that the parameters of legitimacy in armed conflict are set differently.

## Webs of war and MPeg impact

In *Black Hawk Down*, Scott shows a young boy capturing digital images of the incoming Black Hawk assault on a mobile telephone and transmitting them to warlords in Mogadishu, who can ready themselves to ambush the Americans. This is one small example of how the image-communication environment was transformed as the twentieth century gave way to the twenty-first, with the seeming ubiquity of handheld video cameras in the 1990s, which made the Yugoslav War so rich in visual material, being replaced by the even more prevalent presence of digital image capture and transmission. By the middle of the first decade of the new century, digital cameras, including the growing power of both still and video devices on personal mobile telephones, meant that almost anything might be captured in a moment by someone using a digital device, transferred, possibly adapted or doctored and transmitted, either as a multimedia message, or by posting on an internet site for viewing or downloading. This was one of the chief elements enhancing the growth of network organisations such as al-Qa'ida and, as the excellent Abdel Bari Atwan has described, was vital to the working world of the UBL-led net.[22] It was intensified in the course of the conflict in Iraq, with Abu Musab Zarqawi's al-Qa'ida in Iraq, along with other Islamist groups there and around the world, filming events such as suicide operative car-bombing incidents, and using the web to mobilise support and generate recruitment. One of the key stages in the evolution of this approach came in Chechnya. One of the early features that prompted our interest in the topic of images and contemporary conflict was an undergraduate student essay, which drew attention to this phenomenon. The student in question, who was intending to go into the Royal Marines and who was studying on a military bursary, wrote an essay in which he mentioned having received an Mpeg file showing two Russian soldiers' throats being slit in Chechnya. Not only had he received this image, which was an interesting manifestation of the new environment itself, but, perhaps more significantly, in that essay, he expressed doubts about continuing with his career plan, despite the bursary commitment to serve. His nerve had been shaken by what he had seen. This, before Zarqawi and company had been able to move into business against the US presence in Iraq, was an example of what all those using this approach hoped to achieve – undermining the spirit and morale of their potential foes. The fascination with such images, stupefying and mesmerising as watching them can be, is an important trend – one of the things that emerged from audience and public research for the ESRC 'Shifting Securities' project with which the present study is partly associated. This is not a matter of people enjoying the images, but images of beheadings that go around, which seem to prompt a blind fascination in coming to terms with it. There can be no sense of the long-term effect while moving images of an appalling act are viewed repeatedly and continuously – and, as noted in terms of other research in Chapter 1, there is no reason to suppose that viewing will necessarily lead to any particular behavioural consequence. However, there is the potential for some impact, in some cases.

The impact of modern, personal and portable image devices was most evident in the context of the 7 July 2005 attacks on the London transport system. According to a representative of BBCi, the BBC online service, on the day of the London bombings, the BBC received 1,000 images in 300 emails.[23] The images came in three waves: first, those from digital cameras; second, still images from mobile telephones; and finally, moving images from mobile telephones. The advent, in particular, of digital image mobile phone technology heralded an age in which, by the time of the London bombs, it had already become conventional to post invitations on the BBC News website to send in images as soon as possible – a practice not exclusive to the BBC. It was not the first time that this technology had been used – most notably, the Tsunami that devastated South East Asia on 26 December 2004, where both still and moving images gradually emerged. However, speed and scale in the context of the London bombs were unprecedented. Above, all the images were among the most dramatic, while often the quality of the digital moving images in some cases was so high as to be comparable to professional footage.

The first images arrived within 40 minutes and were what became emblematic of the attacks, the devastated number 30 bus in Tavistock Square. But the images of the bus were rapidly complemented by the harrowing images from beneath the ground, in the smoke-filled, wrecked underground carriages and along the tracks in the tunnels. The BBC and other organisations always have to be alert to the possibilities of hoax and fake pictures, but in this case there was little doubt that the images arriving were authentic, not clever fictions resulting from use of Photoshop or similar image-editing software. The BBC showed the images without permission of those depicted, believing that the circumstances justified their use. Despite the justification provided by the circumstances, there were many images deemed not appropriate to reveal through 'normal' channels, given their gruesome content. This censorship, both on television and the web, was consistent with the general practice not to show material deemed likely to be unacceptable by viewers. However, there was no doubt that audiences would want the images that were made available. For news organisations such as the BBC, the images from small portable devices were something that no reporter or camera crew could ever have gained – increasingly, mobile phones, in particular, meant that members of the public could bear testimony and report where professionals could never gain access. Moreover, the importance of the images was really confirmed by information on the BBC News website. Statistical feedback reportedly showed a massive number of visits to the pictures on the BBC News website, far greater than to script material on the site, leading to the inference that, more than ever, 'the pictures tell the story' in the sphere of peace and security.[24]

The appetite for images and their increasingly rich availability, as well as the near impossibility of controlling them, was manifest in the 7/7 London bombings in 2005, which emphasised the diversity of both media and sources. The Security Service and the Special Branch in the UK were trying to keep the images of the nail bombs on the Piccadilly line train to themselves for three reasons: the sake of the investigation; protecting information in advance of possible trials; and with a security concern that people should not see what it was at the time. Yet, all of a sudden, ABC News in New York obtained these images and showed them – because once the images are there, the news broadcasters will show them. ABC was able to show these images from the Piccadilly line because the authorities in the UK had been sharing them with their counterparts in the US. Brian Ross, ABC News' 'special investigative reporter', with good channels into the US Police Departments, the FBI and the CIA, as his 'special investigations' revealed (as well as his listening into the airline and emergency service nets from an undisclosed location on 11 September 2001, as the events of that day unfolded in New York, Virginia and Pennsylvania), had obtained these images through one of those sources – as it turned out, the New York Police Department – and was showing them. Once they had been shown, despite initial reluctance by the BBC and some other UK broadcasters to rebroadcast them – sensitive to the UK authorities' concerns, they were quickly spread around the world, including in the UK itself. This confirmed how difficult it was to control images because of the number of different directions in which they could go. Images of this kind are rather like water, which finds its way into any available hole, nook or cranny.

ABC's *World News Tonight* managed to get hold of images of explosive devices found in cars in the Luton railway station car park on 7 July, the day of the first wave of London bombs, as well as gruesome pictures of the wreckage underground where the bombs had fulfilled their destructive purpose on the Piccadilly line. These clearly had to have come from a US source that had benefited from sharing the images – despite the desire in London to keep the images from public view while investigations continued, and especially despite requests not to show them. After the images emerged, the Metropolitan Police Commissioner Sir Ian Blair said that the images had been shared 'confidentially' with 'colleague agencies in the US', and that their leaking potentially damaged the inquiry into the bombings. ABC had been asked by the Metropolitan Police not to show the images, but ABC claimed that it had asked Scotland Yard why it did not want the pictures to be shown, but had not received a response (although there was no indication of the time frame involved). Executive Producer Jon Banner insisted that *World News Tonight* had only proceeded to air the material after vigorous discussion, saying that ABC news took 'great care' over these matters, discussing them with law enforcement agencies in London and the US, as well as establishing their own judgement that the 'story was newsworthy'.[25]

ABC's *World News Tonight* was not shown in London that night as a result of this request – according to Banner, ABC 'gave the London investigators the benefit of the doubt' in this respect. Yet, the images were shown in the US and, once shown there, were being picked up and used by broadcasters around the world, including British ones. This continued a pattern in which key information, whether substantive or speculative, was emerging in the US when nothing was being said in the UK.

Another instance of the impact of different cultural and political climates emerged with the arrest of one of the second wave of bombers in Rome. The very stylish female lawyer for Isaac Hamdi (also known as Hussain Osman) took the battle for hearts and minds initiative by making public statements and arranging interviews in her plush surroundings which meant matters that would be required by law to be *subjudice*, in the UK, were given a wide public airing in both Italy and the UK, already seeking to shape the attitudes of audiences, casting doubt on the intention of the second-wave bombers – having to concede that her client had carried out the act for political purpose, while asserting that he had no intention of killing anyone, only to cause disruption and make a political point. This was presumably a threefold strategy to sway support in some Muslim audiences, to affect the climate of the Italian courts' investigations over whether to charge her client and deliberations over extradition to the UK, and, in the event of extradition, having already made public statements that could render a fair trial in the UK untenable, as the material in the public domain could be deemed to influence a jury and make a fair trial impossible, or at least very difficult, with the most serious possibly compromised. That the UK could do nothing to influence this meant a significant potential legitimacy gain for Britain's opponents. And while it was the lawyer's words that might compromise future terrorist legal cases in the UK, it was her image – relaxed, svelte, long, dark hair – that ensured the words were broadcast.

Regarding 7 July and, to a lesser extent, the failed attacks of 21 July, while the tapestry of images that emerged from mobile phones on the scene heralded a new phenomenon and a shift in television news reporting, where the broadcasters would immediately be calling for anyone with images to send them, and while websites were checked, two things were quite clear, despite this pattern. The first was that everyone still turned to television news and the second was that, even with digital capture rampant, not everything was caught. In terms of the latter, the aftermath of the failed attacks is illustrative. One of the things about a beast craving images is that talking heads provide the visual element where more dramatic pictures are not available. These talking head visuals, in the wake of an incident such as the shooting of what turned out to be an innocent Brazilian man, Jean-Charles de Menezes, often prominently include eyewitnesses. Yet it was remarkable, in that particular case, after reports of the Independent Police Complaints Commission findings emerged, how inaccurate the initial eyewitnesses had been. And yet, those eyewitnesses, because they were faces confidently, authoritatively talking to us through the television screen shaped most people's understanding of what had happened. Very few people bothered to read the details of the leaked report, or eventually, the report itself. This is always the case with this kind of incident. Often immediate, image-oriented information can be countered with a reasoned, comprehensive approach, but this will have little effect. Those initial images and interpretations have already created a dominant idiom, and it is almost impossible, short of some major countervailing, counter-image, to overcome it. Yet the Stockwell-shooting eyewitnesses were so unreliable. It seems that what most of them saw was the policeman who was restraining Mr de Menezes being dragged away, before another officer actually fired shots into the Brazilian. They thought that the first police officer was actually the victim, because they just could not tell what was happening in the heat of the moment.

The continuing dominance and importance of more traditional news media was evident as the public processed images and other information concerning the initial attacks and their failed follow-on. On 7/7 and 21/7, everyone was watching BBC World, or a similar broadcaster, if they could, as information was emerging. There might well have been a poly-iconography surrounding events, with the internet and digital communication providing any number of options for finding and viewing images and narrative collections of them, but it was still the more conventional and traditional media that carried authority and gave weight to images. This was true of television viewing, but also of website usage – certain websites, primarily those associated with major news broadcasters such as CNN and the BBC, or recognised print authorities, are the ones that are likely to attract those curious for information. As Philip Seib's excellent work indicates, with so many websites, including the large number of 'blogs', available, there is no way for anyone to consult all of them – or however many of those sites have relevant news information on security issues and conflicts.[26] The reality is that people turn to trusted and reliable brands, which are often taken to be those of the well-established major broadcasters.

In this context, however, there was a major shift potentially underway concerning the role of the big internet brands, such as Yahoo! and Google, who had become 'some of the biggest movers and shakers', at the side of which traditional news broadcasters were 'actually nothing': 'Not the BBC, not anybody in comparison with Google and Yahoo!'[27] The scope of these imperial internet brands to exploit their positions in terms of either reach or commerce depended on partnerships. Google could only make the most of its reach if it were to join forces with established news and moving-image producers by 'tying up deals with agencies and broadcasters … basically to pass on their content'. Thus, the new media platforms and actors were not going to be the ones involved in production; they would only be concerned with transmission. This left traditional news, current affairs and moving-image producers in positions of relative strength, albeit challenged by change. All were exploring how to place themselves in relation to the new environment, or by creating multiple media platforms for their business. For example, with the BBC's Online becoming one of the biggest websites in the world, certainly in terms of news reporting, a traditional broadcaster had effectively become one of the major script providers of news globally, but written reporting mingled with sound and image material. In response, traditional print sources began investigating futures as broadcasters, at least via the web. Those working in traditional newspapers were 'worrying like mad about how to – whether to – become broadcasters and to what extent', with the *Guardian*, a major serious news daily newspaper in England, said to be 'panicking' about its website, by one respondent from a television news background, over whether they should be 'putting films on there' or 'doing interviews on tape' because the media available could support these approaches. What is clear from all of the discussion of new media and change is that traditional sources are the ones that stand out and carry credibility in an era of change. This is because the traditional broadcasters are the ones with established reputations and so the ones to which audiences and publics will turn most immediately amid the morass of information available electronically, whether sought out on websites, or received in email news shots, or downloaded as podcasts, on computers, or portable personal organisers, or mobile telephones.

The new media remain a vital and dynamic part of shaping the news and reporting environment, in particular, given their capacities both to provide the immediacy of television with potentially greater depth, or more extensive information, and they are also a means by which journalists who are unable to get their editors to pick up stories, or aspects of them, can 'set a hare running',[28] by using their website 'blogs'. In the end, these sites would be a means of generating sufficient interest and attention to get whatever the issue is into mainstream coverage, or the means of getting authoritative back-up information concerning that which had already found its way on to television news. But it is television news that counts, with its ability to reach large numbers of people with one interpretation, as well as the brand attributes and trust that major broadcasters bring, even when new media are concerned. It is the more traditional broadcast news media that have salience – which is why the bulk of this book has been concerned to build understanding of the common image-narrative elements of moving-image media in the traditional formats of film and television, whether fiction or actuality, and interpretations of particular examples of these moving-image media narratives; the contribution of new media, at least for some time to come, is merely to contribute to conventional media, or to reproduce them in the new form, for example, as download podcasts. Thus, while the new media have importance in relation to legitimacy and success in contemporary warfare, that importance is restricted, for the most part, to the degree to which they inform, influence and penetrate the traditional and conventional media, notably that of the dominant medium, television. It is important, therefore, to understand change in the traditional media, notably television news, and different approaches to capturing warfare with moving images – the topics of the following sections.

### Authors and approaches to representing war on screen: the ABCNNNBCBS of TV news and current affairs

Despite the radical changes heralded by the digital revolution and diversity of outlets and sources, conventional broadcasters and forms retain great importance. Yet, those broadcasters and media are also subject to change. Yet, while change affects them, however much there is change, there is also much that stays the same. Individuals and organisations continue to be important in shaping and presenting war on screen. Even where their particular roles shift, however, there is much that remains the same, it would appear. The purpose of this section is to explore how changes affect those engaged in presenting war on screen, whether organisations, seeking to remain in line with others while at the same time trying to mark their distinctiveness, or individuals – directors, reporters or anchors, or documentary producers or directors – all, in some way, 'authors' in the world of war on screen, contributing to the ways in which images are delivered and frame armed conflict and the issues of legitimacy that will determine success.

A number of filmmakers have begun to develop what might be termed an *oeuvre* of work relating to contemporary war, in both the fiction and non-fiction realms. In some cases, this reveals a somewhat idiosyncratic approach, which engages with conflict in different ways. In others, it reveals a developed approach to making films about contemporary war. All are 'authors', making distinctive films that address aspects of contemporary war. In most cases, armed conflict is just one of a range of topics treated, but for a couple of them, there appears to be a dedicated focus on war. In noting this selection of particularly interesting cases, we do not wish to suggest that this choice is necessarily exclusive. Nor is our intention, in the space of a few paragraphs, to do more than identify the personalities and recognise different approaches to representing war on screen.

The best known of the filmmakers considered here is Ridley Scott, one of the most successful of all contemporary filmmakers, both in terms of box-office revenue and critical recognition. Scott's filmography is extensive, and far wider than concerns with war, but these have loomed large – and, while far from exclusive, Scott himself has acknowledged the presence of war as a theme in his movie-making, rooted in his experiences, first as a child growing up amid Second World War bombing in the northeast of England, and, then as the son of a senior military officer.[29] In *Gladiator* (2000), Scott's depiction of second-century Roman battle was already a treatment informed by America's Vietnam War experience and revealing far more about ideas and images of contemporary armed conflict than the actual scenes he intended to depict.[30] Most obviously, *Black Hawk Down*, discussed already in Chapter 3 (and again, in relation to Africa, in this chapter), is what Scott himself has termed a 'pocket edition' of contemporary warfare – he rightly sees all the aspects of contemporary war, certainly combat – condensed into the 18-hour battle depicted in the film.[31] Finally, in his later film, *Kingdom of Heaven*, even more so than *Gladiator*, the historical setting is a platform for addressing contemporary issues. His purpose in making the film appears clearly to have been to use the great strategist Salahaddin's leadership of Islamic resistance to Christian crusaders' thrust into the Middle East as a vehicle with which to influence legitimacy in the post-9/11 US-led Global War on Terror. In a world easily seduced by ideas of 'clashing' cultures and (falsely) civilisations, divided by responses to events and their counters, it is hard to avoid viewing *Kingdom* as a pitch for understanding and recognition of qualities on all sides. A weak central performance from star Orlando Bloom, who cannot carry the weight of the film, however, meant that Scott's film as a whole could not have the impact it might have done in opening minds and affecting ideas about the continuing contemporary conflict to which it really spoke.

Two other successful fiction feature filmmakers, albeit not on Scott's level of global success, are Michael Winterbottom and Paul Greengrass, both British. The former has created a fascinating, eclectic series of films on a wide variety of topics – if one thing can be said to define his work, it is diversity, with one project seemingly never reflecting the others, except insofar as he invariably produces interesting films. In terms of contemporary conflict, *Welcome to Sarajevo* was discussed in Chapter 3. However, the fairly standard tropes of journalist-outsider and personal transformation used as a vehicle for taking viewers into a conflict used in that film stand in contrast to the radically alternative approach found in at least one other film, *In This World*. That film addresses the security and development sides of contemporary warfare by showing the story of two young Afghan cousins, refugees from conflict there, who journey from a refugee camp in Peshawar Province in Pakistan on foot, making their way to Turkey and then risking suffocation as they take the human smuggling alternative of being in a sealed truck to traverse Europe to Paris,[32] then the Sangatte refugee camp in northern France, before crossing to the UK and ending up in London. This is a fascinating vignette in which two genuine Afghan boys with the same names as the characters they play also perform in a fictionalised version of a journey with parallels to their own experience as by-products of modern war. The decision to use genuine Afghan refugees and to make a film that depicts this human strand away from the conflict itself confirms Winterbottom's status as an imaginative innovator on film, including in the approach he takes to hostilities. In a sense, that independence of approach is shown by the complete absence of conflict in his otherwise disappointing *With or Without You* (1999), which manages to tackle human relations in a mixed marriage in Northern Ireland without making any reference to 'The Troubles' – a bold tack, where the convention is to use them as a backdrop. Despite the title, with its reference to the rock anthem of the same name by U2, itself resonant with echoes of division and trouble, the remarkable aspect of the film is the absence of conflict – in itself a comment on them and their presentation.

The conflict in Ireland also provides the context for *Omagh*, a highly regarded film by one of the most interesting filmmakers engaging with contemporary conflict, Paul Greengrass, whose work is at the cusp of feature fiction and drama documentary. His dramatisation of actual events is unmatched – and perhaps no one else could have made *United 93*, his version of the fourth aircraft in the 9/11 attacks, where the passengers mounted resistance, ending with the United Airlines aircraft crashing in a Pennsylvania field, rather than hitting its target, which the Congressional

9/11 Committee concluded was the US Capitol.[33] While there had been widespread criticism before the film was released in 2006 that it was too soon to tackle the events of that day in a feature film,[34] there was a universal sense, once it had been released, among critics and audiences, that it had been the right thing to do and that it was, indeed, the right film, so well was it accomplished.[35]

Greengrass' origins lay in the path-finding documentary school formed by Granada Television's *World in Action* series, which pioneered drama-documentary, with Leslie Woodhead, who made the first film of the kind, based on the diary of a Soviet dissident General Grigorenko.[36] Woodhead himself has contributed a series of films engaging with atrocities in contemporary conflict – part of a commitment to human rights films, dating back to the days of *World in Action*. *A Cry From the Grave* (1999) detailed the massacre of around 7,000 Muslim men by Serb forces at Srebrenica in Bosnia and Hercegovina in July 1995. This remarkable film benefited from 'the democratisation of image gathering' using camcorder, still or even mobile telephone digital technology (as indeed, did *The Death of Yugoslavia* discussed in Chapter 4). In 2005, he made a follow-up film to mark the tenth anniversary of the massacre, *Srebrenica: Never Again?*, which picked up the stories of relatives of the dead, or presumed dead, seen in the first film, but with a slightly more optimistic final sequence. In addition, in this same period, Woodhead also made a film about Beslan, although as the director himself avows, the stunning *Children of Beslan* owed most to the time producer Ewa Ewart spent with children themselves building their confidence and trust, making it possible to capture the pain and rage revealed in images and expressions of experience.[37] In all the films, Woodhead manages to treat the most appalling human suffering with humanity and understanding for victims of conflict, always focused on content – rather than style or method – and never becoming sensationalist in the face of the most shocking material.

In a similar vein to Woodhead, Dan Reed has used an intelligent, open approach to making films related to contemporary armed conflicts. Among his work, two films particularly stand out (a third, *The 9/11 Liars*, was not what many people might expect from the title and was disappointing). *Terror in Moscow*, in the vein of much contemporary conflict – and as noted specifically with reference to feature fiction films relating to Chechnya and the North Caucasus in Chapter 3 – uses film shot by the protagonists of the Moscow theatre siege in 2001. The seizure of a theatre and its cast and audience by Chechen terrorists was captured hauntingly on film, as were some parts of the Russian authorities' compromised attempt to end the siege, using a gas that killed many of the hostages. *The Valley* (1999) provided an ethnographic picture of the conflict in Kosovo, carefully structured, with parallel scenes from the ethnic Serb and ethnic Albanian communities throughout – funerals, paramilitaries and so on – which funnel into and out of the only scene that does not have a parallel (an ethnic Serb who reflects the only view of common existence between the communities, as well as transformation of the situation), where an ethnic Serb Kosovo and its people are filmed with an aesthetic eye for the landscape (which 'provides an ironic counterpoint to the horrific events'[38]) and shown free of direct voiceover narration, with only occasional on-screen script information. This is a clear example of the art of showing, not telling, as it discovers the equivalents in different communities in conflict.

Where Reed shows-to-tell the ethnic parallels and polarities, drawing on the more traditional, human, emotional and cultural aspects of conflict, another filmmaker, Dodge Billingsley (see also the discussion in Chapter 4), has a mission to show, but with at least two differences. The first is a general commitment to making films where on-screen, or voiceover narrative is eschewed. The other is to capturing and showing aspects of war – particularly combat – that broadly fall outside the conventional realm of filmmaking, and reflecting the genuine realities of war, which are taken to be less the impact of munitions on bodies (as the 'realities' of war are readily understood to mean), as the actual and direct experience of war. In addition to *Virgin Soldiers* (discussed in Chapter 4), which is the antithesis of a conventional contemporary warfare film in its attempt at observational and experiential authenticity, Billingsley's record includes his camerawork and experience on the astonishing *House of War* (2002, directed by Paul Yule), for which he won the 2002 Rory Peck Award (he was nominated again in 2003 for work on *Virgin Soldiers*), along with a colleague and another team, all of whom filmed events in the Qala i Jangi fortress at Mazar i Sharif in Afghanistan, in November 2001. This includes contact with special forces, the two CIA operatives who were at the fortress, which served as a prison for Taliban and (predominantly) 'foreign fighters' with the Taliban, where one of the CIA men was killed as prisoners revolted, beginning with one who blew himself up, and included US B-52 aircraft dropping a JDAM 2000 pound bomb directly on its own special forces. This sees Billingsley getting the kind of footage never usually found in any actuality war film – dropping to the ground in the open with bullets whizzing overhead, as he and the others with him are caught directly in the crossfire raging from one end of the fortress to the other.[39] Billingsley is unusual, in that he is more or less dedicated to making films related to war and issues of international peace and security as part of a company he co-owns, Combat Films and Research. This focus also makes him a peculiar phenomenon, in that he is a filmmaker, but seeks to make a kind of film that is a form of academic defence and foreign affairs analysis, more than it is journalism, where it is evident, in an almost postmodern consciousness, that:

> Filming and reporting on conflict is subject to its own fog and friction, in just the same way that these concepts dominate understanding

of warfare itself for the military – it is almost impossible ever to grasp the whole picture, let alone to picture the whole battlefield, theatre or war. Just as fog and friction enter into the process of conducting military operations, so they have their place in the process of using moving images to record, portray or interpret warfare and war.[40]

However, while documentaries present opportunities for more careful, detailed and fuller image-based interpretation of armed conflict – as some parts of audiences and publics expect[41] – whether by their nature, as Billingsley's view would support, or by the perspective brought to bear on one side of an argument or another by more polemical filmmakers, they do not, and possibly cannot, do more than refract certain aspects of contemporary conflict as authors. And even though Billingsley, in particular, Woodhead and Reed, as well as other directors in both actuality and fiction, present interesting work which will have some impact over time, and, despite the more developed moving-image narratives they can offer, what they produce will rarely, if ever, have the reach and impact found by television news coverage, even if the latter is fleeting, often soon forgotten without the reinforcement brought by longer format work, and usually of quite limited character. Long-format films reach a wider public than books, but nothing like the size of audience found for television news, which makes that element of the moving-image media the most important in terms of channelling images and issues affecting legitimacy in contemporary warfare.

Rather as the state's complete nature has been altered by contemporary processes of globalisation (whether in terms of communications, economics or politics, values and norms), yet the state remains the single most dominant phenomenon in the political realm, so the position of television news has been changed by those same contemporary processes, yet remains the single most important element in the constellation of communications media reflecting and influencing issues of peace and security. While television could dominate almost completely in the age of a small number of terrestrial analogue broadcasters in the real heyday of television, somewhere between 1950 and 1980, the growth of cable and satellite broadcasting, as well as the digital explosion, changed that position decisively forever. Where once upon a time whole peoples might turn to one particular broadcaster at a moment, the reality since the 1990s has been increasing segmentation into specialised niche broadcasting, and at the same time the multiplication of alternatives within those niches. Thus, where once the whole of America (as a figure of speech) might have tuned into Walter Cronkite on the *CBS Evening News* for 15 or, from the time of the Vietnam War, an expanded 30 minutes, in the early twenty-first century the main evening broadcasts by the major networks have come to face competition not only from other major networks. That new competition comes not only laterally from the increasing number of television channels available, but also in other dimensions from the emergence of 24-hour news channels on television and, increasingly, the range of other media through which information (right or wrong) can be available, notably those using the internet. Despite fragmentation of supply, sources, media and markets, with niche versions of each having increased in importance, in most respects, and certainly in the struggle for legitimacy at the heart of contemporary armed conflict, it still matters who delivers the images and messages that count – whether person or brand.

One of the ways in which it became clearest that who delivered images and messages really counted was the emergence of a new brand – al Jazeera,[42] the Arabic satellite news broadcaster based in Qatar, particularly as it moved to set up al Jazeera International, an English language-based version of the channel. Al Jazeera 'original' made a striking impact around the events of 9/11, rather as international handling of Iraq's invasion of Kuwait in 1990 may be seen to have 'made' the nascent CNN by making its 24-hour news coverage important, because for the first time in its history there were world events of such magnitude that viewers – and crucially other broadcasters who would lift CNN footage and spread the brand through their own coverage – had to pay attention. Similarly, al Jazeera, formed in the wake of the BBC Arabic Service's being closed (after the Saudi-linked venture had broadcast a programme on the number of beheadings in Saudi Arabia), the station is entirely funded by the young Emir of Qatar, creating an interesting potential tension and apparent contradiction between the perceived anti-Americanism of the station and the philo-American tendencies of the Emir himself, granting the US its main base in the Middle East there. Al Jazeera really became a household name in the Western world as a result of its coverage of the attacks on America and the subsequent US-led response.

Al Jazeera made its impact by giving an audience what it wanted. That audience was primarily Arabic, as the language used excluded most others (although the phenomenon of watching al Jazeera just through, or for, the images, is not unusual[43]) and wanted a different perspective on stories. The different ways in which that different perspective was provided included lengthier, more detailed and open presentation of scenes of carnage, revealing the images of human damage and destruction that more traditional Western news broadcasters tended to censor out of their coverage, based on their understanding, or perception, of their primary audience's sensibilities.[44] This approach included screening videos of car bomb suicide operations by indigenous insurgents, or al-Qa'ida in Iraq, against Iraqi government, or Coalition targets in Iraq – although this and the screening of decapitation videos was tempered as a result of US pressure.[45] Another very prominent way in which al Jazeera made a mark was through its openness to exclusive tapes from Usama bin Ladin, or Ayman al Zawahiri, the al-Qa'ida leaders. Like any broadcaster given exclusive access to newsworthy material from important political leaders – especially those, such as these two, whose very emitting of messages was newsworthy in itself (let alone what they actually said), al Jazeera enjoyed its pivotal role in making the news, as what it presented was then re-presented by other broadcasters around the world. This confirmed change and continuity at the same time: al Jazeera was different and making its mark, but the way in which it really made its mark – as with CNN before it – was through marketing of its brand as all the mainstream broadcasters around the world showed its logo and struggled with how to avoid identifying the channel while constantly doing so, one way or another, and needing to do so. It was also a trend that reflected the pro-Islamist, pro-al-Qa'ida tendencies of some (by no means all) of the editorial staff at the channel and which continued even when US pressure led al Jazeera not to broadcast the whole of the videos sent, over time – only those parts that were deemed really to be 'newsworthy' and quotable.

The advent of al Jazeera International was set to build on the brand.[46] It was not evident who its primary target audience would be. While there was much to be said for an English language version to make the original available to non-Arabic-speaking Muslims, it seemed likely that there was a far bigger and more lucrative advertising revenue market to be gained by reaching an international audience that was excited by the differences al Jazeera would bring. The second strategy, in many senses, seemed to be confirmed by the trend of recruiting high-calibre, established Western voices, such as the pioneering Sir David Frost, or a range of well-established journalists from news broadcasters such as BBC World or Sky. It was also confirmed by Nigel Parsons, the British managing director of al Jazeera International, reported as telling a Sunday morning talk show in Australia:

> If you go anywhere in the world and pick up the local newspaper, you have a completely different perspective on what's happening in the world. It's like putting on a different pair of spectacles. [Qatar] is very central. It gives us a 360-degreee view on world events.[47]

As the new boys of al Jazeera became an established part of the international news broadcasting landscape, whatever the Islamist political proclivities of some on the editorial staff, by filling a niche, whether with the Arabic service, or if it took off the English language version, they helped to confirm how much television tended to retain its importance, even in the face of immense change. Just as 24-hour news broadcasting had not removed the linchpin, mainstream news broadcasts as the most important part of the news broadcasting imperium, nor did the arrival of new 24-hour news broadcasters who could compete by filling a gap in the market and bringing the excitement of a new approach – and nor, again, were they ever likely to replace the existing 24-hour news channels. In a very agricultural, evolutionary manner, there could be additions to the news broadcasting landscape.

Other changes share this balance with continuity. For example, while 24-hour news channels added a major dimension to the broadcast environment in which war is conducted, and as a result, phenomena such as rolling and breaking news, whenever there is a major development, this creates a context in which there is often what Nik Gowing has described as 'breaking rumour',[48] where anchors and guests indulge in various forms and levels of speculation, often at length, while waiting for firm information of some description. The guests would be pressured by producers to join the speculative flow, as a respondent in research put it, to 'say something – anything – about it' (in that particular case a refugee convoy that had been shot up and 300 people reported killed, with three two-minute slots in one hour).[49] This pressure is the same, whether the 'guest' involves the 'incestuous' expertise of a journalist colleague of the anchor from the same organisation (an increasing trend[50]), or an outside specialist of some kind, usually an academic, or NGO representative, or outside print journalist. While many academic 'experts' might originally have believed that they played a significant 'public education' role, perhaps sometimes backed by a personal or institutional marketing role,[51] there is a trend towards sober recognition that, although the medium means a large audience is reached on one level, messages almost certainly do not, and cannot (for the most part) get through. There is also recognition all round that a hierarchy exists in the realm of the talking head – government or other prominent political figures will always have priority in the news broadcasters' minds over experts of any kind. While the latter may be used simply to fill a gap in coverage with a talking head, or to provide the crucial 15-second quote to support whatever package a journalist is offering as a report and interpretation of events, or, even, genuinely to elucidate issues, they will always be lower in the news production pecking-order to a politician, even if that politician has nothing really to offer but his or her presence.[52] However, while there have been changes regarding the guests, interlocutors with the anchor, or main presenter, remain a mainstay of television news presentation.

At a time of change, the major American news broadcasters appeared acutely aware of this situation. As providers of news and current affairs to a larger and broader public than any other source in any liberal democracy,[53] ABC, CBS and NBC count in any equation of war and peace representation – their standard audience of 22 to 25 million continued to dwarf CNN's success of 3.3 million viewers per 24 hours in the US in the week of September 11, 2001 (ten times its usual audience), and was, of course, even further outstripped by the 80 million audience that events of that day brought to the main evening news broadcasts of the big three traditional, terrestrial newscasts.[54] Yet, in the same period, they all responded to changes in the marketplace of news and current affairs consumption, as well as undergoing a transformation of the personnel involved in the major evening news bulletins. Curiously, despite the changes in market share and the business side of news corporations, these evening news broadcasts retained central importance as the flag bearers of the brands. After decades of familiarity with the faces of Tom Brokaw, Dan Rather and Peter Jennings, everything changed. And yet, in almost all respects, despite attempts at change, it remained the same in the end – with one notable experiment at CBS excepted, as discussed below.

The main evening broadcasts, with familiar, authoritative and reliable anchors, retained and perhaps even enhanced their relevance through the period of change. In terms of news business, by the start of the twenty-first century there had been a pronounced shift from evening to morning, with the big breakfast shows completely outweighing the other branches of news and current affairs output in terms of revenue – the morning programmes generate around three-quarters of the news divisions' profits.[55] Although Bryant Gumbel – whose brave but mixed attempts to handle September 11 live for CBS were discussed in Chapter 4 – had a background in sports reporting, rather than central issues of politics and security, he was not typical. Rather, some of the most serious, hard-nosed broadcast journalists, such as Charles Gibson at ABC, were the breakfast show hosts, mixing news with cute entertainment pieces. Gibson's performance on 9/11 was sterling, fast on to the real thread of story and event, drawing on the qualities shared by the really strong anchor anywhere in any organisation, whether at ABC, CBS, NBC, CNN, the BBC, Sky, al Jazeera or any similar news broadcaster, and irrespective of whether the broadcast is breakfast, evening or middle of the night. Brian Williams, the first 'postmodern anchor' – the first of the new generation to succeed the Vietnam generation (in his case, Tom Brokaw at NBC), presenting in the new environment of diversified sources and means of gaining 'news' – explains in the following terms, to journalism students, the requirements for the role, including rehearsing for pieces that might never need to be broadcast:

> Those of you in this to do what I'm doing make sure, if called upon, you can join me here at the front of the class and give me 30 minutes on the Supreme Court, the current justices, President Ford, President Reagan, the Pope. Because that is what you mentally have to drill for: the time when there is no such thing at a TelePrompTer.... You have to be responsible for the network.... That's when you get measured.[56]

These qualities are what make the major news anchors anywhere important, especially in the representation of war, perhaps the most acute of all events. It is these personalities who carry authority, who are perceived to provide sense and stability in troubled times. They are understood to play a central role in communicating the most important matters, making them clear, indicating in which directions to think (while never quite succumbing to overt political comment), and reassuring their publics in times of disaster. These are iconic foci of trust everywhere, but in American households above all.

## Dropping and weighing anchors: continuity and change in network news

Despite the wonderful puppet caricature of Peter Jennings in Matt Stone and Trey Parker's outrageous but hilarious insight into American and contemporary international security, *Team America: World Police*,[57] where the puppet Jennings presents *World Evening News*, a parody of ABC's *World News Tonight with Peter Jennings*,[58] which sees Jennings as a mouthpiece for strong 'left' liberal direction in reporting (a tendency that surely was there, but was always couched in strong professional ethics regarding standards of reporting), the reality was that Jennings had the trust of his viewers for the most part, and the respect of others. The same was true for his competitors, Tom Brokaw at NBC and Dan Rather at CBS. However, Jennings' illness and death forced change at ABC News, following Brokaw's decision to retire. Brokaw, the legendary presenter who gave America the notion of its 'Great Generation' as he diversified from news anchoring to televisual and written interpretation of the US, moved on to other things. By contrast, Rather's exit as anchor of the *CBS Evening News* was painful, couched in a loss of trust among colleagues and, it may be presumed, the audience.

The changing of the guard at the *CBS Evening News* was not an easy matter. In the wake of Rather's departure under a cloud, celebrations of CBS' proud record as perhaps the 'gold standard' of broadcast news in the US left him out. They pointed to the tradition of Edward R. Murrow, whose work during the Second World War and in the 1950s is regarded as the touchstone of excellence, and whose professional independence was celebrated by George Clooney in his film *Good Night, and Good Luck*, and Walter Cronkite, anchor through the 1960s during the Kennedy assassination and the Vietnam War, whose authority is recognised, albeit ironically, in the wider cultural sphere by a reference in Bob Dylan's *Hurricane*, a long song about a case of injustice. Only a short time before, Rather, Cronkite's heir, would have been included in that same company. However, his enthusiasm to broadcast a story intended to undermine President George W. Bush, in an election year, by claiming that his National Guard service record had been forged, led to his fall from grace. The story was false. This was a major error of judgement, as he was forced to admit when he stepped down as senior editor and presenter of the *CBS Evening News* a few months later. Although he was supposed to continue being involved, in particular, making reports for the current affairs slot *60 Minutes*, it seemed that CBS News and Rather could not identify, or satisfactorily produce, reports for broadcast. After 40 years, Rather drifted out of the CBS orbit he had dominated for most of that period, eventually severing ties completely in June 2006, with Bob Schieffer paying tribute that was respectful but far from fulsome and in a past tense that ran counter to the indication that Rather would 'keep working'.[59]

CBS News showed a marked upturn in the wake of Rather's departure. Elder statesman Bob Schieffer, the corporation's long-time Washington correspondent and host of *Face the Nation*, took the anchor role on an interim basis. His gentle southern style, serious but avuncular, was clearly a winner, with audiences turning to his broadcasts in increasing numbers. The sometimes pompous editorial statements made by Rather gave way to a gentle, friendly smile and a wry twinkle in the eye, while maintaining the strong clear sense of enquiry and explanation that had made Schieffer a tough-but-polite inquisitor of politicians on Sunday mornings, a role to which he returned when he finished an 18-month stint as anchor. After returning to normal duties he continued to be a face on the *CBS Evening News*, not only as its Washington correspondent, but also as a weekly commentator in a new nightly slot called 'Free Speech', where the nice old man could show lucid, hard-hitting insight and judgement, telling people how to think about a topic, such as moral turpitude in a US Congress that had lost its way, far more effectively, for those viewing, than Rather's stentorian tones probably ever did.

Schieffer was a holding-pattern appointment which bypassed Rather's heir-apparent, the excellent John Roberts, who presented the Sunday evening newscast, as well as serving as Chief White House Correspondent and regularly as the stand-in for Rather, anchoring on weekdays, or flying off to an emergency scene, such as to London in the wake of the transport bombings in July 2005. Clearly insulted by the corporation's decision, Roberts, who otherwise probably should have had the appointment, took his good looks and talents to CNN. Schieffer's appointment was not only about holding things together until a more permanent face to present the news emerged, but also about offering stability, putting business into a safe and older pair of hands. This was necessary to restore credibility at CBS. Turning to an older and safer pair of hands is also what happened at ABC, where eventually, after a different kind of interregnum, the impeccable Charles Gibson finally became Senior Editor and anchor of *World News Tonight*, which became simply *World News* under his oversight only a few weeks after he had taken control of the reins.

In the middle of this change in the figures and faces of authority who would tell millions of viewers about how to understand what was happening in their world, radical changes were being explored[60] with youth and gender key issues. When Schieffer ended his temporary duty, he handed over to Katie Couric formally, the first sole, full-time female anchor. However, when the announcement of her appointment was made, as she told viewers at NBC's *Today* that she would be leaving, it was Elizabeth Vargas who reported it as anchor on ABC's *World News Tonight*, notably welcoming Couric, although a 'competitor', to the groundbreaking world of the female anchor.[61] Vargas had become de facto anchor at ABC, although formally hers was a twinning arrangement with her colleague Bob Woodruff. However, early in this code-sharing arrangement, Woodruff was badly injured in Iraq, leaving Vargas to do the job on her own. The two of them had jointly announced their new approach during the 5 December 2005 bulletin, that it would take effect from January, and that the two of them felt 'enormous excitement and a profound sense of responsibility' where they would have to 'preserve the traditions and standards' that viewers could trust and which would 'make Peter proud'. They also said that the broadcast would be evolving, with a separate live West Coast broadcast, a webcast every afternoon and an emphasis on news online all day, but most of all with their arrangement, 'more often than not one of us will be on the road', where they would 'take some chances'. Less than a month into the new role, Woodruff, clearly taking a chance, was knocked out of action by a roadside bomb (see below).

The dual-headed compact at ABC had already started during the many months where the two of them had been the mainstay stand-ins for the dying Peter Jennings, supplemented by Gibson and occasionally others. Officially, Vargas gave up the sole anchor position because she was taking maternity leave to have a second child. However, the issue of her returning to anchor the evening news did not appear even to be considered by ABC management. Instead she was to return to her previous role on the current affairs broadcast *20/20*, after completing maternity leave. This was a disappointment not only for her fans – of which there surely were many going-on middle-aged men, who not only appreciated her intelligence and insight, but also a warm smile and nice-looking face – but for anyone seeking to break the solid, older male mould of broadcast news in the US, in a way similar to that which had occurred in other countries, such as the UK, twenty or more years before – albeit with the crucial difference that the anchors in the US were also senior editors, making the final decisions on what was in the bulletin and how it would be treated, as opposed to British counterparts, where editorial and presentational roles are quite discrete.[62] This makes the US anchor most important and more authoritative. Nonetheless, on one level Vargas had been a breath of fresh air. On another, however, it appeared that neither the younger faces and two-header approach, nor Vargas on her own – albeit always having to sign off 'for Bob Woodruff' as well – satisfied ABC's audience, which dropped away in the post-Jennings era. In part, no doubt, this fall in viewers was explained by the growth in CBS's share of the public, as well as NBC's relatively stronger position, having managed the transition earlier and perhaps better than their competitors, by appointing Brian Williams as anchor of *Nightly News*. Williams had captured at once the image of someone mature and authoritative, but also younger, who connected with the younger members of the evening news-watching audience. Williams came particularly into his own by reporting from inside the New Orleans

Superdome throughout the Hurricane Katrina crisis and by staying in New Orleans for the follow-up after others had begun to move on – also leading to a personal documentary, 'In His Own Words: Brian Williams on Hurricane Katrina'. This carried the same emotional attachment and connection at a human level to individuals who had suffered greatly with which he had covered the disaster, and which characterised his shift from breadth to depth as a newsperson, connecting him strongly with the audience and making his NBC broadcast 'Number 1'.[63]

The real test of change was the *CBS Evening News*, however, where the appointment of Couric was simultaneously radical and apparently safe. It was safe because, over 14 years of presenting the *Today* programme at NBC, she had become one of the most popular figures on American television, reportedly paid $21 million to co-host *Today* alongside Matt Lauer, as well as a person of some influence.[64] Thus, CBS seemed to be backing a winner, a familiar, friendly face, with some authority. However, NBC's long-time position as 'Number 1' in the mornings had been coming under threat, as ABC's *Good Morning America*, fronted by Gibson and Diane Sawyer, had been catching up over recent years, since that pairing had been put in place, initially as a three-month interim step, bringing a faster and, in the first half-hour of the programme, at least, a harder news line. *Today*'s losing ground was attributed to Couric's loss of popularity, whether caused by over-familiarity and her fatigue with the role (she indicated an interest in finding a new role, having become weary, after 14 years in the role at NBC, and needing to refresh herself professionally), or changing attitudes with reports of her income and whispers alleging prima donna attitudes towards her colleagues. However, the CBS anchor role was a potential way of regenerating Couric and her career, taking into account that she was still enormously popular and trusted – a vital aspect for CBS in the wake of Rather's demise, and the work Schieffer had done to restore trust after that dark period – a point he noted when signing off from his last day as anchor, as a prelude to introducing Couric as his successor.[65] The bigger test, following Vargas' transfer from anchor to her old role in current affairs, via maternity leave, was whether the mass audience for mainstream evening news, as the main vehicle for communicating the major political and social information of the day, would positively embrace Couric as indefinite anchor. Would the trust she had built up with morning audiences at NBC translate to the evening at CBS? The real issue was whether a still relatively conservative public would accept a woman as the focal conduit for stories of war and peace from around the world, as well as hard stories from the American homeland. And beyond this there was a further major issue – if they were to accept Couric in that kind of role, would her personality have an influence on how events were presented, and so, possibly, over time, on the shaping of legitimacy in war and politics?

Whether or not Couric proved successful, personalities continued to play a vital role in framing news coverage of war and peace. This was true regarding reporting from the field, where the proximity created by having a personality present, face to camera, was a crucial image linking the audience with the scene (whatever and wherever it was) – especially if that face were experienced and recognisable, but also if it were clear and authoritative, and carrying the stamp of credibility offered by major news channels. However, the quest for proximity in an increasingly insecure and volatile environment for journalists meant far greater risks than perhaps ever before for journalists. In part, this was simply because covering certain stories would mean going where it was risky; in part, it was because, one way or another, as images and the media conveying them became the most important instruments in war, the messengers became protagonists, willingly or otherwise, in a way they never had been before. Journalists were part of any conflict and were vulnerable from either side in it, as ITN's Terry Lloyd's family and colleagues discovered when he and two out of three members of an independent, non-embedded news team were killed, as they rode, unidentified into Iraq's controlled territory, ahead of the Coalition front line during the 2003 advance into Iraq.[66] Three years later, over 80 journalists had been killed. Reporters were seen increasingly as actual, or potential, tools of the enemy: if they were not actually fully under the control of Side A, they were still regarded as enemies of Side B, if, for example, embedded with Side A; and if they were not embedded with Side A, they risked being perceived as attached to, or associated with, Side B, and, therefore, regarded as targets by Side A.

The importance and dangers of presenting personal material from the front line (not that there was necessarily ever a front line, as such, in contemporary warfare) were exemplified by Woodruff's experience and that of CBS's Kimberley Dozier, both very seriously, initially critically, wounded, while reporting from Iraq, and the teams deployed with them. On 29 January 2006, ABC's recently appointed co-anchor Bob Woodruff and his cameraman Doug Vogt were critically wounded while filming for a report from Iraq. The Iraqi military armoured vehicle in which they were travelling was struck by a roadside Improvised Explosive Device (IED). In covering this incident, CBS correspondent Elizabeth Palmer described Iraq as 'the most dangerous place on Earth' for journalists, citing 60 dead there since the US-led operations began in 2003. The *CBS Evening News* followed Palmer's report on Woodruff and his cameraman from Baghdad with a studio to-camera package by Lara Logan, recently returned from Iraq, who led the package with dramatic images of when she and her crew ran into two mines while reporting from Afghanistan in 2004, where she was attached to the US army's 10th Mountain Brigade – confirming that the images were what counted, especially if they involved the journalist personally. Interestingly, the subsequent package reported on the death-toll – US and Iraqi civilian – since 2003, ending by speculating on how the serious injury to a well-known anchor might bring a focus on death in Iraq and possibly have some effect on President Bush's impending State of the Union Address. The answer to this media-centric question was 'none' – and the same was true when CBS's own Kimberly Dozier followed the Woodruff precedent and was initially in a critical condition after an incident in Iraq, when, on 29 May 2006, Memorial Day in the US, she and her CBS crew were caught by a car bomb, along with the military unit they were accompanying. This resulted in the deaths of a soldier, an Iraqi interpreter and two members of the CBS crew, Paul Douglas and James Brolan (cameraman and soundman, respectively, and both British), as well as critical injuries to CBS correspondent Dozier and six troops. Despite the relative lack of impact of these stories themselves, which were subject to updates from time to time as part of the evening news broadcasts, broadcast news organisations continued to seek personal, to-camera, coverage from as close to the action as possible, because the mixture of proximity to events and authority provided were vital both to providing the images craved by the medium and reinforcing the role played by television news in relation to legitimacy.

The nature of moving-image media, coupled with patterns of human interest and experience, were such that some issues will always compete weakly with others. While these media played important roles in shaping legitimacy in contemporary international security, the way in which they operated meant that certain factors, in addition to the structure of narrative image and human experience explored in earlier chapters, were also important for understanding. One of these was that certain regions, such as the whole continent of Africa, would register less than, say, the Middle East, even with the most striking images, for Western broadcast news and their audiences, as shown above – irrespective of the particular branch of the media in question. A further factor was that television news retains the dominant position among moving-image media in terms of reach and potential impact in the contest for legitimacy in war, with the traditional, mainstream broadcasters carrying overwhelmingly more weight than dedicated 24-hour satellite or cable news channels. However, the 24-hour news channels, as well as the various other new media resulting from the digital revolution, all played important roles, particularly in moments of great crisis and security-salient events. Traditional terrestrial television news remained the most important element in the broadcast news media arena, but locked into interaction with other media, where a blog could set a hare running for the major news organisations, or a digital mobile telephone photograph could document a terrorist attack, or important minor broadcasters could be the source of material reproduced throughout the moving-image spectrum, with al Jazeera, for example, having material picked up by all the other broadcasters. The traditional broadcasters remained vital because they retained confidence, even where there were problems, as at CBS News. In addition, even where the importance of mainstream television news was not what it once was, developments made clear that trust and authority still rested with personalities, whether the 'authors' were directors of long-format work, whether fiction or factual, or the presenters and reporters of the daily news, and how they played their part. Reporters were ever more vulnerable in the line of fire as they sought to make all-important reports with personal authority from the field, giving publics proximity, and anchors, as authors, remained mainstays and guides over how to interpret images and other information, above all in the US. These were the elements, in addition to the major aspects of image and experience identified throughout this volume, that fashioned legitimacy in early twenty-first-century armed conflict.

# 7 Image and experience
## Legitimacy and contemporary war

The bulk of this book has been concerned with the nature, or character, of moving-image media, dependent on pictures themselves in the first instance, and human experience, as determinants of content and meaning. This final chapter, as well as drawing together the remainder of the book, first returns to the intellectual space of the contemporary battle-field. Having examined the nature of images as weapons in the moving-image environment in the earlier parts of the book, this chapter explores more fully the nature of contemporary armed conflict, as well as the notion of legitimacy as success, and introduces the key concept of the Multidimensional Trinity Cubed-Plus, and situates the role of images as weapons in this context. The chapter has three sections: the first examines the interaction of contemporary conflict, legitimacy and strategic success; the second section examines the kinetic force aspects of moving images and identifies principles of strategic image containment, suppression and domination; the final section provides the conclusion to the book as a whole, drawing together the different elements it incorporates, adding reflection and confirming our thesis that images are the key weapons in contemporary warfare, because success in contemporary warfare depends on legitimacy in the context of the _**Trinity³(+)**_, and images are the most salient instruments that affect that _**Trinity³(+)**_.[1]

## Contemporary conflict, legitimacy and strategic success

The character and qualities of contemporary armed conflict differ from those of traditional, conventional warfare – although in some respects, as we note below, there are aspects which do not change as such, only in their specific manifestations. The character of contemporary warfare means that conventional warfare between the regular armed forces of states has given way to a range of other factors, among which, for current purposes (given lack of space), the most important may be derived from Rupert Smith's analysis: contemporary warfare is fought not for victory but to create political or strategic conditions, non-state actors are strongly present, and the key to war is the struggle for the will of 'the people', because war is fought among the people.[2] Of course, this was always the case, in one sense or another: as Philip Bobbitt has argued with impeccable insight, law, or legitimacy, and strategy have always been two sides of the victory coin – law is always invoked to confirm military success, while armed force is needed to enforce legal claim, historically. In the contemporary context, even more obviously than in the past, legitimacy is the key to success. However, legitimacy, in the era of contemporary warfare, is affected by the problem of multiple constituencies, which used to be limited to counter-insurgency, but is now the outstanding feature of postmodern war.[3]

The multidimensional character of the type of operation under discussion means that it is important to consider the ways in which an appropriate force might be put together and, in the process of putting it together, how it could be made successful. The key to understanding questions of success is the concept of legitimacy. However, understanding the relevance of legitimacy to all such operations depends on recognising that they are carried out at the strategic level.[4] Operations always involve and affect strategic initiative on the part of those who decide to deploy the forces. Critically, once deployed, however, the force must ensure legitimacy. This is a process of diverse elements, many exterior to the force deployed, of which two factors are vital: the military culture of the forces deployed and the degree to which the force (particularly its political and military chiefs) can seize the strategic initiative at what we identify as 'defining moments'.

This approach is central to contemporary warfare, where major set-piece battles between major armed forces have less relevance than once they did – although this does not mean that they became irrelevant. The military operational environment has become one in which the application of kinetic force to destroy has been supplanted by a greater need for guile in using force to effect. Whereas warfare was principally characterised by the creation of armed force for total war, where the objective was to overcome the enemy by applying a greater wealth of force at the opponent's centre of gravity, in the age from Napoleon to the Cold War (where the advent of nuclear weapons began to alter the paradigm), by the early twenty-first century that had changed. Instead of seeking to destroy the enemy by bringing greater amounts of force to bear, the aim became the establishment of a set of conditions. The purpose became achievement of a quality, rather than objective, physical demand. William S. Lind, and then Thomas G. Hammes, described this shift as 'Fourth Generation Warfare', while Lawrence Freedman, as noted in Chapter 1, has written of the *Transformation of Strategic Affairs*, where winning is about narrative, not sheer brute force.[5] The theorists of contemporary warfare, from a mainly American perspective, have focused on the ways in which the most advanced technical developments coupled with an understanding of the cultural aspects of warfare meant that the accumulation of effects, in a diverse and network-oriented environment, to cause an enemy to collapse, rather than the use of decisive battle to overthrow that opponent, had become the business of soldiers.[6] The sum of this was effects-based warfare, in which the message was as important as the missile – only if the missile sent the right signal did it serve its purpose.

The interaction of meaning and message recalls Freedman's discussion of 'strategic narratives' in the Introduction. In the words of one former US Assistant Secretary for Defense and highly influential intellectual figure, Joseph P. Nye: 'It is not whose army wins, but whose story wins.'[7] Speaking in the context of the US Global War on Terror, Nye pointed out that the 'greatest communications place in history' had been 'outmanoeuvred by guys in caves'. This was a reference to the way in which UBL was successful in getting messages across, using al Jazeera in particular. However, the narratives put forward by al-Qa'ida could be countered, he maintained. The story could be the UNDP report on Arab human development, bringing a positive (though not entirely newsworthy, we would point out) message of international relations that would contrast with the al-Qa'ida appeal to Arab senses of disenfranchisement. In this context, Nye welcomed the US Administration's shift towards using 'soft power' complements to the employment of armed force,[8] noting that the public diplomacy budget bad been hiked enormously from $150 million to $25 billion – but noting that these figures were mere fractions of the defence budgets, indicating that the balance of effort in seeking effect was misplaced. Certainly, this confirmed that the simple metric of victory favoured by US Defense Secretary Donald Rumsfeld – killing more al-Qa'ida personnel and their affiliates than UBL and his followers were able to recruit (and supported, to some extent, by Nye) – was not the true measure of success in contemporary conflict. Certainly, it did not appear that the numbers killed over the number recruited was either working, on its own terms, or the right configuration for legitimacy in either Iraq or the broader Global War on Terror where, on both counts, images threw up critical challenges to legitimacy.

The interpretation of action became more important than the action itself. This combined with a number of other elements to give warfare a new character. The key elements of this new age of warfare were summarised by Rupert Smith in his excellent attempt to come to terms with the issues of using force in what he prefers to call 'war among the people'. The six features he identifies are:

- The ends of war are changing from pursuit of outright victory to the creation of particular sets of conditions in particular situations.
- The fighting occurs among the people, a trend that had been developing throughout a 150- to 170-year period up until the Second World War and after – warfare is no longer about regular armies engaging on set battlefields on behalf of states, but warfare and

attached politics that goes among the people, whether guerrilla or insurgent irregular forces, is the issue, or the impact on civilian, or non-combatant populations, where distinctions blur, as winning means more than securing victory in battle.

- Conflicts are timeless – because of the changing ends, because of the way in which war is conducted among the people without the possibility of a clear-cut victory, it is impossible to be sure how long an engagement will take; there is no chance of making a commitment and saying that 'we will do this for six months', as many missions will be almost interminable.

- From a Western perspective, the means for conducting warfare, in particular, the people who do it are so valuable, given the time and money it takes to recruit them, to train them and, even more, to retain them, that a priority for Western sides is not to lose the force itself; there is a reluctance – in contrast to a different type of conflict where direct survival were at stake, perhaps, and so there would be greater preparedness to make sacrifices – to incur losses while undertaking complex operations to achieve malleable conditions.

- Old weapons are used for new means – a form of adaptation that has always occurred, no doubt, given that adaptability is at the heart of the successful conduct of warfare; however, there is a far greater degree of adaptation involved as the so-called Clausewitzian model of machine war is necessarily adapted to the conflicts among the people of the contemporary era.

- Almost universally, conflict involves non-state actors; this does not mean that no states or state actors are involved at all; it simply notes that there is a variety of non-state actors present and active at the heart of conflicts. Non-state actors can mean the alliances, coalitions and partnerships, including the United Nations, through which most states work alongside others when deployments of armed forces are made, certainly in the Western context that concerns Smith, where armed forces are usually working with those of other states. In this context the focus of clear political control is lost, meaning that clear political purpose and clear political perspectives are harder to identify and sustain. The environment in which that type of force is engaging is also one where there are non-state actors of a different order. That context is very often one of internal conflict, or mixed internal and international conflicts, or one where the actors have a transnational character, such as al-Qa'ida. Non-state actors can also mean that the transnational, or sub-state entity (or community) actors are involved in hostilities against each other, the forces of a state, or the joint forces involving the militaries of more than one state.[9]

Each of these alone, and, above all, all of them taken together, means that the character of warfare is different and the demands on the general have changed in line with this. Each decision on action is to be taken with reference to multiple constituencies.[10] This contrasts with the clarity of the one-time situation where the commander in the field used the armed forces of the state to which they owe allegiance in pursuit of that state's political aims alone against an equal actor of similar composition. In the contemporary era the opponent is rarely, if ever a state, and even where the opponent is formally a state, such as in the cases of Western engagement against Serbia or Iraq, the emphasis is on separating the ruling elite, as the real enemies, from their populations, who are largely interpreted as victims, or prisoners, or their misguided leaders. Hence, the focus on winning 'hearts and minds'. But, winning 'hearts and minds' in that constituency is not enough; decisions have to be gauged against the perspectives of partners and allies with whom the commander is acting, as well as their divided domestic publics, and, indeed, those of the commander's own political leaders and society. In addition to all of this, there is the 'public gallery' of international public opinion, divided at different levels between the political, the security and the popular, which can have an influence on action, whether by restraining it through influence, explicit or implicit, or through perception and interpretation of it afterwards. The bar for success is set high in the context of contemporary warfare, yet the chances of something's being seen to have gone wrong are great.

All of this can be related to the famous Clausewitzian 'trinity'.[11] Clausewitz's secondary trinity of government, armed forces and people retains its relevance,[12] despite its being declared to be past its use-by date, giving rise to the erroneous notion of 'post-Clausewitzian'. With only slight modification, the essential character of the 'trinity' is linked to the importance of legitimacy and of hearts and minds in contemporary war. Martin van Creveld was perhaps the first to consign Clausewitz to the waste heap in an important study, *On Future War*, published in 1991[13] – bravely referencing the title of Clausewitz's classic study. This was a forward-looking study which, although it used the smoke and mirrors of style and structure to make its case in some respects, nonetheless had real merit. Creveld declared that Clausewitzian warfare had gone and that the trinity no longer applied. However, he was wrong. While he was correct in identifying, along with others, that the kind of traditional, direct, state-against-state warfare that had been the mainstay of nineteenth- and twentieth-century thinking was unlikely to be of great relevance, he was wrong to infer that this meant that Clausewitz's principles no longer held force. In fact, they had become increasingly relevant. If the 'hearts and minds' question is considered, it may well be that conventional states with their conventional armed forces are the only, or possibly even the dominant, actors. But the trinity still operates in every single situation: political leaders, an armed element and communities.

But, far more important than the mere continuing relevance of the trinity is its factorial expansion and, so, increased significance. In this era, there is a multidimensional trinity. Clausewitz had in mind the government, the military and the people at home. This was a simple trinity, reflecting key aspects of nineteenth-century statehood. In the twenty-first century, a more complex, Multidimensional Trinity Cubed-Plus operates – expressed as a formula, the Multidimensional ***Trinity³(+)***. First, there is the home front in each case, comprising political leaders, armed forces and people. Second, each aspect of the opponent's triangle of political leaders, armed forces and people needs to be influenced, as well as all of them at the same time. Third, there are multiple global audiences, all being subject to the same information and images, all affecting the environment in which a strategic campaign is going to be conducted.

As Smith correctly asserts, the battle for 'hearts and minds' has gone from being a support activity to military operations to being their central purpose.[14] The key aspect of contemporary warfare is the battle of wills – or rather, we should refine Smith's analysis (which refreshes Clausewitz's), and identify the heart of twenty-first-century conflict as conducting simultaneous multiple battles for multiple wills. The messengers of moving-image media are the main forum, though not the only one, for conducting that battle, and messages – or rather more pertinently – images are the most important instruments in the battle, which is a competition for legitimacy.

In the battle for legitimacy in modern war, the bad outweighs the good – and bad things will always happen. It has been clear from Russell's reports from the Crimea onward that something is always likely to go wrong and so it is essential to avoid it, as far as possible, by ensuring the greatest degree of competent and proper behaviour, and to be ready to acknowledge and deal with it, when, as has happened so often in history, it emerges.[15] Bad things have always happened in the context of expeditionary, or counter-insurgency, missions. This may reflect a lack of appropriate education and preparation in staff colleges and academies, and failing to learn the general lesson from history, to some extent – yet it is also an indication that such things may be expected to occur, come what may, when operations are sensitive and complex. But, in noting this, it is also important to establish an appropriate perspective. The impression that can emerge is that bad or incompetent behaviour is the norm, whereas it is almost always an exception.[16] But as an exception, it becomes especially important and defining in liberal democracies, where the principle of abiding by, and operating within, the law creates greater vulnerability.

Similarly, in the context of contemporary armed conflict, this becomes magnified and multiplied factorially by the numerous environments in which images and issues circulate and have impact, including utilisation by those who would have fewer qualms concerning lawfulness, but who can use a liberal democratic country's fundamental commitment to the rule of law against it. Diverse communities, with embedded belief systems, are much the same: they have positions, and these are not generally changed by information presented by officials, or on television news, as audience research shows.[17] They either acknowledge something by agreeing or disagreeing, depending on the degree to which it fits their belief and value patterns, or, if it does not coincide with those patterns, they ignore what is presented, switching television channels or switching off. There are few things which cut through and get people to change their minds. The image of the Twin Towers in New York was one of these, which appeared, at least temporarily, to cut through because it was so unusual and people did not know what to do. The difficulty is that, while each negative case is only one drop in the ocean, that drop contains a poison, or plutonium, perhaps, that pollutes the whole ocean.

Legitimacy lies at the heart of success in war. The negative drops of image poison affect the legitimacy of contemporary military operations. Destructive brute force, to a considerable extent, might be able to secure victory in warfare through combat – and, indeed, might lead to the control of territory and the physical subjugation of the people on that territory, but success in the modern world is only possible with legitimacy. That is, the complex of socio-political elements that permit those conducting armed forces operations for political purpose to ensure support in whichever population groups might be necessary for the military action.

Legitimacy is a compound concept.[18] It is a quality or phenomenon. It is the result of processes of legitimation, or legitimisation. There are three elements in the compound: bases, performance and support. The bases comprise rules, norms, laws and statements. They can be explicit and stated, or they can be implicit and unstated, and they can be self-ascribed, or ascribed by others. The bases of legitimacy are not only an actor's own beliefs, but those of others – what they believe that actor is doing, or should be doing. Legitimacy is also about performance. Very often, weak, obscure or even doubted bases for legitimacy can be overcome simply by good performance, just as good bases – people believing that something is being done for the right reason – can mitigate poor performance. But neither of those things can go on forever if the other is too severely compromised, and both of them relate to support – the third element in the compound.

While legitimacy is a positive quality, it is not something that is easy to gauge positively.[19] Efforts to gauge it positively suffer from difficulties, such as transience; if the measure of opinion, especially based on polling data, or 'the difficulty of inferring value beliefs',[20] or the problems of identifying consent in complex societies – how broad or deep must this be to register as legitimacy? Where legitimacy can really be identified is in the face of critical challenges. 'At best', it has been correctly suggested, it is possible to 'sense the lack of legitimacy', rather than to struggle positively to affirm it.[21] The issue of legitimacy is really measured by its absence. When legitimacy becomes a question – that is, when there is a legitimacy crisis – then the concept can clearly be identified. In the quasi-medical, quasi-Marxist terms of Jürgen Habermas, the test of legitimacy lies in crisis – the critical challenge, equivalent to the *crise de coeur* of a heart attack, and the strength to withstand that kind of shock and continue, especially with vigour.[22] The ability to withstand is the test of legitimacy.

The discussion surrounding the legitimacy of military engagement and its intensity, therefore, constitutes the measure of how far legitimacy is being questioned. This makes television news, in particular, and cognate media, paramount. Television news' concentration on a topic may be taken as indicative of a salient challenge to legitimacy if the critical approach is adopted. These will not be the only forums in which issues of success and failure or legitimacy will be played out or determined. But in the Western world and most of the rest of it, moving-image media, where television news and film dominate, but also cyber-technology, including digital telephonic vision, will be the principal and key facet in most cases, most of the time. Legitimacy is a function of the interaction of political, legal and strategic elements. All of these will be the focus for the discussion that surrounds events. But it is the images that are going to define and cut through all detail. Where the *jus ad bellum* is questioned, conduct and the *jus in bello* are going to be all the more fragile. This means that legitimacy, overall, is going to be more fragile. That is going to be the case, inevitably, in just about any military operation, or any military-political mission in the twenty-first century. There is unlikely to be any kind of old-fashioned, clear-cut situation.

The television coverage around the globe of the prison abuse at Abu Ghraib, fuelled by outrageous pictures, provides an excellent example of the way in which the intensity and density of television news coverage of a topic confirms and constitutes a critical legitimacy challenge. Not only did that initial coverage raise major questions of legitimacy, but also the longer term, continuing salience of the images, and the accusations of abuse, was evident in the ways in which both political discourse and that within news media continued with the scandal as a major theme, while Western casualties, including fatalities, could be deliberately attributed to the scandal itself, or one of the other incidents of alleged abuse that emerged, such as that involving the Queen's Lancashire Regiment in the UK.[23] The direct link between the publication of pictures of alleged atrocities also applied to the fake pictures of British soldiers supposedly committing abusive acts, which were shown initially by the *Daily Mirror* newspaper in Britain, which was duped into paying for them, and whose editor, Piers Morgan, had to leave over the issue.[24] These negative instances of critical legitimacy challenges confirm the power of images to harm, as well as the capacities of broadcast media (interacting with other media, of course) to impede the prospects of success in warfare, with the images operating across a multidimensional spectrum and affecting attitudes at home, internationally and, crucially, wherever the operations themselves are taking place. Broadcast media provide the delivery mechanism for these weapons, whether inadvertent instances of what might be termed 'friendly film-fire' (such as the self-inflicted damage of bad behaviour and capturing pictures of it at Abu Ghraib), or deliberate cases of image delivery, such as those of the US Rangers' corpses being dragged around Mogadishu in October 1992. They also offer the forum in which the impact resonates and can be identified, as the effect of the images is amplified by repetition, political development in different forums and cultural embedding.

The *Trinity³(+)*, therefore, has particular relevance to images. It is necessary to be aware of the multiple audiences and of the way they spread in international public environments. Crucially, there is a need to be aware of transnational communities – something that is a relatively important and a relatively recent factor, cutting across the boundaries of conventional states, and leading to a whole range of other problems. It is also even more important than ever to be aware that media has always been a plural noun, despite the way in which it is often used. In that context, images are the simplifying element of accessibility that cuts through everything else. No amount of discussion and no amount of explanation is ever going to make up for the presence, or absence, of an image. Although they are unguided missiles, uncontrollable rockets, images constitute the key weapon in contemporary armed conflict. Images certainly constitute the key to legitimacy if there is concern to avoid legitimacy crises. In the end, both at local levels and in international arenas, contested legitimacy becomes the key feature of contemporary armed struggles.

## Kinetic images, kinetic force: image environment domination, containment and suppression

Moving images are, by definition, kinetic. Their narrative structuring is certainly kinetic. This inherent kinesis is not equivalent to the destructive kinetic force available through detonative power. But there is a parallel kinetic effect of this kinetic weapon where the different dimensions of the *Trinity³(+)* are at stake and there is a need to protect against losing legitimacy through negative effects, if not to promote and extend it through positive ones. The kinetic force of film is strong and potentially decisive. The images alone will not necessarily be enough and will likely have narrative or other complements, but they are necessary in striking decisive blows. The images of emaciated Muslim prisoners at Bosnian Serb camp wires, captured by ITN journalists and spread around the world in various types of news media, determined the balance of legitimacy in contemporary warfare. Indeed, the detonative kinesis of conventional military means – bullets, shells, rockets and so forth – can easily be outweighed by the figurative kinesis of moving images. While images will never blow up a bridge or kill a soldier themselves, in the wider context of war in the modern world, they are often more powerful weapons, able to do more harm than consistent, conventionally accomplished victories on the battlefield.

The importance of moving images may be seen in the Yugoslav War of the 1990s, where they formed part of strategic media management by parties to the conflict, as well as inadvertently serving to affect legitimacy.[25] First, as noted earlier in Chapter 4, Slovenia had an integrated military-media strategy geared towards provoking incidents, which could be captured for television news and broadcast around the world to great effect. The Slovenes had established a major media centre in the capital Ljubljana in order to ensure clear direction and flows of information, including images. Former Deputy Defence Minister and at that time Minister for Information Jelko Kacin would inform reporters and cameramen about events which, without lying, did not constitute the whole truth; for example, he would point them to a burned-out armoured vehicle, which his audience then assumed to be the result of anti-armour rocket success, rather than children having set alight an abandoned vehicle – the image of success created, nonetheless, was powerful. Perhaps the greatest moving image coup came in the first hot incident of the conflict in Slovenia, on 27 June 1991, where a Yugoslav military helicopter carrying bread to troops was shot down over the capital Ljubljana, as the Slovenes had threatened, and the Yugoslav army, not believing the Slovenes would deliver on their threats, sought to resupply troops and call Slovenia's bluff at the same time. The incident was perfectly timed, however. The images of the downed helicopter, along with others that Slovenia provoked within those few hours of tanks knocking buses out of their way, made the headlines and the opening scenes of the main evening news bulletins across Europe. There was little time for anyone to check close detail, and the reality was that the Yugoslav military, with its pro-Serbian tendencies, was crushing cars and overturning buses, as well as opening fire with tank canons, in Slovenia in particular, and Croatia. The images were decisive, the die was cast and from the very outset, Belgrade's forces were destined to lose, because the initial moving pictures dealt a decisive blow from which it was almost impossible to recover.

Slovenia's strategy was predicated on showing courage and successful resistance in the face of a brutal aggressor – a strategy with which the Belgrade military complied. The latter also generated negative images in both Croatia and Bosnia over a four-year period. However, in contrast to the idea of an out-gunned small country showing plucky self-defence and calling for assistance if any were available, Croatia and Bosnia both played the image of helpless victims. Of course, both were victims to a considerable extent – each was militarily weaker than the Serbian forces operating against them. In their status as victims there were clear differences between the two predicaments: Bosnia's calamitous fate was not significantly its fault, whereas Croatia had, at least, been a provocative part of the dynamic that led to the war, nationalist sentiment translated into political power, pushing for independence from the Yugoslav federation. Croatia seemingly consciously pursued a victim strategy, most notably in its playing on the images of both the ancient cultural city Dubrovnik, and the eastern town of Vukovar, under siege. The victim strategy was most evident at Vukovar, where a small force inside the town defended against enormously greater forces surrounding it and using artillery to bombard it. The images of devastation and apparent helplessness in the face of the brutal Serbian siege formed part of a victim strategy in which the government in Zagreb failed to get supplies and reinforcements into the town, even though there was movement in and out through the surrounding cornfields. Vukovar was left to eventual capture so that the world could see the work of rapine Serbian forces. Those forces did themselves no favours in Bosnia either, where the Bosnians, in a very weak position for the most part, tried at times to manipulate images to their benefit, but mostly failed because their provocative actions were often identified by the UN force – much to the irritation of the Bosnian government. However, the degree to which Bosnia was genuinely a victim, and to which Serbian atrocities and attacks made it so, was significant, such as the very notable mortar attacks on the Markale Market in Sarajevo, and meant that images were generated by Serbian action anyway, fostering the legitimacy of the Bosnian cause and ultimately provoking the use of armed force by NATO and the UN.[26]

In the Kosovo phase of the Yugoslav War at the end of the 1990s, images were again crucial. The images of dead bodies at Račak, revealed by OSCE-KVM personnel, where Serbian forces had carried out a massacre of ethnic Albanian men in January 1999, were the spur to international action over Kosovo. The images of executed bodies and the ashen expression of the KVM chief, William Walker, were powerful instruments that affected understanding throughout the world. Images were also important to NATO's later air campaign over Kosovo, aimed at strategically resisting ethnic cleansing. At times, the legitimacy of these operations, already questionable because no clear legal grounds for using armed force were stated, was challenged by images of mistakes made – a convoy of refugees on the road, a train crossing a bridge, an apartment block mistakenly destroyed. However, the challenges to the legitimacy of NATO's military mission fell short of the critical pitch, because Belgrade's capacity to inflict blows on itself in images was far greater – for example, ushering tens of thousands of ethnic Albanians on to trains at gunpoint and then taking them to the border with Macedonia created images so redolent of the Nazis that the competition for international public opinion, as with Belgrade's initial actions in Slovenia, was broadly lost by the Serbian side because of these images.

What these examples from the Yugoslav War confirm is a need both to protect and to seize the initiative, as far as possible, in the domain of moving images. Because it is rather difficult to control and it is impossible to guarantee what is going to happen, perhaps the most that can be done in practical terms is to recognise that this is what is going to happen. This also means, where possible, producing an image as well as words to accompany it, but this has to be a genuine image. To a large extent, the 1991 air operations against Iraq were successful because they were perceived as successful, which was because the US Air Force was able to produce weapon-head images up to the moment of impact, unlike anything before. This not only provided crucial images that cut through the words describing operational successes in hitting targets, but also gave the impression of a technically sophisticated campaign with a clinical character – always hitting the target with precision, minimising contingent death and damage. Of course, it emerged later that the impression created did not reflect the whole reality.[27] However, at the time, in terms of the operation, the images penetrated, the perception of success was embedded.

Another example of perceptual success involved Israel's withdrawal from Gaza in summer 2005. This was well presented, whether wholly by intention or not – and offers an example of how positive images can be generated. In television talking head discussion, just after the withdrawal was over, for example, the IDF was said to have been 'brilliantly professional', and it was noticed that there had been no violence – only 'lots of acting out for the media' in the words of Janet Daly, one of the journalistic commentators.[28] The image of withdrawal was powerful and persuasive.

The language surrounding the settlers always labelled them as 'Jewish', not 'Israeli'. This technically accurate use of nouns was nonetheless difficult and dangerous, as well as misleading. On one side, it emphasised the ethno-religious dimension to the issue, characterising an inter-communal, inter-ethnic conflict. On the other, it missed the key point that statehood was the issue and that the settlers were there as part of a would-be expansion of the Israeli state. The settlers were part of a strategy for achieving the maximal Zionist aim of an Israel that would include the whole of Palestine from the Jordan to the Mediterranean, rather than that territory accorded to it by partition. In contrast, commentary always referred to the Palestinians (not all Muslim, it should be noted) by their state-claiming people label – and not a title with religious connotations. The use of language also reflected the tone set by Israeli Prime Minister Ariel Sharon at the start of the withdrawal from Gaza, when he warned against 'Jewish terrorists' – not Israeli – sabotaging the withdrawal, insisting that they would be dealt with as such action was unacceptable. Sharon's approach included expressions of mutuality. This meant that he expected a quid pro quo from the Palestinian leader Mahmoud Abbas (Abu Mazan) in terms of the Palestinian Authority's controlling forces, such as Hamas in Gaza.

The Gaza pull-out was generally seen as representing real change and giving ground for optimism. The images of the IDF bulldozing settler homes provided the key to this. In the words of the BBC's correspondent on the scene, Orla Guerin, the IDF was 'erasing its past'. On one level, this may be seen as a negative presentation of what was happening, consistent with many other tonal aspects of her reporting that caused the BBC trouble. At the same time, there was no insightful comment noting that, while perhaps erasing its past, but far more importantly providing the image-hungry broadcast media with pictures to tell the story and set interpretation of it – decisive action accomplished, leaving no scope for going back – with a little generosity, the Israeli forces could have left the housing as a gift for Palestinian use. As it was, there were some 'gifts', as Guerin noted, slightly contradicting her 'erasing the past' line: some schools and community centres, as well as synagogues, were left intact. In all senses, however, the withdrawal from Gaza was a possible precedent for future developments in the West Bank and Jerusalem. On the Israeli side, concrete withdrawal was shown – quite visibly – to be credible. On the Palestinian side, it created the opportunity to demonstrate responsibility and competence in running territory, and ensuring law and order and public security within that territory, and so security for Israel without it.

During the 1999 Kosovo campaign, there was a successful combination of the two kinetic means, force and film, albeit amid doubt and debate among NATO members and planners about whether or not to hit targets in the centre of Belgrade.[29] The essence of the debate lay in what the impact would be on 'hearts and minds' in Belgrade in particular, and the rest of Serbia. One side of the argument worried that strikes on downtown Belgrade would alienate the local population, whose support needed to be removed, or kept, from the Belgrade authorities. That concern expanded into another one that divisions over this question would affect relations between members of the Alliance adversely, so undermining legitimacy, on a second and multiple level. On the other side, the argument was that strikes in the centre of Belgrade against designated military-related targets would both make the conflict real to the people there, who had otherwise been separated from the direct impact of years of war involving their government, and it would show that it was only military-, security- and regime-related targets, rather than the people as a whole who were being targeted. The latter line of argument proved to be important. Air raids had a big impact locally, because they could not avoid covering them on Serbian television, and internationally, when it was decided to hit the Ministry of Internal Affairs (MUP – which acronym was generally used also to designate the paramilitary special police force units used by Belgrade in Kosovo) and the military headquarters in Belgrade.

Perhaps the most interesting example of a creative combination of the two kinetic forms, stated above, was Rupert Smith's use of deliberate air strikes against Bosnian Serb ammunition dumps outside Pale in May 1995. This was a small incident, but perhaps all the more important because it is small actions of this kind that are the essence of contemporary warfare for Western armed forces, where the use of force must generally be at the tactical level, even if it is intended to have strategic impact. When Rupert Smith was commanding forces in Bosnia on 26 May 1995, he took a very premeditated, deliberate decision to launch an air strike on ammunition dumps outside Pale and did the same thing the following day. Among other reasons, he did this because it would make two great images of two big plumes of smoke sending an uncontestable message to an audience not only in the immediate environment, but which would also be on television and everyone could see that he had done it.[30] The Smith example is striking because it captures the type of situation in which careful decisions need to be taken about the use of force at a tactical level, and how resulting images will have an impact. The key thing in the example is how the impact of using force was calibrated by the positive effect of the images generated, a success, in that case, tempered only by the actions of Smith's superiors who undermined his approach, impairing the degree to which it could succeed, and setting back the strategic rearrangement of which it was part for another three to four months, when Smith would again be able to turn the key of NATO air power to effect.[31]

By contrast, as noted already, when Brigadier General Kimmitt announced the suspected abuse at Abu Ghraib and the investigation into it in January 2004, had he shown just one sample image of such abuse at the time, emphasising that the military was on top of the matter, he would surely have stood some chance of neutralising the impact of the eventual emergence of a whole range of images by journalists. The publication by journalists only helped to reinforce the negative aspects of the affair, cancelling the effort to be up front and inform about the abuse months earlier, making it seem as though the abuse was either being covered up by the US military or, even more damagingly, that the abuse was a policy. Absent a genuine and cutting image with which to engage on the front foot, when images do emerge, as inevitably is bound to happen, the military and the policy makers will be on the back foot and then running around in a mostly futile effort to make up lost ground.

What, then, can be done? What can we learn in terms of strategy and operations once the position of images in a moving image environment is recognised? First, it is necessary to appreciate that the battle for hearts, minds and retinas, or the struggle for the will of multiple peoples, is the core purpose in contemporary warfare, not a subordinate, supporting activity as we note above, echoing Smith. Success is about legitimacy and legitimacy, ultimately, depends on peoples. Second, it is essential to acknowledge that images are central to the battle for hearts, minds and retinas, or the struggles for the will of diverse peoples, and so key to legitimacy and success in contemporary war. Third, it is important to recognise that this is not a matter simply of public relations or 'information warfare', and so it is not a matter of marshalling a single, coherent message and getting it across effectively.

A fine example of this was Israel's campaign against Hizbollah, in

Lebanon, in summer 2006. Israel was enormously successful in getting its message across, particularly in Western news media, where reports from northern Israel, clearly based on good recent briefings, almost meant the reporters were serving as public spokespersons for the Israel authorities at times, so often having iterations and variations of 'what Israel wants', or 'what Israel is doing', all being taken at face value. To some extent, this may well be the result of reporting restrictions imposed by Israel, but never acknowledged.[32] Israel's success in getting a consistent message read across different news media, in different places, was noted by some and taken as something that the US should do, but had not done, in Iraq.[33] However, what this engagement showed was precisely how success in getting across a consistent message and getting it accepted and absorbed by reporters in Israel, and perhaps further afield, made no difference in the multidimensional, multimedia image environment, where images of apparently disproportionate action, seemingly not just against Hizbollah forces or even support targets, came to shape perceptions and legitimacy and contributed to Israel's eventually ceasing operations under a shadow of apparent failure. Of course, the details involved in particular cases were of little relevance due to the power of the images to cut through detailed explanation. And of course, those images were subject to narratives, but the narratives were of different kinds: it was the images, not the narratives, that had impact. For example, one prominent incident at Qa'na resulted in widespread accusations of war criminality by Israeli forces, as a residential block was devastated, resulting in civilian deaths. The initial Israeli release of mobile Katyusha rocket launchers plying their trade from a nearby location a couple of days beforehand served only to reinforce the sense that the attack had, prima facie, been disproportionate, given that the offending launchers had been removed immediately, as seen on the film, and the response had not targeted that particular site. Channel 4 News in the UK, for example, clearly and explicitly posed the question of this constituting a war crime.[34] This report gave the overwhelming sense, despite being framed as a question,[35] that the events depicted were, indeed, criminal.[36] While the detailed evidence was yet to emerge, as an international team was formed to investigate what happened in this and other cases, it transpired that the number of dead was perhaps half that initially reported, and that the apartment block, notwithstanding the injustice to other residents, contained one apartment linked to Hizbollah. However, even if a full report were to emerge utterly exonerating Israel of suspicion, it seems wholly unlikely that this would alter the impression left overall by the conflict and by the moving-image mediation of it: Israel's action was not a measured and proportionate response to the initial taking of hostages, and that, as far as Israel was subject to indiscriminate attacks by Hizbollah rockets and acting in self-defence, the rockets only began to be launched after Israel had commenced operations which appeared an enormous overreaction to the capture of two soldiers. Israel's command of a tightly honed reporting narrative getting its message across was impressive in the circumstances. But it was also irrelevant, because images of apparently excessive action, laying waste to civilian areas, killing civilian non-combatants and so forth utterly wiped out this tactical success. At the strategic level, the weapons of kinetic destruction, in this case, generated largely self-inflicted critical damage by the weapons of kinetic photography. The adverse impact of these images undermined Israel's cause in the multidimensional environment of the **_Trinity_[3]_(+)_**. That adverse impact was partly a result of the inadvertent, uncontrollable nature of images as they spread in that environment, including back into Israel itself (particularly important when the bloody nose received by the Israeli Defence Force in combat and bedraggled, worn troops were shown, and an account of the dead was taken). It was also partly the result of conscious exploitation by Israel's opponents who capitalised on this, even before armed hostilities had actually ceased, by working not only for the hearts and minds of the communities affected by Israel's destruction, notably in Hizbollah's southern Lebanon stronghold, but also ensuring that there were plentiful supplies of positive pictures. Hizbollah's effective victory was cemented by the retinal impact of reconstruction and community support pictures, bolstering legitimacy not only locally, but also internationally. The outcome of this conflict had been determined by images and Israel's success in getting its strong, consistent message into the news media was irrelevant.

In addition to awareness of the centrality of legitimacy, the battle for hearts, minds and retinas, and the importance of understanding how the needs of the image-weapon era transcend traditional notions of public relations and 'information warfare', even when these are comprehensively successful at a tactical level, there are important imperatives for those thinking seriously about operations. These are both negative and positive. On the negative side, there is a need to protect against the improper and wrongful 'detonation' of images in the operational environment. This may well mean rules of engagement that govern the use of all devices capable or making, receiving and transmitting images, much as rules are in place to govern the firing of weapons while troops are on deployment. However, this is a limited measure. It is limited, first, by the reality that soldiers deployed on one side will not be the only ones with access to image-generating technical devices. Second, it is limited by the reality that things will happen and their impact will be uncontrollable.

Ultimately, the contemporary environment, with its multitude of means both to capture and disseminate images, means that complete control, in all circumstances, is impossible to achieve. The examples of the Abu Ghraib abuse pictures, discussed in Chapter 5 and earlier in this chapter, and similar images of abuse from other contexts, or the London tube bomb pictures discussed in Chapter 6, confirm this in different ways. In both instances, the images were being maintained confidentially, as they

were *sub judice* – that is, they were being kept as part of criminal investigations, of which they could potentially become evidence – indeed, in both
cases, they were very likely to do so. Yet the formal, legal restrictions
surrounding them had no effect once they had found their way into the
hands of broadcast news (even if, in the case of Abu Ghraib, as noted in
Chapter 5, CBS News respected military wishes to delay showing them, for
a period, at least). Equally, the way in which mobile telephony and the
internet permitted images of beheadings to be sent and received around
the world, as considered in Chapter 6, or suicide operations (filmed to
become weapons themselves), also constituted evidence of the near
impossibility of controlling the spread of images – authentic or fake. This
was an environment in which journalists, military and policy makers alike
believed,[37] mostly correctly, that 'it gets out there and you have no control
over it anymore', as one journalist put it. This means that material set in
one context can be all too easily translated into others and transformed by
them, as another respondent in the same group noted:

> Something crops up on our bulletin and it's a powerful image … we
> see our material gets re-cut, for example, into a resistance video,
> which then goes out on the internet, where they get 50 times the audi-
> ence our original films did. We've lost control completely. That's
> where it's having an afterlife, which we have no control over.

And just as there is no control over distribution and receipt, there is no
control over effect, as already noted: 'Pictures that we can show here [in
the UK] elicit sympathy, get shown over there [Iraq] and they feel
hatred.'[38]

However, the apparent pessimism on all sides about the inevitable
impossibility of controlling images is not completely beyond question.
Even where, as just noted, it is theoretically possible for an image re-cut to
reach '50 times the audience' an original transmission by mainstream
media might, reflection suggests that 50 times numerically might well be
considerably less than this in terms of effect. Indeed, given the credibility,
reliability and density of mainstream media, their effect may well be considerably greater. In practice, the mainstream media have a multiplier
effect – the equivalent, say, of the force-multiplier effect of quality that
enabled an 8,000-strong British Task Force to overcome 130,000 Argen-
tine troops in the 1982 Falklands Campaign – where traditional, purely
numerical military calculations would suggest a superiority ratio of three
to one to guarantee success. The quality of the recognised and established
mainstream media in the West, for example, acts as a force multiplier in
this context. When images have a mainstream moving-image environment
their effect is immeasurably greater than the more dispersed impact of
images, fragmented and potentially weakened by the multiple means of
transmission and reception, fractured by individual response and

variegated timing. In the military terms used by Rupert Smith to describe the effective application of traditional, destructive, military kinetic force, it is not the amount that counts but the density: is sufficient force applied, in the right way, at the right time, against the right targets, to have a desired effect? Smith uses the classic, biblical example of David and Goliath to exemplify the point. The heart of the issue is 'the way the means are used in relation to the opponent, and whether or not there is the will to use the means in that way'.[39] While equivalent conscious utility cannot be transferred from the destructive kinetic realm to the photographic kinetic realm, a parallel has to be acknowledged: legitimacy is far less likely to be affected by the sparse effects of most mobile telephony or internet dispersal of images than it is by the density of effect achieved when traditional broadcasters present them in a concentrated fashion to a concentrated audience. As we showed in Chapter 6, despite the radical technical changes that have occurred, it is the traditional broadcasters who retain greatest importance, have greatest reach and greatest potential impact.

Given this, it should be possible to qualify the understanding of journalists who might judge that 'the web is where the power is in relation to the image now'. While the web adds dimensions, including speed and potential numerical reach, as indicated in Chapter 6, it is credibility that counts. The web can influence and impact on the images and other forms of information that traditional broadcasters use, as well as providing a supplement to it in some cases, and an alternative in others. But it is the traditional authority that counts. In a world where technical possibilities offer a quasi-democratisation of information gathering and spreading, leading to notions such as the 'citizen journalist', the reality is that only when absorbed by traditional frameworks can such notions really be relevant. Professionalism in all aspects, including an ethos of judgement and restraint, are important aspects of journalism or film production, and are among the key qualities that make mainstream and traditional producers continue to be so overwhelmingly more important than amateur or alternative sources. Thus, for example, in discussion of relations with the military and agreements to withhold the names of dead soldiers for an agreed period, there was a clear and important sense among respondents that if restraint were not shown and an ethical code were not followed in cases such as this, then the professionals would have 'lost the whole thing' and become 'just another blogger'.[40] This sense that those working in the established moving-image media, while subject to scepticism overall, have qualities that set them apart, both in their own self-assessment and that of the audience and publics who most of the time, in most cases, prefer them, is important in understanding some of the possibilities for controlling images, at least, in some circumstances – even, if, ultimately, images will out and their impact will be variable and uncontrolled.

Better relations between government, military and media are important.[41] This is not easily achieved. Broadcast and other moving-image media are generally, though not entirely, sceptical about the intentions and behaviour of those with official positions. Conversely, those working in official capacities are deeply sceptical about the attitudes and behaviour of journalists. However, on both sides of this divide, there is considerable variety and on both sides there appears generally to be an attempt to gain understanding of, and work with, the other. It is evident that both sides bear resentments, at times, against the other, and that there are mixed patterns of belief over whether each makes the effort to understand the other, or not. Certainly, in the UK context, the ham-fisted efforts of the Ministry of Defence to control journalists by using political officers and quasi-journalists who 'try to second guess what we [journalists] might do next', who are 'actually ... not very good at it', generates great hostility – and contrasts radically with the openness of the US military, which insisted on minimal restrictions – no identification of specific persons, places or order of battle, in effect – but otherwise gave completely free access to all levels. Of course, there is some mutual misunderstanding: in the judgement of journalists, the military and their political masters fail to distinguish between, say, the BBC and the tabloid press; in practice, evidence suggests precisely that they do differentiate in this way.[42] However, it is clear that, fundamentally, their professional purposes mean that, on the hardest issues, their aims and actions will pass like ships in the night.

This may be seen in the clearest and most lucid terms by reference to the images of abuse that emerged from the Abu Ghraib prison in Baghdad. Military and media focus groups offered diametrically opposed views over whether the availability of just one image in January 2004, when a US military briefing in Baghdad might have made a crucial difference over how the abuse issues was handled. This reflected their different cultures and concerns and demonstrated the fundamental divide between them. The military rejected the suggestion that publishing just one image would have made all the difference completely, and there was a strong view that the pictures should not have been published at all – both that the media should have exercised self-restraint and that publication should have been prohibited.[43] In contrast, broadcast news journalists concurred absolutely that just one image would have made all the difference, both in drawing attention to the issue when the US military originally reported it, and to the way in which it was reported.[44] Interestingly, however, US General Mark Kimmitt's view, based on direct personal experience and reflection, was also that just one image would have made a great difference.[45] He was directly involved in dealing with the media on the issue. It was he who had originally briefed the press in Baghdad in January 2004 about evidence of abuse, but this was not generally reported.[46] When the images emerged in April 2004 via CBS News, he was at the forefront of handling the fall-out.[47] However, Kimmitt's reflective view, elicited by direct questioning, had little influence on military practitioners who, *inter alia*, believed that 'the media wouldn't have accepted one photo'[48] – a view that was uniformly contradicted by journalists who acclaimed the difference just one image would have made.[49] Recognising that journalists understand what works in broadcast news, and underlining our analysis, in the present volume, of the nature of moving-image media and their dependency on images, as well as recalling our judgement, formed prior to Kimmitt's expressing his view – indeed, the catalyst for seeking that view – that one image could have made all the difference,[50] it is hard not to conclude that something could have been done with just one image. In a world where moving-image media can determine legitimacy and success in armed conflict and those media depend on images, and where images are weapons, there must be a possibility that one photo would have made all the difference, even where the spread and interpretation of those images was beyond the control of Kimmitt, or whoever else had responsibility for introducing them into the public domain.

This is the cue to consider a more positive approach to the kinetic force of images than a despairing fatalism. There is a need to understand the urge to dominate the image environment. Just as there is a need to secure air control and domination of the electro-magnetic spectrum in contemporary warfare, especially in high-intensity, fourth-generation combat, in all types of armed operations in the twenty-first century there is a need to deliver, or neutralise, image impact. It is important to recognise the salience of images in the quest for strategic success and to develop principles of image-environment domination, containment and suppression. There are five such principles regarding one's own side in warfare – two preventive, involving restraint and inhibition, and two reactive, aimed at containment, and finally one that is pro-active, involving risk and judgement.

1   *Preventive behaviour.* This is a far more realistic approach to the problems than seeking a cure. Preventive steps would seek to ensure that nothing equivalent to abuse takes place, although it is almost certainly impossible to guarantee that there will be no examples of bad behaviour by some individuals. This leaves the risk of both wrongful action and images to amplify that action. If the image is there, it is going to have a life of its own. And it is crucial to recognise that that image, as its detonation reverberates, will constitute a strategic crisis, not merely some kind of public relations problem.[51]

2   *Preventive rules of engagement.* The second level of prevention concerns not the images themselves, but the means for capturing information. Rules of engagement are quite developed concerning firearms and using weapons, partly because shooting someone has to be a very considered action, but partly because the implications of getting it wrong are extraordinary. Digital image means are far less controlled, but possibly even more damaging pieces of equipment. If someone is shot incorrectly, that is clearly a major issue. But taking a photograph of it

afterwards raises the issue a level (or more). Therefore, controls and rules of engagement for the use of digital image media need to be developed. The teaching of officers at staff college is extremely good, but the teaching of soldiers, sailors and airmen about what can happen if they play fast and loose with their cameras is less rigorous. However, the training of officers does little in terms of troops further down the command chain and who have mobile phones and digital cameras, as, for example, was seen in the abuse cases – unless of course, such a sense of responsibility is instilled from the trained officers throughout the ranks such as to remove the potential problem.

3   *Containment candour.* The first element of containment is honesty, both when situations are good and when they are bad. There is generally no place for cover-ups, avoidance or fabrication (although completeness may not be necessary). Information and images have to be the truth – as Rupert Smith notes, fabrications will always be found out.[52] Contemporary warfare, especially, where one element concerns trying to build, or rebuild, societies in a post-conflict environment, require a direct and upfront approach. Not to do so will automatically generate doubts. It is better, therefore, to tell the truth, even when it is bad truth.

4   *Containment coverage.* One thing that must be done is, therefore, to avoid leaving gaps. At the same time, it is necessary to look for opportunities that will contribute positively (although the positive will never match the negative; the negative will always outweigh the positive). Do not leave empty spaces. The information media will fill it all. And it is not just the image which excites, it is also confrontation. It is vital therefore, as a measure of containment in the image environment to ensure that, as far as possible, there are no gaps, and that, should any appear, they are filled immediately.

5   *Image environment domination.* As well as minimising the impact of images, generally, in effects-based approaches, it is essential to look for front-foot opportunities as well – to use images to create effect. If there is awareness of the importance of image, image can be employed in positive, pro-active ways, as a weapon of offence. There are times when it can be used positively and it can be relatively controlled, but it is still not possible to guarantee exactly how an attempt at positive image domination is going to be received. That is the real problem. Those engaged can be aware of it and can try, but can never be certain how it will work out. The metrics – or rather, 'immetrics' – and quality control of effects-based approaches mean that there are times when there may be an attempt to dominate by creating a positive image for effect, but always without any guarantee of how it will be received in all directions. Research and development in the area of images will help develop practice significantly in this respect. Sometimes, however, the commander may have to decide simply not to care

what one particular community, or potential audience, will think about a particular action, so long as a problem can be addressed. But this means being crystal clear about where he wants that image to be seen, in particular, and understood and interpreted – and hoping, as with other manoeuvres, that it works.

From all of this, we can observe that probably nothing has ever unified and made such clear sense of the primary Clausewitzian trinity – reason, chance and passion – as do images as weapons in the contemporary era. There is a rational element to their use and control, but there is great possibility that chance will produce collateral effects, and, in either case, nothing so galvanises passions in the age of mass communication as pictures, especially those screened to millions by moving-image media. Moreover, this primary trinitarian view of image effects also unifies the two trinities more clearly than anything else, as the secondary trinity becomes, in effect, the primary one, in real-world terms, and the relationships between governments, armed forces and people are determined largely by focus on the icons of war, affecting legitimacy – and so successful outcome, more than any other factor.

## Conclusion: image and experience, legitimacy and war

The truism that a picture paints a thousand words has a darker twin. For, it is just as likely that while apparently substituting iconic simplicity and clarity in terms of communicating a message, the reality is that the image may well be hiding at least a thousand words. The idea that the simplifying image can be the basis for better communication is strong, but it needs to be balanced with awareness that the simplifying image distorts or disguises. The need for images means that detail and more complex ideas can be easily lost, either because the image simplifies, or even more often because, absent an image, there is no attention whatsoever.

Fictional moving images are important because they can produce salient and lasting interpretations of war in themselves. But they are also significant because how they are used informs usage of their non-fictional counterparts – 'actuality' moving images, whether cinematic, televisual, or, indeed, 'new media'. Actuality moving-image media – whether more reflective current affairs and documentary, or more immediate television news – inherently depend, by their very definition, on the use of moving images. Fictional use of moving images, therefore, defines the parameters of representing contemporary conflict in the various forms of actuality moving-image media – that is how footage is used in the different media. Fictional moving images are important in terms of legitimisation, but the entertainment aspect of fiction also finds its way into the non-fictional. This is in the character of the product produced for the market. The market will be entertained and informed if the material suits the market's tastes. As a blunt instrument of war, the image blows a hole through the dense attrition of complex verbal and conceptual fabrics. Sometimes months or years of discussion, close argument, subtle explanation can be short cut by one set of moving images – as the events of 9/11 proved. In the process of representing war and conflict, and so in the process of legitimisation, fictional narratives with strong, orchestrated images are likely to be as important, in and of themselves, or in the way their structure shapes actuality and news representation, as are those actuality images themselves.

By looking at fictional screen representation of war, we can identify the salience of image and experience, as aspects of war, in determining what can or is likely to be shown. In addition, as noted in Chapter 4, there is an increasing tendency for fiction and factual film to overlap, with each using more of the characteristics of the other. But what is clear is that in every case, in each type within the moving-image media world, the triangulation of interpretation with image and experience constitutes the key. This is what we have shown in the main substantive chapters of this volume, treating the three broad types of feature fiction, documentary and current affairs, and broadcast news, in each case offering interpretation of particular examples in each class, in relation to major cases of modern war. Those interpretations are, we believe, self-standing, each serving as an analysis of the example in its own right, whether the fictional films treated with reference to the Yugoslav War, post-Soviet conflict, or Iraq and the 'War on Terror', or the long-format actuality films dealing with those same wars, or the range of television news illustrations used in Chapter 5 – or, indeed, the discussion of conflict on the African continent related to all types of moving-image media in Chapter 6. However, each individual treatment serves to build the cumulative understandings that all forms share the same, or very similar, basic elements in terms of narrative, for the most part, and that those elements, shown through the examples, are the blend of image and human experience which constitute interpretation. The events of September 11 provide the clearest example of all, combining experience and images unlike any other, because so much of what happened seemed more like scenes from a fictional disaster movie than depiction of actual events. The image made the news.

The visual and visceral character of the medium means that other aspects of war, such as conduct, causes or the highly conceptual strategy, let alone the politics that defines and initiates war, can find little space. These are not inherently visual, whereas the depiction of human experience is. Thus, the available interpretations and understandings of war are limited by the nature of moving-picture media. Once we have identified the salience of both the striking image itself, and human experience, in shaping fictional feature films, or television drama, we can see how, following the nature of the medium, these same aspects define actuality moving pictures, whether current affairs television programming and documentary, or television news coverage. In short, fictional and actuality forms use moving images in the same way. And just as feature fiction film cannot capture important aspects of warfare, neither can actuality film. Yet, despite these limitations, moving-image media constitute the single most important element in representing and interpreting the conduct of contemporary warfare. Images, particularly moving images, or still images presented in a moving image context, do more than anything else to shape understanding of contemporary conflict, and the shape of understanding largely, if not exclusively, determines the outcome of contemporary warfare.

In this context, with a focus on the importance of image and experience, it may be appropriate to offer reflection on some implications for the future regarding aspects of the war moving-image environment that we have not otherwise addressed. These observations, while not essential to this study, have relevance to the topic as a whole, especially in light of the digital developments discussed above. These involve the two trends of reality television and interactive, digital visual computer games, and suggest major questions for the future. These are not ones that can be addressed here, both due to space limitations and because they are emerging developments. However, some comment is appropriate, given the potential salience of this trend. The first is that 'reality war' television seems inevitable, at some point, in some manner – with cameras attached to helmets, as we noted happened for recording purposes in the Russian feature fiction film *War* (*Voina*), and as happens live for operational purposes in some circumstances anyway in the most modern armies, with images relayed back to command positions. The key issue will come, no doubt, when, having taken decisions to relay images from weapon heads, or soldier's heads live on television – or, quite probably, by the time it comes, online, electronically to handheld digital devices, including mobile telephones – those responsible (whether cultural, commercial, military or political) put the decision on one course of action over another to a viewer vote. This will not come until the trend to have alternative endings for feature fictional dramas to be viewed by webcast, or more likely, handheld or mobile phone download or podcast, subject to viewer choice, has become established – which, it seems, is an inevitable development at the time of writing, in the field of computer games and certain types of fictional film. But, once the cultural milieu in which interaction to decide endings has bedded itself in, with choice exercised individually, in some cases, but by collective voting, in others, the next phase of digitally facilitated activity, whether the material is reality or fictional, is very likely to be live choice. And it is hard to see why war, that most all-embracing intellectual and emotional activity, will not be at the core of development – especially as protagonists see the chance to use the images involved as weapons in that war, seeking to generate legitimacy, for a time at least. The potential for associated development in the realm of visually driven computer games is vast – the major visual-image medium among younger genera-tions in the early twentieth century, with the commercial power of games able to bring far greater earnings than either box-office takings or DVD income. Taken together, these dominant visual and information means, both essentially based on interaction and, usually, lowest-common-denominator collective choice, especially when online webcast beheading, say, or helmet-camera combat choices are the material for public partici-pation. 'Big Brother Battlefield' may never happen, but given the trends, it could well be a multi-platform concept just waiting for its time to come – and the time may not be so far off – although continuing deep sensitivities among most broadcasters and much of their publics may mitigate the showing of combat fatalities, at least initially.

The idea of a 'Big Brother Battlefield' is linked to the increasing tend-ency, more often than not without wider context, to scrutinise events in war. This raises potentially thorny questions in terms of the role of images in the conduct of warfare, including ethical and possibly legal concerns about their use. If images are to be understood to be weapons, then can the use of these weapons constitute an armed attack or a war crime? While the immediate and obvious answer to most people would be that neither of these could be the case, after further reflection and probing, it would seem inevitable that these difficult questions would have to be posed and answered. Indeed, in the principles of image-environment domination, containment and suppres-sion identified above, we have begun to address the ethics of using images as weapons in war. The use of any weapon, while always subject to understand-ing the situation in which it is used and the balance between the necessity of the action and the proportionality of its scope and effect, ultimately, is cir-cumscribed by negotiated understandings of 'right' and 'wrong'. This can only mean that, as with developments regarding other dual-use technologies, such as cybernetics, the use of images could be said to constitute an armed attack (in the sense required, but disputed, for claiming the right to self-defence, under Article 51 of the United Nations Charter). And it certainly means that, at some point, at some level, the issue of whether use of images constitutes a war crime is likely to be raised.[53]

A further reflection that should not be overlooked is that moving images as weapons share the same fate as all other technical means in warfare. Human knowledge affects the social sphere in which technology develops and technical means are used. In warfare, this makes adaptation a vital aspect of securing success, as Rupert Smith has pointed out. The advantages of any technology, particularly any new technology, are always overcome by the ingenuity of opponents, either in developing technolo-gies to supersede, or more likely and more important, developing tactical responses to negate the advantages of a particular technology. This means that once the use of images as weapons is understood, then it is inevitable that new tactics will be developed by opponents to deal with any advantage which careful and deliberate use of the graphic realm may bring.

The challenge for predominantly Western forces, who appear generally to be in a weaker position regarding the use of images as weapons, both in terms of conceptualisation and understanding, on one hand, and suffering their blows, on the other, is to devise tactical responses with strategic impact, which will neutralise, overcome or turn use of the image environment to their advantage – notwithstanding the inherent difficulties associated with controlling moving-image media. Moving images will have an impact on modern war, but, whatever the particular detail of that impact is, it will have a critical impact on legitimacy – and so on the prospects of strategic success. There is a basic tension, therefore, between the 'real' war and the 'reel' war. Control of the blunt munitions of moving pictures, as the key weapons of modern war, is the key question of contemporary conflict – yet, as we argue, in contrast to those who have analysed the use of propaganda, that control may well prove increasingly to be illusive and elusive. The challenge is to find ways in which to discipline the image environment and the use of images as weapons.

Without legitimacy, the use of force in anything other than isolated raiding missions will become harder and harder. Yet there is a fundamental problem: it is in the nature of these media to be incapable of reflecting all aspects of warfare. In an age where the character of contemporary conflict, particularly for Western powers, major other powers, and any states engaged on international missions, means that legitimacy is vital to success, it is the moving-image media that, irrespective of intention or reception, constitute the most important factor in potentially shaping the outcome of conflicts. Indeed, the nature of contemporary conflict, coupled with the character of contemporary communications, means that the image, above all the moving image, has become the key weapon in modern war, as we argue in this volume. Identifying this key weapon, as such, and understanding both how it works, on one hand, and its impact and the difficult-to-manage nature of that impact, on the other, is the central issue of contemporary warfare.

# Notes

## 1 Introduction

1 Brian Bond's *The Unquiet Western Front* (Cambridge: Cambridge University Press, 2003) offers an excellent account of how various approaches within the creative and commentating cultural domain transformed victory in the First World War into an account of disaster, resulting in what might be termed the 'Blackadder' view of history, drawing on received understandings of that war as a futile waste of young lives, where the brave-hearted young 'lions' in the ordinary ranks were led by officers who were 'donkeys' in the famous images popularised by the historical interpretation given by Alan Clark in, *The Donkeys: a History of the British Expeditionary Force in 1915* (London: Pimlico, 1991).

2 Although this name is commonly transliterated from Arabic to English as 'Osama bin Laden', Usama bin Ladin is preferred here. There are two reasons for this. First, this corresponds with the version officially used by governments and in international diplomacy – summarised as 'UBL', an abbreviated form we adopt in this volume, and second, experts in those forums regard this form as being a more accurate and authoritative transliteration of the original, and that abbreviation is the one adopted in official circles and documentation.

3 James Gow, for example, was discussing Usama bin Ladin's network, its nature and the threat it posed to international stability on 10 September 2001 to a publisher; a day later, the images had cut through the obscurity surrounding the nexus of the al-Qa'ida network and international security.

4 Among recent titles not otherwise cited here, some of the more interesting include: Stuart Allan and Barbie Zelizer (eds), *Reporting War: Journalism in Wartime* (London, New York: Routledge, 2004); Stephen Hess and Marvin Kalb (eds), *The Media and the War on Terrorism* (Washington, DC: Brookings Institution Press, 2003); Philp Seib, *Beyond the Front Lines: How the News Media Cover a World Shaped by War* (New York: Palgrave, 2004); Daya Kishan Thussu and Des Freedman (eds), *War and the Media: Reporting Conflict 24/7* (London: Sage, 2003); Howard Tumber and Jerry Palmer, *Media at War: The Iraq Crisis* (London: Sage, 2004); Jaap Van Ginneken, *Understanding Global News: A Critical Introduction* (London: Sage, 1998); Barbie Zelizer and Stuart Allan (eds), *Journalism after September 11* (London, New York: Routledge, 2002).

5 Andrew Hoskins, *Televising War From Vietnam to Iraq* (London: Continuum, 2004).

6 Andrew Hoskins and Ben O'Loughlin, *Television and Terror: Conflicting Times and the Crisis of News Discourse* (London: Palgrave, 2007), a volume which relates to research on the Shifting Securities Project.

7 Susan L. Carruthers, *The Media at War: Communication and Conflict in the Twentieth Century* (Basingstoke: Palgrave, 2000).

8 Marion Just, Montague Kern and Pippa Norris (eds), *Framing Terrorism: The News Media, the Government and the Public* (London: Frank Cass, 2003).

9 Stephen Badsey, *Modern Military Operations and the Media* (Camberley: Strategic and Combat Studies Institute, 1994), and the edited volume *The Media and International Security* (London: Frank Cass, 2000); Philip Taylor, *Munitions of the Mind* and *War and the Media: Propaganda and Persuasion in the Gulf War* (Manchester: Manchester University Press, 1995 and 1998 2nd edn).

10 Philip Taylor, *Munitions of the Mind: A History of Propaganda from the Ancient World to the Present Day* (Manchester: Manchester University Press, 2003 3rd edn) p. 7.

11 Although no evidence of serious results emerging from the matchbook drops has emerged, consistent with the assumption about effect and impact here, there is always the possibility that there was some response which, for very good reasons, did not receive the glare of publicity.

12 Where generally homogeneous societies could once be largely shaped by mass communications media with a single point of control – Nazi Germany or the Soviet Union – the growth of diversity within countries and transnationally means that this is increasingly hard to archive for any regime, though it remains possible. But it is all but impossible in open, liberal, Western societies. The message is no longer the medium – the media fragment and refract the message.

13 Kate Utting, 'The Strategic Information Campaign: Lessons from the British Experience in Palestine, 1945–1948', *Contemporary Security Policy*, Vol. 27 No. 4, April 2007.

14 Peter Pachnicke and Klaus Honnef (eds), *John Hartfield* (New York: Harry N. Abrams, 1994).

15 James Gow, 'Hearts, Minds and Retinas', Counter Insurgency Issues Conference Joint Service Command and Staff College, 1 September 2005.

16 Among the more important books treating the epiphenomena of 'new wars' are the following: Mary Kaldor, *New and Old Wars* (Cambridge: Polity Press, 1999); Martin Shaw, *The New Western Way of War* (Cambridge: Polity Press, 2005), and *War and Genocide* (Cambridge: Polity Press, 2003); Colin S. Gray, *Modern Strategy* (Oxford: Oxford University Press, 1999); Chris Hables Gray, *Postmodern War: The New Politics of Conflicts* (London: Routledge, 1997); Michael Ignatieff, *Virtual War: Kosovo and Beyond* (London: Chatto & Windus, 2000); Martin van Creveld, *On Future War* (London: Brassey's, 1991); Lawrence Freedman, *The Transformation of Strategic Affairs*, Adelphi Paper 389 (London: Routledge for the IISS, 2005); General Sir Rupert Smith, *The Utility of Force: the Art of War in the Modern World* (London: Allen Lane, 2006).

17 Freedman, *Transformation*, pp. 22–26.

18 Ibid., p. 79.

19 Ibid., p. 87. It should be noted that 'torture' is a particular term, with a narrow legal definition, involving the infliction of significant physical or mental pain, under the Torture Convention, and that, in these terms, the US categorically rejected description of the events depicted at Abu Ghraib as 'torture', recognising, nonetheless, that serious abuse had taken place, which brought shame on the US military and the country as a whole, even if it was not 'torture'. The perceptual reality was that, in terms of competing strategic narratives, while far from complete in its acceptance, the narrative of 'torture' took hold in various parts of the international public imagination.

20 Indeed, in the course of empirical research, this notion was rejected – perhaps surprisingly – by one of the clearest and most imaginative thinkers on contemporary warfare, General Sir Rupert Smith (Ret), although, on reflection, his position would surely change. Rupert Smith, Interview, Strand C. Shifting Securities Project.

21 John Stone, in discussion with Gow, and whose understanding of technology helpfully informed the present discussion; on tanks and their uses other than as paperweights, see John Stone, *The Tank Debate: Armour and the Anglo-American Military Tradition* (Amsterdam: Harwood Academic, 2000).

22 Keith Grint and Steve Woolgar, 'Computers, Guns and Roses: What's Social About Being Shot?', *Science, Technology and Human Values* Vol. 17 No. 3 (summer 1992), pp. 366–380, and Keith Grint and Steve Woolgar, *The Machine at Work: Technology, Work and Organization* (Cambridge: Polity Press, 1997), ch. 6; Rob Kling, 'When Gunfire Shatters Bone: Reducing Sociotechnical Systems to Social Relationships', *Science, Technology and Human Values* Vol. 17 No. 3 (summer 1992), pp. 381–385.

23 On the crucial importance of understanding 'the constant adaptation' (p. 197) in the use of technical means, see Smith, *Utility*, where he points out that almost no technical means in warfare is used in the manner for which it was intended, and that finding appropriate ways to adapt tactics and technology lies at the core of success in war – therefore, adaptation of one means or another must be anticipated.

24 The dual kinetic aspect is seen clearly in *The Peacemaker*, a fictionalised setting, where the power entailed in satellites and the images they can both capture and relay is shown in an operational context, where George Clooney's character summarises the developments in capability by telephone for one particular target, whom he knows from the past and locates in the Russian province of Dagestan, in the North Caucasus, neighbouring Chechnya, carrying a 'loose nuke': he reminds him how he watched CNN during the Gulf and saw the images where it was possible almost to see faces on the ground, but then 'you don't know what happens next – well you're about to find out!' This embraces the two forms of kinesis and relies on the images associated with the use of one type of kinetic force to have an impact on the implied basis of how they were rendered by the other type. This of course, corresponds to the realities created by those images up to the point immediately before kinetic impact found in real-world, high-tech, US operations in particular.

25 We originally used the term 'expert' as part of Strand C on the Shifting Securities Project; however, one panel of experts included a voice rejecting the label 'expert' for that of 'specialist'. 'Experts Panel' Transcripts, Symposium, Strand C, Shifting Securities Project.

26 Morton G. Ender, 'Military Brats: Film Representations of Children From Military Families', *Armed Forces and Society*, Vol. 32 No. 1 (October 2005), esp. pp. 27–30, which includes useful, reflective information and discussion on the methodology used.

27 Richard Dyer, 'Introduction to Film Studies', in John Hill and Pamela Church Gibson (eds), *The Oxford Guide to Film Studies* (Oxford: Oxford University Press, 1998), pp. 3–10.

28 'Editorial', *Film Studies*, Issue 2 (spring 2000), p. 3.

29 Where titles for these texts exist in more than one language, we generally use the English version to facilitate reading a book written in that language, while indicating the original language title, unless the titles are the same, or the original language title is commonly used.

30 Ender, 'Military Brats', p. 27.

31 Leslie Woodhead, Interview, Strand C, Shifting Securities Project.

32 Richard Taylor, *Film Propaganda: Soviet Russia and Nazi Germany* (London: I.B. Tauris, 1998), p. 62.

33 The one exception concerns those devoted specifically to fiction film of the Vietnam War, where there is a dedicated literature and general availability on

DVD and VHS of the major films – but the Vietnam focus necessarily provides a limitation.

34  This is not to say that actuality films, any more than fictional ones, are 'false', or necessarily 'untruthful' or 'inaccurate' – although they may be any or all of these, they may well also be the opposite. It is to argue that whatever they are is driven by the nature of the medium – and a highly accessible and influential element of legitimisation in contemporary conflict is necessarily not dependable.

35  This is in contrast to the much-vaunted 'CNN Effect' notion that media drive policy in a 24-hour satellite news age. This was an idea largely discredited by Nik Gowing; see also Piers Robinson, *The CNN Effect: The Myth of News, Foreign Policy and Intervention* (London: Routledge, 2002); and Steven Livingstone, 'Beyond the "CNN Effect": The Media–Foreign Policy Dynamic', in Pippa Norris (ed.), *Politics and the Press: The News Media and its Influences* (Boulder, CO: Lynne Rienner, 1997).

## 2  Moving images and meaning: the nature of the weapon

1  Anthony Aldgate and Jeffrey Richards, *Britain Can Take It: the British Cinema in the Second World War* (Edinburgh: Edinburgh University Press, 1994, 2nd edn).

2  Although the Vietnam War has attracted more attention than most others, that attention has been limited in scope and uneven in quality. See e.g. Jack Hunter (ed.), *Search and Destroy: An Illustrated Guide to Vietnam War Movies* (place unknown: Creation Books, 2002). See also Mark Taylor, *The Vietnam War in History, Literature and Film* (Edinburgh: Edinburgh University Press, 2003), a broader, but more systematic enterprise that reflects the interaction of different cultural elements in shaping meaning and understanding.

3  *Millennium Journal of International Relations*, Vol. 34 No. 2 (2006).

4  *Apocalypse Now*, directed by Francis Ford Coppola was the text; this is discussed in James Gow, 'Strategic Pedagogy and Pedagogic Strategy: Film, Fact and Fiction', *International Relations*, Vol. 20 No. 4 (December 2006).

5  Paul Jenkins, Interview, Shifting Securities Project, London, June 2006.

6  Of course, even this kind of distinction can present intellectual and classificatory challenges, as well as ethical issues – for example, Brian Winston writes of the difficulties inherent in an actuality film, where the filmmaker fuses two moments on film, taken six months apart, in order to create narrative coherence and not obscure the 'truth' in question; this is seen as an acceptable practice by filmmakers, as it does not detract from the essential 'truth' at stake (an issue treated in relation to *The Death of Yugoslavia*, in Chapter 4); but it is also, clearly, a form of fictionalisation, albeit for possibly good reason and effect, and can be criticised as such: Brian Winston, *Lies, Damn Lies and Documentaries* (London: BFI, 2000), p. 17.

7  Fred Shook, *Television Field Production and Reporting* (Boston, MA: Pearson, 2005, 4th edn), p. 13.

8  This can be seen by looking at almost any report, either current or found via searching the archive, at news.bbc.co.uk. The BBC planned also to make all its output available online at some stage, although there were likely to be significant copyright issues in doing so – as one veteran pointed out in our research, the problems and costs of obtaining copyright clearance to use library footage in making documentaries was likely to be a recipe for trouble, making the attempt impossible at times (Leslie Woodhead, Interview, Strand C, Shifting Securities Project).

9  Paul Jenkins, Interview, Strand C, Shifting Securities Project.

10  Paul Jenkins, Interview, Strand C, Shifting Securities Project; the education

perspective cannot translate realistically into market benefits, given the tiny amounts of money involved in selling such films after their initial production and showing – for example, a BBC film with a small budget of £150,000 might be sold on for as little as £800 to £1,000 (Leslie Woodhead, Interview, Strand C, Shifting Securities Project).

11 For further discussion of documentary filmmaking, see the following selection: Bill Nichols *Representing Reality: Issues and Concepts in Documentary* (Bloomington: Indiana University Press, 1989), and *Introduction to Documentary* (Bloomington: Indiana University Press, 2001); Kevin MacDonald and Mark Cousins, *Imagining Reality: the Faber Book of Documentary* (London: Faber and Faber, 1998); Brian Winston, *Fires Were Started* (London: BFI, 1999), and *Lies, Damned Lies*; Ian Aitken, *Film and Reform* (London: Routledge, 1990); John Corner, *The Art of Record* (Manchester: Manchester University Press, 1996).

12 MacDonald also made the highly successful docudrama *Touching the Void*, showing his flair and panache for exploring form, before moving on to make fact-based feature 'fiction', *The Last King of Scotland*, about the Idi Amin regime in Uganda and the atrocities committed by it. MacDonald's grasp for the form is also shown in his excellent book on documentary films with the critic Mark Cousins: *Imagining Reality*.

13 There are partial exceptions, at least, to the notion of narrative in actuality film. For example, abstract and avant-garde filmmakers may well eschew 'narrative' form. Abstract filmmaking remains the preserve of a tiny community interested in film for its own sake. To reach a wider audience of any kind – and for most filmmakers it is the mixture of having something to say and the possibility of reaching an audience at least fifty times the size of a best-selling factual book that impels them – it is vital to have a clear sense of what the story is, in order to work on making it accessible to the audience. (Leslie Woodhead, Interview, Strand C, Shifting Securities Project).

14 Nichols, *Representing Reality*, pp. 32–33; the typology is extended in Nichols, *Introduction to Documentary*.

15 Leslie Woodhead, Interview, Strand C, Shifting Securities Project.

16 See: Iurii Mikhailovich Lotman, *Struktura khudozhestvennogo teksta* (Moscow, 1970), particularly pp. 60–61. A passage from this is quoted in translation by Benjamin Rifkin in his assessment of the film/literature debate in the first chapter of his excellent study, *Semiotics of Narration in Film and Prose Fiction. Case Studies of "Scarecrow" and "My Friend Ivan Lapshin"* (New York, 1994), p. 10.

17 William de Mille, quoted by Lewis Jacobs in *The Rise of the American Film – A Critical History* (New York, 1956), p. 128, as cited in V.F. Perkins, *Film as Film: Understanding and Judging Movies* (London, 1972), p. 9.

18 See Perkins, *Film as Film*, p. 9.

19 Béla Balázs, *Theory of the Film: Character and Growth of a New Art*, trans. Edith Bone (London, 1952), p. 46, as cited in ibid., p. 13.

20 See the entry on 'Soviet montage' in Ginette Vincendeau (ed.), *Encyclopedia of European Cinema* (London, 1995), pp. 397–398.

21 Kristin Thompson and David Bordwell, *Film History. An Introduction* (New York, 1994), p. 140.

22 Ibid.

23 Zorkaya, *The Illustrated History of the Soviet Cinema*, p. 75.

24 Paul Burns, 'Linkage: Pudovkin's Classics Revisited', *Journal of Popular Film and Television*, vol. 9 no. 2 (1981), pp. 70–77 (p. 70).

25 Thompson and Bordwell, *Film History*, p. 140.

26 For more on Vertov see Vlada Petrić, *Constructivism in Film. The Man with the Movie Camera: A Cinematic Analysis* (Cambridge, 1987).

27 See in particular: 'Word and Image', in Sergei M. Eisenstein, *The Film Sense*,

trans. Jay Leyda (London and Boston, 1986), pp. 13–59 (pp. 29–33 and pp. 54–58 on Leonardo da Vinci and Milton respectively).

28  Eisenstein, *The Film Sense*, p. 18.

29  See: Thompson and Bordwell, *Film History*, p. 141.

30  See: Eisenstein, *The Film Sense*, pp. 13–59 (p. 34).

31  Robert P. Kolker, 'The Film Text and Film Form', in John Hill and Pamela Church Gibson, *The Oxford Guide to Film Studies* (Oxford: Oxford University Press, 1998), p. 15.

32  See: S. Eizenshtein, V. Pudovkin and G. Aleksandrov, 'Zaiavka', *Zhizn´ iskusstva* (5 August 1928), pp. 4–5 and, in translation, 'Sergei Eisenstein, Vsevolod Pudovkin and Grigorii Alexandrov: Statement on Sound', in Taylor and Christie (eds), *The Film Factory*, pp. 234–235.

33  John Ellis, *Visible Fictions* (London, New York: Routledge. 1982).

34  Fred Shook, *Television Field Production and Reporting* (Boston, MA: Pearson, 2005, 4th edn), p. 1.

35  George Bluestone, *Novels Into Film* (Berkeley and Los Angeles: California University Press, 1968), p. 1.

36  See André Bazin, *Qu'est-ce que le cinéma?* (Paris, 1958), vol. 1; and Christian Metz, *Film Language: A Semiotics of the Cinema*, trans. Michael Taylor (New York, 1974).

37  Metz, *Film Language*, p. 95.

38  For more on Metz and a survey of criticism on Metz see: Pam Cook (ed.), *The Cinema Book* (London, 1985), pp. 229–230.

39  See Bazin, *Qu'est-ce que le cinéma?*, p. 132, as quoted in Cook, *The Cinema Book*, p. 225.

40  Siegfried Kracauer, *Theory of Film: the Redemption of Physical Reality* (London, 1960), pp. 237 and 242.

41  See: Cook, *The Cinema Book*, pp. 137–138.

42  See: Boris Eikhenbaum, 'Problems of Cine-stylistics', trans. Richard Sherwood, in Richard Taylor (ed.), 'The Poetics of Cinema', *Russian Poetics in Translation*, vol. 9 (1982), pp. 5–31 and in particular p. 24. Eizenshtein noted the connection between the cinema of Griffith and the literature of Charles Dickens, focusing on the role Dickens' narrative style had as a proto-montage device, rather than on the treatment of character and theme that went with the writer's technique. See S.M. Eizenshtein, 'Dikkens, Griffit i my', in his *Izbrannye proizvedeniia v shesti tomakh*, vol. 5 (Iskusstvo, Moscow), 1968, pp. 129–180.

43  See Joy Gould Boyum, *Double Exposure: Fiction into Film* (New York, 1985), pp. 6–23.

44  Seymour Chatman, *Coming to Terms: The Rhetoric of Narrative and Fiction in Film* (Ithaca and London, 1990), p. 40.

45  This may be seen with the French *noveau roman*, which tried to provide every conceivable detail of a scene. Alain Robbe-Grillet is one exponent of this method; he has written novels, such as *La Jalousie* (1957), which are referred to as 'cinematic' due to their emphasis on the visual, as well as film scripts, including *L'Année dernière à Marienbad* (directed by Alain Resnais, 1961), which retain this technique of emphasising images rather than ideas.

46  See David Bordwell, *Narration in the Fiction Film* (Madison, 1985); Bordwell finds the Russian Formalist distinction between 'fabula' (the actual events of a story) and 'siuzhet' (the presentation of the story's events) indispensable to his theory of narration (pp. 48–53).

47  See: Perkins, *Film as Film*, p. 24.

48  Ibid., p. 24.

49  Avrom Fleishman, *Narrated Films: Storytelling Situations in Cinema History* (Baltimore, 1992), p. 9.

50  See Chatman, *Coming to Terms*, pp. 124–135 and pp. 80–83 respectively; Wayne

C. Booth, *The Rhetoric of Fiction* (Chicago and London, 1961), and Bordwell, *Narration in the Fiction Film.*

51  See Chatman, *Coming to Terms,* p. 133.

52  Ibid., pp. 134–135.

53  See James Griffith, *Adaptations as Imitations: Films from Novels* (Newark and London, 1997), particularly pp. 35–40.

54  Griffith, *Adaptations as Imitations,* p. 71.

55  This is in line with Boris Eikhenbaum's writing in the 1920s that turning liter-ature into cinema is neither to stage it nor to illustrate it, but to translate it into film language. See: Boris Eikhenbaum, 'Literature and Cinema (1926)', in Stephen Bann and John E. Bowlt (eds), *Russian Formalism: A Collection of Articles and Texts in Translation* (Edinburgh, 1973), pp. 122–127 (p. 123).

56  This was also implicitly linked to Soviet author and scenarist Iurii Olesha's and director Abram Room's aims in making *Strogii iunosha:* this was an attempt to create a new art form at once literature and cinema, the combination of ele-ments which would permit a narrative that worked simultaneously as an independent artistic creation in both media. See Milena Michalski, 'Promises Broken, Promise Fulfilled: The Critical Failings and Creative Success of Abram Room's *Strogii iunosha'*, *Slavonic & East European Review,* vol. 82 no. 4 (October 2004).

57  Chatman, *Coming to Terms,* p. 162.

58  See Kenneth Portnoy, *Screen Adaptation: A Scriptwriting Handbook* (Boston and London, 1991), *passim.*

59  It was this set of difficulties that Olesha was, in essence, trying to overcome by creating his 'new art form' combining literature and film.

60  See James Gow, Richard Paterson and Alison Preston (eds), *Bosnia by Television* (London: British Film Institute, 1997), *passim,* where Gow was the only person involved with a lasting and embedded background in war studies. Stephen Badsey of the Strategic and Combat Studies Institute at the Royal Military Academy, Sandhurst, is a notable exception. See Badsey, *Modern Military Opera-tions and the Media* (Camberley: Strategic and Combat Studies Institute, 1994), and the edited volume *The Media and International Security* (London: Frank Cass, 2000).

61  Philip Taylor, *Munitions of the Mind* and *War and the Media: Propaganda and Per-suasion in the Gulf War* (Manchester: Manchester University Press, 1995 and 1998, 2nd edn).

62  James Gow, 'Hearts, Minds and Retinas', Counter Insurgency Conference, Joint Services Command and Staff College, 1 September 2005.

63  See, for example, *Mark Thompson Forging War: the Media in Serbia, Croatia and Bosnia and Hercegovina* (London: Article 19, 1994).

64  'National' memory entails association with events in history; whereas 'public memory' pertains to the political discourse of rulers at a given time. While the former is largely based in symbolic understanding of the past, the latter derives from education in the present. See Paul Connerton, *How Societies Remember* (Cambridge: Cambridge University Press, 1989), pp. 21–23.

65  Sandra Basić-Hrvatin, 'Television and National/Public Memory', in Gow *et al.* (eds), *Bosnia by Television,* pp. 63–71.

66  See, for example, Thomas Patterson and Robert D. McClure, *The Unseeing Eye. The Myth of Television Power in National Politics* (New York: Putnam, 1976).

67  *After September 11: TV News and Multicultural Audiences* (London: British Film Institute, 2002).

68  George Grubner *et al.*, 'The Mainstreaming of America: Violence Profile Number 11', *Journal of Communication,* vol. 30 no. 3 (summer 1980).

69  Albert Bandura and Richard Walters, *Social Learning and Personality* (New York:

Holt, Rinehart & Winston, 1963); see also Leonard Berkowitz, *Aggression: A Social Psychological Analysis Development* (New York: McGraw Hill, 1962).

70 Joseph Klapper, *The Effects of Mass Communication* (New York: The Free Press, 1960).

71 Aristotle, *De Poetica*, in W.D. Ross, *The Works of Aristotle*, Vol. XI (Oxford: Clarendon Press, 1924), ch. 6; Seymour Feshbach, 'The Stimulating vs. Cathartic Effects of a Vicarious Aggressive Experience', *Journal of Abnormal and Social Psychology*, vol. 63 (1961); S.W. Jackson, 'Catharsis and Abreaction in the History of Psychological Healing', *Psychiatric Clinics of North America*, vol. 17 no. 3 (1994), p. 475; Thomas J. Schiff, *Catharsis in Healing, Ritual and Drama* (Berkeley and Los Angeles: University of California Press, 1979), pp. 20–24.

72 Robert Karl Manoff, 'Telling the Truth to Peoples at Risk: Some Introductory Thoughts on Media and Conflict', Unpublished paper presented at the 'Legitimacy of Intervention for Peace by Foreign Media in a Country in Conflict' Conference, Fondation Hirondelle, Geneva, 3–4 July 1998.

73 Aurélien Colson, 'The Logic of Peace and the Logic of Justice', *International Relations* (2000).

74 Stan Le Roy Wilson, *Mass Media/Mass Culture* (New York: McGraw-Hill, 1992, 2nd edn), pp. 16–17.

75 For discussion on film and various aspects of reality, evidence and the relationship with academic study the following are useful, though by no means exhaustive: Natalie Zemon Davis, *Slaves on Screen: Film and Historical Vision* (Cambridge, MA: Harvard University Press, 2000); Milton Bates, *The Wars We Took to Vietnam: Cultural Conflict and Storytelling* (Berkeley: University of California Press, 1996); M. Blumenson, 'Can Official History be Honest History?', *Military Affairs*, vol. 26 (1962); Joanna Bourke, *An Intimate History of Killing: Face to Face Killing in 20th Century Warfare* (London: Granta, 1999); Roland Barthes, *The Death of the Author* (New York: McGraw Hill, 1977); Robert A. Rosenstone, 'A History in Images/History in Words: Reflections on the Possibility of Really Putting History onto Film', *The American Historical Review*, vol. 93 no. 5 (1998), pp. 1173–1185; John O'Connor, 'History in Images/Images in History: Reflections on the Importance of Film and Television Study for an Understanding of the Past', *The American Historical Review*, vol. 93 no. 5 (1988), pp. 1200–1209.

## 3 Feature fiction film

1 The term 'Yugoslav War' is discussed in Chapter 1, as are the different aspects of war and the capacities of moving-image media to come to terms with, and represent, them. The Yugoslav War provides the best and most coherent body of cinema for the purposes of this study because it attracted more and more consistent attention from feature fiction filmmakers than any of the other many areas of conflict in the contemporary era. Thus, while later in the chapter we give attention to films concerning conflict in the Caucasus, Iraq and the Middle East, and the African continent, it is notable that fewer films have emerged prominently regarding these areas, and that, where they have, their appearance has been more spread out and their scope more diffuse.

2 The present analysis is limited to discussion of four films. We have developed this analysis through earlier presentations of our research. Constraints of time and space mean that films such as *Vukovar: Jedna Priča* directed by Boro Drašković and *Before the Rain* directed by Milcho Manchevski, one of the most acclaimed, elegiac and ultimately dismal films linked to the Yugoslav War, are not treated here.

3 See *Guardian*, 7 March 1996.

4 Dina Iordanova's 'Kusturica's "Underground" (1995): historical allegory, or

propaganda?', *Historical Journal of Film, Radio and Television*, vol. 19 no. 1 (1999), pp. 72–73 and Dina Iordanova's *Cinema of Flames: Balkan Film, Culture and the Media* (London: BFI, 2001). Iordanova goes beyond the Yugoslav War in arguing for a Balkans cinema, but that conflict and the cinema surrounding it is clearly the impetus for the book – to be understood in its title. This makes the treatment of those films very important. Disappointingly, she does not fully grasp the problems surrounding Emir Kusturica's major film *Underground*. While there is a very interesting and important treatment of the film and of the controversy that surrounded it – there was a major public debate in France connected to its winning the Palme d'Or at the Cannes Films Festival – in the end, the judgement is uneven. On the issue of the film as propaganda, the author's exculpatory conclusion is that 'nobody cared much ... the film was perceived [by critics] as a gargantuan [*sic*] metaphor of the messy state of Balkan affairs rather than as a finely crafted propagandistic insinuation that would work in favour of one of the warring sides.... In the minds of reviewers, these Balkan nations were all the same.' This conclusion, however, misses the point – that set of messages was exactly what the Belgrade leadership wanted: in the contest for hearts and minds, a circus of confusion would mean no clear judgements and, it was hoped, no strong international action. However, in the wider discussion, there is a slightly awkward but still very useful 'moral' question-and-answer creation to discuss wider issues, such as the film's financing and production. However, the book is both about a particular area and the culture claimed for it, and also about areas studies and cultural studies and makes for stimulating reading, away from issues such as that of Kusturica. Discussion in earlier parts of the book – which does not concur with our views entirely – should be considered by all interested in these topics.

5  See David Robinson's interview with Kusturica in *The Times* (5 March 1996).

6  These allegations were made, for example, in questions to the actors after a showing of the film at the London Film Festival in 1996.

7  Michael Nicholson, *Natasha's Story* (London: Pan, 1994), p. 29.

8  It should be noted that this fictional scene occurs while the war is underway and is not a filmic representation of an actual shooting at an Orthodox wedding which occurred prior to the onset of armed hostilities, as suggested by some, such as Martin Bell.

9  Interestingly, in the screenplay by Frank Cottrell Boyce, what the boy actually says is not written. Instead, there is an indication. 'What he is saying seems urgent. Is he angry, or is it some kind of warning?': Frank Cottrell Boyce, *Welcome to Sarajevo* (London: Faber and Faber, 1997), p. 9.

10  This reflects the screenwriter's own transmutation. In his introduction to the published text, Cottrell Boyce notes that he first accepted the commission to write the film for purely professional reasons – 'because I needed the money and because I wanted to work with Michael Winterbottom [the film's director]'. However, he continues by reporting the sense of mission which grew with the project. He had ignored Bosnia until starting on the film, but long before he finished, his mission had become to write a film which would 'make it impossible for people to go on ignoring it' (Cottrell Boyce, *Welcome*, pp. vii and xi–xii).

11  This incident derives from a real situation in which cellist Vedran Smailjović played this theme and organised musicians in many places to play at the same time.

12  Such films include Oliver Stone's *Under Fire*.

13  Frank Cottrell Boyce, speaking at the showing of *Welcome to Sarajevo* at the London Film Festival, 15 November 1997.

14  In fact, in the UK, the film was only moderately received at the box-office, sug-

gesting no more than limited accomplishment of this mission. It should be noted, however, that the film was originally conceived while the war continued, but was only made and shown after its end.

15 This was confirmed by Kenović himself in an extract from an interview in *Souvenir Programme. 41st London Film Festival, 1997* (London: BFI, 1997), p. 92.

16 James Gow, The ICTY, War Crimes Enforcement and Dayton: The Ghost in the Machine', *Ethnopolitics*, vol. 5 no. 1 (2006).

17 See Sabrina Ramet, *Thinking about Yugoslavia: Scholarly Debates about the Yugoslav Breakup and the Wars in Bosnia and Kosovo* (Cambridge: Cambridge University Press, 2006), ch. 10; Brendan Simms, *Unfinest Hour: Britain and the Destruction of Bosnia* (London: Penguin, 2001); Gow, *Triumph of the Lack of Will: International Diplomacy and the Yugoslav Crisis* (New York: Columbia University Press, 1997), pp. 174–182.

18 The title actually translates as 'Prisoner of the Caucasus', but was released for a US audience as *Prisoner of the Mountains*. The story by Lev Tolstoy is also entitled 'Prisoner of the Caucasus'. Tolstoy's story is also the basis for *Prisoner of the Caucasus* (dir. Yuri Khashchavatski (2002)), discussed in Chapter 4, which includes several voiced quotations directly from the original.

19 The son of the director of *Prisoner of the Mountains* appears in *Voina* as the experienced and noble wounded soldier Captain Medvedev – a rough equivalent to Sasha in *Prisoner*, on one level, but wounded and confined to the pit, on another.

20 This is one of several instances in the film which involve cooperation with the military – as also occurs in other films. The production relationship with the military is treated during a short, informative and entertaining documentary film, *Behind the Scenes*, which appears on the DVD version of the film. In that film, Balabanov bemoans the importance of money when making contemporary war films and requiring cooperation with the Russian military; in the old days, whole parts of the military would have been made available, wholesale, for use in making films (for example, Sergei Bondarchuk's *War and Peace* probably could not have been made without the legions of Soviet conscripts assigned to the film – not an example that Balabanov cites). This marks the changes in both filmmaking and defence in relation to Moscow, where the certainties of Soviet command provision, while still, perhaps, a part of cultural expectation, are no longer a part of the economic and political reality. Planes, helicopters, detonations and so forth, all of which occur in *War* (and some of which are seen being coordinated and filmed in the documentary), cost – although Balabanov also tells us that the military is unreliable and that payment does not guarantee delivery; this is perhaps why helicopters are shown firing flares and rockets as, summoned by the Captain, they approach to rescue the liberators and their former hostages; the latter are under siege by Chechen forces in a tower where they have sought refuge as they try to escape, but, unlike any major action film, the rescue itself is not shown, as Balabanov skips to a military base at sunset, where they have been taken ('Behind the Scenes' Extra Feature Documentary on the Making of *Voina. Voina* DVD).

21 'Behind the Scenes' Extra Feature Documentary on the Making of *Voina.*

22 *Jarhead*. Dir. Sam Mendes, Germany, USA, UK, 2005. Screenplay by William Broyles Jr. (a former Marine who served in Vietnam), based on the book *Jarhead* by Anthony Swofford.

23 The attention to the long wait during the build-up to operations and the frustration that this engenders, as well as not seeing real combat action, in this feature fictional presentation based on an autobiographical account of 1990 to 1991, has strong parallels with the experience shown in Dodge Billingsley's *Virgin Soldiers*, a very different kind of film, as a documentary, discussed in Chapter 3.

24 One commentator, interviewing Mendes, suggested that *Jarhead* is a 'perverse war' movie, essentially because the film does not deal with, or rather, show combat directly (Andrew Graham-Dixon, *The Culture Show*, BBC2, 8 December 2005).

25 Mendes, *Culture Show*, 8 December 2005; Graham-Dixon turns this into a 'sense of blood-lust' running throughout the film.

26 The director used photographic research rather than the paintings of Edward Hopper that influenced the visual style of his previous films as a guide to *Jarhead*'s design, and did not use storyboards or pre-compose shots. While he says that this is 'un-painterly', there is a look of Andrew Wyeth's bleached rural landscapes, on the one hand, and John Keane's work as official war artist with UK forces in the Gulf conflict during 1990 to 1991 on the other. Mendes used handheld cameras and improvisation to work with the desert as a 'blank canvas', responding to the challenge of composing shots when there 'are no structures around you to compose anything to' (Mendes, *Culture Show*).

27 In her 'Film of the month' review of Mendes' film, Leslie Felperin suggests that it is 'quite likely' that Mendes and his team watched Werner Herzog's 1992 documentary about Kuwait's burning oilfields *Lessons of Darkness* while researching the film, and that this 'leaves its mark not just in *Jarhead*'s rendition of the ecological disaster of the war, but also in its weird, Stygian visual poetry' (Leslie Felperin, 'The longest days', *Sight and Sound*, January 2006, p. 47).

28 Walter Murch was Sound Editor on both *Jarhead* and *Apocalypse Now*.

29 Mendes admitted that he had little idea of how long the military build-up in Saudi Arabia took before the American-led campaign to evacuate, including that the Marines he depicts in the film had been there for over six months before their four-and-a-half days of full combat deployment without actually seeing action. However, rather than absorbing this lesson and demonstrating a greater understanding of the realities of war – preparing to go somewhere that the forces then went, achieving the operational objectives of evicting Iraqi forces from Kuwait and restoring the legitimate exercise of sovereign rights in that country – the director appears to see this as a metaphor for that particular military conflict and for war, in general. His film, in a sense, does not go any-where because 'it is a war that doesn't go anywhere … and do any wars go any-where? That's the point,' adding that the last line of the film is: 'We're still in the desert.' That last line, in effect, becomes a comment on the 2003 Iraq engagement, as Mendes suggests, adding politics to an otherwise apolitical film. Mendes claims he could have made a polemic about how both 1991 and 2003 were wrong, but chose to let the audiences make up their own minds (Mendes, *Culture Show*).

30 David O. Russell, 'Commentary', *Three Kings* DVD. Quotation in the following section is from the same source.

31 The transition to responsibility is also reflected in the dialogue, where early talk of 'rag heads' or 'towel heads' gives way to support and understanding, as Archie and his team find meaning in their mission – meaning that was clearly missing for Archie in his early statements asking what the war had been about and in the emptiness of the others. The disparaging language about Iraqis upset Arab members of the cast initially (all Iraqi refugees in the US), until Russell explained that this was necessary not only to capture reality, but as a vehicle for showing how the troops gain understanding and grow morally.

32 Tom Doherty, 'The New War Movies as Moral Rearmament: *Black Hawk Down* and *We Were Soldiers*', *Cineaste* (summer 2002), pp. 4–8.

33 *Black Hawk Down*, DVD Extras.

34 Information in the following paragraphs is taken from *Black Hawk Down – Hol-lywood's Greatest FX* Five, 28 February 2005.

35 The DVD version of *Black Hawk Down* includes an excellent extra feature in which Scott shows and discusses his artwork and storyboards, which does much to draw out the importance of understanding images and getting them right, as well as highlighting Scott's great talent.
36 Scott, Commentary.

## 4  Documentary and current affairs

1 *The Fall of Milošević* (Brook Lapping for the BBC, 1995).
2 Ivan Stambolić, an articulate, moderate political figure, was later ousted from power by Milošević in a party coup – also brilliantly captured in *Death*. A decade later, on the eve of NATO action over Kosovo, Milošević's mentor disappeared while jogging one morning. His remains were uncovered in April 2003, having been murdered – and with suspicion falling overwhelmingly on his protégé.
3 In 1999, at the beginning of NATO operations against Serbia, CNN interviewed James Gow for a special programme on Milošević. In the interview the crucial point about the two visits was made and appeared to be ready to be included in the film. Then, at the eleventh hour, there was a phone call to ask for corroboration, as none of the books mentioned this seemingly salient information (the exception, which had clearly not been consulted, was Laura Silber and Allan Little's *The Death of Yugoslavia* (aka *Yugoslavia: Death of a Nation*) (London: Penguin, 1995), which was written to accompany the series and used the material available for the production. Despite being referred to the primary evidence, the information was cut from the final film, as the producers appeared unable to view the material. Thus, the weight of false understanding handed down through the literature as received wisdom counted for more than the reality.
4 The footage came into their possession as part of a collection of tapes handed over by one of the interviewees. Had the directors not been both assiduous and astute in reviewing all the footage available to them, the KOS material might have been overlooked completely. As it is, they viewed the material, found it to be of great interest, understood what it was and put it to good use. They were uncertain as to whether the interviewee could have been aware of exactly what was being handed over for use in making the films.
5 Robert Hayden, for example, has raised questions over the English language subtitles that appear as the talking heads of the protagonists tell the tale in their own South Slavic tongues (with the exception of Tupurkovski, who speaks with sharpness and humour in English). On several occasions, the translation is not literal, with more appearing in writing on screen than is said verbally. However, the translations were faithful to the sense and to that which was said in the film interviews, but which would take too long to show on screen. Thus, the essential information was included in the speakers' native language, while additional material might be included from parts of the interview around the extract used. Thus, the 'product' was faithful and accurate, but not necessarily in an immediate and literal sense. This device, driven by production needs, does not invalidate what is said, as Hayden judges. But it does tarnish it in some way.
6 This appears to be material-driven, although there could be a chance that the change of director, from the well-worn team of Angus MacQueen and Paul Mitchell to Dai Richards, also resulted in a slight change of style and emphasis.
7 The absence of American film interviewees on this topic appears to suggest that there was a policy decision not to permit such interviews. US Envoy Charles Redman is the only relevant official figure who gave an interview at all for the first five programmes. However, the contrast with *Death* Part 4 and *Fall* is striking: the US actors are out in full.

8 On the nature of politics in Russia and other key former Soviet states, see Andrew Wilson's superb *Virtual Politics: Faking Democracy in the Post-Soviet World* (London: Yale University Press, 2005).

9 Evgenii Tsymbal, Moscow, May 2005.

10 Ian Christie, The Other Cinema, 1 February 2004.

11 See Richard Taylor, *Film Propaganda: Soviet Russia and Nazi Germany* (2nd revised edn London: I.B. Tauris, 1998), chs 4, 5 and 6; and Emma Widdis, *Alexander Medvedkin* (London: I.B. Tauris, 2005).

12 Ian Christie, The Other Cinema, 1 February 2004.

13 A significant comparative point in the Yugoslav War was the presentation of identical images on Serbian and Croatian TV, but with the victims labelled as Serbs in Serbia and as Croats in Croatia. See James Gow *et al.*, *Bosnia by Television* (London: British Film Institute, 1996).

14 As noted in Chapter 4, what made the al-Qa'ida attacks on the World Trade Center towers so remarkable was that the strikes and the collapse were caught on film as they happened.

15 The International Helsinki Federation was a Cold War product. With no official peace treaty signed between the Soviet Union and the West at the end of the Second World War, while the Cold War quickly emerged, and Soviet territorial occupation, border changes and domination of Central and Eastern Europe, Moscow had pushed for a formal agreement when, in 1975, the Helsinki Final Act resulted from the Conference on Security and Cooperation in Europe (CSCE – a diplomatic process that continued and became the formal Organisation for Security and Cooperation in Europe at the start of 1995, after the Cold War had finished). The Soviets sought a political-military deal and economic cooperation, while the Western countries, prepared to accommodate political-military agreement that would mean arms controls measures, at a late stage added a humanitarian basket. This was not expected to have any significant impact, but along with the other non-legally binding but hard-to-walk-away-from political agreements it was an addition that would mean, in principle, at least, that the communist countries would have acknowledged individual human rights and civil liberties, including freedom of expression. In practice, however, the human rights basket took on a significant life of its own, becoming a benign Frankenstein that contributed enormously to the undermining of communist control and Moscow domination in Central and Eastern Europe. One part of this was the development of 'Helsinki' organisations throughout the CSCE region, non-governmental organisations, associated internationally by the federation, focused on the protection and promotion of human rights and free expression. Thus, its continuing role and presence as an international force in Moscow was geared towards ensuring awareness of issues such as Chechnya and the human rights abuses taking place there.

16 The festival had been organised by the Museum and Cultural Centre 'Andrey Sakharov', Memorial, the Moscow Helsinki Group, the All-Russia Cultural Movement 'For Human Rights', the Russian PEN Centre, the Citizens Action group, the Fund for the Protection of Openness, the Mothers of Russia, the Trans-Village Forums Organisation, the Foundation for Citizens Freedom, the Holocaust Foundation, and ANO Internews.

17 The film's original title is *Il était une fois la Tchétchénie*, but the Russian version of it is known as *Chechenskaia kolybel'naia*, meaning 'Chechen lullaby', a reference to the song used in the film.

18 These figures are given with authority in the film by Putin's negotiator sent to deal with the hostage crisis, who was clearly working with specific information – which information was clearly known, but in an act of Soviet-heritage falsity is

given as 354 by a regional official to press and public on camera, with public declamations regarding the impossibility of there being such a low number inside the school, which, again in Soviet fashion, he ignores. Ironically, the total figure given for hostages was about the same number as the actual number of dead at the end of the crisis.

19 Another, even more striking film on the horror of Beslan is Leslie Woodhead's *The Children of Beslan*. This extraordinary film is not discussed here due to the combination of space limitation and pertinence of Sim's film in terms of using the hostage taker's footage, although reference is made to it in Chapter 6, and it will be treated in future work.

20 *Beslan: Siege of School No. 1*, Filmmaker Notes: Meet Director Kevin Sim, www.pbs.org/wnet/wideangle/shows/beslan/filmmaker.html at 22 August 2006.

21 The circumstances in which the siege began to be broken are glossed over with brief explanation in the film; given the remarkable, honest and telling interviews made with the victims, as well as those with the official negotiator and the police investigators (who show and comment on plans of the school), it is interesting to note that there appear to be no interviews with members of the local 'vigilantes' over their role in events and precisely how the denouement unfolded – while this might well have been a different film and is not imperative to the film Sim makes in the end, it would have provided fascinating material.

22 And, in a curious way, fire fighters connect the two films. The Naudets film is clearly about New York fire-fighters and their experiences. The Moore film alludes to the seminal feature fiction film *Fahrenheit 411*, directed by François Truffaut, based on a novel by Ray Bradbury. The title refers to the Imperial-American measured temperature at which paper burns, and the plot turns around the conscience of a fireman in a world where the fire service's job is to start fires by burning books, so as to eliminate independent sources of knowledge and reflection. It is somewhat ironic, therefore, that Moore has opted to make a film in which he at once seeks to be a dissident in a political world he sees as seeking to control information, and at the same time his manipulative film is the one that, in the end, more takes on the mantle of corrupting information, despite its success as a film.

23 Gédéon Naudet, quoted in J. Max Robins, 'The Robins Report: A Film Built From a Bond of Brotherhood', *TV Guide* (New York Metropolitan Edition, vol. 50, no. 8, 23 February 2002), p. 54. This comment is made in response to comments that the brothers had negotiated a $1m contract with CBS to make the film, which they argued was only to cover costs and allow for any residue to be paid to the Uniformed Firefighters Association Scholarship Fund, which would also benefit from advertising spots while the film was shown on the CBS network (an arrangement that meant the film was not associated with CBS News). The brothers also kept their word to be true to the spirit of their project and the fire-fighters themselves by making one of fire-fighters, James Hanlon, a producer on the film. See also David Friend, 'Bond of Brothers', *Vanity Fair*, no. 499 (1 March 2002), pp. 74–78.

24 Robert de Niro does not appear in the commercially available DVD, which is another version again, containing more of the original footage shot that day at 'Ground Zero'.

25 Dan Trigotoff, '*9/11* [*sic*] 'not exploitive', *Broadcasting and Cable*, vol. 132, no. 11 (18 March 2002), p. 25.

26 See the discussion in Maarten Pereboom and John E. O'Connor (chairs) *et al.*, 'Michael Moore: Cinematic Historian or Propagandist?', A Historians Film Committee Panel Presented at the 2005 American Historical Association Meeting, *Film and History*, vol. 35, no. 2 (2005), pp. 7–16.

27 Steven Mintz, 'Michael Moore and the Re-birth of the Documentary'; and Ron Briley, '*Fahrenheit 9/11*: Michael Moore Heats it Up', respectively – the latter following David Bordwell and Kristin Thompson; both pieces are from *Film and History*, vol. 35, no. 2 (2005), p. 11.

28 Andrew Roy, 'Images de guerre et guerre des images', *24 Images*, no. 118 (1 September 2004), p. 4.; the view Roy reports is that of the great Jean-Luc Godard, who raged against the film when it was shown and became a prizewinner at the Cannes Film Festival in 2005.

29 Ken Nolley, '*Fahrenheit 9/11*: Documentary, Truth-telling and Politics', *Film and History*, vol. 35, no. 2 (2005), p. 13.

30 Nolley '*Fahrenheit 9/11*', p. 13.

31 Richard Porton points out that Moore's treatment of the Carlyle Group–Saudi connection with the Bushes is effectively a simplified primer derived from *Exposed: The Carlyle Group*, a film made in the Netherlands by VPRO, available online at www.informationclearinghouse.info/article3995.htm; see Porton, 'Weapon of Mass Instruction: Michael Moore's *Fahrenheit 9/11*', *Cineaste*, vol. 29, no. 4 (2004), p. 5.

32 This is discussed by Nolley in '*Fahrenheit 9/11*', p. 13.

33 One of the notable coups in the counter-film *Fahrenhype 9/11* is to have the class teacher whose class Bush heard reading *My Pet Goat* saying how much admiration she had for his calm and reflective demeanour at that moment. While others raise the reasonable questions about what else Bush might have done in those moments, it is her sense of the respect he showed and the tenor he set that is winning, footnoted, as it is, in effect, by her assertion that she did not vote for him to be president, but that she would have done that day.

34 As Porton notes '(Weapon', p. 4), the use of 'found' footage in this way for 'didactic purposes' is common in the tradition of the documentary essay, of which *Fahrenheit 9/11* forms an important and successful part.

35 Gilles Marsolais, 'Tout est affaire de montage', *24 Images*, no. 118 (1 September 2004), p. 56.

36 Porton, 'Weapon', p. 6.

37 Focus Group 2, Strand C, Shifting Securities Project. London. A military participant in this mixed military and civilian policy-maker group introduced the term 'letter-box' in this discussion. Other aspects of the present paragraph are informed by this Focus Group in particular.

38 Focus Groups 11 and 12, Strand C, Shifting Securities Project.

39 The trial at the Iraq High Tribunal started on 21 August 2006.

40 *Fighting the War* Press Release, www.bbc.co.uk/pressoffice/pressreleases/stories/2003/05_may/30/fighting_the_war.shtml at 18 August 2006.

41 In a film made at a much later stage, in 2005, for Channel 4 *Dispatches*, print journalist Peter Oborne, presenting an on-screen personal account of Iraq, begins by explaining that the only way to get around Iraq safely is with protection from the American or British military, that getting that protection means being embedded, and then, he extends, being embedded means that the reporter only gets to see and hear what the military want. He then asserts that there are two stories in Iraq, one of a country beset by civil war and the other the version that the Americans want to tell, implying, apparently disingenuously, that there is no chance to tell the 'civil war' version due to military control, and that the version the American or British military allow is, somehow, false. Leaving aside the realities of Iraq at the time, which were that four out of eighteen provinces were the focus of trouble and much of the rest of the country, as a US diplomat tells Oborne, is trying to get on with something approximating a normal life (clearly, a difficult thing to do when other parts of the country are subject to protracted political violence). Strikingly, it is

the US military (one of whom is shown to have a shoulder escutcheon – commenting on who sent him to Iraq – who help him by explaining a three-pronged vehicle-bomb attack around the Palestine Hotel in Baghdad, with images of each of the three blasts, which Oborne's film uses to punctuate dramatically a soldier's explanation. This hardly seems as though he is prevented from reporting Iraqi political violence – which remained some considerable way short of a 'war' threshold; nor does it seem as though the US military wants to prevent his reporting this, as it is they who take him through the moving pictures with analysis of the attack.

42 See the excellent study of this effect by Brian Bond, *The Unquiet Western Front: Britain's Role in Literature and History* (Cambridge: Cambridge University Press, 2002).

43 In many respects, *Jarhead* could have been informed by *Virgin Soldiers*, and it would be quite surprising and coincidental if Mendes had not viewed the film and been informed by it; however, given that both relate to authentic Marine experiences, and given the eponymous book on which *Jarhead* is based (see Chapter 2), this may simply be a reflection of the genuine Marine experience.

44 It is notable that, even in what are clearly intended to be, and are acknowledged as, the most authentic depictions of high-intensity combat, such as Steven Spielberg's *Saving Private Ryan*, John Irvin's *Hamburger Hill*, Oliver Stone's *Platoon*, and, above all, Ridley Scott's *Black Hawk Down*, the precision-guided anatomy of the combat scene shows not only intercut close-ups of what are American troops in each case, but also includes the narrative reference points and relief of showing the enemy, at least fleetingly.

45 Dodge Billingsley, Interview, Strand C, Shifting Securities Project. Billingsley, at one stage, worked on military-related documentaries for that channel.

46 The increasing tendency for actuality films to adopt the characteristics of fiction films and for the latter increasingly to use elements of the former is confirmed by empirical research, as well as observation. Focus Group 5, Strand C, Shifting Securities Project.

## 5 Television news

1 The following selection of works provides various relevant discussion: Glasgow University Media Group, *War and Peace News* (Milton Keynes: Open University Press, 1985); Piers Robinson, *The CNN Effect: The Myth of News, Foreign Policy and Intervention* (London and New York: Routledge, 2002); James Hoge, 'Media Pervasiveness', *Foreign Affairs*, vol. 73 (1994), pp. 136–144; Steven Livingston, *Clarifying the CNN Effect: An Examination of Media Effects According to Type of Intervention*, Research Paper R-18 (Cambridge, MA: The Joan Shorenstein Barone Center on the Press, Politics and Public Policy, JFK School of Government, Harvard University, 1997); Nik Gowing, *Real-time Television Coverage of Armed Conflicts and Diplomatic Crises: Does it Pressure or Distort Foreign Policy Decisions?*, Working Paper 94–1 (Cambridge, MA: The Joan Shorenstein Barone Center on the Press, Politics and Public Policy, JFK School of Government, Harvard University, 1994); Philip Seib, *Beyond the Frontlines: How the News Media Cover a World Shaped By War* (New York: Palgrave, 2004); Andrew Hoskins, *Televising War: From Vietnam to Iraq* (London: Continuum, 2004).

2 Other parts of the ESRC-funded research project, which provide the context for this volume, deal with both the nature of news production and of audience reception and interpretation. Both parts of that research challenge and disprove the arguments put forward by many scholars concerning the nature of power–media relations and assumed audience behaviour. Certainly concerning contemporary war coverage, audiences do not generally change their views in

response to immediate television news coverage – rather there is variegated reaction, mostly based on predisposition towards an issue or event. News producers, aside from basing overall output on an actual or imagined understanding of their audience, and the inevitable presence of some personal perspective at times, are generally primarily concerned with getting a news broadcast, or a package, in a viewable form and sufficiently ready to be broadcast at the allotted time, See www.mediatiningsecurity.com for further information, including on further publications, both books and articles, in preparation at the time of writing, as well as *After September 11* (London: British Film Institute, 2002). On changes in news production and values, see also Donald R. Shanor, *News From Abroad* (New York: Columbia University Press, 2003), pp. 30–31 and 64ff.

3 The title for this section echoes James Gow, Richard Paterson and Alison Preston's *Bosnia by Television* (London: British Film Institute, 1996), although much of the material covered here is different and from a later stage in the Yugoslav War.

4 See James Gow and Cathie Carmichael, *Slovenia and the Slovenes: A Small Country in the New Europe* (Bloomington, IN: Indiana University Press, 2000), ch. 6.

5 Marjan Malešič (ed.), *The Role of the Mass Media in the Serbian-Croatian Conflict* (Stockholm: SPF, 1993), p. 11.

6 Nik Gowing, 'Real-time TV Coverage from War: Does it Make or Break Government Policy?' in Gow *et al. Bosnia*, p. 89.

7 James Gow, *The Serbian Project and Its Adversaries: A Strategy of War Crimes* (London: Hurst & Co, 2003).

8 Much of the original research presented in this chapter has its genesis in the BFI's *After September 11* project – see Preface. The material presented here is primarily original work excluded from the *After September 11* report due to tight space constraints and availability of comparable material, as well subsequent research developing that original work for this volume. However, some material here draws on that study, including Alison Preston's work, as indicated below. See *After September 11* (London: BFI, 2002); see also Milena Michalski and Alison Preston, 'Le 11 septembre vu de Grande Bretagne: Comparison des journaux télévisés' in Marc Lits (ed.), *Du 11 septembre à la riposte: les debuts d'une nouvelle guerre médiatique* (Brussels: De Boeck, 2004), pp. 61–85.

9 As stated in the Introduction, although this name is commonly transliterated from Arabic to English as 'Osama bin Laden', Usama bin Ladin is preferred here. There are two reasons for this. First, this corresponds with the version officially used by governments and in international diplomacy – summarised as 'UBL', an abbreviated form we adopt in this volume, and this is because, second, experts in those forums regard this form as being a more accurate and authoritative transliteration of the original.

10 *After September 11.*

11 *After September 11.*

12 Hoskins, *Televising War*; Robinson, *The CNN Effect.*

13 It should be noted that what applies regarding CNN over September 11 might be shared with, or fall to, other 24-hour international news channels at other times, regarding other crises in the world. While CNN held a pretty unique position in 1990 to 1991, by 2001 there were others engaged in the international 24-hour news arena, notably BBC World (and its domestic counterpart News 24), and the emerging Arabic language service al Jazeera, which really came to prominence in the wake of 9/11. Of course, these major examples do not represent the totality of 24-hour news broadcasting, with a range of others engaged in the field, but perhaps with less salience, given lesser resources, and especially in terms of their being adopted as a source of reportage by domestic and other services around the world.

14 This could be seen in research for the *After September 11* study.
15 The following is based on Ivan Zveržhanovski, 'Croatian TV News', *South Slav Journal* (forthcoming). That analysis covers news bulletins for six specific dates in 2001: 11 September, 7 October, 19 October, 10 November, 13 November, 13 December, and was originally conducted as raw research for the *After September 11* project.
16 This process has been dubbed 're-mediation'. See Hoskins, *Televising War*, pp. 16 and 20–21.
17 'CBS News Videos: September 11, cbsnews.com/htdocs/september11/video_ 0911.html; 'Special Report: September 11', cbsnews.com/sections/september11/main500249_overflow.
18 The CBS News *9/11 Archive* continued to include a section called *What We Saw* after other parts of the archive became inactive. However, this did not include the edited portions of live coverage in the DVD, but the accounts of CBS journalists' experiences on the day, many of which were also included in the book version.
19 Indeed, having viewed the footage as preparation for class, this was how some first-year students reacted in presenting accounts of the experience.
20 Kay's appearance on NBC with Brokaw, as well as coverage in relation to it of what was termed 'the Bush "Dodge"' by Ben Froomkin, appeared in the *Washington Post* on 28 January 2004.
21 Corporal Lawrence Shane Colton was known as Shane, but the original Fallen Heroes slot presented him as Lawrence. The corrected version in the follow-up report did not comment on the original.
22 'A Mother Mourns' *inter alia* cbsnews.com/elements/2003/22/06/Iraq/ videoarchive582 at 11 August 2006.
23 *CBS Evening News*, 20 August 2005.
24 *CBS Evening News*, 28 May 2005.
25 The report also noted that the ban on images of the dead returning had been introduced in 1991 by then Assistant Defense Secretary Dick Cheney, using archive film of Cheney's making some kind of announcement, and noted that the ban had continued under the Clinton presidency, reinforced by a sombre image of Clinton sideways on descending the steps of Air Force One – which could have given the impression that Cheney was the aggressive initiator of the policy while Clinton perhaps regretfully did nothing to change it.
26 The 'forgotten war' label was introduced in the UK by ITV News to refer to continuing operations in Afghanistan. See, for example, *ITV News*, 11 August 2005.
27 Gow, Interview with Michael di Paula Coyle, Special Assistant (Security), US Department of Commerce, London, July 2006.
28 Rich Noyes, *TV's Bad News Brigade: ABC, CBS and NBC's Defeatist Coverage of the War in Iraq*, Media Research Center, October 2006, www.mrc.org/SpecialReports/2005/report101405_pl.asp at 11 August 2006.
29 See the discussion of major changes in television news broadcasting and organisations in Chapter 6.
30 www.cbsnews.com/blogs/2006/08/03/publiceye/entry1863139.shtml.
31 The latter is assumed to have been the widest vehicle for trying to get across whatever the intended message was. However, it is quite possible that other US concerns regarding al Jazeera aside, that al Arabiya had the largest audience in Iraq, making it the preferable choice – and also suggesting that there was an intention on the part of the White House to reach an audience in Iraq, as well as, it might be presumed, the primary audience in the US itself. Confidential comment to Gow by an Arabic international news channel journalist, London, November 2005.

32 This theme is developed in Chapters 6 and 7.

33 In focus group research with senior defence practitioners, it should be noted, there was a strong sense that Secretary of Defense Donald Rumsfeld was the one responsible for setting the tone. Focus Group Research conducted by James Gow and King's College London War Crimes Research Group, London March 2003.

34 It is unlikely that in other cases the politicians will behave otherwise, however.

## 6 The alphabet of images

1 When armed conflict erupted involving Hizbollah in Lebanon and Israel during July 2006, scheduled seminars on Africa, in Brussels, had been suddenly supplanted by Israel–Lebanon meetings, reflecting the way in which the European Commission and the news media had focused on that topic. Gerard Prunier, conversation with Gow, July 2006.

2 *Daily Telegraph*, 12 January 2003.

3 Focus Group 18, Strand C, Shifting Securities Project.

4 The figures for dead are initially given as 'tens of thousands' and later as 'hundreds of thousands'. Channel 4 News, 16 September 2006, www.channel4.com/news/special-reports/special-reports-storypage.jsp?id=3290.

5 Focus Group 18, Strand C, Shifting Securities Project; a variant on this distinction offered by one journalist was 'people like us' and 'people not like us' (Jennifer Glasse, Interview, Shifting Securities Project).

6 Focus Group 18, Strand C, Shifting Securities Project.

7 Focus Group 8, Strand C, Shifting Securities Project.

8 Focus Group 8, Strand C, Shifting Securities Project; Focus Group 12, Strand C, Shifting Securities Project.

9 Focus Group 8, Strand C, Shifting Securities Project.

10 Focus Group 12, Strand C, Shifting Securities Project.

11 Focus Group 8, Strand C, Shifting Securities Project.

12 Focus Group 12, Strand C. Shifting Securities Project.

13 Focus Group 8, Strand C, Shifting Securities Project.

14 CNN, 6 June 2005, available at CNN Pipeline.

15 *Hotel Rwanda*, dir. Terry George (2004).

16 Trailer, *Hotel Rwanda*, M Kigali Releasing Company Ltd. MGM Home Entertainment LLC (2005); the box also included a card insert for supporting Amnesty International USA.

17 See Gerard Prunier, *Darfur: the Ambiguous Genocide* (London: Hurst and Co, 2005). This is an exceptional account of the history and circumstances surrounding the case, and makes clear the nature of the campaign. The book's strength in terms of its impeccable handling of the detail of Darfur is let down by its inaccurate, ill-informed and confused handling of the concept of genocide.

18 Michael Gibbons, 'Chasing the Game', *Screen International*, no. 1490 (25 February 2005), p. 9; see also Terry George, 'Look Back in Anger', *Premiere*, vol. 18, no. 4 (1 December 2004), pp. 46–50.

19 Romeo Dallaire, *Shake Hands With the Devil: The Failure of Humanity in Rwanda* (London: Arrow, 2005). In addition, a feature fiction film, based on Dallaire's autobiography and, again, using its title, was reported in 2006 – us.imdb.com/title/tt0472562/ at 25 October 2006.

20 We are grateful to Gerard Prunier who drew Gow's attention both to the film and its more overtly political character.

21 The film was fairly well received by an audience of victim-survivors to whom it was shown in Rwanda and who were then interviewed by Fergal Keane, the

BBC television news reporter who memorably covered the genocide in Rwanda at the time and who made a very interesting package about *Shooting Dogs* and the events of the genocide for BBC *Newsnight*, 30 March 2006.

22 Abdel Bari Atwan, *The Secret History of al-Qa'ida* (London: Saqi Books, 2006), ch. 4.

23 Vicky Taylor of BBCi, interviewed on *Go Digital*, BBC World Service, 1900 GMT, 12 July 2005. The following is based on information from that interview.

24 Vicky Taylor of BBCi, interviewed on *Go Digital*, BBC World Service, 1900 GMT, 12 July 2005.

25 *Reuters*, 1 August 2005.

26 See Philip Seib, *Beyond the Front Lines: How the News Media Cover a World Shaped by War* (New York: Palgrave, 2004), p. 88ff.

27 Focus Group 8, Strand C, Shifting Securities Project, on which the current discussion is based.

28 Focus Group 14, Strand C, Shifting Securities Project.

29 Ridley Scott, *Mark Lawson Interviews Ridley Scott*, BBC4, Broadcast 22 October 2006.

30 Philip Sabin's expertise on the conduct of warfare in ancient times informs this point gratefully.

31 Ridley Scott, *Mark Lawson Interviews.*

32 This form of pitiful human trafficking is also handled, against a backdrop of social change and human security concerns in Slovenia, in *Rezervni Deli* (aka *Spare Parts*, 2004) by Damjan Kozole.

33 *Report of the 9/11 Commission: Final Report of the National Commission on Terrorist Attacks Upon the United States, Official Government Edition* (Washington, DC: Government Publications Office, 2004), p. 166.

34 On the first weekend that trailers appeared in New York cinemas, before the film was released, there were reports of deeply upset customers.

35 According to one view, 'Greengrass is currently the place where drama docs best work is being done' (Leslie Woodhead, Interview, Strand C, Shifting Securities Project).

36 Leslie Woodhead, Interview, Strand C, Shifting Securities Project; our treatment of Woodhead's work here is informed by this interview.

37 Producer Ewa Ewart, a native Russian speaker, spent a long time getting to know some of the surviving children very well, building confidence with them, so as to make an extraordinary film, directed by Woodhead (also a Russian speaker, who spent some of the Cold War years monitoring Soviet air force communications). *The Children of Beslan* and Woodhead's other films will be treated in an article in progress and in a further book in development under the title *Watching War Crimes*, also connected to the Shifting Securities Project. On the director's experience as a Cold War eavesdropper, see also Woodhead, *My Life as a Spy* (London: Macmillan, 2005).

38 *Variety* (8–14 May 2000), p. 67.

39 This same film used in the documentary originally shown on Channel 4 in the UK and then CNN was also initially used by CBS News.

40 Dodge Billingsley, Interview, Strand C, Shifting Securities Project. His latest film, released just as this volume was being completed, bore the title *Fog and Friction*. In terms of the characterisation of what he does as academic research using film, some of Billingsley's films have been made with a direct academic connection to Brigham Young University, Utah.

41 Interview, Set 2.5, Strand A, Shifting Securities Project.

42 Mohammed el Nawawy and Adel Iskandar, *Al Jazeera: The Story of the Network that is Rattling Governments and Redefining Modern Journalism* (Cambridge, MA: Westview/Perseus, 2003).

43 As non-Arabic speakers, we were fascinated to watch some of al Jazeera's coverage of the Asian Tsunami at the end of 2004 – notably, the first images of US military helicopters in connection with the US humanitarian relief effort we saw on any of the international coverage appeared on al Jazeera, where this was the first item. Research indicates that we are not alone in watching al Jazeera without understanding Arabic, although instances of this are very limited. For example, some respondents in non-Arabic households may only watch Jazeera. Interviews A.1 and K4, for example, Strand A, Shifting Securities Project.

44 Focus Group 12, Strand C, Shifting Securities Project; Marie Gillespie *et al.*, *Shifting Securities: News Cultures Before and Beyond the Iraq 2003 War – Preliminary Findings Report* (June 2006).

45 Mohammed Chebaroo, Interview, Strand C, Shifting Securities Project.

46 Al Jazeera International commenced broadcasting on 15 November 2006.

47 Quoted in Charlotte Eagar, 'The Sultans of Spin', *ES Magazine* (16 December 2005), p. 31.

48 Nik Gowing, Presentation, 'Communicating the War on Terror: Are we Getting the Balance Right Between Being Alert and Being Alarmed?', Conference, King's College London-Royal Institution, 6 June 2003.

49 Focus Group 1 Strand C, Shifting Securities Project.

50 Focus Group 17, Strand C, Shifting Securities Project; see also Andrew Hoskins and Ben O'Loughlin, *Television and Terror: Conflicting Times and the Crisis of News Discourse* (London: Palgrave, 2007).

51 Focus Groups 11 and 15, Strand C, Shifting Securities Project; the focus group respondents revealed a trend away from initial belief in really making a difference through public education, to recognising that recognition was perhaps one of the main reasons to take part in the production of television news, especially where there was no editorial control over what would be said or how interviews would be presented. However, scepticism was reported even regarding the value of 'marketing' expertise and organisational existence – although this was a point that split opinion where it was a contention; other respondents challenged this, noting that, although no one could ever say what an interviewee had said at an interview, they were recognised for having done the interview, while another participant registered when competitors had provided interviewees who received brand awareness impact by appearing on the large screens at Waterloo Station, for example (Focus Group 16, Strand C, Shifting Securities Project). This suggests that, as with other aspects of moving-image media handling of war, it is the talking head as image that counts, not the verbal aspect of what was actually said – a judgement supported by empirical research (Focus Group 17, Strand C, Shifting Securities Project).

52 Focus Group 15, Strand C, Shifting Securities Project.

53 It was notable that despite the appearance of news satellite and cable news channels, as well as the impact of the internet, the three big news broadcasts attracted nightly audiences collectively of 22 to 25 million. However, in the changing environment, emphasis on the internet was also regarded as a vital supplement or, in the case of NBC's 24-hour news channel MSNBC, mainstay, as fairly weak audiences were more than offset by having one of the most visited news websites (*New York Times*, 27 October 2005). This is consistent with research on the UK as part of the Shifting Securities Project, which indicated that of the great variety of sources available, including satellite and cable channels in various languages and from various perspectives, the traditional terrestrial mainstream broadcasters retained the key position in news publics' use of the medium, with the BBC *10 O'Clock News*, for example, being both a mainstay and a first port of call for news. Gillespie *et al.*, *Shifting Securities – Preliminary Findings* (June 2006).

54 Donald R. Shanor, *News From Abroad* (New York: Columbia University Press, 2003), p. 4.

55 The most significant of these shows was NBC's *Today*, presented by Katie Couric, until summer 2006, and Matt Lauer, reaching an audience of six million viewers, mostly younger, and generating $250 million annually nationally and the same amount again in advertising revenues paid to local affiliates. This was significantly more than its rivals at ABC and CBS (Ken Auletta, 'Annals of Communications – The Dawn Patrol: The Curious Rise of Morning Television and the Future of Network News', *New Yorker* (8 and 15 August 2005), p. 68).

56 Sridhar Pappu, 'On the Heir', *Arrive* (March/April 2004), p. 24.

57 For a wider reading of *Team America*, see James Gow, '*Team America* – World Police: Down-home Theories of Power and Peace', *Millennium: Journal of International Relations*, vol. 34, no. 2, 2006.

58 Parker and Stone also include a similar, though less biting caricature of a report on BBC World, although not labelled as such.

59 *CBS Evening News*, 20 June 2006.

60 These radical changes briefly seemed possible at CBS, when Leslie Moonves, the CBS Chairman, said he wanted to replace the 'Voice of God anchor' (meaning Dan Rather) with something reported as 'radical and even revolutionary' (*New York Times*, 27 October 2005, quoting Moonves from January 2005).

61 It might be noted that the usual broad, natural smile on Vargas' face (unless inappropriate to the material in a report) was not evident, as she seemed to curl her lip and utter her words through gritted teeth!

62 The 'auto-cuties', as the British female news presenters were called, brought bitter comment from old-time male journalists, such as Michael Buerk, a former BBC news anchor, who suggested bitterly that their roles were about appearance, not professionalism, and that it took nothing to read an autocue.

63 *New York Times*, 27 October 2005.

64 *Time*, 30 April 2006, available at www.time.com/time/magazine/article/0,9171,1187398,00.htmml, at 8 May 2006.

65 *CBS Evening News*, 31 August 2006.

66 A Coroner's Inquiry in the UK found that Lloyd had been 'unlawfully killed', while confirming the seriousness with which his employer's at ITN had taken care through training and other precautions to ensure security in dangerous circumstances. The principal facts in the case were that Lloyd and his team had been travelling close to an Iraqi vehicle which had been firing; US fire contingently hit the journalists' vehicle; Lloyd had been wounded, as had Iraqi personnel; a white mini-bus picked up the soldiers and Lloyd; US forces then opened direct fire on the white mini-bus, killing Lloyd and others; the Coroner clearly interpreted this vehicle as an ambulance, concluded that US forces were aware of this, and that, because the vehicle and the people inside it were not, or no longer, engaged in armed hostilities, the killing was unlawful. However, the judgement perhaps misses the complexity of combat situations, where details such as the absence of symbols, for example, a red crescent, to indicate that the mini-bus was an ambulance, the absence of surrender, and US forces Rules of Engagement, might all pose question marks against the judgement.

### 7  Image and experience: legitimacy and contemporary war

1 Parts of this chapter develop arguments made on images and legitimacy in James Gow, 'Hearts, Minds and Retinas', Counter Insurgency Issues Conference, Joint Service Command and Staff College, 1 September 2005, the notion

of **_Trinity_**<sup>3</sup>(+) also appears there, but is more developed in James Gow, *War and War Crimes* (London: Hurst & Co, 2007).

2  Lieutenant General Sir Rupert Smith, *The Utility of Force: The Art of War in the Modern World* (London: Allen Lane, 2005), ch. 7.

3  This is not just about counter-insurgency operations; it is about the nature of all types of conflict in the contemporary era.

4  This issue can be understood by references to change in military peacekeeping, where a shift occurred also in the 1990s from traditional peacekeeping to new strands, including what may be termed 'strategic peacekeeping'. James Gow and Christopher Dandeker, 'Strategic Peacekeeping: Military Culture and Defining Moments', in S.D. Gordon and F.H. Toase (eds), *Aspects of Peacekeeping*, (London: Frank Cass & Co, 2001). Thus, in contrast to the strategically static nature of traditional peacekeeping, where the initiative lies with parties to the conflict, the type of situation with which we are concerned is strategically dynamic not static. It is one in which, although maximal consent is still the ideal, consent may well be challenged, even where there is some consensual basis for the deployment, as in Bosnia and Hercegovina, there are still some parts of the mandate which go beyond that and which are subject, for example, to Chapter VII enforcement measures authorised by the UN Security Council. Thus, there is a complex: the mission is based on the need to maximise consent, as far as possible, while recognising that there is a situation in which consent is not likely easily to be forthcoming – therefore, the Security Council has authorised those enforcement measures as part of the mandate (it should be stressed, only as one part of the mandate) to enable certain things to be permissible. The strategic initiative lies with the external actors. By comparison, in a conventional peacekeeping operation, the strategic initiative lies with the parties to the conflict who have made clear that whatever strategic objectives they had, they have come to the conclusion that they will not be able to get any further and so have said 'Please, help us' and the forces are deployed at the initiative of the parties. In this context there is a difference and that difference is that, at the strategic level, a response is being made to a conflict.
 Whether or not strategic peacekeeping is the right term is open to discussion. Although it is a useful term for carrying the discussion forward, it may not be definitive. But it is a problematic term, given that peacekeeping could be seen entirely as a passive activity in which there is no strategic initiative taken by the force, or its international sponsors. Similarly, terms such as peace enforcement, or the more generic peace support operations, are used in different ways, depending on the authors involved. The virtue of the label we have adopted for this activity is that it does put the focus at the strategic level.

5  Lawrence Freedman, *The Transformation of Strategic Affairs*, Adelphi Paper 379 (London: Routledge for the IISS, 2006); William S. Lind, 'Understanding Fourth Generation War', *Military Review* (September–October 2004), pp. 12–16; Thomas G. Hammes, *The Sling and the Stone: On War in the 21st Century* (St Paul: Zenith Press, 2004), and 'War Evolves into the Fourth Generation', *Contemporary Security Policy*, vol. 26, no. 2 (2005).

6  Of course, it should be noted that this phenomenon of warfare was new in terms of technical means and in relation to that which had gone immediately before, but that it was an entirely new feature of strategy that factors other than decisive battle contributed to victory, and that the purpose of battle itself was to create a set of strategic conditions. Indeed, this was a dominant mode of strategy in the era of Frederick the Great that was outmoded by the advent of Napoleonic mass armed forces.

7  Joseph P. Nye, 'Soft Power and the Struggle Against Terrorism', Lecture, The Royal Institute of International Affairs, Chatham House, London, 5 May 2005.

8  Nye, 'Soft Power'; see also Nye, *The Paradox of American Power: Why the World's Only Superpower Can't Go It Alone* (Oxford: Oxford University Press, 2002), and 'US Power and Strategy After Iraq', *Foreign Affairs*, vol. 82, no. 4 (July–August 2003).

9  Rupert Smith, *The Utility of Force: The Art of War in the Modern World* (London: Allen Lane, 2005).

10  This phenomenon was identified in James Gow and Christopher Dandeker, 'Strategic Peacekeeping', *The World Today*, vol. 51, nos 8–9, (August–September 1995), pp. 171–174; however, for an excellent treatment of the diverse global publics that constitute one of the markers and dynamics of contemporary armed conflict, see Martin Shaw, *The New Western Way of Warfare* (Cambridge: Polity Press, 2005).

11  Carl von Clausewitz, *On War*, trans. J.J. Graham, Introduction and Notes by Colonel F.N. Maude, CB (Late RE). Introduction to the New Edition by Jan Willem Honig (New York: Barnes & Noble, 2004). The following draws on Gow, *War and War Crimes*, where the notion of the *Trinity³(+)* is developed.

12  This is Clausewitz's secondary trinity, which is a reflective derivative of the primary trinity of reason (linked mainly to government), chance (linked mainly to the military) and passion (linked mainly to the people). See Beatrice Heuser, *Reading Clausewitz* (London: Pimlico, 2002), pp. 53–54.

13  Martin van Creveld, *On Future War* (London: Brassey's, 1991) (also known as *The Transformation of War*).

14  Smith, *Utility*, p. 278.

15  Andrew Lambert and Stephen Badsey, *The Crimean War* (Dover, NH: Sutton Press, 1994).

16  Rt. Hon. John Reid MP, Secretary of State for Defence, 'The Uneven Playing Field', Lecture, King's College London, 20 February 2006.

17  *After September 11: TV News and Multicultural Audiences* (London: British Film Institute, 2002).

18  This treatment of legitimacy draws on James Gow, *Legitimacy and the Military: The Yugoslav Crisis* (London: Pinter, 1992). For further discussion on the concept, the following provide a selected introduction: Max Weber, 'Science as a Vocation', in Weber, *From Max Weber: Essays in Sociology* ed. H.H. Gerth and C. Wright Mills (London: Routledge & Kegan Paul, 1948), p. 145ff.; Dolf Sternberger, 'Legitimacy', *International Encyclopaedia of the Social Sciences* (New York: Macmillan, 1968), p. 247; Arthur L. Stinchombe, *Constructing Social Theories* (New York: Harcourt, Brace & Jovanovich, 1968); Guigliemo Ferroro, *The Principles of Power: The Great Political Crises of History* (New York: Puttnam's, 1943); J.G. Merquior, *Rousseau and Weber* (London: Routledge & Kegan Paul, 1980).

19  This is discussed more extensively in Gow, *Legitimacy and the Military*, where the difficulties of positively affirming, or measuring, legitimacy are identified (pp. 14–21). For an attempt to re-engage with a positive approach to legitimacy, in contrast to the critical method identified here, but related to the work research project with which this volume is associated, see Marie Gillespie, 'Security, Media, Legitimacy: Multi-ethnic Media Publics and the Iraq War 2003', *International Relations*, vol. 20, no. 4 (December 2006).

20  Merquior, *Rousseau and Weber*, p. 5.

21  Alfred G. Meyer, 'Legitimacy of Power in East Central Europe', in S. Sinnanian *et al.* (eds), *Eastern Europe in the 1970s* (New York: Praeger, 1972), p. 66.

22  Jürgen Habermas, *Legitimation Crisis* (London: Heinemann Educational Books, 1970).

23  Focus Group 11, Strand C, Shifting Securities Project.

24  *Daily Telegraph*, 15 May 2004.

25  Freedman, *Transformation*, sets two of these examples (from Croatia and

Bosnia) in the context of strategic narratives in contemporary warfare, without actually focusing on the salience of the images involved; in doing so, the analysis follows James Gow and James Tilsley, 'The Strategic Imperative for Media Management', in Gow *et al.* (eds), *Bosnia by Television* (London: BFI, 1996), pp. 103–111, which analysis also included Slovenia; and was later enhanced in Gow, *The Serbian Project and Its Adversaries: A Strategy of War Crimes* (London: Hurst & Co, 2003), ch. 9 *passim*, on which the present treatment draws.

26 There have been allegations that the most famous mortar attacks, in February 1994 and August 1995, were fired by the Bosnian Army itself, not by Serbian forces. However, there was ultimately conclusive evidence, in each case, that Serbian forces had fired the rounds, despite suspicions and reservations. The suspicions arose because of the degree to which the Bosnian Army had been identified firing on its own people, or on the UN, in what were presumed to be efforts to provoke greater international action. An early incident, an alleged bread-queue massacre, was by far the most suspicious of the major incidents. The immediate scenes, approximated in Michael Winterbottom's fiction film *Welcome to Sarajevo* (discussed in Chapter 3), were consistent not with a mortar attack, but with an anti-personnel device (although this cannot be conclusive, as there is a theoretical possibility that the mortar could detonate in an unusual way), which, along with the immediacy of the images captured, suggested that the incident had been a self-inflicted, dark provocation, not a Serbian mortar blow.

27 See Philip Taylor, *War and the Media: Propaganda and Persuasion in the Gulf War*, 2nd edn (Manchester: Manchester University Press, 1998), esp. pp. xiv–xvi.

28 *Dateline London*, BBC News 24, 21 August 2005.

29 James Gow, *The Serbian Project and Its Adversaries: A Strategy of War Crimes* (London: Hurst, 2003), pp. 298–299; see also Ivo Daalder and Michael O'Hanlon, *Winning Ugly: NATO's Kosovo War* (Washington, DC: Brooking's Institution, 2000).

30 Smith had started with the ammunition dumps furthest from Pale, and had intended to work his way through them, sequentially getting closer to Pale itself, but was prevented from doing so by the UN hierarchy, which intervened and disrupted his scheme. General Sir Rupert Smith, Interview, Strand C, Shifting Securities Project.

31 Smith had already shown himself to be a creative thinker, in terms of using moving images, in the run-up to operations against Iraq in 1991. Smith had arranged a television news opportunity to film British troops by the coast, before they were then deployed inland for the eventual assault. However, Smith calculated that without fresh images, these same shots would be used from the library for days, and, as far as the Iraqis were paying any attention, they would assume that the British part of the main assault into Kuwait would come along the coast rather than from the desert, deep inland. This was a manoeuvre that journalists regarded as 'extraordinary'. Focus Group 8, Strand C, Shifting Securities Project.

32 Focus Group 12, Strand C, Shifting Securities Project. Journalists appeared completely familiar with the agreements that had to be signed to report from Israel, taking it as a matter of course and presuming that this would explain why reporters appeared to be mouthpieces for the Israeli government. However, these agreements and restrictions are never noted in broadcasts – in contrast, say, to reports from Saddam's Iraq, where prefatory, or coda labels such as 'this report was filed under government reporting restrictions' would be added. We can speculate that this does not occur in the case of Israel because those agreements themselves, perhaps, preclude declarations of this kind as a condition of access and ability to report.

33 Jennifer Glasse, 'War of Ideas: The Need for a Coherent US Message About Iraq', Research Paper, RCDS, July 2006; and Glasse, Interview, Strand C, Shifting Securities Project.

34 Channel 4 News, 31 July 2006 www.channel4.com/news/special-reports/special-reports-storypage.jsp?id=2894 at 1 September 2006.

35 One of the experts used in this package was used to reinforce the judgement that this action was a war crime, with reporter John Sparks answering the self-posed question of whether or not it was, with 'Some experts think so', before the talking head is shown saying that elements in this present a 'prima facie case' to answer. That in itself is short of the point it was intended to support. However, the sound bite used omitted the context provided by the full film interview that, although there was a 'first sight' or surface case, any judgement on lawfulness had to be made with full understanding of the context and detail, and how issues of necessity and proportionality were weighted in light of them (James Gow, Field Observation Note 3, Strand C, Shifting Securities Project).

36 Focus Groups 13 and 17, Strand C, Shifting Securities Project; Interview 2.4, Strand A, Shifting Securities Project. In the latter, respondents were in no doubt that the action, as revealed by the report, was 'disproportionate' and 'uncalled for', with one saying that 'I don't think anyone would think that it was not disproportionate. It didn't leave a lot of ground to think otherwise. I think it was objective somehow, but under the table objective. And on the surface you only saw the disproportionality of the event and not the both sides.' In a similar vein, respondents said, 'the impression it left me with was that Israel was in the wrong.' This engendered the response: 'Exactly. Basically, you watch it, you get that feeling, you switch off the TV, go do something and in your mind you have it that Israel was wrong.' There was some sense in both the Strand C focus groups and the Strand A interview that there could be more to understanding this and similar events in the case of this particular conflict, and that there could be more to the Israeli action than was apparent.

37 Focus Groups 8, 11, 12, 13 and 14, Strand C. Shifting Securities Project.

38 Focus Group 8, Strand C, Shifting Securities Project.

39 Smith, *Utility*, p. 241.

40 Focus Group 8, Strand C, Shifting Securities Project.

41 The points in this paragraph are informed by: Focus Groups 1, 2, 3, 4, 7, 8, 11, 12, 13, 14, Strand C. Shifting Securities Project.

42 Focus Groups 8 and 13, with the latter confirming that, for military and civilian officials, there was absolutely no question of a 'one-size-fits-all' approach to the media, and, reflexively, that there were 'just as many misconceptions in the media of the military as the other way round'.

43 Focus Groups 11 and 13, Strand C, Shifting Securities Project.

44 Focus Groups 12 and 14, Strand C, Shifting Securities Project.

45 Brigadier General Mark Kimmitt, Interview, Strand C, Shifting Securities Project.

46 Barbara Starr, on CNN, made the only report of which we are aware. However, that report was made on 20 January, and based on further enquiries by her in Washington DC, and without reference to Kimmitt's original briefing four days earlier, on 16 January 2004. edition.cnn.com/2004/US/01/20/sprj.nirq.abuse/ at 18 June 2006; Donald H. Rumsfeld, 'Testimony', House Armed Services Committee, 7 May 2004, www.defenselink.mil/speeches/2004/sp20040507-secdef0421.htm and www.defenselink.mil/Speeches/Speech.aspx?SpeechID=118, at 18 June 2006; and 'Chronology of Investigations', www.defendamerica.mil/articles/may2004/a050704h.html, at 18 June 2006.

47 *60 Minutes II*, CBS News, 28 April 2004, www.cbsnews.com/stories/
2004/04/27/60II/main614063.shtml, at 31 August 2006; *CBS Evening News*, 28
April and 5 May 2004.

48 Focus Group 13, Strand C, Shifting Securities Project.

49 Focus Group 12, Strand C, Shifting Securities Project.

50 James Gow, 'Hearts, Minds and Retinas', Counter-insurgency Issues Conference, Joint Service Command and Staff College, 1 September, 2005, which
became the basis for Gow, 'Hearts, Minds and Retinas: Legitimating
Contemporary Warfare', *Contemporary Security Policy*, vol. 27, no. 4 (April 2007),
as well as both enquiries for, and parts of, this volume.

51 There is no doubt that, as a public relations question, the US Marines' public
affairs policy of getting information out immediately makes sense. However, in
the context of a multi-service and multi-agency environment, because this is a
strategic question there needs to be a strategic approach, unified at the highest
levels. A retired US Marines' Colonel pointed out the Marines' approach to
Gow during a conference at the Joint Services Command and Staff College,
1–2 September 2005.

52 Smith, *Utility*, p. 393.

53 To be clear, the point here is the use of images constituting alleged war crimes,
not the fact that images might portray and provide evidence of particular acts
that may be alleged war crimes in themselves.

# Selected filmography and bibliography

## Filmography

*9/11* dirs Jules and Gédéon Naudet (2002)
*A Cry from the Grave* dir. Leslie Woodhead (1999)
*ABC News Presents War with Iraq – Stories from the Front* no dir. (2004)
*Before the Rain* dir. Milcho Manchevski (1994)
*Beslan: Siege of School No. 1* dir. Kevin Sim (2005)
*Black Hawk Down* dir. Ridley Scott (2001)
*Chechnya: Separatism or Jihad?* dir. Dodge Billingsley (2005)
*CNN Presents – War in Iraq – The Road to Baghdad* no dir. (2003)
*CNN Tribute – America Remembers – The Events of September 11th* (Commemorative Edition) no dir. (2002)
*Fahrenheit 9/11* dir. Michael Moore (2004)
*Fahrenhype 9/11* dir. Alan Petersen (2004)
*Fault Lines and Pipelines* dir. Dodge Billingsley (2004)
*Fighting the War* (7 parts) dir. Neil Hunt (2003)
*Hotel Rwanda* dir. Terry George (2004)
*House of War* dir. Paul Yule (2002)
*Il était une fois la Tchétchénie* dir. Nino Kirtadze (2004)
*Immortal Fortress* dir. Dodge Billingsley (1999)
*In This World* dir. Michael Winterbottom (2002)
*Independence Day* dir. Roland Emmerich (1996)
*Jarhead* dir. Sam Mendes (2005)
*Kingdom of Heaven* dir. Ridley Scott (2005)
*No Man's Land* dir. Danis Tanović (2001)
*Operation Enduring Freedom: America Fights Back* no dir. (2002)
*Perfect Circle* dir. Ademir Kenović (1995)
*Pretty Village, Pretty Flame* dir. Srdjan Dragojević (1995)
*Prisoner of the Caucasus* dir. Yuri Khashchavatski (2002)
*Prisoner of the Mountains* dir. Sergei Bodrov (1996)
*Rezervni Deli* (aka *Spare Parts*) dir. Damjan Kozole (2004)
*Shake Hands with the Devil: The Journey of Romeo Dallaire* dir. Peter Raymont (2005)
*Shooting Dogs* dir. Michael Caton Jones (2006)
*Srebrenica: Never Again?* dir. Leslie Woodhead (2005)
*Terror in Moscow* dir. Dan Reed (2002)
*The Children of Beslan* dir. Leslie Woodhead (2005)

*The Death of Yugoslavia* (6 parts) dirs Angus MacQueen and Paul Mitchell (1995)
*The Fall of Milošević* (3 parts) dir. Dai Richards (1999)
*The Life and Death of Colonel Blimp* dir. Michael Powell (1943)
*The Peacemaker* dir. Michael Schiffer (1997)
*The Valley* dir. Dan Reed (1999)
*Three Kings* dir. David O. Russell (1999)
*Underground* dir. Emir Kusturica (1995)
*United 93* dir. Paul Greengrass (2006)
*Virgin Soldiers* dir. Dodge Billingsley (2003)
*Vukovar* dir. Boro Drašković (1994)
*War* dir. Aleksei Balabanov (2004)
*War With Iraq* ABC News (2003)
*Welcome to Sarajevo* dir. Michael Winterbottom (1995)
*What We Saw* CBS News (2002)

# Bibliography

Adie, Kate, *The Kindness of Strangers: The Autobiography*, London: Headline, 2002

*After September 11: TV News and Multicultural Audiences*, London: British Film Institute, 2002

Aitken, Ian, *Film and Reform*, London: Routledge, 1990

Aldgate, Anthony and Richards, Jeffrey, *Britain Can Take It: The British Cinema in the Second World War* (2nd edn), Edinburgh: Edinburgh University Press, 1994

Allan, Stuart and Zelizer, Barbie (eds), *Reporting War: Journalism in Wartime*, London, New York: Routledge, 2004

Alsanjak, Metin, '(Un)real Versions of Experience: The Cross-cultural Trade in Media Imagery During the Invasion of Iraq', *Vertigo*, vol. 2, no. 5, summer 2003

Anonymous, *Through Our Enemies' Eyes: Osama bin Laden, Radical Islam, and the Future of America*, Washington, DC: Brassey's, 2002

Atwan, Abdel Bari, *The Secret History of al-Qa'ida*, London: Saqi Books, 2006

Auletta, Ken, 'Annals of Communications – The Dawn Patrol: The Curious Rise of Morning Television and the Future of Network News', *The New Yorker*, 8 and 15 August 2005

Badsey, Stephen (ed.), *The Media and International Security*, London: Frank Cass, 2000

Badsey, Stephen, *Modern Military Operations and the Media*, Camberley: Strategic and Combat Studies Institute, 1994

Balázs, Béla, *Theory of the Film: Character and Growth of a New Art* (trans. Edith Bone), London: Dennis Dobson, 1952

Bandura, Albert and Walters, Richard, *Social Learning and Personality*, New York: Holt, Rinehart & Winston, 1963

Barthes, Roland, *The Death of the Author*, New York: McGraw Hill, 1977

Basić-Hrvatin, Sandra, 'Television and National/Public Memory', in Gow *et al.* (eds), *Bosnia by Television*, London: BFI, 1996

Basinger, Jeanine, *The World War Two Combat Film: Anatomy of a Genre*, Middletown: Wesleyan University Press, 2003

Bates, Milton, *The Wars We Took to Vietnam: Cultural Conflict and Storytelling*, Berkeley: University of California Press, 1996

Berkowitz, Leonard, *Aggression: A Social Psychological Analysis Development*, New York: McGraw Hill, 1962

Bluestone, George, *Novels Into Film*, Berkeley and Los Angeles: University of California Press, 1968

Blumenson, M., 'Can Official History be Honest History?', *Military Affairs*, vol. 26, 1962

Bond, Brian, *The Unquiet Western Front: Britain's Role in Literature and History*, Cambridge: Cambridge University Press, 2002

Boon, Kevin, 'Human 911: Spectacle and Tragedy', *Creative Screenwriting*, vol. 9, no. 2, March 2002

Bourke, Joanna, *An Intimate History of Killing: Face to Face Killing in 20th Century Warfare*, London: Granta, 1999

Boyce, Frank Cottrell, *Welcome to Sarajevo*, London: Faber and Faber, 1997

Briley, Ron, '*Fahrenheit 9/11*: Michael Moore Heats it Up', *Film and History*, vol. 35, no. 2, 2005

Burns, Paul, 'Linkage: Pudovkin's Classics Revisited', *Journal of Popular Film and Television*, vol. 9, no. 2, 1981.

Carruthers, Susan L., *The Media at War: Communication and Conflict in the Twentieth Century*, London: Palgrave, 2000

CBS News with an Introduction by Dan Rather, *What We Saw*, New York: Simon & Schuster, 2002

Clark, Alan, *The Donkeys: A History of the British Expeditionary Force in 1915*, London: Pimlico, 1991

Clausewitz, Carl von, *On War* (trans. J.J. Graham), Introduction and Notes by Colonel F.N. Maude, CB (Late RE). Introduction to the New Edition by Jan Willem Honig, New York: Barnes & Noble, 2004

Colson, Aurélien, 'The Logic of Peace and the Logic of Justice', *International Relations*, vol. 15, no. 1, April 2000

Connerton, Paul, *How Societies Remember*, Cambridge: Cambridge University Press, 1989

Corner, John, *The Art of Record*, Manchester: Manchester University Press, 1996

Creton, Laurent, *L'économie du cinéma*, Paris: Nathan, 2003

Creveld, Martin van, *On Future War*, London: Brassey's, 1991

Daalder, Ivo and O'Hanlon, Michael, *Winning Ugly: NATO's Kosovo War*, Washington, DC: Brooking's Institution, 2000

Dallaire, Romeo, *Shake Hands With the Devil: The Failure of Humanity in Rwanda*, London: Arrow, 2005

Davis, Natalie Zemon, *Slaves on Screen: Film and Historical Vision*, Cambridge, Mass.: Harvard University Press, 2000

Doherty, Tom, 'The New War Movies as Moral Rearmament: *Black Hawk Down* and *We Were Soldiers*', *Cineaste*, summer 2002

Dyer, Richard, 'Introduction to Film Studies', in John Hill and Pamela Church Gibson (eds), *The Oxford Guide to Film Studies*, Oxford: Oxford University Press, 1998

Eisenstein, Sergei, *The Film Sense* (trans. Jay Leyda), London and Boston: Faber and Faber, 1986

Eisenstein, Sergei, Pudovkin, Vsevolod and Alexandrov, Grigorii, 'Statement on Sound', in Richard Taylor and Ian Christie (eds), *The Film Factory*, Cambridge, MA: Harvard University Press, 1988

Eizenshtein, S., Pudovkin, V. and Aleksandrov, G., 'Zaiavka', *Zhizn' iskusstva*, 5 August 1928

Ender, Morton G., 'Military Brats: Film Representations of Children From Military Families', *Armed Forces and Society*, vol. 32, no. 1, October 2005

Felperin, Leslie, 'The Longest Days', *Sight and Sound*, January 2006

Fenton, Tom, *Bad News: The Decline of Reporting, The Business of News, and The Danger To Us All*, New York: Regan Books, 2005

Ferroro, Guigliemo, *The Principles of Power: The Great Political Crises of History*, New York: Putnam, 1943

Feshbach, Seymour, 'The Stimulating vs. Cathartic Effects of a Vicarious Aggressive Experience', *Journal of Abnormal and Social Psychology*, vol. 63, 1961

Freedman, Lawrence, *The Transformation of Strategic Affairs*, Adelphi Paper 379, London: Routledge for the IISS, 2006

Friend, David, 'Bond of Brothers', *Vanity Fair*, no. 499, 1 March 2002.

Gates, Philippa, ' "Fighting the Good Fight:" The Real and the Moral in the Contemporary Hollywood Combat Film', *Quarterly Review of Film and Video*, vol. 22, no. 4, October 2005

George, Terry, 'Look Back in Anger', *Premiere*, vol. 18, no. 4, 1 December 2004

Gibbons, Michael, 'Chasing the Game', *Screen International*, no. 1490, 25 February 2005

Gillespie, Marie, 'Security, Media, Legitimacy: Multi-ethnic Media Publics and the Iraq War 2003', *International Relations*, vol. 20, no. 4, December 2006

Gillespie, Marie *et al.*, *Shifting Securities: News Cultures Before and Beyond the Iraq 2003 War – Preliminary Findings Report*, June 2006

Ginneken, Jaap van, *Understanding Global News: A Critical Introduction*, London: Sage, 1998

Glasgow University Media, Group *War and Peace News*, Milton Keynes: Open University Press, 1985

Glasse, Jennifer, 'War of Ideas: The Need for a Coherent US Message About Iraq', Research Paper, RCDS, July 2006

Gordon, S.D. and Toase, F.H. (eds), *Aspects of Peacekeeping*, London: Frank Cass, 2001

Gow, James, 'Hearts, Minds and Retinas', Counter Insurgency Issues Conference, Joint Service Command and Staff College, 1 September 2005

Gow, James, *Legitimacy and the Military: the Yugoslav Crisis*, London: Pinter, 1992

Gow, James, *Triumph of the Lack of Will: International Diplomacy and the Yugoslav Crisis*, New York: Columbia University Press, 1997

Gow, James, *The Serbian Project and Its Adversaries: A Strategy of War Crimes*, London: Hurst & Co, 2003

Gow, James, '*Team America – World Police*: Down-home Theories of Power and Peace', *Millennium: Journal of International Relations*, vol. 34, no. 2, 2006

Gow, James, 'The ICTY, War Crimes Enforcement and Dayton: The Ghost in the Machine', *Ethnopolitics*, vol. 5, no. 1, 2006

Gow, James, *War and War Crimes*, London: Hurst & Co, 2007

Gow, James and Carmichael, Cathie, *Slovenia and the Slovenes: A Small Country in the New Europe*, Bloomington: Indiana University Press, 2000

Gow, James and Dandeker, Christopher, 'Strategic Peacekeeping', *The World Today*, vol. 51, nos 8–9, August–September 1995

Gow, James and Dandeker, Christopher, 'Strategic Peacekeeping: Military Culture and Defining Moments', in S.D. Gordon and F.H. Toase (eds), *Aspects of Peace-keeping*, London: Frank Cass, 2001

Gow, James and Tilsley, James, 'The Strategic Imperative for Media Management', in James Gow *et al.* (eds), *Bosnia by Television*, London: BFI, 1996

Gow, James, Paterson, Richard and Preston, Alison (eds), *Bosnia by Television*, London: BFI, 1996

Gowing, Nik, *Real-time Television Coverage of Armed Conflicts and Diplomatic Crises: Does it Pressure or Distort Foreign Policy Decisions?*, Cambridge, MA:, Harvard University: Shorenstein Center, 1994

Gowing, Nik, 'Real Time TV Coverage of War: Does it Make of Break Government Policy', in James Gow, Richard Paterson and Alison Preston (eds), *Bosnia by Television*, London: BFI, 1996

Gowing, Nik, Presentation, 'Communicating the War on Terror: Are we Getting the Balance Right Between Being Alert and Being Alarmed?', Conference, King's College London-Royal Institution, 6 June 2003

Gray, Chris Hables, *Postmodern War: The New Politics of Conflicts*, London: Routledge, 1997

Gray, Colin S., *Modern Strategy*, Oxford: Oxford University Press, 1999

Grint, Keith and Woolgar, Steve, 'Computers, Guns and Roses: What's Social About Being Shot?', *Science, Technology and Human Values*, vol. 17, no. 3, summer 1992

Grint, Keith and Woolgar, Steve, *The Machine at Work: Technology, Work and Organization*, Cambridge: Polity Press, 1997

Grubner, George *et al.*, 'The Mainstreaming of America', *Violence Profile Number 11, Journal of Communication*, vol. 30, no. 3, 1980

Hammes, Thomas G., *The Sling and the Stone: On War in the 21st Century*, St Paul: Zenith Press, 2004

Hammes, Thomas G., 'War Evolves into the Fourth Generation', *Contemporary Security Policy*, vol. 26, no. 2, 2005

Hess, Stephen and Kalb, Marvin (eds), *The Media and the War on Terrorism*, Washington, DC: Brookings Institution Press, 2003

Heuser, Beatrice, *Reading Clausewitz*, London: Pimlico, 2002

Hill, John, 'Film and Television', in John Hill and Pamela Church Gibson (eds), *The Oxford Guide to Film Studies*, Oxford: Oxford University Press, 1998

Hill, John and Church Gibson, Pamela (eds), *The Oxford Guide to Film Studies*, Oxford: Oxford University Press, 1998

Hoge, James, 'Media Pervasiveness', *Foreign Affairs*, vol. 73, 1994.

Hoskins, Andrew, *Televising War: From Vietnam to Iraq*, London: Continuum, 2004

Hoskins, Andrew and O'Loughlin, Ben, *Television and Terror: Conflicting Times and the Crisis of News Discourse*, London: Palgrave, 2007

Hunter, Jack (ed.), *Search and Destroy: An Illustrated Guide to Vietnam War Movies*, Unknown place: Creation Books, 2002

Ignatieff, Michael, *Virtual War: Kosovo and Beyond*, London: Chatto & Windus, 2000

Iordanova, Dina, 'Kusturica's "Underground" (1995): Historical Allegory, or Propaganda?', *Historical Journal of Film, Radio and Television*, vol. 19, no. 1, 1999

Iordanova, Dina, *Cinema of Flames: Balkan Film, Culture and the Media*, London: BFI, 2001

Izod, John and Kilborn, Richard, 'The Documentary', in John Hill and Pamela Church Gibson (eds), *The Oxford Guide to Film Studies*, Oxford: Oxford University Press, 1998

Jackson, S.W., 'Catharsis and Abreaction in the History of Psychological Healing', *Psychiatric Clinics of North America*, vol. 17, no. 3, 1994

Jacobs, Lewis, *The Rise of the American Film – A Critical History*, New York: Harcourt, Brace, 1956

Just, Marion Montague Kern and Norris, Pippa (eds), *Framing Terrorism: The News Media, The Government and the Public*, London: Frank Cass, 2003

Kaldor, Mary, *New and Old Wars*, Cambridge: Polity Press, 1999

Kibbey, Ann, *Theory of the Image: Capitalism, Contemporary Film, and Women*, Bloomington: Indiana University Press, 2005

Kinney, Katherine, *Friendly Fire: American Images of the Vietnam War*, Oxford: Oxford University Press, 2000

Klapper, Joseph, *The Effects of Mass-communication*, New York: The Free Press of Glencoe, 1960

Kling, Rob, 'When Gunfire Shatters Bone: Reducing Sociotechnical Systems to Social Relationships', *Science, Technology and Human Values*, vol. 17. no. 3, summer 1992

Lambert, Andrew and Badsey, Stephen, *The Crimean War*, Dover, NH: Sutton Press, 1994

Lind, William S., 'Understanding Fourth Generation War', *Military Review*, September–October 2004

Livingstone, Steven, 'Beyond the "CNN effect": The Media–Foreign Policy Dynamic', in Pippa Norris (ed.), *Politics and the Press: The News Media and its Influences* Boulder, Col.: Lynne Rienner, 1997

Livingston, Steven, *Clarifying the CNN Effect: An Examination of Media Effects According to Type of Intervention*, Research Paper R-18, Cambridge, MA: The Joan Shorenstein Barone Center on the Press, Politics and Public Policy, JFK School of Government, Harvard University, 1997

Lotman, Iurii Mikhailovich, *Struktura khudozhestvennogo teksta*, Moscow: Iskusstvo, 1970

MacDonald, Kevin and Cousins, Mark, *Imagining Reality: The Faber Book of Documentary*, London: Faber and Faber, 1998

Malešič, Marjan (ed.), *The Role of the Mass Media in the Serbian–Croatian Conflict*, Stockholm: SPF, 1993

Manoff, Robert Karl, 'Telling the Truth to Peoples at Risk. Some Introductory Thoughts on Media and Conflict', Unpublished paper presented at the 'Legitimacy of Intervention for Peace by Foreign Media in a Country in Conflict' Conference, Fondation Hirondelle, Geneva, 3–4 July 1998

Marsolais, Gilles, 'Tout est affaire de montage', *24 Images*, no. 118, 1 September 2004

Merquior, J.G., *Rousseau and Weber*, London: Routledge & Kegan Paul, 1980

Meyer, Alfred G., 'Legitimacy of Power in East Central Europe', in S. Sinnanian *et al.* (eds), *Eastern Europe in the 1970s*, New York: Praeger, 1972

Michalski, Milena and Preston, Alison, 'Le 11 septembre vu de Grande Bretagne: Comparaison des journaux télévisés', in Marc Lits (ed.), *Du 11 septembre à la riposte: les débuts d'une nouvelle guerre médiatique*, Brussels; De Boeck, 2004

Mintz, Steven, 'Michael Moore and the Re-birth of the Documentary', *Film and History*, vol. 35, no. 2, 2005

Nawawy, Mohammed el and Iskandar, Adel, *Al Jazeera: The Story of the Network that is Rattling Governments and Redefining Modern Journalism*, Cambridge, MA: Westview/Perseus, 2003

Nichols, Bill, *Representing Reality: Issues and Concepts in Documentary*, Bloomington: Indiana University Press, 1989

Nichols, Bill, *Introduction to Documentary*, Bloomington: Indiana University Press, 2001

Nicholson, Michael, *Natasha's Story*, London: Pan, 1994

Nolley, Ken, '*Fahrenheit 9/11*: Documentary, Truth-telling and Politics', *Film and History*, vol. 35, no. 2, 2005

Nye, Joseph P., 'Soft Power And The Struggle Against Terrorism', Lecture, The Royal Institute of International Affairs, Chatham House, London, 5 May 2005

Nye, Joseph P., *The Paradox of American Power: Why the World's Only Superpower Can't Go It Alone*, Oxford: Oxford University Press, 2002

Nye, Joseph P., 'US Power and Strategy After Iraq', *Foreign Affairs*, vol. 82, no. 4, July–August 2003

O'Connor, Joseph, 'History in Images/Images in History: Reflections on the Importance of Film and Television Study for an Understanding of the Past', *American Historical Review*, vol. 93, no. 5, 1988

Pachnicke, Peter and Honnef, Klaus (eds), *John Hartfield*, New York: Harry N. Abrams, 1994

Pappu, Sridhar, 'On the Heir', *Arrive*, March/April 2004

Paris, Michael (ed.), *The First World War and Popular Cinema: 1914 to the Present*, Edinburgh: Edinburgh University Press, 1999

Patterson, Thomas and McClure, Robert D., *The Unseeing Eye. The Myth of Television Power in National Politics*, New York: Putnam, 1976

Pereboom, Maarten and O'Connor, John E. (chairs) *et al.*, 'Michael Moore: Cinematic Historian or Propagandist? A Historians Film Committee Panel Presented at the 2005 American Historical Association Meeting', *Film and History*, vol. 35, no. 2, 2005

Perkins, V.F., *Film as Film: Understanding and Judging Movies*, London: Penguin, 1972

Petrić, Vlada, *Constructivism in Film. The Man with the Movie Camera: A Cinematic Analysis*, Cambridge: Cambridge University Press, 1987

Poole, Elizabeth and Richardson, John E. (eds), *Muslims and the News Media*, London: I.B. Tauris, 2006

Porton, Richard, 'Weapon of Mass Instruction: Michael Moore's *Fahrenheit 9/11*', *Cineaste*, vol. 29, no. 4, fall 2004

Prunier, Gerard, *Darfur: The Ambiguous Genocide*, London: Hurst & Co, 2005

Ramet, Sabrina, *Thinking about Yugoslavia: Scholarly Debates about the Yugoslav Breakup and the Wars in Bosnia and Kosovo*, Cambridge: Cambridge University Press, 2006

Reid, Rt. Hon. John, MP, Secretary of State for Defence, 'The Uneven Playing Field', Lecture, King's College London, 20 February 2006

*Report of the 9/11 Commission:Final Report of the National Commission on Terrorist Attacks Upon the United States*, Official Government Edition, Washington, DC: Government Publications Office, 2004

Rifkin, Benjamin, Semiotics of Narration in Film and Prose Fiction. Case Studies of 'Scarecrow' and 'My Friend Ivan Lapshin', New York: Peter Lang, 1994

Robinson, Piers, *The CNN Effect: The Myth of News, Foreign Policy and Intervention*, London: Routledge, 2002

Rosenstone, Robert A., 'A History in Images/History in Words: Reflections on the

Possibility of Really Putting History onto Film', *The American Historical Review*, vol. 93, no. 5, 1998

Ross, W.D., *The Works of Aristotle*, vol. 11, Oxford: Clarendon Press, 1924

Roy, Andrew, 'Images de guerre et guerre des images', *24 Images*, no. 118, 1 September 2004

Scheff, Thomas J., *Catharsis in Healing, Ritual and Drama*, Berkeley and Los Angeles: University of California Press, 1979

Seib, Philip, *Beyond the Front Lines: How the News Media Cover a World Shaped by War*, New York: Palgrave, 2004

Shanor, Donald R., *News From Abroad*, New York: Columbia University Press, 2003

Shaw, Martin, *War and Genocide*, Cambridge: Polity Press, 2003

Shaw, Martin, *The New Western Way of War*, Cambridge: Polity Press, 2005

Shook, Fred, *Television Field Production and Reporting* (4th edn), Boston: Pearson, 2005

Silber, Laura and Little, Allan, *The Death of Yugoslavia* (aka *Yugoslavia: Death of a Nation*), London: Penguin, 1995

Simms, Brendan, *Unfinest Hour: Britain and the Destruction of Bosnia*, London: Penguin, 2001

Sinnanian, S. *et al.* (eds), *Eastern Europe in the 1970s*, New York: Praeger, 1972

Smith, General Sir Rupert, *The Utility of Force: The Art of War in the Modern World*, London: Allen Lane, 2006

Sternberger, Dolf, 'Legitimacy', in *International Encyclopaedia of the Social Sciences*, New York: Macmillan, 1968

Stinchombe, Arthur L., *Constructing Social Theories*, New York: Harcourt, Brace & Jovanovich, 1968

Stone, John, *The Tank Debate: Armour and the Anglo-American Military Tradition*, Amsterdam: Harwood Academic, 2000

Swofford, Anthony, *Jarhead: A Marine's Chronicle of the Gulf War and Other Battles*, New York: Scribner, 2003

Tanović, Danis, 'No Man's Land', interview with Arzie Dobko, *Creative Screenwriting*, vol. 8, no. 6, November 2001

Taylor, Mark, *The Vietnam War in History, Literature and Film*, Edinburgh: Edinburgh University Press, 2003

Taylor, Philip, *War and the Media: Propaganda and Persuasion in the Gulf War* (2nd edn), Manchester: Manchester University Press, 1998

Taylor, Philip, *Munitions of the Mind: A History of Propaganda from the Ancient World to the Present Day* (3rd edn), Manchester: Manchester University Press, 2003

Taylor, Richard, *Film Propaganda: Soviet Russia and Nazi Germany* (2nd revised edn), London: I.B. Tauris, 1998

Thompson, Kristin and Bordwell, David, *Film History. An Introduction*, New York: 1994

Thompson, Mark, *Forging War: The Media in Serbia, Croatia and Bosnia and Hercegovina*, London: Article 19, 1994

Thussu, Daya Kishan and Freedman, Des (eds), *War and the Media: Reporting Conflict 24/7*, London: Sage, 2003

Tishkov, Valery, *Chechnya: Life in a War-torn Society*, Berkeley: University of California Press, 2004

Trigotoff, Dan, '*9/11* [*sic*] "not exploitive"', *Broadcasting and Cable*, vol. 132, no. 11, 18 March 2002

Tumber, Howard and Palmer, Jerry, *Media at War: The Iraq Crisis*, London: Thousand Oaks; New Delhi: Sage, 2004

Utting, Kate, 'The Strategic Information Campaign: Lessons from the British Experience in Palestine, 1945–1948', *Contemporary Security Policy*, vol. 27, no. 4, April 2007

Valentin, Jean-Michel, *Hollywood, The Pentagon and Washington: The Movies and National Security from World War Two to the Present Day*, London: Anthema Press, 2005

Vincendeau, Ginette (ed.), *Encyclopedia of European Cinema*, London: Cassell/BFI, 1995

Virilio, Paul, trans. Patrick Camiller, *War and Cinema: The Logistics of Perception*, London: Verso, 1989

Weber, Max, 'Science as a Vocation', in Weber, *From Max Weber: Essays in Sociology*, ed. H.H. Gerth and C. Wright Mills, London: Routledge & Kegan Paul, 1948

Weber, Max, *From Max Weber: Essays in Sociology*, ed. H.H. Gerth and C. Wright Mills, London: Routledge & Kegan Paul, 1948

Westwell, Guy, 'Lights, Camera, Military Action ...: Considering Celluloid Conflicts', *Vertigo*, vol. 2, no. 5, summer 2003

*What does Al-Qaeda Want? Unedited Communiques*, Commentary by Robert O. Marlin IV, Berkeley, Calif: North Atlantic Books, 2004

Widdis, Emma, *Alexander Medvedkin*, London: I.B. Tauris, 2005

Wilson, Andrew, *Virtual Politics: Faking Democracy in the Post-Soviet World*, London: Yale University Press, 2005

Wilson, Stan Le Roy, *Mass Media/Mass Culture* (2nd edn), New York: McGraw-Hill, 1992

Winston, Brian, *Fires Were Started*, London: BFI, 1999

Winston, Brian, *Lies, Damned Lies and Documentaries*, London: BFI, 2000

Woodhead, Leslie, *My Life as a Spy*, London: Macmillan, 2005

Zelizer, Barbie and Allan, Stuart (eds), *Journalism after September 11*, London, New York: Routledge, 2002

Zveržhanovski, Ivan, 'Croatian TV News', *South Slav Journal*, forthcoming

# Index